THE
HITLER
YEARS

THE HITLER YEARS

VOLUME 1
TRIUMPH
1933–1939

FRANK McDONOUGH

HEAD
of ZEUS

An Apollo Book

In loving memory of:
Brother Michael McDonough (1951–2018)
Sister Carol Ann McDonough (1953–2017)

For Ann – with love

This is an Apollo book, first published in 2019 by Head of Zeus Ltd

Copyright © Frank McDonough 2019

The moral right of Frank McDonough to be identified as the author
of this work has been asserted in accordance with the
Copyright, Designs and Patents Act of 1988.

A catalogue record for this book is available
from the British Library.

3 5 7 9 10 8 6 4 2

ISBN (HB) 9781784975920
(E) 9781784975913

Picture research Juliet Brightmore
Designed by Isambard Thomas, Corvo
Printed and bound in Wales by Gomer Press

Head of Zeus Ltd
5–8 Hardwick Street
London ECIR 4RG
WWW.HEADOFZEUS.COM

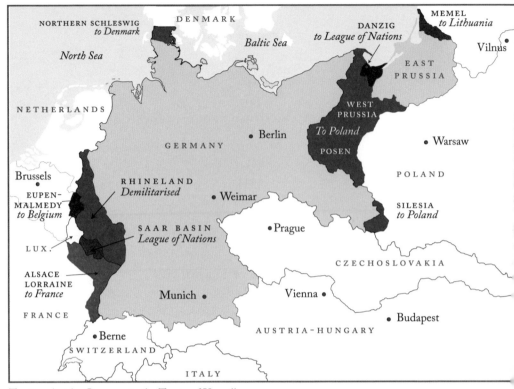

Territory lost by Germany in the Treaty of Versailles

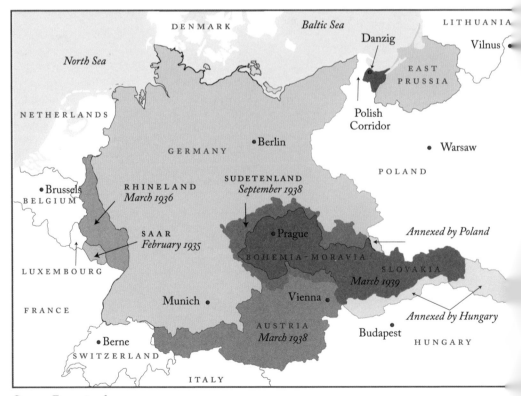

German Expansion from 1933–1939

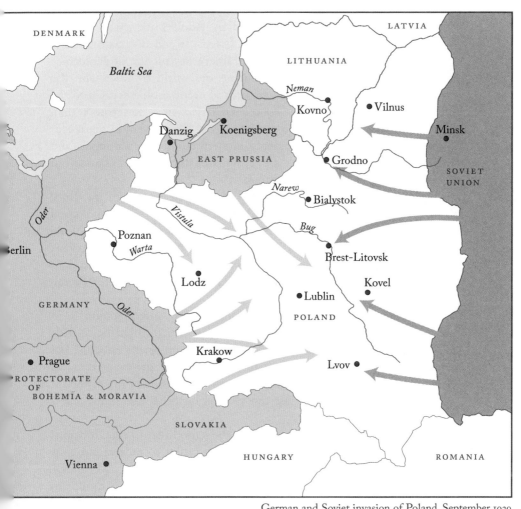

German and Soviet invasion of Poland, September 1939

INTRODUCTION

The Third Reich was dominated by Adolf Hitler, who boasted that it would last for a thousand years. It ended catastrophically twelve years and four months later. Hitler's destruction of democracy in Germany, his attempt to dominate the world by force, and the horrific Holocaust he ordered are central events in history. Up to the end of 1941 Hitler's armies conquered larger areas of territory than Julius Caesar, Attila the Hun and Napoleon. The ghost of Hitler is ever present in political discussions, in modern culture, in the media and throughout historical debate. Hitler remains the epitome of horror, but also a source of endless fascination.

The Hitler Years aims to tell the story of the history of the Third Reich from 1933 to 1945 in two volumes. I adopt a chronological explanation. Each chapter deals with a particular year to give a blow-by-blow account. Sections in each of the chapters explore various themes to provide further context to the events under discussion. This allows the reader to see how events evolved and fitted into the overall development of Hitler's rule.

Narrative history incorporating analysis and interpretation is, in my view, preferable to a thematic structure, which might be suitable for students looking at various aspects on a university module, but can become extremely difficult to follow for the general reader. So many new books appear each year on various aspects of the history of the Third Reich but there are few general histories and a new one is thoroughly warranted.[1]

This first volume, *Triumph*, covers the period 1933 to 1939. It begins with the dramatic intrigues that brought Hitler to power, and ends shortly after his swift conquest of Poland in 1939. The second volume, *Disaster*, starts with the build-up to the attack on Western Europe in 1940, then moves on to examine the key battles of the Second World War and the Holocaust and concludes with the catastrophic German defeat in 1945. Each volume can be read as a distinct examination of each period but taken together they make up a comprehensive history of the period Hitler ruled Germany between 1933 and 1945.

These two volumes draw on a wide range of sources, including letters, speeches, newspapers, government documents, party records, army
memoranda, SS and Foreign Ministry documents, war-trial evidence,
interviews with contemporary witnesses, diaries and memoirs. Some
sources give the view from the top, others the reaction of ordinary
people from below. The way these different viewpoints interact gives us
a rich and vivid picture of events as they unfold. These books would have
been impossible to write without drawing on the major achievements
of recent political, diplomatic, economic, social and military historians.

The monumental events related in the following pages are not, in
my view, susceptible to any simple thesis. However, my interpretation
of each episode, which grows out of the sources assembled, makes clear
my position at every stage and new insights emerge repeatedly. These
two books will correct many of the myths that have developed over
many decades concerning Hitler's foreign and racial policies and life
inside the Third Reich.

There are hundreds of thousands of historical studies of Hitler's
Germany. Old disagreements among academic historians – between the
'intentionalists', who believe Hitler was an all-powerful 'master of the
Third Reich', and the 'structuralists', who view him as a 'weak dictator'
presiding over a chaotic political system – now seem inconclusive. It
is possible to argue in favour of either case in different policy areas.[2]

There were some historians who argued that Germany followed
a *Sonderweg* or 'special path' of abnormal development over centuries
that rejected democracy and modernity in favour of a militaristic and
aristocratic will to create a European empire. This made German
militarism and its association with Hitler seem wholly inevitable.
However, this idea that Germany's politics and economy developed
differently from other major European nations is now viewed as flawed
and too deterministic.[3]

The same is true of writers who depicted the Third Reich as a
totalitarian dictatorship. One of the prime examples was Hannah
Arendt in *The Origins of Totalitarianism* (1951) which suggested that
Hitler's regime was very similar to Joseph Stalin's Soviet Union. In
practice, however, Nazi government was much less totalitarian than
the USSR. The German public had far greater latitude to grumble
and criticize than was previously supposed. The original concept of
totalitarianism now seems a deeply flawed way to explain Hitler's rule.[4]

Even if Hitler had never come to power Germany would probably
have had a right-wing nationalist coalition during this period.

Conservative power brokers in German politics had never accepted Germany's defeat in the Great War and they had utter contempt for democracy. A right-wing nationalistic regime, supported by the army, would have almost certainly attempted to revise the Treaty of Versailles, which was regarded by most Germans as a gross injustice, and they may even have done so with the blessing of the British and the French governments. However, without Hitler as leader, it is extremely doubtful that such a conservative-nationalist regime would have resorted to mass genocide founded upon racist and anti-Semitic ideas.

Hitler and his radical National Socialism was therefore central to what happened in Germany from 1933 to 1945. It is impossible to believe that German – or indeed world – history would have taken the same course had Adolf Hitler never lived. Yet Hitler did not create the very specific circumstances that persuaded him to pursue a career in politics and which crowned him leader. Without the Great War and Germany's strong sense of humiliation, the Nazi Party would not have needed to exist.

Germany's defeat in 1918 resulted in the establishment of the Weimar Republic, which lasted from 1918 to 1933. From the very beginning it was beset by economic and political difficulties. It only survived between 1919 and 1923 with the help of the army. Germany was almost bankrupted by the Great Inflation of 1923. Between 1924 and 1929 US loans gave the Weimar Republic some economic stability, but these loans were quickly recalled during the Stock Market Crash of 1929. There was then a 'run on the banks' in Germany and unemployment soared from 1.6 million in October 1929 to 6.12 million by February 1932. The government could not afford to pay unemployment benefits, which only added to the misery of the population. Those still in work saw their wages cut. There was starvation in rural areas as agricultural prices plummeted. The collapse of the German economy led to a further mistrust of democracy among the people, many of whom now yearned for a strong leader to revitalize the nation.

On to this stage stepped Adolf Hitler. The popularity of his Nazi Party had increased dramatically during this severe economic downturn as he moved from the radical fringe to the political mainstream. In 1928 just 2.8 per cent (810,000) voted for the Nazis. In 1930 this jumped to 18 per cent (6.4 million). By July 1932 the Nazi Party was polling at 37.2 per cent (13.7 million). This proved the peak of electoral popularity before he came to power. In the November 1932 election support for the Nazi Party fell by 4 per cent. Similarly, the German Communist Party (KPD) saw its vote share increase from 10 to 17 per cent between 1928 and 1932. Combined, this meant that by July 1932 the two parties that promised to destroy democracy were supported by 54.2 per cent of German voters.

The National Socialist German Workers' Party (*Nationalsozialistische Deutsche Arbeiterpartei* or NSDAP) was founded on 24 February 1920 in Munich. It was primarily composed of ex-soldiers who believed that Germany had not lost the Great War, but had been 'stabbed in the back' by communists and Jews on the home front. They were defined as the chief enemies of the National Socialist or Nazi Party.

Drawing upon this discontent, the Party's leader Adolf Hitler, an accomplished public speaker, tried to seize power in November 1923 by overthrowing the Bavarian local government. However, the bungled 'Beer Hall Putsch' in Munich was easily suppressed by the army. Hitler was arrested and sentenced to five years for 'high treason'. During his 264-day imprisonment, he changed tack and decided to seek power legally through democratic elections. He also accepted that he would need the support of the traditional conservative right if he wanted to win power legally.

Support for the Nazi Party came at first from the lower-middle-class voters in rural Protestant areas. By 1932 Hitler was attracting the middle classes in Germany's big cities: white-collar workers, doctors, civil servants and independent traders and small businessmen all contributed to the huge upsurge in voting support. Hitler had managed to unite conservative voters. No party in a large modern democratic state had ever risen from such obscurity so quickly.

Hitler's promise to his followers was that he alone could bring order and stability to the chaos of Germany by creating a stable, united, classless 'National Community'. He would ease the hardships of the Great Depression through public works programmes and job-creation schemes. The German economy would be reorganized to serve the interests of the nation. The perceived grip of Jewish capitalists on the nation's finances would be weakened. Hitler's ideas were popular and appealed most markedly to the German middle classes.

Alarmed by Hitler's popularity and the strong performance of the Nazis in elections, the elderly President Paul von Hindenburg tried to establish a right-wing authoritarian regime, which excluded Hitler and the Nazi Party. Article 48 of the flawed Weimar constitution gave him unlimited emergency powers, so he appointed three conservative chancellors: Heinrich Brüning (1930–32), then Franz von Papen (June–November 1932), and finally General Kurt von Schleicher, who lasted just fifty-seven days. All proved deeply unpopular and none were party leaders.

Hitler later claimed to have 'seized power' on 30 January 1933, but in fact his appointment as Chancellor was entirely legal and constitutional. Hindenburg had been persuaded by his narrow conservative group of advisers that Hitler should be given the chance to rule and perhaps he could even be controlled to serve their own ends. So there was no violent revolution in Germany in 1933 as there had been in Russia in 1917 or France in 1789.

Hitler faced a huge dilemma when he came to power which he never fully resolved. His rule began as a coalition involving himself and the Nazi elite working alongside the traditional, conservative elite, the army, the bureaucracy of the civil service and the interests of big business. He was never the puppet of conservative forces, but he constantly had to seek their consent in order to push through his policies.

Furthermore, his utopian vision of a classless, harmonious National Community was never matched by any fundamental social or economic change in Germany. Capitalism was central to the old conservative order and under Hitler it remained largely unchallenged and unreformed. Civil servants – provided they were not Jewish or left-wing – remained in post, their career prospects largely unaffected. The judiciary and prison governors were still old-fashioned conservatives, while the German police remained state employees. Indeed, the newly created Gestapo, which hunted down political opponents, drew its recruits from the existing police force. Finally, the army remained independent of Hitler's government and he needed its support to remain in power.

Rearmament was an agreed policy. It was popular because it promised to reduce unemployment and aid heavy industry. Hitler thought strong armed forces would improve his bargaining power in diplomatic negotiations. His key aim had always been to avenge Germany's humiliation after the Great War. Hence, his key allies were the army and big business, both non-Nazi organizations.

A further point of unity for Hitler and his conservative partners – as well as for the Nazi Party and most of the German population – was the desire to revise the Treaty of Versailles, which was generally viewed as an Allied conspiracy to keep Germany weak and humbled. Hitler's underlying long-term aim was to instigate a racial war in order to gain *Lebensraum* or 'living space' for the German people, but he could not openly reveal this while Germany was militarily weak. In public he suggested modest and reasonable treaty revisions. In private he preached expansion through brutal conquest and racial superiority.

One main area of conflict between Hitler's government and the conservative elites was church policy. Hitler originally wanted to Nazify the Lutheran Protestant Church, but he was forced to drop this proposal after fierce organized resistance. The Catholic Church remained in continuous conflict with Hitler's government and German Catholics experienced persistent persecution. By 1939, however, it was clear that Hitler's plan for Nazism to supplant Christianity in the German people's hearts had failed.

Even radical Nazi groups such as the SS and the violent storm troopers (SA) were not guaranteed access to the centre of power, but had to operate alongside existing conservative-dominated state institutions. The SS under Heinrich Himmler became a progressively more powerful organization, but its officers were recruited from young, university-educated people, many of whom had not been Nazi Party members in 1933.

Hitler also promised to improve German society by removing the 'enemies' of national unity. These included communists, trade unionists, liberals and Jews, as well as 'anti-social' outsiders such as vagrants, hardened criminals, the long-term unemployed, prostitutes; also those defined as 'racially unfit', most notably, the physically and mentally handicapped. All of these groups were progressively marginalized and excluded from the National Community.

Hitler understood that Nazifying German society was a long-term project that would probably take decades to achieve. In the short term he needed to win popular support for his ideas, which is why propaganda became so integral to the Nazi regime. Hitler's loyal Minister of Propaganda Joseph Goebbels seized control of the press, radio and all aspects of German culture in order to promote the Führer and his aims.

The Hitler Years acknowledges the central importance of Adolf Hitler to the ideological and especially the military prerogatives of his government and restores him to the centre-stage. However, it will also be revealed that he was often forced to compromise and display political flexibility much more than is generally appreciated. Hitler's actions were often premeditated, but sometimes he had to react to events beyond his control. In the period 1933 to 1939 he was not so much a master planner as a master of flexibility and improvisation.

1933

·

DEMOCRACY AND COMMUNISM DESTROYED

·

•

It was icy cold in Munich on New Year's Day. Adolf Hitler was drinking coffee over breakfast at his luxurious apartment at 16 Prinzregentenplatz. The morning papers made gloomy reading about his political prospects in the coming year. A critical article in the social democratic newspaper *Vorwärts* headlined 'Hitler's Rise and Fall' suggested the Nazi Party's electoral popularity had peaked in the July 1932 federal election.[1] The *Berliner Tageblatt* mockingly observed: 'Everywhere in the world people were talking about – what was his name: Adalbert Hitler. Later? He's vanished!'[2] The official Nazi Party newspaper, the *Völkischer Beobachter*, printed Hitler's 'Battle Message for 1933' in which he refused to compromise his principles for 'a couple of ministerial posts', and promised to continue his 'all or nothing strategy' of remaining in opposition until he was offered the post of Chancellor.[3]

During the evening of 1 January Hitler attended a performance of Richard Wagner's comedic opera *Die Meistersinger von Nürnberg* (*The Master-Singers of Nuremberg*) at Munich's Court Theatre.[4] Accompanying him were his deferential personal assistant Rudolf Hess, his photographer Heinrich Hoffmann, and Eva Braun. Hoffmann had 'a weakness for drinking parties and hearty jokes'.[5] Braun, tall, blond and strikingly attractive, was an assistant in Hoffmann's photography studio. This is where she first met Hitler when she was just seventeen. She had slowly emerged as Hitler's primary female companion after the tragic and somewhat suspicious death of his half-niece Geli Raubal, whose corpse had been found in Hitler's apartment on 18 September 1931. The inquest concluded that she had shot herself through the heart, using Hitler's own pistol. Braun's employment by Hoffmann meant that she could accompany Hitler socially without arousing public suspicion of any romantic involvement between them.

After the performance, they all went to a party at the opulent Munich residence of Hitler's witty and wealthy friend Ernst 'Putzi' Hanfstaengl, a Harvard graduate who joined the Party in the early 1920s. Hitler was in a very optimistic mood that night, Putzi later recalled.

After criticizing the talented young conductor Hans Knappertsbusch's handling of Wagner's opera, Hitler turned to Putzi and said: 'This year belongs to us. I will guarantee that to you in writing.'[6]

At the start of 1933 democratic government in Germany had virtually collapsed. The previous year had seen three different German chancellors: Heinrich Brüning, Franz von Papen and General Kurt von Schleicher, and two inconclusive national elections in July and November. Each Chancellor failed to establish a government that could command a majority in the German parliament, known as the Reichstag. Papen's government fell after a vote of no confidence, losing by 512 votes to 42. He was replaced by Schleicher, who took office on 3 December 1932.[7] Schleicher was appointed by Germany's 85-year-old President Paul von Hindenburg using the arbitrary power granted to him under Article 48 of the flawed Weimar constitution. This allowed him to appoint not merely the German Chancellor, but also the other members of the cabinet. As a result, the democratically elected members of the Reichstag were sidelined in the decision-making process. Hindenburg wanted to establish a stable and popular right-wing authoritarian government, excluding all left-wing parties, but since 1930 he had failed to make this a reality.

Schleicher had only a few weeks to put together a coalition government that could survive a potential vote of no confidence in the Reichstag. He envisaged an authoritarian regime which would appeal to the working classes, but this was completely out of step with what Hindenburg wanted. Schleicher spent most of December 1932 trying to persuade Gregor Strasser – a high-profile figure on the socialist left of the Nazi Party – to join his cabinet, with the aim of splitting the Nazi Party. On 3 December he offered Strasser the posts of Vice Chancellor and Minister-President of Prussia,[8] but Strasser refused both offers. Strasser resigned from the Nazi Party on 8 December, claiming that he could no longer accept Hitler's uncompromising refusal to become the Chancellor of a coalition government. In his diary Joseph Goebbels, the leading Nazi propagandist, summed up Gregor Strasser's predicament in two words: 'Dead man!'[9]

Franz von Papen, who had not forgiven Schleicher for helping to bring down his own government, wanted to return to power, but he realized that in order to create a viable coalition he needed the cooperation of Adolf Hitler. As the leader of the most electorally popular political party Hitler's claim to be Germany's Chancellor was very strong, but he still needed help to get into power.

It was the businessman Baron Kurt von Schröder who opened a fresh dialogue between Hitler and Papen. In evidence presented at the Nuremberg trials after the end of the Second World War, Schröder said Papen asked him to arrange a meeting with Hitler on 10 December 1932.[10] In his testimony, Papen claimed that Schröder had simply relayed Hitler's own request for a meeting.[11] Hitler and Papen duly met on 4 January at Schröder's home in Cologne. Although they arrived separately, they were both photographed entering the house.[12] Papen claimed that it was not a press photographer who took the photos, but a policeman tipped off by Chancellor Schleicher.[13]

The meeting started just before noon.[14] Hitler began by criticizing Papen for preventing him from becoming Chancellor in July 1932. Papen responded by claiming that it was Schleicher who blocked Hitler's appointment.[15] Hitler made it clear he would join the cabinet only if he was made Chancellor. However, he was willing to accept a prominent role for Papen and other positions for his conservative allies in his government provided they accepted the need to remove social democrats, communists and Jews from leading positions in German life.[16]

Schröder later recalled that during their two-hour meeting Papen proposed a conservative-nationalist coalition involving Hitler and the Nazis.[17] However, Papen later claimed that the question of Hitler becoming Chancellor was never discussed. Papen was merely suggesting Hitler should cooperate responsibly with the current government, according to his own recollection. All Papen promised was to ask Schleicher to consider bringing Hitler into the cabinet.[18] Papen gave Hitler the impression of being 'dead set against Schleicher', Goebbels noted in his diary after talking to Hitler. 'Wants to topple and eradicate him. Has the old man's [Hindenburg's] ear. Even stays with him.'[19]

As they left the house, Papen and Hitler were photographed once again. It was suggested in the newspapers that Hitler had asked Papen to persuade Hindenburg to appoint him as Chancellor.[20] The *Tägliche Rundschau*, a Berlin newspaper sympathetic to Schleicher, led with the headline 'Hitler and Papen against Schleicher'. The communist newspaper *Die Rote Front* (*The Red Front*) claimed that the meeting was part of 'a capitalist plot to create a fascist dictatorship'.[21]

After reading these reports Schleicher went to see Hindenburg and accused Papen of extreme disloyalty. Hindenburg told Schleicher that Papen would not meet Hitler in future without his express agreement. In an act of duplicity, Hindenburg secretly authorized Papen to continue his dialogue with the Nazi leader.[22] Business interests were alarmed by

Schleicher's willingness to court trade unions and the socialist left. The Agricultural League (*Reichslandbund*), a pressure group representing Germany's biggest landowners, suggested that Schleicher was not doing enough to help farmers either.

On 6 January the atmosphere was so febrile that Hitler and Papen were forced to issue a joint press statement denying that they were plotting to bring down the Schleicher government.[23] Papen visited

the German Chancellor on 9 January to convince him that he was trying to persuade Hitler to join the current government, but Schleicher was not convinced.[24] Nevertheless, he told a group of journalists at a dinner on 13 January that according to Papen Hitler wanted to be made Minister of the Interior and Defence Minister.[25]

After meeting Papen, Hitler gave a speech in Detmold in North Rhine-Westphalia on the evening of 4 January. He made no secret of wanting power, 'not through the back door but rather through the main gate'.[26] This was the starting point of a brief election campaign in the tiny German state of Lippe-Detmold, which had an electorate of 117,000. It was the sort of area where the Nazi Party normally fared well, because it was 95 per cent Protestant and predominantly rural. Over the next eleven days Hitler spoke in sixteen small towns in the region. He was concentrating on this local election in the hope of dispelling the view that the Nazi Party was in electoral decline. In the November 1932 federal election the Nazi Party saw its popular vote fall from 13,745,680 in July 1932 to 11,377,395, which resulted in it losing thirty-four Reichstag deputies. As the local newspaper the *Lippische Landes-Zeitung* wryly observed: 'The NSDAP [Nazi Party] must be in serious trouble if the great "Führer" himself is travelling to small villages.'[27] On his speaking tour, Hitler offered the German people a utopian vision of a racially pure Germany that would ruthlessly eradicate the threat of Marxism.[28]

Hitler waves to cheering crowds below at the window of the Reich Chancellery on 30 January 1933.

Hitler's ploy paid off. The Nazis saw their vote increase in the Lippe-Detmold election from 34.7 to 39.5 per cent. This was 6,000 votes up on November 1932, although 3,000 lower than the peak of July 1932. Most of the Party's gains came at the expense of the conservative-nationalist German National People's Party (DNVP), which was led by an austere businessman called Alfred Hugenberg.[29] The election result proved once again that the Nazis had still not been able to win votes from the two main working-class parties: the Social Democratic Party (SPD) and the German Communist Party (KPD). In private, Hitler claimed the Lippe-Detmold result was a success 'whose importance it is impossible to underestimate', because it was evidence of a resurgence of popular support for the Party.[30] Behind the scenes, however, there was pessimism about the Nazi Party's future electoral prospects. Secret Nazi internal polling suggested that the Party's popular appeal had peaked in July 1932. Hitler was now acutely aware that he needed to gain power if he was to revive his party's fortunes. According to the *Völkischer Beobachter* Hitler had denied reports in the left-wing press that he had received 4 million marks from Markus Wallenberg, a Swiss banker, to bolster the Nazis' election funds. In retaliation, Hitler vowed to rid the nation of 'the sensationalist press' if he ever came to power.[31]

Hitler's pleasing election result sealed the fate of 'dead man' Gregor Strasser. He resigned his Reichstag seat and promised to avoid all political activity for two years. 'The Strasser case is over,' Goebbels wrote in his diary. 'Poor Gregor! His best friends have turned against him.'[32] On that same evening Schleicher gave a speech on national radio in which he claimed to support 'neither socialism nor capitalism' and promised to boost the wages of working people.[33] At a cabinet meeting the next day he suggested it might be a good idea to ask Hindenburg to dissolve the Reichstag and postpone new elections. It would be an unconstitutional move, but the cabinet agreed all the same.[34] Schleicher admitted that a majority in the Reichstag could be attained only with Hitler's cooperation.[35] Goebbels noted in his diary: 'Everything is still up in the air regarding the ongoing negotiations to form a new government.'[36] He was concerned about the strain upon Hitler of all this political manoeuvring: 'The boss doesn't feel well at all. He gets too little sleep and doesn't eat enough.'[37]

On 17 January Hitler met the DNVP leader Alfred Hugenberg and his parliamentary secretary Otto Schmidt-Hannover in Hermann Göring's opulent apartment in Berlin. Hugenberg regarded Hitler and the Nazis as a street-fighting rabble, but he had become disillusioned with Schleicher and was keen to have talks with Hitler about the possibility of entering a new coalition government. Hugenberg felt that he and Hitler had found some 'common ground', but nothing concrete was agreed. Hugenberg told Hitler there was little hope of him being appointed Chancellor because of Hindenburg's opposition. 'Rubbish,' Hitler replied.[38]

The next day Hitler met Papen again. Hitler requested the meeting and not Papen as is often supposed.[39] Papen denied it ever happened which was untrue.[40] They met at the plush villa of Joachim von Ribbentrop, which was located in the affluent Berlin suburb of Dahlem. Goebbels once said that Ribbentrop had 'bought his name and married his money'. He was a wine merchant with a diplomatic and military background, but had only recently joined the Nazi Party. Ribbentrop and his wife took notes at Hitler and Papen's meeting.

More care had been taken over the security arrangements for this Hitler-Papen encounter. Ribbentrop's chauffeur picked up Papen from his home, while Hitler's chauffeur-driven limousine was driven into the garage of the house. This allowed Hitler to enter the house through the back garden. With Hitler that day were Ernst Röhm, the chief of the *Sturmabteilung* (SA) or Brownshirts, the Nazi Party's paramilitary wing, and Heinrich Himmler, the leader of the *Schutzstaffel* (SS), which began as a branch of the SA, but was destined to become far more powerful and deadly.[41]

'Hitler insists on being Chancellor,' Ribbentrop noted in his diary. 'Papen again considers this impossible. His influence with Hindenburg was not strong enough to affect this.'[42] Hitler told Papen that he was reluctant to engage in any further talks unless Papen agreed to make him Chancellor.[43] Papen prevaricated, because he still thought Hitler could be persuaded to take the post of Vice Chancellor. In the evening, Hitler went to see *The Rebel*, a new film released in Berlin on 22 December 1932. It told the tale of Austrian mountaineer Severin Anderlan's heroic resistance to Napoleon's occupation of the Austrian Tyrol. Hitler loved it. According to Goebbels, the film really 'fired him up'. What Hitler had most admired while watching it was how Anderlan had rejected all offers to compromise.[44]

On 20 January the Reichstag Steering Committee postponed the opening of the first Reichstag session of 1933 from 24 to 31 January. On the same day a Nazi-sponsored resolution on foreign policy was passed in the Reichstag thanks to the combined support of the Nazi and the Communist parties.[45] This gave a clear indication that Schleicher's

[overleaf] Hitler with leading members of the Nazi elite at the Hotel Kaiserhof in Berlin on the day he came to power. *From left to right:* Justice Minister Hanns Kerrl, Joseph Goebbels, Adolf Hitler, Ernst Röhm; Hermann Göring, Minister Walter Darré, Heinrich Himmler, head of the SS, Deputy Führer Rudolf Hess, Finance Minister Wilhelm Frick.

government stood little chance of winning a parliamentary vote of no confidence. In the evening Hitler spoke before a full house at the Berlin Sport Palace (*Sportpalast*). Hitler told his supporters they should not be discouraged by setbacks, but instead work for the establishment of a 'new ethnic-popular community'.[46] The Nazi newspaper *Der Angriff* observed that at the end of his speech: 'A storm of applause erupted such as cannot be described in words.'[47]

The most important day of clandestine discussions to bring Hitler to power was undoubtedly 22 January. It began with Hitler unveiling a memorial at the St Nicholas and St Mary I Cemetery (*St. Marien- und St. Nikolai-Friedhof I*) in Prenzlauer Berg, Berlin. The memorial was dedicated to Horst Wessel, an SA street-fighter who had been murdered by communists in February 1930 and subsequently elevated to martyrdom via a hugely popular Nazi battle song called 'Raise the Flag' ('*Die Fahne Hoch*'), popularly known as the 'Horst Wessel Song'.[48] Afterwards, 35,000 Brownshirts demonstrated noisily outside Karl-Liebknecht House on Bülowplatz, the headquarters of the KPD. The social democrat newspaper *Vorwärts* noted: 'The fact that on 22 January 1933 in Berlin Hitler's brown hordes were allowed to march outside the windows of the KPD headquarters with the conscious intention of challenging and humiliating their enemies, and that they were able to do so without any possibility of effective resistance, was a very bitter blow for the *entire* labour movement.'[49]

In the evening Hitler gave another rabble-rousing speech at the Sport Palace, primarily dedicated to the memory of Horst Wessel. He left just before 10 p.m. and travelled by limousine in the company of Wilhelm Frick and Hermann Göring for yet another secret meeting with Papen, once again at the home of Ribbentrop, who was emerging as a key player in the dark art of clandestine political intrigue. Papen later recalled that it was Hitler who had requested this meeting. Papen told Hindenburg about it and gave his consent for him to attend.[50] Accompanying Papen was Hindenburg's son Oskar, as well as Otto Meissner, Hindenburg's State Secretary. Papen had invited them both,[51] because they had considerable influence over Hindenburg. Meissner, who was secretive and devious, had been a member of the presidential staff since 1920. Oskar was once described by the French ambassador André François-Poncet as 'tall and massive as his father, but without the gracious demeanour'.[52] Oskar was, however, very close to his father and he trusted his judgement. Oskar had previously been friendly with Schleicher, but their relationship had recently cooled.

Up to this this point, Oskar had shown little sympathy for Hitler and National Socialism. In a prescient memorandum just two months before this meeting Oskar had warned his father that Hitler's appointment as Chancellor would inevitably lead to a one-party dictatorship.[53] Meissner told the Nuremberg trials that the key reason why Hitler was brought into discussions about a future coalition was because it had become clear that Schleicher had failed to gain Nazi support or to create a viable right-wing coalition.[54]

It seems that Oskar had other worries on his mind at this time. The SPD and the Catholic Centre Party (Zentrum) had set up a Reichstag enquiry into recent dodgy property deals under the so-called Eastern Aid programme. This had been created to bail out ailing Junker farming estates in East Prussia, but serious allegations began to emerge indicating that government funds were diverted from the scheme to buy property, racehorses, cars and luxury goods. Some of those under investigation were friends and relatives of President Hindenburg. These revelations were front-page news. Oskar's involvement in this scandal might have come to light under parliamentary scrutiny. This raises the distinct possibility that during their meeting Hitler promised to drop the Eastern Aid investigation if he became Chancellor.[55]

Elaborate arrangements were put in place to ensure the secrecy of this meeting. Oskar and Meissner, accompanied by their wives, began the evening by attending a performance of Richard Wagner's two-act opera *The Ban on Love* (*Das Liebesverbot*), based on William Shakespeare's *Measure for Measure*, at the Prussian State Opera House on the Unter den Linden. During the interval, both were seen talking to guests, but when the lights went down for the final act to begin they collected their overcoats from the cloakroom and slipped away by a side entrance, taking a taxi to Ribbentrop's house. It was snowing very heavily when they finally arrived.[56]

At the meeting Papen stressed that Hindenburg remained unconvinced of Hitler's suitability as Chancellor. Hitler said that he would not join Schleicher's cabinet and the Nazi Party would not support Schleicher's government in the Reichstag. He was prepared to cooperate only in a coalition in which he was appointed Chancellor.[57] Once this brief exchange of views was over, Hitler invited Oskar to an adjacent room for a private talk. This meeting reportedly lasted for just over an hour. Neither man kept a record of what was said, but at the Nuremburg trials Oskar said that Hitler had dominated the conversation. He stressed that he alone could save Germany from civil

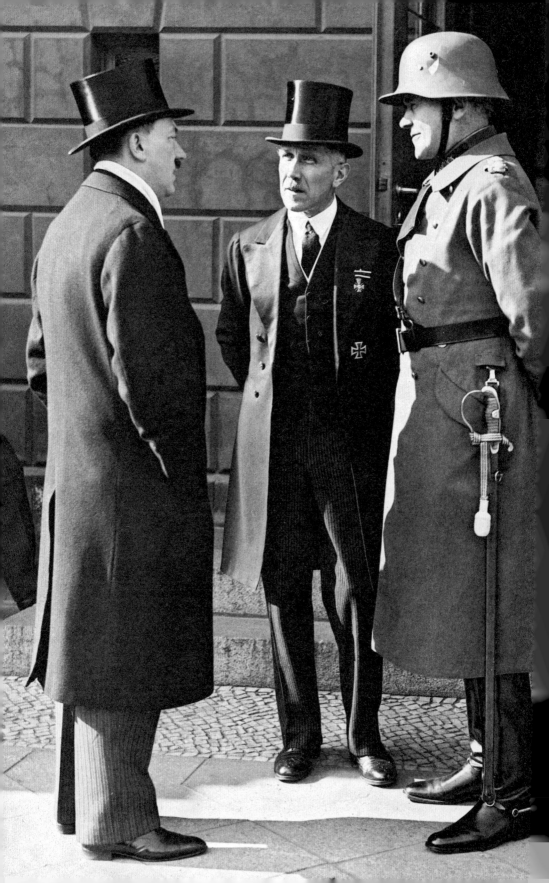

war and crush the communist threat and he reminded Oskar that no government could survive without the support of the Nazi Party.[58]

A one-pot dinner followed, accompanied by champagne, although Hitler stuck to his usual tipple of mineral water. Oskar and Meissner were the first to leave. 'In the taxi on the way back,' Meissner recalled, 'Oskar von Hindenburg was very silent; the only remark he made was that there was no help for it, the Nazis had to be taken into the government. My impression was that Hitler had succeeded in getting him under his spell.'[59] Hitler told Goebbels two days later that he doubted whether he had really won over Oskar, whom he described as the 'personification of stupidity'.[60] For his part, Papen later commented: 'I want to make it clear the actual question of forming a cabinet with Hitler as Chancellor was not discussed by Oskar Hindenburg, Meissner or myself.'[61] This is contradicted by Ribbentrop's more reliable contemporary diary entry. 'Papen will now press for Hitler as Chancellor,' he wrote, 'but tells Hitler he will withdraw from these negotiations forthwith if Hitler has no confidence in him.'[62]

In Papen's own report of the meeting, which he submitted to Hindenburg, he suggested Schleicher should be given more time to secure support in the Reichstag. Papen also ruled out taking over as Chancellor himself. Significantly, he did not recommend that Hitler should be made Chancellor at this stage.[63] Meissner later recalled that despite Papen's persuasive arguments, Hindenburg remained 'extremely hesitant' about appointing Hitler as Chancellor. He still wanted Papen to assume that role again.[64]

In spite of all the secrecy surrounding the meeting, Schleicher's spies found out about it. Schleicher bluntly asked Meissner in a telephone call if he had enjoyed his meal at Ribbentrop's house. On 23 January Schleicher met Hindenburg and told him that his negotiations to form a coalition, which might survive a vote of no confidence in the Reichstag, had failed.[65] Now the only alternative to a Hitler-led government, Schleicher said, was a 'military dictatorship'. He asked Hindenburg for a permanent suspension of the Reichstag and to cancel all further elections. He also wanted the Nazi Party and the German Communist Party banned. His dictatorship would be kept in power by the army.[66] Hindenburg rejected Schleicher's proposals out of hand. Even worse for Schleicher, his plan for a military dictatorship was leaked to the press, which led to a general outcry from all his political opponents.

On 27 January the Reichstag Steering Committee met again and affirmed that the parliamentary session would begin on 31 January.[67]

Franz von Papen, German politician *(centre)*, with Adolf Hitler *(left)* and Werner von Blomberg *(right)* on 12 March 1933, a day of general mourning for German soldiers killed in the First World War.

On that same day Hitler met the DNVP leader Alfred Hugenberg, informing him that Papen now supported his appointment as Chancellor. Hugenberg objected to Hitler's demand that a Nazi should be appointed Prussian Interior Minister, because this would give the Nazis full control of the police force.[68] Ribbentrop was present and noted the meeting ended 'in a quarrel' between Hugenberg and Hitler with nothing decided. Hitler described the leaders of the DNVP as 'one gang of swindlers'.[69]

Meanwhile, Göring met Meissner at the presidential palace to reassure him that Hitler had no intention whatsoever of violating the Weimar constitution if given power and the Nazi Party would oppose any attempt by Schleicher to govern without parliamentary support.[70] Even at the last minute Hitler thought that Papen might double-cross him. Ribbentrop noted in his diary: 'Hitler very indignant, wants to leave for Munich immediately. Göring persuades him to stay.'[71] At 11 a.m. on this very eventful day, Ribbentrop met with Papen and told him that after a long talk with Hindenburg he now believed that Hitler's appointment as Chancellor was a real possibility.[72]

At an emergency cabinet meeting on 28 January Schleicher told his colleagues that he would ask Hindenburg to dissolve the Reichstag, then to delay elections and allow him to govern in a 'presidential cabinet'. If Hindenburg refused, Schleicher would immediately resign.[73] He then asked the President to carry out his plans. 'No,' was Hindenburg's blunt reply. Schleicher was left with no alternative but to resign. Hindenburg explained that he needed to find a majority government that could stabilize Germany. 'Whether what I am doing now is right, my dear Schleicher,' he added, 'I do not know, but I shall know soon enough when I am up there, [pointing heavenward].' Schleicher pondered this statement before replying: 'After this breach of trust, sir, I am not sure that you will go to heaven.'[74]

Hindenburg next summoned Papen, in the presence of his son Oskar and Meissner, and urged him to take the post of Chancellor. Papen declined the offer, and he, Oskar and Meissner said Hitler was now the only logical choice. Hindenburg finally conceded defeat. 'It is my unpleasant duty,' he replied, 'to appoint this fellow Hitler as Chancellor.' However, he insisted that if Hitler became Chancellor it must be in a coalition arrangement under which he could be contained by reliable conservatives. Furthermore, Hitler's cabinet must include General Werner von Blomberg as Minister of Defence. Hindenburg mistakenly believed that Blomberg was a 'non-political soldier' and therefore a safe pair of hands. In fact he was a pro-Nazi and a passionate advocate of rearmament.[75] Hindenburg had been deeply influenced by Papen in finally agreeing to appoint Hitler as Chancellor. As Otto Meissner put it: 'Papen finally won him [Hindenburg] over to Hitler with the argument that the representatives of the other right-wing parties, which would belong to the government, would restrict Hitler's freedom of action.'[76]

A hectic day of discussions followed concerning the composition of Hitler's cabinet on 29 January. At 11 a.m. Hitler met Papen and agreed to the formation of a national coalition government, containing only two other Nazis. After coming to power, Hitler wanted to call an immediate general election and pass an Enabling Act to dispense legally with the Reichstag. Papen relayed these proposals to Hindenburg, who was surprised by how moderate they were.[77] 'Don't worry, we've hired him,' Papen told Hindenburg.[78] In the afternoon Hitler was informed by Papen that he would be appointed the Chancellor of Germany at 11 a.m. on the following day.

It was -4°C on 30 January. Hitler had just one more problem left to resolve before he took office. Hugenberg, the DNVP leader, had raised a last-minute objection to Hitler's desire for a general election. A frustrated Papen shouted at Hugenberg: 'If the new government is not formed by eleven o'clock, the army is going to march. Schleicher may establish a military dictatorship.'[79] Hitler tried to appease Hugenberg by assuring him that whatever the result of the election every cabinet minister would keep his job.

At 11.15 a.m. Hitler's Reich cabinet (*Reichsregierung*) finally walked into Hindenburg's office and the President gave a short speech, emphasizing the need for cooperation in this new government.[80] At 11.30 a.m. Hitler took the oath of office to become the German Chancellor. In an impromptu speech, he vowed to uphold the Weimar constitution. After speaking, Hitler waited for Hindenburg to say a few positive things about him, but all Hindenburg could say was: 'And now gentlemen, forward with God.'[81] Hitler went to the Hotel Kaiserhof for lunch. 'We all had tears in our eyes,' Goebbels noted in his diary. 'We shook Hitler's hand. He deserved this. Enormous celebrations.'[82]

Hitler had become the Chancellor of what was officially described as 'A Government of National Concentration'. Only two other Nazis were included in Hitler's cabinet: Wilhelm Frick, Minister of the Interior, a career civil servant and a moderate Nazi. The other was the Reichstag President (Speaker) Hermann Göring, effectively Hitler's deputy, who was given the role of Minister without Portfolio, plus the additional post of Prussian Deputy Minister of the Interior. Papen was appointed Vice Chancellor, but he remained Prime Minister of Prussia and was nominally Göring's line manager.[83]

Hitler took over a highly sophisticated state machine, but he had no cabinet or civil service experience. He had been brought in by the conservative elite as the front man for a popular authoritarian regime. This is why his cabinet, which had been chosen by Hindenburg and Papen, was predominantly conservative. Hitler had never even met several of his cabinet colleagues before. Four of them had served in Schleicher's outgoing cabinet: Konstantin von Neurath (Foreign Minister), Lutz Graf Schwerin von Krosigk (Finance Minister), Paul von Eltz-Rübenach (Postmaster General and Transport Minister) and Franz Gürtner (Justice Minister). The new non-Nazi entrants were: Werner von Blomberg (Minister of War), Alfred Hugenberg (Economics and Food and Agriculture Minister) and Franz Seldte, the Labour Minister and leader of the paramilitary Steel Helmet League of Front Soldiers (*Stahlhelm*). Although Papen sat in the cabinet as Vice Chancellor, he had no ministry of his own. Hugenberg, the head of the DNVP, was the only other party leader in the cabinet. In addition, Dr Perecke attended cabinet as Reich Commissar for Procurement of Labour. Two state secretaries – Dr Hans Lammers of the Reich Chancellery and Otto Meissner of the Presidential Chancellery – also attended. Walther Funk was appointed Reich Press Chief, a post that had been expected to go to Joseph Goebbels, the Nazi propaganda chief.[84]

Many of these conservative individuals remained in Hitler's cabinet for long periods.[85] Typical was Lutz Graf Schwerin von Krosigk, the Finance Minister. The first time he ever met Hitler was on the day he became Chancellor. He was an upper-class conservative, who kept his comments in cabinet 'short, clear and always to the point'.[86] He remained in office from 1933 to 1945. A loyal German bureaucrat, he did not even regard himself as a politician. André François-Poncet, the French ambassador, knew him well and described him as 'the embodiment of a reliable, correct and decent German official'.[87] Schwerin von Krosigk later told Hans Luther: 'Before National Socialism came to power I had great respect for its idealistic goals, but serious reservations about its violent methods and rowdy followers.'[88]

The first meeting of Hitler's cabinet took place on 30 January at 5 p.m. Hitler simply asked his colleagues for their full support at this difficult time.[89] Hugenberg suggested that the Communist Party should be banned immediately. 'It is nothing short of impossible to ban six million people who stand behind the KPD,' Hitler replied.[90] Hugenberg never developed a close relationship with Hitler. Indeed, their mutual dislike was obvious to other cabinet members.

At the time of Hitler's appointment, Papen had said in an off-the-cuff remark: 'Within two months we will have pushed Hitler so far in the corner that he'll squeak.'[91] This comment is repeated in nearly every general history of the Third Reich,[92] but it is unfair to Papen. Hitler's modest personal manner in face-to-face encounters, and his diffidence in private, misled Papen into thinking he could be easily controlled. When he saw Hitler addressing the cabinet, Papen began to appreciate how quickly the Nazi leader was 'able to dominate and to impose his opinion on everyone who came into contact with him. Even people who differed with him fundamentally became convinced of his sincerity.'[93] Hitler impressed other cabinet colleagues, too. Schwerin von Krosigk observed: 'In cabinet meetings, one could not but recognize and admire the qualities that gave him a mastery of discussions: his infallible memory, which enabled him to answer with the utmost precision.'[94]

Before Hitler came to power the Reich cabinet proceeded on the basis of majority decisions, but Hitler decided that policy should now be agreed by the Chancellor in liaison with individual ministers. This was allowed under Article 26 of the existing Weimar constitution.[95] Hitler did not remove power from the cabinet and devolve it to ministers who then created competing empires, as is often supposed. He simply followed existing practice. Each Reich minister in the Weimar era had enormous independence to control their ministries. No minister could interfere with the policy-making of another. The only minister who acted in liaison with other ministers was the Finance Minister, who was responsible for the budget of each ministry. Hitler tended to work closely with the Finance Minister in deciding the allocation of funds. Again, this was similar to what had occurred during the Weimar period.[96]

It was a wintry evening on 30 January when Nazi Party supporters celebrated Hitler's rise to power with a torchlight parade through Berlin. Jubilant storm troopers carrying flaming torches and holding aloft swastika flags marched triumphantly through the Brandenburg Gate, singing the 'Horst Wessel Song'. Manfred von Schröder, the pro-Nazi son of the banker who had played a role in bringing Hitler to power, later recalled: 'The young were enthusiastic and optimistic and believed in Hitler.'[97] Melita Maschmann, a fifteen-year-old schoolgirl who idolized Hitler and was taken to the parade by her parents, remembered: 'The crashing tread of the feet, the sombre pomp of the red and black flags, the flickering light from the torches on the faces and the songs with melodies that were at once aggressive and sentimental.' She was drawn to National Socialism because Hitler promised that 'people of all classes would live together, like brothers and sisters'.[98] 'Naturally we were excited,' claimed Gabriele Winckler, a young secretary. 'We thought now everything will be different and everything will be better.'[99] Claus Moser, the ten-year-old son of a wealthy Jewish banker, was having supper with his parents in a plush Berlin hotel that evening: 'We saw the torchlight procession, and then I learned from talking to my parents as it was going on that this was a peaceful change. I don't think I did politics at school, but I knew about revolutions and violence and of course Hitler was clever: he came to power constitutionally.'[100]

Papen witnessed the triumphant parade of storm troopers as it reached the illuminated windows of the Reich Chancellery: 'It was an extraordinary experience, and the endless cry "Heil, Heil, Sieg Heil" rang in my ears like an alarm bell.'[101] Hans Frank stood behind Hitler as he leaned out of the window and acknowledged the cheering crowds below: 'God knows our hearts were pure that day, and if anyone had told us of the events to come, no one would have believed it, least of all I. It was a day of glory and happiness.'[102] In a speech on national radio that evening Göring said: '30 January will go down in German history as the day the nation found its way back to itself, because a new nation emerged and made short work of all the agony, humiliation and treachery of the past fourteen years.'[103] 'The new Reich has been born,' Goebbels wrote in his diary. 'Fourteen years of work have been crowned with victory. The German revolution has begun.'[104]

Hitler's appointment provoked a variety of reactions. The British *Sunday Times* commented: 'Have President von Hindenburg and his "comrade" Herr von Papen got Hitler into a cage before they wring his neck or are they in a cage?'[105] In Germany the *Frankfurter Zeitung* noted: 'The make-up of the cabinet shows that Herr Hitler had to accept significant restrictions.'[106] In America the *New York Times* concluded that Hitler had 'no scope for the gratification of his dictatorial ambitions'.[107] The German SPD newspaper *Vorwärts* commented: 'With the appointment of this cabinet, the President has assumed the most dreadful responsibility ever taken by a statesman. It is up to him to see this cabinet does not depart from the constitution and that it immediately resigns if it does not attain a majority in the Reichstag.'[108]

Sir Horace Rumbold, the British ambassador to Berlin, observed: 'On the whole the press has taken the appointment of Hitler to the chancellorship with almost philosophic calm.'[109] He informed the British Foreign Office that because the Nazis were in a minority position in the cabinet Hitler would be 'unable to embark on dangerous experiments'.[110] A Czech diplomat stationed in Berlin gave a similar upbeat assessment in his diary: 'No Nazi government, not even a revolutionary one, even though it carries Hitler's name. No third Reich, hardly even a second and a half.'[111] Similarly, Kurt Schumacher, an SPD Reichstag member, observed: 'The cabinet is called Adolf Hitler. But the cabinet is Hugenberg's.'[112] Perhaps Siegmund Weltlinger, a member of the Berlin Jewish council, best summed up the mood at the time: 'When Hitler came, I regarded him as just one of the many political idiots which were springing up all over the place, as far back as I could remember in recent times and I did not take him seriously.'[113]

On 31 January Hitler held a cabinet meeting. He informed its members that no agreement was currently possible with the Catholic Centre Party to get the Enabling Act through the Reichstag, and therefore a fresh national election was required. Papen said that 'a return to the parliamentary system was to be avoided permanently'.[114] A few hours later, Hindenburg granted Hitler a dissolution of the Reichstag and a new general election. In his diary Goebbels wrote: 'For the present we intend to refrain from direct countermeasures [against the communists]. First, the Bolshevik attempt at revolution must flare up. Then we will strike.'[115] Hitler felt confident that with Hindenburg's support he could bring about a legal revolution that would destroy democracy.

On 1 February Hitler delivered his 'Appeal to the German Nation' live on national radio. It was his first major speech as Chancellor. The leading banker Hjalmar Schacht was present as Hitler spoke and he noticed 'his whole body quivered and shook' as he delivered the speech in a surprisingly calm and restrained voice.[116] There was no mention at all of Hitler's favourite subject, the Jewish question. Instead, Hitler argued that Germany's current political and economic problems were primarily due to Germany's defeat in 1918 and the unstable Weimar Republic that followed. It was the communists who had ripped Germany apart, he argued, and he vowed to end the 'communist menace'.

The first aim of his government, he said, was to restore to the German people unity of mind and will. He would preserve and defend the foundations on which the strength of the nation rested. He would protect Christianity and from now on the family would be the nucleus of the nation and state. His government would stand above states and classes and 'bring back to our people the consciousness of its racial and political unity and its attendant obligations'. German youth would be educated to respect 'our great past and have pride in our old traditions', he said. Furthermore, he would declare war on 'spiritual, political and cultural nihilism'. He announced a four-year programme to rescue the German peasantry from impoverishment, to overcome unemployment, and to reform the German state and local authorities. On foreign policy he struck a moderate tone, even stressing that he was willing to listen to disarmament proposals from the Allies.[117]

On 3 February Hitler dined at the home of General Kurt von Hammerstein, commander-in-chief of the *Reichswehr*, the Weimar Republic Armed Forces, who had previously been an outspoken critic of the Nazi Party. After dinner Hitler gave a two-and-a-half-hour speech to the German military establishment who were also present. The audience response was polite but restrained. For once Hitler had been honest about his real foreign policy aims and his key objectives. First, Marxism and democracy would be eradicated. Second, rearmament would be pushed forward at a rapid pace to escape the restrictions imposed by the Treaty of Versailles. Third, he would reintroduce conscription. Fourth, Germany would seek the 'the conquest of land', *Lebensraum* or 'living space' in Eastern Europe at the expense of the Soviet Union. This would be achieved gradually, step by step, because of Germany's weak military standing at present. He promised them that the army would be placed above politics.[118] The naval leader Admiral Erich Raeder later claimed to have found Hitler's speech 'extraordinarily satisfying'.[119]

On 8 February another cabinet meeting took place to decide on budget priorities for the next five years. Hitler stressed that rearmament was his chief priority. Germany would not be content simply with equality of rights in armaments: 'The next five years in Germany had to be devoted to rendering the German people capable of bearing arms again. Every publicly sponsored measure to create employment had to be considered from that point of view.' This would be the 'dominant thought, always and everywhere', he said.[120]

At another cabinet meeting on 16 February Hitler announced the creation of a State Commissariat for Aviation. It was a camouflage organization for channelling funds towards the creation of a German air force or *Luftwaffe*, which had been prohibited since 1919 under the terms of the Treaty of Versailles. A secret fund of 127 million Reichsmarks was allocated to this project.[121] Thus, within days of coming to power, Hitler had begun plans for rearmament.

Hitler began the general election campaign with a speech at the Berlin Sport Palace on 10 February, although this was not going to be a fully democratic campaign. Six days earlier Hitler had issued a 'Decree for the Protection of the German People', with Hindenburg's blessing, which gave his government the power to ban the public meetings, newspapers and even the election literature of rival opposition parties.[122] Hitler opened his speech with a familiar complaint that the fourteen years of the democratic Weimar Republic had brought nothing but ruin to Germany. He described his rivals the German Communist Party and the Social Democratic Party as the 'political parties of disintegration' and promised to root out Marxism and to replace democracy with 'the virtue of personality and the creative power of the individual'.[123] Give me four years in power, he said, and a new Germany of 'greatness and power and glory and justice' would rise again.[124]

The government's key election slogan was 'Build with Hitler'. He flew around the country on a speaking tour to seventeen different cities, including Breslau, Cologne, Dortmund, Kassel, Leipzig, Munich, Nuremberg and Stuttgart. Hitler later recalled that the German people 'thirsted for order', so he had hammered home this theme in every speech during the election campaign.[125] In Kassel he said: 'The period of international babble, the promise of reconciliation among nations is over and done with: its place will be taken by the people's community.'[126] In Stuttgart, he claimed his central ambition was to liberate Germany from the restrictions of an 'impossible parliamentary democracy'.[127] In the crowd that night was Alfred Haussen, a communist mechanic, who later recalled: 'The local inhabitants gathered in the city centre. The speech was supposed to be broadcast on German national radio, but after a few minutes no one could hear anything, as some local comrades with axes, working at the local post office, cut the electric wire. The local Nazis were deeply outraged.'[128]

On 20 February Hitler broke off from his election tour to meet several key industrialists at the official residence of Hermann Göring in Berlin. The aim was to persuade big business to fund the Nazis' election

[*overleaf*] Policemen assess the fire damage to the Reichstag in the aftermath of the fire on 27 February 1933.

campaign. In a ninety-minute rambling speech Hitler declared that after his victory he would uphold private property and private enterprise and crush communism. Göring then asked the businessmen to fund the election campaign. In return, he promised this election would be 'the last for the next ten years, probably for the next hundred years'.[129] An estimated 2 million Reichsmarks was raised at this meeting from several major German companies, most notably, Hoesch, IG Farben, Opel, Siemens and United Steel. Further contributions from the business elite brought the Nazi electoral campaign fund to a whopping 3 million Reichsmarks. Big business was reluctant to support the Nazi Party before Hitler came to power, but was now willing to work with him as Chancellor.[130]

On 22 February Göring set up an auxiliary police force of approximately 50,000 men. They were recruited from the SS and the unruly and uncontrollable storm troopers of the SA. These Nazi squads began a violent reign of terror against the socialist left. Furthermore, the Prussian police were told by Göring to cease all surveillance of Nazi activists. The relationship between the state police forces and the SA was extremely strained. Many police officers unsympathetic to Nazism were often intimidated by the storm troopers.

The violence and fear that accompanied the election campaign should not be underestimated. Gangs of storm troopers broke up the meetings of the KPD and the SPD. On 24 February a former SPD police commissioner in Berlin wrote to SPD leaders in Altona, Dortmund and Kiel complaining several of his own public meetings had been disrupted. Large numbers of the audience were attacked by the thuggish SA. He decided not to speak at further events, because 'there is obviously no longer police protection sufficient to check the aggressive actions of the SA and the SS at my meetings'.[131] On that same day a mob of SA men raided Karl Liebknecht House, the Berlin headquarters of the KPD, on the pretext a communist uprising was in the offing. Supposedly 'treasonous' documents were seized. The KPD had not been officially banned, but its normal electioneering activities were so hampered that it might as well have been.

On 27 February the Reichstag was set on fire.[132] The person charged with this crime was Marinus van der Lubbe, an unemployed, working-class Dutch communist. He was born in Leiden in the Netherlands on 13 January 1909, the product of a poverty-stricken, dysfunctional background. His drunken father deserted the family soon after his birth and his mother died when he was twelve. Afterwards, he drifted from job to job, but soon became active in various left-wing groups. His involvement with communists gave some meaning to an otherwise lonely and rootless existence. When he heard Hitler had been appointed German Chancellor, he thought he would protest by travelling to Germany and setting fire to public buildings.[133]

On 18 February he arrived in Berlin, having walked on foot all the way from the Netherlands in ten days. He was seen in a shop on Müllerstraße buying four boxes of firelighters. His actions in the days beforehand were not those of someone fixated merely upon burning down the Reichstag. He started his haphazard arson campaign at three other government buildings on 25 February: the welfare office in the Labour Ministry building, Schöneberg Town Hall and the Imperial Palace. Each time he managed to evade arrest.

His fourth target was the glass-domed Reichstag on the evening of 27 February.[134] Security at the building's western entrance was extremely lax. Van der Lubbe nimbly climbed a wall, broke a window and was soon on the first floor of the deserted building. A witness on the street down below, a theology student, heard breaking glass as he walked by and noted the time: 9.30 p.m. Looking up, he saw a person at the window with a burning object in his hand. He ran to alert a policeman. Van der Lubbe, stripped to the waist, dripping with sweat, was quickly apprehended by the police inside the burning Reichstag. It was some time before the fire brigade was alerted, however. The first fire engine did not arrive until 10 p.m., by which time the blaze was completely out of control.[135]

In his opulent Berlin apartment opposite the Reichstag, Hitler's friend Ernst 'Putzi' Hanfstaengl was asleep in bed, suffering from a severe cold, when his housekeeper suddenly woke him up, screaming the Reichstag was on fire. He telephoned Joseph Goebbels, who was hosting a dinner party for the Chancellor at his home. They had been listening to music and sharing anecdotes when he rang. Goebbels thought Putzi was joking at first. Then Hitler looked out of the window, saw the flames in the sky and shouted: 'It's the communists!'[136] Hitler and Goebbels set off towards the burning building.

Already at the scene was Göring. 'When I entered [the Reichstag],' Rudolf Diels, the head of the Prussian Gestapo later recalled, 'Göring strode forward to meet me. His voice rose with all the fateful emotions of that dramatic hour: "This is the beginning of the communist uprising. Now they are going to strike. Not a minute must be lost."'[137] Historians have often wondered whether the Nazis were responsible for the Reichstag fire. Was it part of a secret plan to destroy democracy? Göring's sudden arrival on the scene makes him a prime suspect. After all, there was an underground passage connecting his official residence to the Reichstag building. He certainly had the motive, the means and the opportunity. However, in the summer of 1945 in Mondorf internment camp near Luxembourg, Göring confided to Schwerin von Krosigk: 'I would have been proud to have set the Reichstag on fire, but I was innocent of that crime.'[138] Later, while awaiting execution at Nuremberg in 1946, Göring told William Donovan, the head of the US Office of Strategic Services: 'You must at least be convinced that with death staring me in the face, I have no need to resort to lies. I give you my word that I had nothing to do with the Reichstag fire.'[139]

Conspiracy theorists have also considered Hitler's reaction on the night of the fire. Rudolf Diels thought Hitler was genuinely shocked.[140] After arriving at the building, Hitler began shouting hysterically. 'Now there can be no mercy,' he said to Diels. 'Every communist functionary will be shot wherever we find him. The communist deputies must be shot this very night. Everyone in alliance with the communists must be arrested.'[141] On the other hand, Hitler shed no tears for the Reichstag. 'Good riddance to that trashy old shack,' he said.[142] At the time Papen was convinced it was the Nazis who started the fire, but he changed his mind after the war and accepted that van der Lubbe acted alone.[143] There is no evidence Goebbels knew anything about the fire in advance, but he saw immediately how it might be used to Hitler's advantage. It was a 'huge stroke of luck', he wrote in his diary.[144]

The foreign press corps and many foreign diplomats suspected the Nazis were behind the Reichstag fire. After all, it was the perfect pretext to destroy the communists and justify the end of democratic government. Foreign journalists investigated the story in great depth. However, when interviewed by Sefton Delmer of the British *Daily Express*, Hitler rejected the suggestion that the fire was a calculated move to give the Nazis a pretext to crush communism. The Nazi Party, he said, had nothing to do with it.[145] Nevertheless, the pressure intensified for the truth to be revealed. Hitler sanctioned a full-scale show trial of Marinus van der Lubbe. He wanted to prove that he was the stooge in a complex communist conspiracy which involved Ernst Torgler, the leader of the German Communist Party in the Reichstag, along with three Bulgarian communist accomplices: Georgi Dimitrov, Blagoi Popov and Vasil Tanev, all of them leading figures in the Communist International (Comintern). Dimitrov, for instance, was the leader of Comintern activities in Western Europe. Dimitrov, Popov, Tanev and Torgler were arrested and held in custody until a trial date could be set.[146]

On the day after the Reichstag fire the cabinet met to discuss its implications. Hitler was in a ruthless mood. He insisted the communists must be suppressed. The cabinet agreed to the introduction of the far-reaching 'Decree of the Reich President for the Protection of People and State'. This suspended most of the civil rights granted under the Weimar constitution, including free speech, a free press, the right to assemble, imprisonment without trial, and the privacy of mail and telephone calls. It also gave the Reich Minister of the Interior the power to seize control of any state government unable to keep order.

Papen was the only cabinet minister to raise any objection to this turn of events, observing that it might compromise the autonomy of federal state governments. However, the original idea for the emergency decree had come not from a Nazi but from Ludwig Grauert, a leading conservative official in the Prussian Ministry of the Interior. Furthermore, Hindenburg signed it without raising any objections. The 'Reichstag Fire Decree', as it became known, was a spontaneous response to an act of terrorism, but it also provided Hitler with the fundamental, quasi-legal basis for the conquest of the Weimar state and its swift transformation into a dictatorship. It would remain in place for the entire duration of the Third Reich.[147]

Violence against the left now escalated dramatically. 'Mass Arrests Everywhere' declared the *Völkischer Beobachter* on 2 March.[148] On 3 March Ernst Thälmann, the Communist Party leader, was seized. He would spend the next eleven years in solitary confinement until, on 18 August 1944 on Hitler's direct orders, he would be executed in Buchenwald concentration camp. In Leipzig 474 people were taken into 'protective custody', a favourite Nazi euphemism for imprisonment without trial. By April the SA and the police force had arrested 8,000 Communist Party functionaries in the Ruhr and the Rhineland alone. In Bavaria 3,000 people were captured. Over the course of the year more than 100,000 'political prisoners' were detained in what were known as 'wild' concentration camps located in the larger cities.

It's been estimated that the SA ran more than 240 such camps in Berlin alone during the early months of Hitler's rule. Conditions were extremely brutal. All types of buildings were converted to house political prisoners, including old workhouses, derelict army barracks, warehouses and factories, and even the cellars of beer halls. Prisoners rarely had beds or running water and barely survived on the meagre rations available. Punishment beatings and verbal bullying were frequent. As Wilhelm Murr, the Nazi state president of Württemberg, put it: 'We don't say an eye for an eye, a tooth for a tooth. No, if someone knocks out one of our teeth, we will smash in his jaw.'[149]

The British writer Christopher Isherwood observed how the SA went about cracking down on opposition in Berlin, where he lived: 'The whole city lay under an epidemic of discreet, infectious fear. I could feel it, like influenza, in my bones. The city was full of whispers. They told of illegal midnight arrests, of prisoners tortured in SA barracks, made to spit on Lenin's picture, swallow castor oil, eat old socks.'[150] Local neighbours could hear the blood-curdling screams of inmates being beaten with iron rods, truncheons and whips. Doctors in local hospitals were confronted with battered and tortured victims who were scarcely recognizable and very often beyond medical care.

It's difficult to establish how many prisoners were killed during this orgy of violence. Estimates vary between 500 and 1,000.[151] Often people knew about this violence and even witnessed it on the streets, but as Lucie Baumann, who lived in Essen at the time, put it: 'Everyone knew what would happen if the Nazis gained power, but most people didn't want to know, they didn't want to see. See nothing, hear nothing, that was the order of the day.'[152]

Hitler concluded his hectic election campaign tour with a speech in Königsberg, which was broadcast live on German national radio. He told the audience that people would have more freedom under his rule. 'Now hold your heads high and proud once again!' he said. 'You are no longer enslaved and unfree; now you are free again.'[153] Victor Klemperer listened in horror. He was an academic professor based in Dresden, he had been born into a Jewish family that converted to Protestantism and he was married to a German Christian. He described Hitler's speech in his diary as the 'unctuous bawling of a priest'.[154]

The general election took place on 5 March, dubbed by the Nazis 'The Day of the Awakening Nation'. When the results were declared the Nazi Party had secured 43.9 per cent of the vote, up by 10.8 per cent, and with 5.5 million more votes than in November 1932. The Nazi Party now had an additional 92 seats in the Reichstag, which made a total of 288.

Some historians of the Third Reich like to observe that because 'only 43.9 per cent' of the German people voted for the Nazi Party in the March 1933 election it was no great triumph for Hitler.[155]

However, in the context of German elections since 1918 it was quite an exceptional success. It was the highest vote of any political party in any democratic election in Germany from 1919 to 1932; the second highest being 37.9 per cent for the SPD in January 1919. It also exceeded by 6.7 per cent the July 1932 total for the Nazi Party, which itself was the third largest Weimar share of the vote. The turnout at 88.8 per cent was also a record in any post-1918 national election. The Nazi Party received 17.2 million votes, way ahead of the 13,745,000 it had achieved in July 1932. The highest popular vote achieved between 1919 and 1932 by any other German political party was 11,509,048, again by the SPD in January 1919. This huge increase in the popular vote in March 1933 was almost entirely attributable to voters who had not voted in the previous election.

The main message of the Nazi election campaign had been a promise to crush the communist threat, a promise that brought the Party a flood of new middle-class and rural voters. The Nazi vote increased in many Catholic areas, too, although the working-class districts once again bravely and stubbornly rejected Nazism. The votes of the two leading left-wing parties held up surprisingly well. The socialist SPD took 18.2 per cent, a fall of just 2.1 per cent, so that they had lost just one Reichstag seat since the November 1932 election. The KPD polled 12.3 per cent, down only 4.5 per cent, with a loss of 18 seats. The two left-wing parties retained a combined vote of 30.5 per cent. Considering the extraordinary violence and intimidation suffered by the left during the campaign, this was a pretty remarkable result.

The Catholic Centre Party (Zentrum) took 11.2 per cent, holding 74 seats: an increase of four seats on the previous election. The German National People's Party (DNVP), Hitler's coalition partners, won 52 seats: 7.9 per cent of the popular vote, with no gain in seats. Overall, this gave Hitler's coalition government 51.9 per cent of the popular vote. Hitler still needed the votes of the Catholic Centre Party to pass the Enabling Act, which required the support of 66 per cent of Reichstag deputies. In another outrage to democracy, however, the 81 Communist Party deputies were banned from serving in the new Reichstag and from voting on the Act, even though they had all been legally elected.

On 6 March the *Frankfurter Zeitung*, in reflective mood, observed that 'The intensive propaganda of the right had succeeded in creating a nervous, feverish atmosphere. The feeling of oppression among the population was great.'[156] In Britain, by contrast, the *Daily Mail* celebrated Hitler's victory: 'In Germany, the elections have brought some relaxation of tension in the Fatherland. Herr Hitler has won his majority clearly. If he uses it prudently and peacefully, no one here will shed any tears over the disappearance of German democracy.'[157] Many in Germany hoped that Hitler would reunite the country. As the industrialist Hans Kehrl observed, the Nazi Party was 'the only party that promised to get us out of the hole and the idea was principally that it would be possible if we developed as a nation a team spirit and solidarity, pulling on the same rope'.[158]

At a cabinet meeting on 7 March Hitler claimed his success in the general election amounted to a revolution. What was now required, he said, was the swift passing of the Enabling Act to end parliamentary democracy now and forever.[159]

In the days that followed, Nazi activists seized power in all the federal states. Before 5 March only Hamburg, Hesse, Prussia and Württemberg had Nazi-dominated local governments. After the election the states of Baden, Bremen, Lübeck, Saxony and Schaumburg-Lippe all turned Nazi in quick succession. Nazis no longer had to wait for conservative nationalists to invite them into office, they could take the law into their own hands.

In the vanguard of this 'revolution from below' were Ernst Röhm's storm troopers and the sequence of events in each region was usually the same. Major public buildings were occupied, then the local Nazi leadership demanded control of the police. The SA occupied government offices and the swastika flag was soon visible on public buildings. The Reich Interior Minister would then invoke emergency measures and appoint Reich commissioners to take charge, usually Nazi Gauleiters.* Local government civil servants and the police were powerless to stop any of this from happening.

The Bavarian state government was dissolved on 8 March. The following day the Nazi General Franz von Epp took power as state commissioner, after President Heinrich Held, a member of the Bavarian People's Party, was forced to resign and members of his party were arrested and beaten up by the SA.[160] SS leader Heinrich Himmler became Police President for Munich, while Reinhard Heydrich took over as head of the political police. In Nuremberg Julius Streicher, the editor of the rabidly anti-Semitic newspaper *Der Stürmer* (*The Stormer*), seized power. 'Today, all of Nuremberg celebrates Adolf Hitler,' he told a packed council chamber. 'The flags now being raised at the top of this building will fly there forever. He who sins against them deserves

---

* Political officials governing a district under Nazi rule.

death.'[161] Hitler later claimed that it was only when he seized local government that he truly controlled the whole of Germany.[162]

Two laws to coordinate the German federal states were introduced on 31 March and 7 April and they also ended the sovereignty of these previously autonomous regions. The aim was to bring the state legislature under the central control of Hitler's government. These laws ended the role of the Reich commissioners. They were replaced by Reich Governors (*Reichsstatthalter*) in each of the federal states, who were directly responsible to the central Reich government. All governors were appointed by Adolf Hitler himself from the existing Nazi Party regional Gauleiters and they were instructed to uphold policies laid down by the Reich Chancellor in the States (*Länder*). However, disputes often arose between the Reich governors and the ministers of the Reich cabinet. Finally, on 10 April, Göring was named the Prussian State President, thereby ending Franz von Papen's dominance of Prussia. To complete the Nazis' monopoly of power, Hitler became the Prussian Reich Governor.[163]

The Nazi 'seizure of power' in the federal states was extremely violent. Revenge against political opponents was the order of the day. Gangs of storm troopers roamed the streets looking for rival party members. An SPD report from the state of Brunswick listed numerous beatings carried out by the SA in the region. The socialist left had no defence against the ferocity of the SA. Richard Neunfeldt, a former police lieutenant, was beaten on the head and face with sticks, steel pipes, revolver butts and metal tools until he collapsed unconscious.[164] Hermann Liebmann, the former SPD Minister of the Interior in Saxony, was forced by storm troopers to read out his old anti-Nazi speeches, before they beat him up and stabbed him. He died of the lingering medical effects of this assault in 1935.[165]

Hitler did not want his Nazi revolution to be led by a mob in the streets, but he was not unduly concerned about attacks on communists. On 10 March he issued a carefully worded appeal to the SA to end their arbitrary use of violence: 'The molesting of individuals, the obstruction and disturbance of business life must cease on principle. You, [Nazi] comrades, must see to it that the national revolution of 1933 cannot be compared with the revolution of the [communist] Spartacists in 1918. Apart from this, do not be deterred for a second from our watchword. It is: the extermination of Marxism.'[166] The SA and SS understood from this that Hitler would turn a blind eye to the ruthless persecution of communists.

One Gestapo official who questioned a number of communists after they had been held in a makeshift SA 'wild' concentration camp near Wuppertal observed that 'The SA had tortured the communists in a particularly "original" way. They were forced to drink a salty herring solution and then left to pant in vain for a sip of water throughout the hot summer days.'[167] In the end this Nazi brutality went unpunished. A general pardon was issued on 21 March for all crimes committed by the SA, the SS and any other Nazi organization during the 'seizure of power'.[168]

Papen wrote to Hitler to complain about the unbridled violence of the SA in the German federal states. In reply, Hitler claimed that the SA men had in fact shown 'unprecedented discipline'. No one would stop him, he continued, from fulfilling his mission to eradicate Marxism. He concluded by stating: 'I most insistently request of you, my dear Herr Vice Chancellor, to refrain from addressing such complaints to me in the future.'[169] This final rebuke shows just how quickly things had changed in Germany. As André François-Poncet, the French ambassador, observed: 'When the Hitler-Papen cabinet came to power, there were assurances that Hitler would be kept in check. Six weeks later we find that all the dams that were supposed to hold back the waves of the Hitler movement have been washed away.'[170]

In a speech in Munich on 12 March Hitler promised that Germany would now undergo a process of coordination (*Gleichschaltung*). In essence, this meant Nazification, but it was presented as a positive transformation that would unite the nation. Many people who worked in the public services quickly fell into line. Victor Klemperer had a friend who worked in a hospital in Dresden and he told him that most of the nurses had quickly become fanatical Nazis. They sit around the radio during breaks, he said, and when the 'Horst Wessel Song' comes on 'they stand up and raise their arms in the Nazi greeting'.[171]

Other public sector workers were less enthusiastic. One long-standing SPD party member, who resigned on 9 March, summed up the dilemma that he faced when Hitler came to power:

> As a civil servant I have to make a choice. On the one hand,
> I see how the tendency is growing on the part of my employer,
> the Reich, not to tolerate those employees belonging to anti-
> government associations. On the other hand, there is my loyalty
> to the [SPD] Party. Unfortunately, I see no other solution but my
> resignation. The existence of my family is at stake.[172]

The promising careers of socialists and Jews were wrecked. Arnold Biegelson, a German Jew who later emigrated to Argentina, remembered: 'I was twenty-five years old and employed as a clerk when trouble began in 1933. I held a good position. But when Hitler arrived on the scene, my career plans went up in smoke.'[173]

It was a similar situation in higher education. The universities were state funded, so it proved relatively easy to purge them of Jews and left-leaning academics. By September, 313 full professors had already been dismissed. In total 1,145 out of 7,758 university lecturers were sacked, which represented 15 per cent of university employees.[174] Those who stayed soon jumped on the Nazi bandwagon. A prime example was the eminent German philosopher Martin Heidegger. In his inaugural speech as the Rector of the University of Freiburg on 21 April he told staff that 'academic freedom' would no longer be the basis for the life of a lecturer in the university. He expected academics to play their full part in the 'historic mission' that Hitler was now leading. At the end all the academics present sang the 'Horst Wessel Song'.[175]

By the end of May all non-Nazi paramilitary organizations were banned. The Steel Helmets (*Stahlhelm*) were incorporated into the SA on 21 June. Their leader Franz Seldte had joined the Nazi Party on 26 April and pledged the total allegiance of the Steel Helmets to Hitler's new government. In fact they changed their name to the National Socialist German Front Fighters' League and retained their membership of half a million people.[176]

In Hitler's Germany some individuals became persona non grata overnight. A typical example was the prominent Jewish sexual reformer Magnus Hirschfeld, who had championed abortion, sex education in schools, birth control and the legalization of homosexuality in the Weimar years. Hirschfeld was the director of the internationally renowned Institute of Sexual Science, which was located in Berlin's affluent Tiergarten district. On 6 May a number of pro-Nazi students marched into the Institute and vandalized it. Four days later they stole books from its library, which they ceremonially burned in a huge fire nearby. The police did nothing to stop them. Luckily, Hirschfeld was abroad when the raid occurred. He never returned to Germany, dying in Nice on 14 May 1935.[177]

With continued 'coordination' now a chief priority, Hitler appointed Joseph Goebbels as Minister for the People's Enlightenment and Propaganda on 13 March. 'I'm so happy,' Goebbels wrote in his diary. 'Minister at 35. Unimaginable.'[178] He would come to dominate German cultural life in the years that followed. As Papen observed: 'Despite the disability of a club foot, he seemed to suffer no inferiority complex. He had a biting wit and a gift for venomous sarcasm.'[179] Goebbels said that his key aim was to 'work on the people until they accept our influence'.[180] He sought to bring the press, radio, film, theatre, music, the visual arts, literature and all other cultural organizations under Nazi control.

Goebbels's new ministry consisted of seven departments. At its heart was the propaganda department, which oversaw all of its activities. There were other sections devoted to the press, film and radio. It was staffed by existing civil servants, few of them were committed Nazis. Here was Goebbels, a zealous Nazi, leading a bunch of adaptable and compliant middle-class conservatives. Erich Greiner, who led the administrative section, was typical: he was a conservative-nationalist who never joined the Nazi Party.[181]

The purge within German culture was much more extensive than in many other areas of society. The removal of Jews was the central priority. Otto Klemperer, Victor's cousin, was a prominent classical musician during the Weimar period. But when the Nazis came to power, his concerts were cancelled. On 4 April he left Germany for good. In fact, there was an extensive purge of classical Jewish musicians. On 6 April the Hamburg Philharmonic Society announced that no Jewish soloists would participate in any of its future concerts.[182]

A prominent critic of this purge of Jews from classical music was Wilhelm Furtwängler, the star conductor and composer with the Berlin Philharmonic Orchestra, which was not a state-owned organization. On 11 April Furtwängler published an open letter to Goebbels in a liberal daily newspaper, declaring his unwillingness to purge any Jewish players from his orchestra. Goebbels responded in a surprisingly measured tone. He told Furtwängler that if he opposed the modernist trend in classical music, then he 'would always have a place in the Third Reich'.[183] Once this disagreement had died down, the Berlin Philharmonic was brought under state control. Furtwängler remained its conductor for the entire duration of the Third Reich. He was never a Nazi Party member or even a supporter, but his decision to remain in post undoubtedly bestowed a certain prestige upon classical music in the Third Reich. It brought him severe criticism from Jewish musicians and others beyond Hitler's Germany.

The German film industry proved even easier for Goebbels to bring into line. A few large companies dominated, including the giant UFA

(*Universum Film Aktiengesellschaft*) film studios, which were owned by Alfred Hugenberg. On 14 July Goebbels created the Reich Film Chamber, which oversaw the coordination of the entire film industry. It vetted scripts and purged the movies of Jewish and left-wing actors, writers and directors. Some big stars and directors left Germany for Hollywood, most notably Fritz Lang, the director of the classic silent films *Die Nibelungen* (1924), *Metropolis* (1927), *M* (1931) and the talking picture *The Testament of Dr Mabuse* (1933), a subtle satire on the Nazis, which was banned in the spring of 1933. The popular Hungarian-born actor Peter Lorre, the star of *M*, left Germany, too, but not because he was opposed to Nazi ideology. He wanted more money. In fact, the exodus of film stars from Hitler's regime was not as extensive as might be supposed. Of the seventy-five most popular box-office stars in Germany in 1932, only thirteen emigrated after Hitler came to power.[184] Movie-going actually increased during the Nazi period, perhaps because the great majority of films avoided any overtly political content. Of the 1,100 films produced between 1933 and 1944 the majority were comedies, love stories, thrillers and musicals.[185]

The purging of radio, which Papen had brought under state control in 1932, proved equally straightforward. At least 270 Jewish, liberal and socialist radio employees were dismissed by the end of July 1933, roughly one in eight of all employees. Those who remained were willing to compromise with Hitler's regime.[186] Goebbels was convinced that radio would replace newspapers as the most important influence on public opinion in future.[187] The number of households with radios increased from 4 million in 1933 to 16 million by 1944. Hitler's speeches were broadcast live and to encourage group listening loudspeakers were installed in factories, workplaces and railway stations. Domination of the airwaves was crucially important for the Nazis, although the ideological content of radio broadcasts was usually kept to a minimum. About 75 per cent of programmes were devoted entirely to music.[188]

Germany had more daily newspapers than Britain and France combined, so Goebbels understood how important they were as a means of influencing public opinion. Most papers had a regional or city focus, reaching about 20 million households. Bringing such a diverse press into line was an enormous task. Any newspapers supportive of the Communist Party or the SPD were closed down, swiftly followed by the Catholic press. However, Goebbels had to move more gradually to successfully 'coordinate' all of the centre-right newspapers and periodicals. Some of the major liberal newspapers – notably the *Frankfurter*

Zeitung and the *Berliner Tageblatt* – survived, but their left-wing and Jewish journalists were sacked.[189] Newspaper proprietors were persuaded to cooperate by the Reich Press Chamber. The Reich Association of the German Press and the Union of Journalists converted to Nazism and assisted in the purge of Jews and leftists. The German Newspaper Publishers' Association appointed the Nazi Party publisher Max Amman as its chairman and he soon brought newspaper editors into line.[190] On 29 March Goebbels held a reception for all the major newspaper publishers and told them that he regarded the German press as 'a piano on which the government can play'.[191]

The German literary world, too, was cleansed of all anti-Nazi writers and editors, many of whom fled abroad. The world-famous communist playwright Bertolt Brecht went to Switzerland. Erich Maria Remarque, the author of the pacifist novel *All Quiet on the Western Front*, and Thomas Mann, who won the 1929 Nobel Prize for Literature, also left Germany, as did the leading poet Stefan George. It has been estimated that some 2,500 novelists and playwrights abandoned the country in 1933. Those who stayed accommodated themselves to the political needs of Hitler's regime. Typical was the obsequious 'Oath of Loyalty of German Poets to the Reich Chancellor', which was delivered to Hitler in the spring of 1933.[192] Of the twelve best-selling authors of the Weimar period, the works of seven of them were banned. It might be assumed that this purge of literature led to a decline in reading, but the opposite is the case. State-run libraries increased from 6,000 in 1933 to 25,000 during the 1940s and the borrowing of literary works soared.[193]

The art world was of great interest to Hitler, who viewed himself as an artist and who had painted realist watercolours in his youth. However, he hated modern art with a passion. As a result, modernist representations of anguish and pain were branded 'degenerate' by the Nazis and removed from art galleries. Some were ritually burned. In 1933 twenty-seven gallery and museum curators were sacked. Max Liebermann, a Jew and Germany's leading impressionist painter, was forced into retirement. Paul Klee, a key advocate of modernist abstraction, lost his professorship in Düsseldorf. A similar fate befell Otto Dix, whose paintings were taken down from the walls of art galleries.[194] The Reich Chamber of Art vetted all artists, architects and sculptors. Officially sanctioned artists tended to portray family scenes in rural settings or physical beauty in the classic style.

The dynamic influence of Goebbels was felt just days after his appointment, during the lavish opening ceremony of the German parliament, which was held at Potsdam on 21 March. Hitler chose the Potsdam garrison church for the event, because its crypt contained the tombs of the Hohenzollern Prussian kings, most notably Hitler's military hero, the soldier-king Frederick the Great. Furthermore, the great German statesman Otto von Bismarck had opened the first German Reichstag to inaugurate the Second Reich at this venue on the same day in 1871. For Hitler this seemed the perfect place to begin his Third Reich. The black, white and red flags of the old empire flew side by side with Nazi swastikas. The whole ceremony was designed to reassure Germany's conservative power brokers that Hitler intended to remain subservient to Hindenburg, who wore his grand field marshal's uniform. Hitler was dressed soberly in a dark morning suit.[195]

Hitler's speech inside that crowded church was broadcast live on national radio. He summarized the 'sorry legacy' and 'national decay' of the Weimar period, which had culminated in economic depression and high unemployment. Ending this crisis was his chief objective, he said. The German people were crying out for a new Reich and a new life. Goebbels, seated near Hindenburg, noticed with satisfaction that the President had 'tears welling up in his eyes' as Hitler spoke.[196] In fact, Hitler turned to Hindenburg during his speech and said: 'We consider it a blessing to have your consent to the work of the German rising.' When he had finished speaking, Hitler, with due deference, walked to Hindenburg's chair and bowed deferentially, before warmly shaking his hand. The old man seemed genuinely moved by this gesture.[197]

Afterwards, Goebbels noted in his diary: 'His best speech. At the end, everybody very moved. I have tears in my eyes. This is how history is made.'[198] It proved to be a key moment in the relationship between Hitler and Hindenburg. The fears about Hitler that Hindenburg had expressed in January had by now evaporated. Gottfried Fährmann, just ten years old at the time, was not alone in remembering that moment in the church: 'I vividly recall Hitler bowing to Hindenburg. In my mind, this gesture resulted in the identification of National Socialism with Prussia and Germany.'[199]

The German writer Erich Ebermayer noted in his diary:

> It cannot be denied: he [Hitler] has matured. Surprisingly enough for his opponents, the demagogue and party leader, the fanatic and rabble-rouser seems to be developing into a real statesman [...] The government declaration [at Potsdam] stands out in its striking moderation. Not a word of hatred against opponents, not a word of racial ideology, no threats directed inside and outside of the country.[200]

Two days later at the Kroll Opera House in Berlin (a temporary alternative to the burnt-out Reichstag building) the Reichstag met to debate and vote on the Enabling Act, entitled: 'The Law for Removing the Distress of People and the Reich'. It was not, as is often supposed, a distinctly Nazi innovation. Enabling Laws had been passed by the democratic Weimar Republic on 13 October and 8 December 1923 to deal with the crisis caused by the great inflation and the disruption caused by the French occupation of the Ruhr. In fact, Hindenburg had used Article 48 of the Constitution to bypass the Reichstag on numerous occasions between 1930 and 1933.[201] The difference was that Hitler wanted this state of emergency to be permanent. Henceforth, he could issue decrees and laws and sign foreign treaties without needing the blessing of either the Reichstag or the President.

German democracy was about to come to an end. As if to stress this was a Nazi victory, Hitler wore his brown-shirted paramilitary uniform. Any non-Nazi Reichstag deputies who entered the building found the atmosphere personally intimidating. As the social democrat Wilhelm Hoegner put it: 'Young lads with the swastika on their chests looked us up and down, virtually barring the way for us. They made us run the gauntlet, and shouted insults at us like "centrist pig"'.[202]

Inside the packed auditorium a huge swastika banner dominated the stage. Armed SA, SS and *Stahlhem* guards were positioned by every exit. None of the 81 communist deputies were allowed to attend. The SPD was the only opposition party brave enough to oppose the Enabling Act, but only 94 of its 120 elected representatives had turned up. The others were either ill, in custody or feared for their lives. Nobody quite knew how the deputies of the Catholic Centre Party (Zentrum) would vote, but their support was vital if Hitler was to secure the required two-thirds majority to pass the Act. It seemed likely that they would support it, because Hitler had promised their leader Ludwig Kaas, a Catholic priest, that the rights of the Catholic Church would not be affected by the Act.[203]

At 2.05 p.m. Hermann Göring, the speaker, called Hitler to the podium. This was Hitler's first ever speech before the Reichstag and it lasted for two and a half hours. He spoke in a quiet and moderate tone and after delivering his familiar denunciation of Weimar democracy, he promised the German people a 'moral renewal'. He would respect private property, he said, and individual initiative. He would help the German peasants, the middle classes and end unemployment. He singled out the army for special praise. The rights of the Christian

Adolf Hitler and Reichspräsident Paul von Hindenburg on the Day of Potsdam.

churches would be respected too. On foreign policy, he promised to promote peace with Britain, France and the Soviet Union, but said he wanted Germany to be treated equally with them. The position of the Reich President would remain untouched. The federal states (*Länder*) would not be abolished. To achieve all of these things he needed to pass the Enabling Act. Hitler made it all sound reasonable: 'there are times when emergency legislation is necessary'.[204] When he had finished, the Nazi deputies gave Hitler a standing ovation and sang '*Deutschland über alles*'. Göring then announced a two-hour recess. During this hiatus, the Centre Party confirmed that it would vote in favour of the Act.

The Reichstag session resumed shortly after 6 p.m. The first deputy to speak was Otto Wels, the leader of the SPD. He walked to the podium in complete silence. In a brave speech, Wels defended the social achievements of the Weimar Republic. He claimed that the Nazi revolution amounted to little more than an attempt to destroy socialism in Germany, and he observed: 'If the gentlemen of the National Socialist Party wanted to perform socialist acts they would not need an Enabling Act.' A vote in favour of this Act, he added, would spell the end of parliamentary democracy, the rule of law, the principles of humanity, justice, freedom and socialism. 'No Enabling Act', he concluded defiantly, 'gives you the power to destroy ideas that are eternal and indestructible.'[205]

Hitler was rattled by this impressive defence of parliamentary democracy. He was seen by foreign newspaper reporters feverishly scribbling down notes during the speech. When the SPD leader finally sat down, Hitler jumped theatrically to his feet, to wild cheering, strode back to the podium and issued the following angry warning to Wels: 'I don't want your votes. Germany will be free, but not through you. Do not mistake us for the bourgeoisie. The star of Germany is in the ascendant, yours is about to disappear, your death knell has sounded.'[206] Goebbels felt that Hitler had given Wels 'a fierce lambasting. You don't [usually] see such a slaughter.'[207] Hitler's spontaneous rant was a clear example of how his uncontrolled anger could rouse his supporters and silence his opponents.

After its third reading the Enabling Act passed by 441 votes to 94. Every vote against came from the SPD. Otto Wels and other leading figures in the SPD fled Germany for Prague soon afterwards, where a party headquarters in exile had already been established.[208] Dr Karl Bachem, a historian of the Centre Party, felt that its deputies had little choice but to vote in favour, or else 'All civil servants belonging to the Centre Party would have been dismissed. There would have been a great fracas in the Reichstag and the centrists would probably have been beaten up and thrown out.'[209] Centre Party leader Ludwig Kaas received a letter from Hindenburg congratulating him on his support for the Act. Even if the Communist Party deputies had been allowed to vote against it, the Act would have passed anyway.

The Enabling Act provided the key legal basis for Hitler's personal dictatorship. In just one day Hitler had dispensed with the President's authority to issue emergency decrees and made himself independent of the Reichstag. The cabinet had no power to restrain him now. There would be no more openly democratic elections. It was the beginning of the end for every political party except the Nazi Party. The Act was initially limited to four years and only applied to Hitler's government, but it was extended in 1937, then 1941 and again in 1943, when Hitler declared it to be perpetual. Henceforth, the Reichstag became primarily a venue for Hitler's speeches. Only seven laws were voted upon by the Reichstag before 1939. As Hugh Greene, the British *Daily Telegraph*'s Berlin correspondent, observed: 'The Enabling Law made it possible for civil servants and other elements, respectable elements in the state, to think that Hitler's dictatorship was basically legal and constitutional.'[210]

While these momentous political events were taking place at Potsdam and in Berlin, the first purpose-built concentration camp opened in Dachau. Nothing symbolizes the collective memory of the Third Reich more than the *Konzentrationslager* or concentration camps. They acted as a deterrent to political opponents who might fear being sent to one, but also as a kind of shock treatment, often accompanied by arbitrary violence, for anyone unfortunate enough to find themselves inside one.[211]

On 20 March the SS leader Heinrich Himmler announced at a press conference the establishment of the Dachau concentration camp in a former munitions factory on the outskirts of Munich. Dachau derived its name from *dah* ('mud') and *au* ('meadow'), so it means 'Muddy Meadow'.[212] The camp was opened because Himmler wanted to bring some order to the chaos that prevailed in the 'wild' camps run by the SA. Dachau would not just house communists, Himmler said, but all those who threatened the Nazi state.[213] On 22 March the first 200 detainees arrived at the camp. 'I still maintain', Papen later commented, 'that it was impossible to imagine that these first concentration camps would ever become the murder factories which were later to disgrace Germany.'[214]

Dachau was enclosed by a ten-foot-high perimeter wall topped with high-voltage electrified barbed wire. The guard towers were mounted with machine guns. The interior of the wall was patrolled by armed guards. Prisoners were initially housed in one-storey barracks made

out of brick, concrete and wood. Each barracks contained five rooms with three-tier bunk beds, a straw mattress and a blanket. Each housed forty-five prisoners. There was a washroom, toilets and sinks. The concentration camp contained work areas, a laundry and an infirmary. There was also a large square where prisoners gathered every morning for a lengthy roll call.

The first guards at Dachau were a mixture of Bavarian state police, the SA and the SS. By May the SS had assumed complete control. This became the norm for all of the Nazi-organized concentration camps.[215] Inmates sent to the camps were held under the usual 'protective custody' orders. The official line was that these 'enemies of the state' had to be 'protected' from the anger and violence of the loyal National Community, Himmler argued. Protective custody ran in parallel with the existing criminal justice system. Serious cases still went through that formal system. Prisoners in the concentration camps did not serve out a specific sentence. They could be held for days or weeks or even years. Those deemed to be 're-educated' or 'no longer a danger to the National Community' were released.[216]

Twelve prisoners died in custody in Dachau from 12 April to 26 May 1933. The most notorious of these cases involved four Jewish prisoners: Rudolf Benario, a lawyer, and Ernst Goldmann, a businessman, as well as Erwin Kahn and Arthur Kahn (no relation to Erwin). All of them were in their early twenties and opposed to Nazism, but they were not committed communists. After being brought to the camp, they were ordered by SS guards on 12 April to walk to a nearby wooded area to undertake heavy gardening duties. The SS later claimed the prisoners

Inmates at the notorious Dachau
Concentration Camp, which opened on
22 March 1933.

tried to escape, so the armed guards opened fire. Three were killed instantly, but Erwin Kahn, who received two bullet wounds to his face, was taken to a Munich hospital, where he died a few hours later. In total, fifteen bullets were recovered from the bodies of the victims. The local police accepted the SS's version of events, but Josef Hartinger, a lawyer from the state prosecutor's office, did not. He concluded that 'The entire story of the escape was invented.'[217] All four victims had received fatal bullet wounds to the head. Post-mortems confirmed that they had all been shot at close range, which cast further doubt on the official story, which claimed they were running away when they were shot. Hartinger bravely attempted to bring those responsible to justice, even in the face of fierce opposition from local Nazis, Himmler and the SS. 'I was intent on making the public aware of what was going on in the camp, especially abroad,' Hartinger later commented.[218] Then files related to the case began to go missing, witnesses refused to speak and the evidence disappeared.

The Hartinger investigation caused unrest in the Bavarian government. Himmler referred the matter to Hitler, who intervened personally and ordered that the investigation be terminated. After the war, however, an SS guard called Hans Steinbrenner admitted that the four Jews had been summarily executed. He was charged with their murders, but the case was dropped by the West German authorities. In 1952 Steinbrenner was sentenced to ten years for his involvement in other killings.[219]

In Chemnitz in Saxony the chief of the criminal investigation department Albrecht Böhme was also appalled by the lawless violence of the storm troopers in this early period of Nazi rule. Like Hartinger he was a politically conservative official disgusted by the breakdown of law and order. In a report on the illegal actions and killings that had occurred in Chemnitz, he identified the main culprits as an SA group and arrests did follow.[220] However, brave individuals like Böhme and Hartinger were the exception. It was more typical for local police and judiciary officials to turn a blind eye to the escalating violence.

By the summer of 1933 it had become unnecessary to recruit auxiliary police from the SA. The parties of the left had been dissolved and their most 'dangerous' members were now in concentration camps. As a result, German states began to disband their SA auxiliary forces. Bavaria was the last to do so on 21 December. This did not mean that the SA suddenly stopped their violent activities. The stand-off between the official police authorities and the SA would rumble on.

Violence was the norm in the SS-run concentration camps. The American journalist Edgar Mowrer, a fearless investigative reporter for the *Chicago Tribune*, gave details of SS beatings at Dachau and quoted a Jewish inmate who told him that he had been 'beaten to a pulp'. On 20 April a tour of Dachau was arranged for a group of foreign journalists. It was conducted by Hilmar Wäckerle, the camp commandant, who explained that his camp held 530 detainees who ranged in age from seventeen to very elderly men. Wäckerle described the camp as an 'orderly detention facility' where detainees were treated fairly and received three meals a day. A *New York Times* reporter described the atmosphere at Dachau as being 'halfway between that of a severely disciplined regiment and a hard-labour prison'.[221]

Jews suffered dreadfully during this early period of SA violence. It's been estimated that storm troopers had murdered forty-three Jews by the end of June 1933.[222] Jews were a very small minority, numbering just 525,000 or 0.76 per cent of the German population and a great majority of them lived in the large cities, particularly Berlin. In 1933, 37,000 Jews left Germany. Hans Peter Herz, who was defined by the Nazis as a 'half-Jew', recalled: 'We didn't belong any more. They [SA] broke our kitchen windows and the glass in the front door. On the wooden part of the door they scrawled a Star of David and wrote Jews Get Out [*Juden Raus*].'[223]

Several pressure groups represented Jewish interests, most notably, the Central Association of German Citizens of the Jewish Faith, the National League of Jewish Front-Line Veterans and the League of National-German Jews. All of these groups were patriotic and German in outlook and tended to underplay their 'Jewishness'. The only Zionist pressure group was the German Zionist Federation, but it represented only a very small minority of German Jews.

Anti-Semitism was rife among the rank and file of the Nazi Party. One SA fighting song contained the chilling line 'When Jews' blood spurts from the knife, good times are once more here.'[224] In the week after Hitler came to power, Nazi storm troopers took the law into their own hands. They attacked Jewish shops, vandalized synagogues, beat up Jews, and brutally attacked lawyers in court buildings. Hitler did not personally sanction this violence, but the police did little to stop it. There were few legal prosecutions for anti-Jewish acts of violence.[225]

In the last days of March there was a fresh wave of anti-Jewish demonstrations. In Dortmund the SA smashed the front windows of thirteen Jewish shops and singled out Orthodox Jews for public humiliation and beatings. In some instances their beards were crudely and humiliatingly shorn off in front of baying gangs of storm troopers.[226] In Strauberg, a small city in Lower Bavaria, the SS abducted Otto Selz, a Jewish shop owner. He was later found dead in a local wooded area.[227]

In Hamburg Kurt Rosenberg, a Jewish lawyer, saw a Jewish man and a German woman paraded through the streets. The woman had a cardboard sign pinned to her chest with the slogan: 'I am a pig because I took up with a Jew.'[228] Gaston Ruskin, who later survived being incarcerated in the notorious Auschwitz-Birkenau concentration camp, recalled: 'I remember very clearly that in 1933 the Nazis were already beating up Jews. That year, an SA man put a sign in front of my grandfather's store which read, "Don't buy from Jews" [...] That guy beat up my sixty-year-old grandfather and left him lying there on the ground.'[229]

The foreign press reported incidents of anti-Semitic violence in Germany. There was extensive coverage in American newspapers, especially the *Chicago Times*, the *Los Angeles Times*, the *New York Times* and the *Washington Post*. Most British papers also carried detailed articles.[230] Under the headline 'Judea Declares War on Germany!' the *Daily Express* reported on 24 March that Jewish business leaders in America had launched an international boycott of German goods in response to the attacks on German Jews.[231] On 27 March the *New York Daily News* reported on a huge anti-Nazi demonstration held in Madison Square Garden in New York City.[232] As Victor Klemperer noted in his diary on the same day in Dresden: 'The [Hitler] government is in hot water. "Atrocity propaganda" from abroad because of its [anti-] Jewish campaign. It is constantly issuing official denials, there are no pogroms [the Nazis claim] and it has Jewish associations issue refutations.'[233]

In defiance of these concerns, the Nazis doubled down on their oppression of Germany's Jews. On 28 March Goebbels announced that in response to these international protests in support of the Jews, a one-day boycott of Jewish businesses would take place throughout Germany on 1 April.[234] Hitler met leading members of the Nazi elite in Berchtesgaden and Munich to coordinate the protest. A Central Committee for the Defence against Jewish Atrocity and Boycott Agitation, led by the Nazi and anti-Semite Julius Streicher, planned and organized the boycott in conjunction with thirteen party functionaries.[235] In a cabinet meeting on 29 March Hitler gave it his full support. Konstantin von Neurath, the conservative Foreign Minister, was uneasy about the boycott, which he worried would be 'disastrous for Germany's foreign prestige'.[236] To lessen its economic impact, Hitler exempted large Jewish businesses, including the popular city centre department stores, from the boycott.[237]

On the eve of the protest, Victor Klemperer went to the cinema. He overheard an off-duty soldier and his girlfriend discussing the upcoming boycott: 'He: One really shouldn't go to a Jew to shop. She: But it's terribly cheap. He: Then it's bad and it doesn't last. She, reflective, quite matter-of-factly, without the least pathos: No, really, it's just as good and lasts just as long, really just like in Christian shops – and so much cheaper.'[238]

The Jewish economic boycott on 1 April was the first openly anti-Semitic act of Hitler's new government. It offered a chance for Hitler's regime to placate the more unruly rank-and-file members of the SA, who were already demanding radical action on the Jewish question. Goebbels drove through Berlin on the day of the boycott. 'All Jewish shops are shut,' he recorded in his diary. 'SA sentries are standing in front of the entrances. The public has declared its solidarity.' However, Sir Horace Rumbold, the British ambassador to Berlin, thought the boycott had not been popular among the general public.[239] Elsewhere, there was a mass demonstration of 150,000 workers opposing the so-called 'foreign smears' of the international press, while 100,000 members of the Hitler Youth paraded through the streets of Berlin in the evening to express their support for the boycott.[240] Many Jewish shop owners avoided trouble by closing for the day. Some brave Jewish veterans of the Great War had opened their shops and worn their military medals. In Dortmund the German Jew Friedrich Ernal recalled that his father was convinced that because he had fought in the war 'Nothing will harm us.'[241]

Hitler came to see this high-profile economic attack on the Jews had generated nothing but negative publicity abroad. Germany's standing in the world was still relatively weak, he concluded, so a less openly confrontational approach was required for the time being. He would turn instead to the law. By using orderly acts of government legislation, drafted by non-Nazi civil servants, he could gradually and peacefully erode the legal status of Jews and diminish their position in society without recourse to violence. This process began on 7 April when the 'Law for the Re-establishment of a Professional Civil Service' was passed. It made legal the purging of Jews, non-Aryans and political

A National Socialist Election poster from 1933 identifying Hitler with Hindenburg. The caption states: *Never will the empire be destroyed if you are united and loyal.*

„Nimmer wird das Reich zerstöret — wenn ihr einig seid und treu"

1 Nationalsozialisten

opponents. Jewish civil servants, academics and schoolteachers were fired or forced into early retirement. Paragraph III of the law enforced the retirement of all officials of 'non-Aryan' descent. It was the first specifically anti-Semitic law to be passed in Germany since unification in 1871. On 22 April Jewish doctors were banned from working in the state health service, although Hitler vetoed a proposal to ban all Jewish doctors from practising.[242]

On 25 April the 'Law Against Overcrowding of German Schools and Universities' was introduced. It aimed to reduce the number of 'non-Aryan' students by applying a quota of 1.5 per cent to new entrants to schools and colleges. In practice, this meant reducing the number of Jews. At the time of the law's enactment 3.6 per cent of students were Jewish. The law aimed to cut those numbers in half. Jews were also forbidden from entering the legal profession, but those already qualified and practising were left untouched for now. The purge of

Hitler speaking at the Sport Palace,
Berlin, October 1933.

Jews in the judiciary was not initially comprehensive. Out of 717 Jewish judges, 336 kept their jobs, as did, for the moment, 3,167 out of 4,585 Jewish lawyers. This provoked criticism from Nazi activists, particularly in the SA.[243]

President Hindenburg personally intervened on behalf of Jewish veterans of the Great War. 'If they were worthy of fighting and bleeding for Germany,' he wrote in a letter to Hitler, 'they must be considered worthy of continuing to serve the Fatherland in their profession.'[244] Still keen to placate Hindenburg, Hitler agreed to exclude from the anti-Jewish legislation all Jews who joined the civil service since 1914, plus any Jew who had lost a father or son in the Great War, and also Jewish soldiers who had served in the war. This pleased Victor Klemperer, who noted in his diary: 'The new civil service law leaves me, as a front-line veteran, in my post, at least for the time being.'[245]

On 22 April the members of the cabinet were informed that they were no longer required to vote on anything. 'The Führer's authority is now completely in the ascendant in the cabinet,' Goebbels commented. 'There will be no more voting. The Führer's personality decides. All this has been achieved much faster than we anticipated.'[246]

In Prussia on 26 April Hermann Göring established the *Geheime Staatspolizei* (secret state police) or Gestapo, declaring: 'Its task is to investigate all political activities in the entire state that pose a danger to the state.'[247] The Gestapo was confined to Prussia initially, with the central aim of tracking down political opponents. The day-to-day running of the Prussian Gestapo was devolved to Rudolf Diels, a conservative career policeman and experienced administrator. The Gestapo began therefore as an outgrowth of the Prussian political police. Its officers were state employees drawn from police ranks. There was no wholesale Nazification of the Gestapo or the existing criminal police force, with only 1,453 police officers losing their jobs in the first year of Nazi rule. Diels later recalled that the Gestapo was originally composed of 'old civil servants, not Nazis'.[248]

Contrary to popular myth, the Gestapo was not an all-powerful, Orwellian thought police. It did not have enough staff to spy on everyone. Most of its investigations began with a tip-off from the public. It was under-resourced and overstretched. The number of active, full-time Gestapo officers reached a peak of 16,000 officers during the Second World War. In most small rural towns there were usually no Gestapo personnel at all. To make up for its shortage of staff the Gestapo targeted its resources against clearly defined opposition groups, most notably communists, religious dissidents, Jews, foreign workers and a broadly defined group of 'social outsiders'.

Among the other 'enemies of the state' were the trade unions, who represented a powerful force in German society, united under the General German Trades Union Federation (ADGB) and the General Independent Employees' Federation (AFA). These were the last bastion of the organized working class. Hitler was initially uncertain about what to do about them. The Nazi Party's original aim had been to win over the workers, but working people had stayed loyal to the parties of the socialist left. The National Socialist Factory Cell Organization (NSBO) was created as a Nazi alternative to the trade unions, but it remained in a minority among workers in industrial areas. In March 1933 NSBO candidates won only 25 per cent of the votes in the work council elections.

Theodor Leipart, the ADGB chairman, wrote a conciliatory letter to the German Chancellor on 23 March requesting a meeting with him. There was no reply. On 9 April the ADGB offered to place the union at the service of the state. By now Hitler was convinced that the unions would offer no opposition if they were banned.[249] On 21 April plans were drawn up by Dr Robert Ley for a Nazi takeover of the trade unions. The day set for their execution was 2 May when the SA and NSBO would occupy trade union offices and arrest their leaders.[250]

Secrecy surrounded this plan. In a deliberate diversionary tactic, Hitler's government announced a new National Labour Day on 1 May. It would be accompanied by parades of workers and employers, marching together with Nazi storm troopers. May Day was the traditional socialist celebration of workers. Hitler wanted to turn it into an annual National Socialist festival. A huge May Day ceremony took place in Berlin, organized by Goebbels with the help of a young architect called Albert Speer.

In the evening Hitler gave a keynote speech at the Tempelhofer Field in Berlin before a crowd estimated at 1 million. 'May Day,' he said, 'once the symbol of class warfare, has become once more the symbol of the great unification and rebirth of the nation.' The great task he now set out to achieve was to 'lead the German people back to themselves, and, if need be, to force them back'. The whole world had turned against Germany, he added, so 'it is even more important that we join together as one'. Finally, he promised: 'We are determined to earn our nation's return to greatness through our diligence, our tenacity and our unshakable will.'[251]

The following day the SA, supported by the NSBO, raided trade union offices all over Germany. They arrested officials, seized documents and confiscated funds. Labour newspapers were shut down. ADGB leader Theodor Leipart was taken into 'protective custody' and sent to a concentration camp. In one day the strongest and best organized trade union movement in Europe was destroyed. Hitler claimed the banning of trade unions was not directed against the workers, but was part of his struggle against the communists. He told the *Völkischer Beobachter* that Marxists would not be allowed to hide behind the trade unions any more.[252]

To compensate for the loss of trade union rights, workers were offered a Nazi substitute: a quasi-union organization called the German Labour Front (*Deutsche Arbeitsfront* or DAF). It was set up on 6 May, led by Dr Robert Ley, a hard-drinking, plain-speaking Hitler acolyte. The DAF aimed to create a harmonious relationship between employers and employees. The NSBO was quietly marginalized.

Stormtroopers operating a picket
outside a Jewish-owned shop during
the 1 April 1933 boycott.

Workers' employment rights were greatly eroded, as was the right of the new DAF to negotiate wages. Most importantly, the right to strike was withdrawn. In practice the DAF was a vital means of controlling employees. Wages were set and imposed by DAF trustees, who nearly always followed the wishes of the employer. Hourly wages for skilled factory workers fell by 1 per cent and by 3 per cent for the unskilled between 1933 and 1939. The number of hours worked increased by 15.2 per cent in the same period. Under the Nazis the average worker was working more hours for less pay.

The DAF made cosmetic efforts to improve leisure activities for workers through a sister organization called Strength through Joy (*Kraft durch Freude* or KdF). It organized subsidized holidays, offered adult-education courses, musical and theatrical performances, as well as hiking and sports facilities, including sports grounds, swimming pools and fitness centres. There were even cruises to Italy, Norway or Spain on twelve ocean liners owned by the KdF. Green spaces were created in workplaces under a 'Beauty of Labour' banner, and there were new canteens. By 1939, 43 million Germans had been on a holiday organized by the KdF. It had been inspired by the Italian Fascist leisure organization *Dopolavoro* (After Work), which managed the leisure time of Italian workers in a similar way.

The KdF presented its activities as clear evidence of the benefits to all of the National Community, which it suggested also broke down class barriers.[253] Walter Ehlery, a sheet-metalworker from Essen and a committed trade union member before the Nazis came to power,

later recalled: 'There were no quarrels. Everybody joined the DAF as a matter of course. Nobody wanted to risk their jobs by refusing to join.' Walter enjoyed the excursions and holidays provided by the KdF and he welcomed the longer holiday leave on offer. He felt this was some compensation for the loss of trade union rights.[254]

On 10 May many ceremonial book burnings of 'un-German' authors took place throughout Germany. Lists were drawn up of Jewish and left-wing authors whose works were viewed as 'unacceptable', including Einstein, Freud, Mann, Marx and Remarque. Book burnings were organized by university students, who viewed them as part of the general Nazi 'coordination' process in Germany's universities. Goebbels said to a crowd of students at a book burning in Berlin: 'Here sinks the intellectual basis of the November Revolution to the ground.'[255] Students publicly undermined lecturers whom they viewed as politically suspect and they organized public talks by enthusiastic Nazi academics. Eduard Klemt, the student union leader at the University of Leipzig, declared: 'We have got the university in our hands and we can do with it what we will.'[256]

Book burnings took place in small towns, too. A huge crowd gathered in the market square in Northeim, a small rural town in Lower Saxony, for what was described as the 'burning of filthy literature'. Hundreds of books were piled up and set alight. The Hitler Youth took a leading role. One speaker said that books and newspapers written by 'racially foreign elements' would no longer be tolerated. As the flames engulfed the books, the crowd sang *'Deutschland über alles'*.[257]

On 17 May Hitler gave his first major speech on foreign policy since coming to power. He had outlined a clear set of foreign policy objectives in his 1925 book *Mein Kampf* (*My Struggle*). In many foreign translations these sections were often omitted. The first of Hitler's aims was to abolish the Treaty of Versailles, but this was merely the first stage in the resurgence of a more extreme German militarism made possible through rearmament. Hitler ultimately wanted to gain *Lebensraum* or 'living space' in Eastern Europe, a goal that implied a final showdown with the Soviet Union. Along the way, he would see to it that all German-speaking people in Austria, Czechoslovakia and Poland were brought within a Greater German Reich. Hitler realized that such a programme would be opposed by France and probably Britain, but he hoped that Britain would allow him a free hand in Europe in return for German guarantees concerning the British Empire and naval supremacy.

A ritual book burning of banned authors organised by pro-Nazi students and Stormtroopers in May 1933.

The German Foreign Ministry agreed with many of Hitler's foreign policy aims, although its officials were concerned the Nazi leader might move too quickly to achieve them, thereby provoking Britain and France into a preventive war. Foreign Minister Konstantin von Neurath, a traditional conservative, presented a detailed foreign policy paper at a cabinet meeting on 7 April in which he explained that the first objective of German foreign policy had to be the revision of the Treaty of Versailles. However, because Germany's army and navy was so weak at present, it would take five years to achieve military parity even with Poland. Therefore, he said, it was 'inadvisable to broach the question of the territorial revision of frontiers' for the 'foreseeable future'.

Provoking France was also to be avoided, Neurath added. The central goal was to revise the Treaty of Versailles as it applied to Eastern Europe. German-speaking minorities should be encouraged to agitate in Austria, Czechoslovakia and Poland. Friendly relations with the Soviet Union ought to be maintained for the time being, because Germany was its biggest supplier of industrial goods, and also because the Soviets were 'anti-Polish'. Any agreement with Poland would 'not be desirable'. A period of tranquillity would 'allow us to recover our [military] strength far more effectively'. Neurath also advised close cooperation with Britain and Italy. In short, Neurath advised the main task during this 'first phase of the regime was to provide diplomatic cover for the consolidation of Nazi power at home and for an acceleration of the rearmament programme'.[258] These views from the German Foreign Minister show Hitler's views on foreign policy were part of a broad consensus, especially the promise to revise the Treaty of Versailles.

During his speech to the Reichstag on 17 May Hitler drew heavily on Neurath's memorandum, while also giving every impression he was a man of sweet reasonableness. It was a brilliant exercise in duplicity. It is important to recognize that what Hitler believed privately and what he said in public on foreign policy were two different things. The private Hitler was a warmonger but the public Hitler seemed a peace seeker. Hitler began his so-called 'Peace Speech' by stating that deficiencies in the Treaty of Versailles had caused the current unrest in international relations. The imposition of reparation payments on Germany in 1919 had proved self-defeating, because they had caused severe economic problems which made it impossible for Germany to pay. The branding of Germany as the guilty party for the Great War was another major error by the Allies. Totally disarming Germany after the war was also unfair and indeed unheard of in the whole history of European nations.

Hitler stressed that his revolution aimed primarily to restore harmony within Germany in three ways. First, by ending communist subversion and creating a classless National Community. Second, by solving the unemployment problem. Third, by creating a stable authoritarian leadership that could act as a legitimate partner with the rest of the world.

Hitler went on to say how much Germany supported the principle of disarmament, but only if other states treated Germany as an equal partner in negotiations with equal rights. Germany's ultimate aim was not offensive war, he added, or to somehow 'Germanize' parts of Eastern Europe, but to ensure its own security. He ended by warning the rest of the world that it would be impossible for Germany to remain a member of the League of Nations if it were not granted equality of treatment.[259]

In Britain *The Times* believed that Germany's claim to be treated equally with other nations was 'irrefutable'.[260] Few foreign observers realized that Hitler would not be content with merely revising the Treaty of Versailles. Louis P. Lochner, an American journalist and head of the Berlin Bureau of the Associated Press, was typical of many in observing far too blithely: 'That's the interesting thing about dictators, when it comes to foreign policy, they are tame as lambs (witness Mussolini, Hitler, Stalin, Piłsudski),* for they know they have so much trouble consolidating their power at home.'[261] Those who didn't take Hitler at his word were rare. George S. Messersmith, the US consul general in Berlin, shrewdly observed that Hitler would publicly espouse peace while he was militarily weak, but that ultimately Germany would 'strive to impose its will on the rest of the world'.[262]

On 18 May, continuing his charm offensive with the international press, Hitler was interviewed by Thomas Ybarra for the popular US magazine *Collier's Weekly*. Hitler, who was described as 'courteous, measured and statesmanlike', was quoted as saying: 'Whatever violence there was is now past. Perfect calm reigns in Germany. Not a street has been destroyed, not a house. Where is this terror they talk about?' He denied any Nazi involvement in the Reichstag fire and issued a very lengthy tirade on the importance of dealing with the communist threat.[263]

---

* Józef Piłsudski (1867–1935) the Polish general and statesman.

On 28 May Hitler enjoyed another foreign policy success when the Nazi Party polled 50.1 per cent of the vote in the Polish Free City of Danzig elections, holding 38 out of the 71 seats in the parliament. The Nazi vote rose by 33.7 per cent. A new Nazi government was formed in Danzig under the Nazi Senate President Dr Hermann Rauschning, supported by local Nazi leader Albert Forster. This development clearly boosted Hitler's long-term aim of returning Danzig to German control.

On 31 May an ambitious work-creation scheme was approved at a cabinet meeting. The 'First Reinhardt Programme' was part of the highly publicized Nazi drive to reduce unemployment. A total of 1 billion Reichsmarks – an enormous chunk of government expenditure – was allocated to the project, which was primarily focused on house- and road-building. It was expected that some 600,000 people would find employment.

On 1 June the 'Law for the Reduction of Unemployment' was passed, using the slogan 'Battle for Work' (*Arbeitsschlacht*). Erich Koch, the Gauleiter of East Prussia, became a champion of this campaign to put people back to work. It met with remarkable success in this region. When Hitler came to power there were 130,000 registered unemployed in this backward rural area. On 16 July that figure had fallen to zero.

This was surely evidence of a Nazi economic miracle. In fact, the whole thing was stage-managed and achieved through coercion. Local unemployed men were ruthlessly dragooned into so-called 'Camps of Comradeship' (*Kameradschaftslager*), then forced to work long days ploughing up wasteland and planting seeds to grow crops.[264] Northeim, another rural enclave, received 160,000 marks for a similar public works programme. In January there were 653 registered as unemployed in the town. By 24 July not a single unemployed person remained on the register. Once again the men had been coerced into work. They were offered the choice of taking poorly paid agricultural work or receiving no unemployment benefits.[265] Unemployment did fall in rural areas, because of these work-creation schemes, but only by press-ganging workers into back-breaking labour.

On 8 June in Berlin secret details of a huge rearmament programme were laid bare at a cabinet meeting. The enormous sum of 35 billion Reichsmarks was allocated over an eight-year period from 1933 to 1941, at a rate of 4.4 billion per year. It represented a vast increase in armament spending. For instance, the previous annual army budget had been between 700 and 800 million Reichsmarks.[266] Hitler was prepared to allocate almost unlimited funds to rearmament without any real consideration of the consequences for the German economy.

The most important figure in the rearmament programme from 1933 to 1937 was Dr Hjalmar Schacht, who was highly respected in business circles and regarded as a safe pair of hands. On 17 March he replaced the conservative Hans Luther as president of the Reichsbank, a post he had previously held between November 1923 and March 1930. Schacht's appointment was viewed as a welcome sign of moderation in Hitler's new government and was widely welcomed by the financial markets. But how moderate was Schacht? Since 1931 he had openly aligned himself with the Nazi Party and he was trusted by Hitler. He had even introduced Hitler to key business figures during the Führer's ascent to power.

It was Schacht's financial wizardry which made German rearmament on a vast scale possible. He came up with the ingenious idea of printing secret government bonds (Mefo bills). These IOUs were then issued to arms manufacturers through a holding company called the Metallurgical Research Company *(Mefo GmbH)*. The Mefo bills were used to pay contractors, who could then convert them into currency at banks. The first bills were issued in autumn 1933, but the scheme did not roll out fully until the spring of 1934. It was a buy now, pay later scheme that simply added billions to the government deficit. Hitler intended to pay off these debts through territorial conquests in war. At the Nuremberg trials Schacht claimed to have opposed the idea of gearing the whole German economy towards war preparations. He had called for 5 to 10 per cent of GDP to be devoted to defence spending. Nevertheless, his scheme was the starting point of a vast military-industrial complex dedicated to the creation of a huge arms industry. It was this rearmament programme that reduced unemployment, not cosmetic work-creation schemes.[267]

On 17 June Hitler appointed Baldur von Schirach, the head of the Hitler Youth, as Youth Leader of the German Reich. He was only twenty-six, but the promotion of relatively young men to important positions was a feature of Hitler's government. Most of the leading figures in the Nazi elite were under forty. The average age of party members was thirty. Schirach, the son of a German aristocrat, had joined the Nazi Party in 1925. He appeared regularly at Nazi rallies, particularly the Hitler Youth Day at the annual Nuremberg Rally, and he often introduced Hitler's speeches to German youth.

It was a key aim of Hitler's regime to win over young people. The Hitler Youth (*Hitlerjugend*) was founded in the 1920s as a younger

[overleaf] Hitler in Berlin in May 1933, before delivering his 'Peace Speech'.

sub-group of the storm troopers. In 1932 the Hitler Youth had 35,000 members. By the end of 1933 some 2 million young people had joined. By 1936 this had grown to 6 million. In 1939, when it was compulsory to join, 90 per cent of German youths were members. 'You have to remember,' recalls Elisabeth Hartnagel, a schoolgirl from Ulm, 'there was great excitement when Hitler came to power. All the school books, newspapers, films and radio were all putting out Nazi ideas. It was very difficult for young people not to want to be a part of that.'[268]

The Hitler Youth encouraged young Germans to accept Nazi concepts of racial purity, discipline and obedience. At weekly meetings and summer camps the focus was on physical fitness, rifle practice and team-building games. For some boys it had unintended consequences. School discipline was disrupted because Hitler Youth leaders often challenged their teachers and questioned their loyalty to Hitler. Parents who were critical of the government risked being denounced by their own children and school performance suffered because the Hitler Youth members had been told that physical fitness mattered far more than academic qualifications. On the whole, however, most of the boys seemed to enjoy the sports and camping trips more than any ideological message.

The German Girls' League (*Bund Deutscher Mädel* or BDM) was the female equivalent. The BDM encouraged girls to improve their physical fitness, although it concentrated primarily on developing the domestic skills required of a future wife and mother. The girls generally found the experience much more liberating than the boys in the Hitler Youth. As one BDM member later recalled:

> Almost all German women get excited when they think of their
> time as BDM leaders. For us, it was a kind of emancipation, even
> if no one today believes us. As a leader I received an instruction
> booklet every two to four weeks, even if this was oversimplified,
> I related these to the younger girls. There were tales about the
> German farmer who lives in the east, motherhood, the brave mother
> who makes sacrifices for Germany and other sentimental stuff.[269]

The destruction of Germany's party political system was the inevitable next step on Hitler's road to a personal dictatorship. 'All parties will have to be destroyed,' Goebbels wrote in his diary on 3 June.[270] In thirteen days – from 22 June to 5 July – every German political party except the Nazi Party disappeared. The German Communist Party had already been eliminated. On 22 June the SPD was ordered to dissolve itself and its Reichstag deputies were summarily dismissed. The SPD's property and assets had been seized on 10 May. On 21 June the SA converged on the Berlin suburb of Köpenick. They rounded up 500 social democrats and beat and tortured them over the following bloody week, resulting in ninety-one deaths. Over 3,000 SPD functionaries were sent to the concentration camps, where they suffered violence, torture and murder.[271]

On 27 June the German National People's Party was formally dissolved after its leader Alfred Hugenberg resigned from the cabinet. It had changed its name to the German National Front (DNF) in early May and even adopted the Nazi leadership principle, but this did not appease Hitler. Members of the DNVP had been progressively hounded out of office in the federal states, while its student and youth organizations had been wound up long before the party was dissolved. Goebbels summed up the general cabinet response to Hugenberg's resignation in three words: 'No tears shed.'[272]

On 28 June the State Party (DStP) – formerly the Democratic Party (DDP) – was dissolved. On 4 July the People's Party (DVP) voluntarily ceased its operations. The Party had moved to the right after the death of the liberal statesman Gustav Stresemann in 1929. The DVP had only two seats in the Reichstag after the 5 March elections. The Bavarian People's Party (BVP) ceased operating on the same day. On 5 July the Catholic Centre Party (Zentrum) was voluntarily wound up. In early May Ludwig Kaas, its leader, resigned, citing poor health, and was succeeded by Heinrich Brüning, the former German Chancellor. Zentrum's Reichstag deputies resigned their seats or meekly transferred their allegiance to the Nazi Party.[273] Germany's Catholic bishops had already agreed to recognize Hitler's government in return for the passing of a concordat with the Vatican, which would be signed later in the month.[274]

On 6 July Hitler said in a speech to Reich governors: 'The political parties have now been abolished. This is an historical event, the meaning and implication of which has not been completely understood.' However, he warned: 'Revolution is not a permanent state, it must not develop into a lasting state. The full spate of revolution must be guided into the secure bed of evolution. In this, the most important part is played in the education of the people.'[275] This speech was not welcomed by Ernst Röhm, the radical leader of the storm troopers. He wanted to move on to a 'second revolution', which would Nazify the police, the civil service and the army. There was so much more to be done, as he wrote in the SA monthly journal: 'The national uprising has thus far travelled part

[overleaf] Hitler Youth Gathering, 1 May 1933.

of the way up the path of German revolution.' Röhm promised that the SA 'would not tolerate the German revolution falling asleep'.[276]

On 9 July Victor Klemperer mourned the end of party politics in his diary: 'And now this monstrous internal tyranny, the break-up of all the parties, the emphasis on the idea that "We the National Socialists have power. It is *our* revolution." Hitler is the master.'[277] In a speech in Dresden on 13 July Franz von Papen – the man who had promised to have Hitler squeaking like a mouse when he came to power – formally admitted defeat: 'Who among us thought it possible that the irresistible force of National Socialism would completely subdue the whole German Reich in four short months? The political parties have been dissolved, the institutions of a parliamentary democracy have been abolished by the stroke of a pen and the Chancellor possesses powers not even accorded to the German Kaisers.'[278] On 14 July the 'Law Against the Establishment of Political Parties' decreed that the Nazi Party was the only legal political party. Germany was now a one-party state controlled by a single leader.

By now a cult of hero worship had developed around Hitler. As Paul Dinichert, the Swiss envoy in Berlin, noted: 'Unlimited trust in the Führer has undoubtedly spread to broad segments of the public in the preceding few months.'[279] Thousands of fan letters arrived daily at the Reich Chancellery. Streets, animals and children were named after him. Images of Hitler appeared everywhere. There was also a growing trade in Hitler-related products, including ashtrays, beer jugs, board games, china, comics, photographic books, pillows, playing cards, tea towels and much more. Most people voluntarily adopted the 'Heil Hitler' greeting to one another before it became legally compulsory. Victor Klemperer noticed that people were 'constantly raising their arms to one another'.[280]

Foreign correspondents clamoured for 'exclusive' interviews with Hitler, although he was also a figure of fun in many foreign reports, some suggesting he looked like the comedy film star Charlie Chaplin. The American *Literary Digest* concluded: 'While the myth of the leader is growing by leaps and bounds in Germany, certain European dailies and weeklies are stressing the comic aspects of Germany's dictator. They picture Hitler as a comedian, all the more laughable because of his seriousness.'[281]

On 10 July the *New York Times* put Anne McCormick's detailed interview with Hitler on the front page, under the headline 'Hitler Seeks Jobs for All Germans'. McCormick put a wholly positive spin on

Hitler's plan to solve unemployment through public works programmes. She found him to be a 'rather shy and simple man, younger than one expects, more robust, taller', with a voice as 'quiet as his black tie and his double-breasted black suit'. Hitler expressed sympathy with President Franklin D. Roosevelt, 'because he marches towards his objective over Congress, over lobbies, over stubborn bureaucracies'. He justified his banning of all democratic political parties in Germany by pointing to the British republican Oliver Cromwell as his role model: 'I myself assume absolute authority,' he said. 'If I fail, I'll retire to a villa in Switzerland.' Hitler also paid tribute to women, describing them as 'among my staunchest supporters'. On the so-called 'Jewish question', he adopted a very moderate tone. He merely hoped that other nations would 'open their gates to them'. His discriminatory laws were not directed against Jews personally, he said, but were for the benefit of the German majority. Above all, he told her, the main aim of his government was the 'elimination of unemployment'. He expressed admiration for the US motor manufacturer Henry Ford for producing a cheap car for the working man and he said that he would like to do something similar for the German worker. As for his critics abroad, he concluded by saying that 'no outside criticism will deflect me from the course I have mapped out'.[282]

On the same day that Germany became a one-party state, two other important laws were enacted. The first was the 'Law on the Revoking of Naturalization and the Deprivation of German Citizenship'. This meant some German Jews and Gypsies were deprived of their German citizenship. Their names were listed in the *Reich Law Gazette* (*Reichsgesetzblatt*). The second law was even more far-reaching. It was called the 'Law for the Prevention of Hereditarily Diseased Offspring', and became operative from 1 January 1934. It allowed for the compulsory sterilization of anyone deemed to be suffering from what was described as 'hereditary disabilities'. These included blindness, 'congenital feeble-mindedness' (a very elastic concept), deafness, epilepsy, Huntingdon's chorea, manic-depressive psychosis, schizophrenia and severe physical or mental disability. Further legislation denied secondary education to the disabled and prohibited marriage for anyone with a hereditary illness.

Hitler's regime used the 'Unification of Health Affairs Law' to bring the entire public health system under state control. Local health officials and doctors were encouraged to monitor the 'genetic health' of patients and they were given the authority to nominate individuals for compulsory sterilization. New so-called 'biological diseases' were invented, such as 'hereditary feeble-mindedness' and 'moral feeble-mindedness'. This widened the net considerably for sterilization to include career criminals, Gypsies, homosexuals, prostitutes, severe alcoholics, vagrants and women known to have had several sexual partners. Perhaps surprisingly, Jews were not specifically targeted under this legislation.[283]

In his speeches before 1933 Hitler had made no secret of his desire to create a 'racial state' based upon eugenic 'racial laws'.[284] Eugenics – the theory that the human gene pool can be improved through selective breeding – was not a Nazi invention, but it was at the heart of the Nazis' drive to create a 'biologically pure race'. Eugenics can be traced back to social Darwinism in the 1850s. A Eugenics Educational Society was founded in Britain in 1907 to campaign for sterilization and marriage restrictions for the 'weak' to prevent the degeneration of the population. Such ideas were not only popular, but were respectable in Germany and beyond. Sterilization laws were introduced in Switzerland (1928) and Denmark (1929), while no less than thirty-nine American states had voluntary sterilization laws when Hitler came to power. Compulsory sterilization had been suggested in Germany before the Nazis. In 1920 two German professors Karl Binding and Alfred Hoche had published a very influential book called *Permitting the Destruction of Life Unworthy of Life*, which discussed euthanasia and the legality of killing the mentally ill. In 1932 the Prussian Health Council had proposed a compulsory sterilization law, which found widespread support among German doctors.

Compulsory sterilization under the Nazis could be recommended by a local doctor, a social worker or a director of a state mental asylum, prison or care home. The chosen individual was then asked by letter to attend a medical at which the doctor would decide whether or not to sanction a sterilization order. A total of 220 Hereditary Health Courts were established to administer this system, each presided over by a lawyer and two doctors. There were a further eighteen appeal courts for anyone who wished to contend a decision. Statistics compiled by the Reich Ministry of the Interior in 1934 – the first full year in which the compulsory sterilization law became operational – show that 32,268 people were forcibly sterilized. There were 4,000 appeals, but only 441 were upheld.[285]

On 20 July a *Reichskonkordat* (Concordat between the Holy See and the German Reich) was signed in Rome. There had been no concordat between the Vatican and the German states since the Reformation. It seemed like a victory for the 20 million Catholics in Germany and it was well received by the international community. It added to the growing impression of Hitler as a conciliatory statesman when it came to foreign affairs. The Vatican ordered all of its bishops in Germany to swear allegiance to Hitler's regime.[286] In reality, however, Nazism and Catholicism were to prove completely incompatible. As Goebbels put it: 'The Führer is deeply religious, though completely anti-Christian. He views Christianity as a symptom of decay. It is a branch of the Jewish race.'[287]

From 30 August to 3 September Hitler attended the fifth Nazi Party rally to be held in Nuremberg.* The Nuremberg Rally had been a high point of the National Socialist calendar in the late 1920s, although none had been held between 1930 and 1932. Hitler decided to revive it in 1933. Hundreds of thousands of Nazi Party functionaries and activists arrived in Nuremberg, including the leaders of the SA, the SS and the Hitler Youth. The rally was not like a traditional party conference at which policies are discussed. It was primarily an opportunity to glorify the leader and stress the unity of the Nazi movement. In his closing speech, Hitler declared that Germany's anti-Bolshevik struggle was a European challenge and he reminded his audience that his mission in government was not to 'conserve but to liquidate'.

Goebbels hired a 31-year-old director called Leni Riefenstahl to film the 1933 Nuremberg Rally. The result, *Der Sieg des Glaubens* (*Victory of the Faith*) was sixty-four minutes long and released on 1 December. Following the events chronologically, the movie showed Hitler and the radical SA leader Ernst Röhm on friendly terms. After watching it, Goebbels felt that a better film could be made which focused exclusively on Hitler.

On 13 September Hitler announced the introduction of the Winter Aid Fund. The idea was to ask the public to donate money towards helping pensioners and 'deserving' poor people to cope with 'hunger and cold' in the winter months. Hitler claimed all the credit for the scheme, although it had been pioneered by Heinrich Brüning, the former German Chancellor, in 1931. Under the Nazis, the Winter Aid Fund became an annual, high-profile charity fundraising event. In 1933 alone the campaign raised 358 million Reichsmarks. The scheme distributed winter hampers, as well as Christmas presents for the old and the children of the poor.[288]

---

* Nuremberg had been chosen because of its medieval associations with Germany's past.

[*overleaf*] Hitler performs the ceremonial shovelling of dirt for the beginning of work on the Frankfurt *Autobahn* on 23 September 1933.

On 21 September the Reichstag Fire Trial opened in Leipzig. The leading judge was Dr Wilhelm Bünger and the trial lasted for just over thirteen weeks.[289] The five accused were Marinus van der Lubbe, the Dutch communist arrested at the scene, plus four alleged communist 'co-conspirators', including the former German Communist Party member Ernst Torgler. The other three – Georgi Dimitrov, Blagoi Popov and Vasil Tanev – were Bulgarian senior members of the Communist International (Comintern).

It suited the Nazis to blame the Reichstag fire on communists. The prosecution case suggested the four communists used van der Lubbe to carry out their plot against the Hitler government. International interest in the trial was considerable. In Paris in August a Soviet agent called Otto Katz published *The Brown Book of the Reichstag Fire and Hitler Terror* in which it was argued that the fire had been planned and ordered by the Nazis as a false flag operation. A mock trial was held in London, starting on 14 September and presided over by the British barrister Dennis Pritt and the US attorney W. Arthur Hays. That mock trial also concluded that the fire was the work of the Nazi Party.

The star of the real Reichstag Fire Trial was undoubtedly Georgi Dimitrov, who proved to be a very impressive debater and acted as his own lawyer. He cast severe doubts on Göring's elaborate conspiracy theory. Göring frequently lost his temper during Dimitrov's forensic and often witty cross-examination. During one exchange Göring shouted at him: 'You wait until we get you outside the court, you scoundrel.'[290] The foreign press was not impressed by this outburst.

Marinus van der Lubbe made matters worse for the Nazis by doggedly sticking to his original story. 'I can only repeat,' he told the court, 'I set fire to the Reichstag all by myself. After all, it has been shown in this trial that Dimitrov and the others were not there.'[291]

On 23 December Judge Bünger read out his judgement: van der Lubbe was found guilty and sentenced to death, but it was decided that he had acted alone.[292] The four communist defendants were sensationally acquitted. The Nazi press branded it a major 'miscarriage of justice'. In a letter to Hitler, Göring observed: 'You would think we were on trial.' Hitler replied: 'We shall soon have those old fellows [the judges] talking our language. They are all ripe for retirement anyway and we will put in our own people. But while the old gentleman [meaning President Hindenburg] is alive, there is not much we can do.'[293]

On 23 September Hitler ceremonially shovelled some dirt for Germany's first ever *Autobahn* near Stuttgart. The creation of this

Poster promoting the Nazi created trade union: the German Labour Front (*Deutsche Arbeitsfront*, or DAF).

Deutsche Arbeitsfront

network of new motorways was portrayed in Nazi propaganda as central to reducing unemployment, but the idea had been discussed frequently by the Weimar governments in the 1920s. It was decided back then that German car ownership would not grow sufficiently to warrant motorways until the 1950s. Hitler claimed the idea for his own, however, and appointed Fritz Todt, a civil engineer and committed Nazi, to coordinate the heavily trumpeted *Reichsautobahn* scheme. A total of 5 billion Reichsmarks was allocated to the project over a five-year period. Hitler was still thinking ahead, because the underlying rationale of the programme was to build roads to speed up military transport during a war. Unemployment was not greatly reduced by the scheme. In the autumn of 1933 no more than 1,000 workers were employed on the scheme. Even a year later only 38,000 were working on *Autobahn* construction.[294]

One group that expected to benefit from Nazi rule were Germany's farmers. Support for the Nazi Party was strongest in rural areas. On 26 September the 'Hereditary Farm Law' was discussed in cabinet. Under this legislation a farm between 7.5 and 125 hectares was declared to be 'hereditary' and had to pass on death from the father to the eldest son and could not be mortgaged or sold. The owner was also required to be of 'German stock' and able to trace his ancestry back to 1800. Thus Nazi racial law was enshrined into land ownership. The German peasantry had long wanted to remain on the land that they farmed, although only about 1 million farmers fell under the new legislation, which favoured middle-ranking farmers rather than peasants with smallholdings.

On 1 October Hitler gave a speech announcing the new 'Hereditary Farm Law' at the first Reich harvest festival on the hillside of Bückeberg near Hamelin. The festival was attended by 500,000 people and the day became a national holiday for the duration of the Third Reich. Hundreds of special trains from every farming area in Germany converged on the town. Hitler marched through cheering crowds before reaching the speaking podium flanked by loudspeakers.[295] Goebbels noted in his diary: 'Fantastic teeming mass [of people]. After dusk the searchlights and beacons flare up [...] The moon over it all. The crowd sings: Now thank we all our God! Emotional moment.'[296]

On 14 October Hitler felt that the time was ripe for him to make his first major gamble in foreign affairs. In a live radio broadcast he announced that Germany was going to leave the League of Nations and withdraw from the World Disarmament Conference. He blamed

Hitler with Ernst Röhm.

the Western Allies for these decisions, particularly the French government for refusing to grant Germany equal rights. Of course, Hitler knew he could only act unilaterally in foreign affairs by leaving the League of Nations. Similarly, he had no desire to negotiate Germany's rearmament with foreign countries that might one day be his enemies.

Hitler sought to strengthen his hand further by asking the German public to endorse his bold move. In a surprise announcement he said that the Reichstag would be dissolved and that a referendum would take place on 12 November, the day after the fifteenth anniversary of the signing of the Armistice in 1918. It would be up to the German people to approve or disapprove of Hitler's decision to walk out of the League of Nations and the Disarmament Conference. At the same time they would be voting on the performance of his government.

On 19 October, in an 'exclusive' interview with George Ward Price in the *Daily Mail*, Hitler sought to reassure the British government and public that his decision to leave the League of Nations was not antagonistic. He wanted cordial relations with Britain and France, he said, and he had no aggressive designs towards Poland whatsoever. Hitler promised that Germany would abide by all existing international treaties. He did not even rule out returning to the League of Nations in the future, provided Germany was treated as a fully equal member.[297] On 23 October Victor Klemperer noted in his diary:

> When the withdrawal from the League of Nations took place a few days ago, I believed for a moment that this could accelerate the fall of the government. I no longer believe it. The plebiscite and the splendid Reichstag 'election' on 12 November are magnificent advertising. No one will dare *not* vote, and no one will respond with a No in the vote of confidence.[298]

The question in the referendum was: 'Do you approve, German man, and you, German woman, this policy of your national government, and are you willing to declare as the expression of your own opinion and your own will and solemnly profess it?'

On 22 October Hitler opened the election campaign with a speech at Kelheim, near Regensburg. Once again, he flew to several major cities to deliver speeches, including Berlin, Breslau, Cologne, Ebling, Essen, Frankfurt am Main, Hannover, Kiel, Neumarkt, Stuttgart and Weimar. On 8 November, at a celebration of the tenth anniversary of the Munich Beer Hall Putsch at the Bürgerbräukeller, Hitler declared: 'We are a revolutionary movement, we shall win power, we shall break this state in pieces and subdue it to our will, and yet we refuse to desert the path of legality.'[299]

On 10 November Hitler gave a speech to workers at the Siemens plant in Berlin. He talked about foreign policy: 'If Germany does not want to remain as an outcast it must insist on equal rights and that can only be accomplished if all Germans hold together as one man.'[300] On the day before the referendum, 11 November, President Hindenburg gave a radio broadcast: 'Tomorrow show your national honour and identify with the Reich government. Speak up with me and the Chancellor for the principle of equality and show the world that we have restored German unity.'[301]

On 12 November, 96.1 per cent of all registered voters (43,492,735 people) turned out to vote. Of these, 95.1 per cent overwhelmingly approved of Hitler's decision to leave the League of Nations and the Disarmament Conference, with just 4.9 per cent (or 2.1 million people) registering their disapproval, while 757,876 were spoiled or invalid votes. In East Prussia, 97.3 per cent favoured withdrawal. Hamburg, formerly a German Communist Party stronghold, recorded the lowest vote in favour of Hitler's leadership, although that was still a very decisive 83.9 per cent.

1934

·

BLOOD PURGE

·

At the beginning of 1934 Ernst Röhm and the unruly hooligans of the paramilitary SA were still demanding a 'second revolution'. These Brownshirts – with a membership exceeding 4.5 million – outnumbered the German army, which was limited to 100,000 men, because of the restrictions imposed by the Treaty of Versailles.[1] Hitler had appointed Röhm as Minister without Portfolio just before Christmas 1933 in yet another attempt to appease him, but Röhm interpreted this as an endorsement of his growing power and influence.

On New Year's Day Hitler sent a glowing personal letter to Röhm, which was published in the official Nazi newspaper the *Völkischer Beobachter* on 2 January:

> When I appointed you, my dear chief of staff, to your present
> post, the SA was undergoing a grave crisis. It is primarily to your
> credit that within a few years this political instrument was able to
> develop the strength that made it possible for me to finally win
> the struggle for power by overcoming our Marxist opponents.
> Now that the year of the National Social Revolution has ended,
> therefore, I feel impelled to thank you, my dear Ernst Röhm,
> for the imperishable services you have rendered the National
> Socialist movement and the German people, and to assure you
> how grateful I am to destiny to be privileged to call men like
> you my friends and comrades in arms. In cordial friendship and
> grateful appreciation, yours, Adolf Hitler.[2]

It appeared to be a huge public endorsement of Röhm. In reality Hitler and Röhm were becoming increasingly estranged from each other. Röhm was disillusioned with what he saw as Hitler's accommodation with the traditional conservative right and the army. As he told Hermann Rauschning: 'Adolf is rotten. He's betraying us all. He only goes around with reactionaries. So, he brings in these East Prussian generals. They're the ones he pals around with now.'[3] Röhm wanted the SA to replace the traditional elites within the army and the state. This went some way beyond Hitler's more pragmatic 'legal revolution', which sought the consent of the existing conservative power brokers to consolidate his hold on power.

Ernst Röhm (light uniform) inspecting his Stormtroopers on 1 January 1934.

[overleaf] Hitler and, second from left, Albert Speer inspect an architectural model.

The SA was undoubtedly disrupting the smooth running of the Nazi state. As one SA leader admitted: 'Everyone is arresting everyone else, avoiding the prescribed official channels. Everyone is threatening everyone else with protective custody. Everyone is threatening everyone else with Dachau. Right down to the smallest police station, the best and most reliable officials have become uncertain about the hierarchy of authority.'[4] Hindenburg and leading figures in the army felt the SA was becoming much too powerful and needed to be reined in.

On 24 January Hitler attended the funeral of Paul Troost, his chief architect, who had died suddenly and unexpectedly three days earlier. Troost favoured the neoclassical architectural style which Hitler adored. Hitler not only admired Troost's work, but had become friendly with his wife and family. A young architect called Albert Speer, aged twenty-eight, took Troost's place and soon became a key member of Hitler's inner circle. Speer, the product of an affluent upper-middle-class family from Mannheim, had only joined the Nazi Party in 1931.

On 26 January Hitler surprised everyone by signing a ten-year German-Polish Non-Aggression Pact. It was yet another bold move in his foreign policy. Poland was a new state in its post-1918 form, with a population of 35 million. It drew together disparate territory acquired from Germany, the Habsburg Empire and the Soviet Union, all of which had been allocated under the 1919 Paris Peace Conference. In November 1932 Poland's authoritarian military leader General Józef Piłsudski appointed Józef Beck as his Foreign Minister. Beck, a shrewd diplomat, realized that he needed to position Poland's foreign policy in between Germany and the Soviet Union, while attempting to retain Polish independence. Poland had already signed a non-aggression treaty with the Soviet Union in July 1932 and Beck had been the instigator of a similar agreement with Germany.

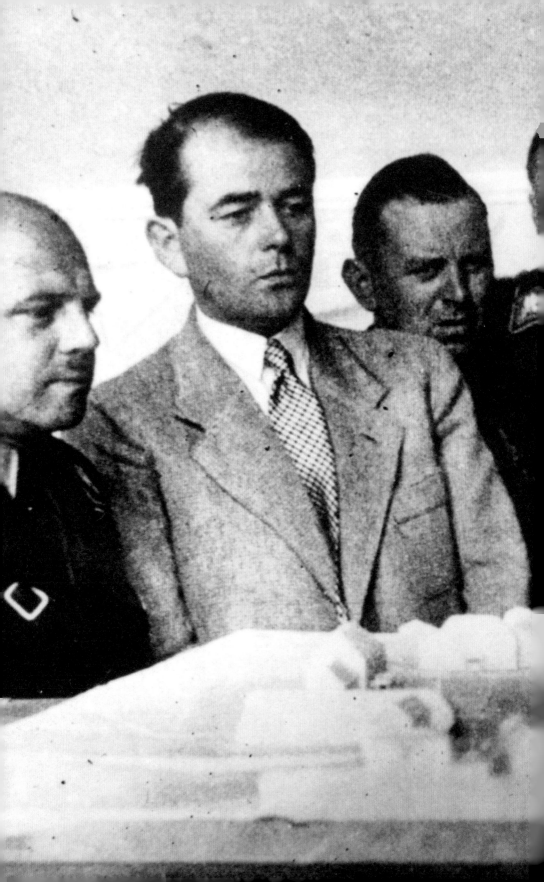

Two of the most contentious clauses of the Treaty of Versailles related to Germany's loss of territory to this new Polish state. The first was the creation of the so-called Polish Corridor, which cut off East Prussia from the rest of Germany. The second was the creation of the Free City of Danzig, which was under the control of the League of Nations and denied Germany access to the Baltic Sea. Leading

officials at the German Foreign Ministry expressed opposition to such an agreement. The German public, which regretted the loss of territory to Poland after the Treaty of Versailles, was also antagonistic to a new German-Polish accord. Sir Eric Phipps, the British ambassador to Berlin, sent a detailed report to the British Foreign Office pointing out that Hitler had sacrificed some of his popularity in Germany by signing the Non-Aggression Pact.[5]

Hitler was willing to risk some unpopularity at home, because he appreciated the propaganda value of a pact with a nation everyone assumed to be Germany's sworn enemy. He also hoped the agreement would move Poland out of the orbit of the Soviet Union and France. Hitler wanted Poland to become a German satellite state, which could act as a launch pad for his long-term plan to attack the Soviet Union. The agreement showed Hitler's tactical flexibility in foreign affairs. He was willing to sacrifice what seemed to be an unshakable ideological principle in the short term if it gave him the advantage in the long run.[6]

On 27 January Hanns Johst's lengthy interview with Hitler on the nature of National Socialism was published in the *Frankfurter Volksblatt*. Nazism was not a complete rejection of the bourgeois way of life, Hitler said, but such affluent surroundings encouraged a disinterested way of thinking, which in turn led to the growth of 'armchair politicians'. It created the sort of people who criticize all the time, but do nothing to improve their community. In contrast, National Socialists saw Germany as an organic unity, like a body, and there could be no such thing as 'non-responsibility in this organic being, not a single

Left to right, German Ambassador to Poland Hans-Adolf von Moltke, Józef Piłsudski, Polish leader, Joseph Goebbels, Propaganda Minister and Józef Beck, the Polish Foreign Minister, meeting in Warsaw on 15 June 1934, five months after the signing of the German-Polish Non-Aggression Pact.

cell that is not responsible, by its very existence for the welfare and well-being of the whole'. There was no room in the new Germany for the 'apolitical bourgeois man' who has 'a deep-seated aversion towards what goes on in the streets' but is addicted to life 'within his four walls'. The National Community was an expression of this unified vision, he said, building the 'unity of all vital interests, that means overcoming the bourgeois retreat into private life and the unionized, mechanically organized masses, that means equating individual fate and the nation, the individual and the *Volk.*'

Asked why he used the word 'worker' in the title of the National Socialist German Workers' Party, Hitler explained it was because that word had been hijacked by communists. He wanted to recapture it to explain the role of every individual in his new classless society. Hitler denied being the brutal dictator. He viewed himself as 'an educator' who discussed his ideas solely with the aim of winning over the public. He even claimed that his rule in Germany reflected the will of the public.[7]

The popular American *Time* magazine ran a series of articles outlining the generous financial assistance Hitler gave to a German war veteran living in America. Ignaz Westernkirchner went there after the Great War, but lost his job during the Great Depression. He wrote to Hitler outlining his plight. Hitler not only provided him with a return sea passage to Germany, but secured him a job as a caretaker in the Brown House, the Nazi Party headquarters in Munich. Westenkirchner described Hitler as a 'kind man' who was 'raising Germany's poor without permitting the upper classes to be leveled down – which is real socialism.'[8]

On 30 January Hitler delivered a speech to the Reichstag exactly one year on from the day he came to power. This would become an annual tradition. Hitler warned that opportunists who 'pounce on every successful movement' to further their own egotistical interests would be purged from the state and the party. He then discussed the introduction of the controversial 'Sterilization Law', which became operative on 1 January 1934. It was necessary, he said, because 'the army of the unfortunate' (as he described those suffering from hereditary illnesses and disabilities) was 'growing to such an extent that it would ultimately be too much of a burden on government expenditure' to sustain in the long term. He dismissed objections raised by church leaders as mere rhetoric, because the established churches were not prepared to bear the cost of caring for those with congenital conditions.

Sterilization would prevent these conditions from being passed on to future generations and was therefore 'a humane measure and would benefit the general health of the population'.[9]

On 1 February Röhm sent a letter to the Minister of War Werner von Blomberg demanding that the SA take over the functions of national defence, thereby reducing the army (*Reichswehr*) to a mere 'training army'.[10] Around this time Fritz Günther von Tschirschky, a close associate of Franz von Papen, overheard a blazing row between Hitler and Röhm in the Reich Chancellery:

> It was clear that a very heated argument was in progress in Hitler's room. After a short while, I said to Brückner [a Hitler aide]: 'Who's in there, for God's sake? Are they killing each other?', to which Brückner replied: 'Röhm's in there. He's trying to talk the old man [Hitler] into going to the Reich President to grant him [Röhm] his requests.' So I waited [outside the door]. Again and again I heard [Hitler saying]: 'I can't do that, you're asking the impossible of me.'[11]

On 2 February Hitler openly attacked the rabble-rousing leadership of the SA in a speech at a conference in Berlin. Only 'fools' would suggest that 'the revolution was not yet at an end', he said, and he suggested that such individuals had leadership ambitions.[12]

As part of his ongoing drive to project a more positive image of his government abroad, Hitler gave a wide-ranging interview to George Ward Price of the British *Daily Mail*. They discussed various subjects, including recent unrest in Austria. Hitler denied that any German National Socialists had been involved, but he was critical of the current Austrian government leadership: 'We sympathize neither with Herr Dollfuss [the Austrian Chancellor] or his opponents. Both sides are using the wrong methods. Nothing of permanence can be achieved by the violent methods they have resorted to.' Price moved on to discuss the recently signed German-Polish Non-Aggression Pact. Price asked if it was the basis for a future attack on the Soviet Union of the sort Hitler had described in *Mein Kampf*. 'What?' replied an incredulous Hitler. 'We take territory from Russia? Ridiculous!'

The problem was, Hitler said, that all attempts at laying the groundwork for lasting peace in Europe had failed, because everybody viewed Poland and Germany as irreconcilable enemies. He had never subscribed to this gloomy view and when he became Chancellor he was determined to make fresh negotiations with Poland a key foreign policy aim. It was his sincere hope, he added, that 'the new understanding would signify that Germany and Poland had permanently abandoned the idea of resorting to arms, not only for ten years, but for all time'.[13]

Three days later Anthony Eden, the British Lord Privy Seal, arrived in Germany for a two-day official visit. During his talks with Eden, Hitler once again repeated his offer of an Anglo-German Naval Treaty. He also alluded to his troubles at home with the SA, telling Eden that he would never tolerate the creation of a second army in the country.[14] Hitler made quite a deep initial impression on Eden, not only by wearing a very well-cut suit, but also because he displayed an impressive and extensive knowledge of foreign affairs. 'He knew what he was speaking about,' Eden observed, and 'as the long interview proceeded, he showed himself completely the master of his subject'.[15]

At a lunch at the British Embassy on 21 February, Hitler floated a proposal to limit German aircraft expansion to a maximum of 60 per cent of the French air force.[16] The idea of a controlled German rearmament programme negotiated by diplomatic agreement appealed to the British government. Sir John Simon, the British Foreign Secretary, felt that Hitler was 'very convincing' when he spoke on international affairs. When he told Hitler that the British government liked countries that adhered to treaties, Hitler replied: 'That was not always the case. In 1813 the German army was prohibited by treaty. Yet I do not recollect that at Waterloo Wellington said to Blücher: "Your army is illegal, kindly leave the field."'[17]

German rearmament was by now an open secret. The *New York Times* reported that German munitions factories were working at full capacity, while American aeroplane manufacturers were already selling aircraft and aviation technology to the Germans. Hitler's Germany, the *New York Times* concluded, would soon have a 'powerful air force'.[18]

Anthony Eden's brief visit to Germany was a convivial diversion for Hitler from Ernst Röhm's ongoing campaign to give his Brownshirts equal military status with the German army. Indeed, leading generals in the army were deeply concerned about it. In an attempt to come to a negotiated settlement, Hitler held a meeting at the Ministry of the *Reichswehr* at the Bendlerblock on Bendlerstraße in Berlin. He invited all the leading SA and SS leaders, plus army officials to the gathering.

In a gripping speech, delivered in the marble-pillared lecture hall, Hitler made an impassioned appeal for all sides to compromise. At the same time he made it clear that he completely ruled out Röhm's demand for the creation of a People's Militia. The SA had to accept the authority of the *Reichswehr*. A document was drawn up defining the future roles within Nazi Germany of the SA and the army. The SA would take charge of domestic, 'pre-military training', but it would have no direct responsibility over military matters. The army would remain the sole bearer of arms in the nation.[19] Hitler made Werner von Blomberg (for the army) and Röhm (for the SA) sign this apparently binding agreement. Röhm signed and shook hands with Blomberg, giving the clear impression to those present of having accepted Hitler's proposals in full. Later in the day, however, in an unguarded moment, he told the SA official Viktor Lutze that he had no intention whatsoever of accepting Hitler's agreement. This sounded like treason to Lutze, who informed Hitler of Röhm's outburst.[20]

While this heated dispute between the SA and the army rumbled on, there was another debate taking place of even greater significance: who should become President of the German Reich after the death of Paul von Hindenburg? Hindenburg had developed lung cancer and his demise seemed likely to happen sooner rather than later. Many influential conservatives and military figures were seriously considering the restoration of the German monarchy. The conspiratorial Vice Chancellor Franz von Papen was at the centre of these clandestine deliberations. 'I realized that his [Hindenburg's] death would have serious consequences,' he later recalled.[21] Papen felt that restoring the monarchy would act as a useful brake on Hitler's dictatorial style.

In March Papen talked to Hitler about the succession to Hindenburg. It would be difficult for Hitler to become president, he said, because to do so he would have to surrender the leadership of the Nazi Party to assume the role of a 'non-political head of state'. In these circumstances, Papen argued, a restoration of the monarchy 'provided the only real solution'.[22] Papen was 'pleasantly surprised' when Hitler seemed quite keen on the idea. He told Papen that he had no objections to the restoration of the Hohenzollern dynasty, although he felt that there were no suitable candidates among the current exiled German royal family.[23] In private, however, Hitler was horrified by the idea of restoring the monarchy. He had recently described pro-monarchists as 'more dangerous than the communists'[24] and warned Goebbels about the 'spread of monarchist propaganda' by conservative 'reactionaries'.[25] On another occasion, when Göring told him he'd written a book called *I am a Monarchist*, Hitler's angry response was such that the title was hastily changed to *The Building of a Nation*.[26]

Around this time Hitler discussed the monarchy with the architect Albert Speer:

I've permitted the social democrat ministers to continue receiving their [occupational] pensions. Think whatever you like about them, you have to grant there is one thing to their credit: they did away with the monarchy. That was a great step forward. To that extent they paved the way for us. And now we are supposed to bring back the monarchy? Am I supposed to divide my power? Look at Italy! Do they [the German conservatives] think I'm that dumb? Kings have always been ungrateful to their foremost associates. We need only remember Bismarck. No, I'm not falling for that.[27]

On 21 March Hitler turned his attention to domestic policy and a national drive devoted to the Battle for Work (*Arbeitsschlacht*). He launched a new motorway-building project at Unterhaching near Munich. The ministries of Propaganda and Economics had organized many other events around the country to promote the scheme, including speeches on the radio, rallies, and activities in factories and schools. Newly employed men marched through city centres and then gave speeches praising Hitler for ending the misery of unemployment. In reality, however, the Battle for Work was more Nazi propaganda and window-dressing rather than reality. Hitler's government had already decided to cut domestic work-creation schemes by 16 per cent and to allocate no new money to these projects. The major government spending priority was now the financing of rearmament. By 1934 military spending would account for 50 per cent of all central government spending.[28]

On 4 April Hitler's interview with Louis Lochner, an Associated Press correspondent in Germany, was published and reported in numerous newspapers around the world. Hitler told Lochner that his primary aim as Chancellor was 'to eliminate the scourge of unemployment', because this would lead to a better standard of living for the entire population. He did not want to make 'everyone the same', but wanted to give every German a chance to 'climb the ladder of opportunity', as was possible in America.

Turning to foreign policy, Hitler adopted a moderate tone. He was opposed to 'secret diplomacy', he said, and much preferred open, 'man-to-man' diplomacy. 'Any representative of a foreign power will find when he confers with me,' Hitler continued, 'that I am absolutely frank in stating what Germany is willing to do and I do not make my demands any higher than is necessary. For instance, if I say we need a *Wehrmacht* of 300,000 men, I will not condescend to reduce the number to 250,000 afterwards.' Above all, he hoped to 'make

Germany's word and signature respected once more'. He only wanted Germany to have 'an armed force that fulfils the requirements of general defence'. He denied being surrounded by yes men. Before he passed any law he discussed it with his cabinet colleagues and always sought their opinions: 'I do not want them to simply say amen to everything. They are of no value to me unless they are critical and do not tell me what defects might, under certain circumstances, detract from our measures.'[29]

Between 11 and 14 April Hitler attended naval manoeuvres on board the pocket battleship the *Deutschland*. He spoke with leading officials of the army and navy and reiterated his pledge to curb the disruptive influence of Röhm and the SA, in return for their support of his bid to succeed Hindenburg as president when he died.

Meanwhile, Papen had met with Hindenburg and advised him to write a political testament outlining his own wishes on the question of the succession. Hindenburg asked Papen to prepare for him a draft document, suggesting that a constitutional monarch should be appointed after his death and stating his opposition to any merging of the offices of President and Chancellor. A few days after seeing Papen's draft, Hindenburg suddenly changed his mind. He had decided, he told Papen, that 'the nation as a whole should make up its mind as to the form of government it desires' after he died. Nevertheless, Hindenburg did sanction the publication of two documents upon his death. The first was a political testament focusing on his service to the nation. The second was a personal letter to Adolf Hitler, advising him to restore the monarchy.[30] However, Blomberg warned Hitler that Papen was positioning himself to replace Hindenburg after his death.[31] If anyone was secretly conspiring against Hitler at this time, it was not Röhm, but the slippery political operator Papen.

On 20 April all the police forces in Germany, including the Prussian Gestapo, came under the unified command of the ruthless SS leader Heinrich Himmler and his close associate Reinhard Heydrich. These two, along with Göring, were bitter enemies of Röhm. Himmler had spent the previous six months expanding his control of the political police in Bavaria to include all the federal German states outside Prussia. Gaining control of the Prussian Gestapo offered Himmler the opportunity of overseeing all of Germany's security forces in addition to his leadership of the SS and the concentration-camp system.

In early 1934 Göring had ordered the Gestapo to start collecting incriminating material on Ernst Röhm.[32] The *Reichswehr* intelligence

Heinrich Himmler *(left)*, head of the SS with his close aide Reinhard Heydrich.

department was also feeding derogatory information about Röhm to the Gestapo. The focus of this character assassination centred on Röhm's well-known homosexual leanings.[33] Even the foreign press was well aware of this. *Time* magazine, for instance, described Röhm in April 1934 as 'that arrant Nazi queer'.[34] Hitler had tolerated Röhm's homosexuality for many years, but the new Gestapo allegations of the SA being dominated by a 'homosexual clique' worried him. There is little doubt some of Röhm's inner circle were gay. As the art historian Christian Isermayer later recalled: 'I got to know some people in the SA. They used to throw riotous parties. I once attended one. Someone I knew had taken me along. It was quite well behaved, but thoroughly gay.'[35] Even so, the number of gay men at the top of the SA was extremely small. For a storm trooper to come out at all was almost impossible. In spite of the rumours, the majority of the SA leadership was essentially homophobic.

Over 1.5 million people attended Hitler's speech at the National Labour Day celebrations in Berlin's huge Tempelhof airfield on 1 May. Hitler looked back with satisfaction on the past year which had witnessed the destruction of party politics and the trade unions. They had to be removed, he said, because 'we were forced to regard them as breeding grounds for phenomena that undermine the self, cause discord in the *Volk* and lead ultimately to national and economic ruin'. Hitler claimed the working classes were now liberated from the 'destructive influence' of socialist parties, as well as the trade unionism which had caused nothing but 'internal strife and discord' within the greater National Community. He was pleased that millions of 'our former opponents are now standing in our ranks and thanks to their skill as helpers in our reconstruction are held in no less regard than our own longstanding comrades'.[36]

What Hitler failed to mention was a rising tide of public discontent over Germany's poor economic outlook. On 11 May Goebbels launched a national campaign against 'grumblers and critics' at the Berlin Sport Palace. The campaign slogan was 'Don't Whine – Work'. In his speech Goebbels castigated all the critics (*Kritikaster*) of Hitler's government and warned the Jews of Germany also needed to understand their place in the new German order: 'They are guests in the country and they should quietly and modestly retire within their four walls.'[37] Leading Nazi ideologue Alfred Rosenberg noted in his diary that Goebbels's campaign against critics was likely to prove counter-productive, because

Leading Nazis Hermann Göring *(left)*,
President of the Reichstag, and
Reichsführer-SS Heinrich Himmler.

it informed the wider world that there was 'widespread discontent' in Germany and appeared to suggest that the German people had 'backed the wrong pony'.[38]

Public support for Hitler's government undoubtedly began to fall during the early part of 1934. The promise of a brave new world outlined during the frenetic year of 1933 now seemed like airy rhetoric. Unemployment remained high at 4 million and the old middle class of craftsmen, small traders and peasant farmers had seen little real improvement in their standard of living. A wage and price freeze had shrunk living standards still further. In rural areas the process of 'coordination' had caused deep conflicts, especially in Catholic regions, as the Nazis attempted to suppress Catholic social groups and youth organizations, both of which remained popular.

The main economic crisis of 1934 was a dramatic fall in Germany's foreign currency reserves. It meant Germans could take only 50 Reichsmarks with them when travelling abroad. Germany's industry and consumers were still heavily dependent on foreign imports. High-priced food imports were pushing up the cost of staple foods in the shops. By the summer Germany's foreign currency reserves had been reduced to just 100 million Reichsmarks. It was only enough to pay for one week's imports. It was a dire situation for any major industrial power to find itself in.

On 14 June Hjalmar Schacht, the President of the Reichsbank, suddenly announced that Germany would suspend all of its foreign currency payments on international debts. German foreign trade threatened to grind to a halt. Neville Chamberlain, the British Chancellor of the Exchequer, responded by allowing his Treasury to impound German funds in Britain in order to pay creditors. Germany soon backed down and agreed to a reduced payment plan with its chief creditors, although this did not immediately solve the crisis. Exports continued to decline, especially to France, Switzerland, the Netherlands and the United States. This particularly affected German export-orientated consumer industries, especially those producing food and textiles.

To add to this gloomy economic picture, the German mark was seriously overvalued. This pushed up the price of German exports, making them even more uncompetitive. Hitler's government was now faced with a stark choice: boost exports to the main capitalist economies or prioritize certain imports over others. Hitler's solution was the introduction of an import quota system (giving top priority to raw materials for rearmament), accompanied by a system of bilateral trade agreements, particularly with Southeast European countries and those in Latin America.

This process has been described as a move towards self-sufficiency or autocracy. In practice, it meant a reduction in trade with the three major democratic capitalist economies: Britain, France and the United States. In 1929 Germany had run a huge trade deficit with America of 800 million Reichsmarks. By 1934 this was reduced to 230 million Reichsmarks. The response of the United States to Germany's reduced debt repayments was to cut off any new loans, to reduce exports of raw materials and to adopt a generally antagonistic attitude towards German traders.

Germany was still Britain's biggest European export market, so the British government adopted a much more conciliatory approach. The Anglo-German Payments Agreement was signed on 1 November, which helped Britain and Germany to continue trading with each other. The City of London even offered German exporters generous lines of credit and fresh bank loans.[39]

The public mood was still one of economic gloom in the summer of 1934, according to Gestapo surveillance reports. One of these noted: 'The housewives in the markets still hold their tongues. But if one of them protests – which happens quite often – no one contradicts her.' There were reports of worker unrest on motorway construction sites, too. Goebbels's campaign against critics of Hitler's government had not gone down well either and its meetings were poorly attended. Goebbels quietly abandoned the whole thing, telling a meeting of newspaper editors: 'I want to hear nothing, I want to see nothing, I want to know nothing [about the Nazi regime's critics]. I know what is going on. But you don't need to tell me about it. Don't ruin my nerves.'[40]

Germany's underlying economic problems were not the only problem facing Hitler. Ernst Röhm's dispute with the army continued as he tried to strengthen his own hold on power. Hitler was under pressure to do something about the unruly leader of the Brownshirts. On 5 June Hitler summoned Röhm to a showdown meeting in his office at the Reich Chancellery, where they talked for five hours. Hitler accused Röhm of plotting a revolution and he warned him to 'abandon this madness' before it was too late. Röhm claimed to be suffering from neuralgia. He would go on holiday on 1 July, he said, to the Bad Wiessee spa on the Tegernsee Lake in Upper Bavaria. As

Goebbels noted in his diary: 'He [Hitler] no longer trusts the SA leadership. We all need to be on our toes.'[41]

On 7 June Röhm released a public statement, announcing a rest cure for himself and a 'collective holiday' for the Brownshirts:

> I have decided to follow the advice of my doctors and take a cure in order to restore my energies, which have been strained by a painful nervous complaint [...] Therefore, for a limited number of SA leaders and men, June, and for the majority of the SA, July, will be a period of complete relaxation in which they can recover their strength. I expect the SA to return on 1 August completely rested and refreshed in order to serve in those honourable duties which the Fatherland and nation expect of it.[42]

Hitler went to Italy between 14 and 16 June. It was his first official visit overseas and it was mostly confined to the Venice region. It was the first meeting between Europe's two Fascist dictators. Hitler arrived at the Lido airfield on 14 June looking extremely nervous, wearing an ill-fitting raincoat over a gawdy blue suit. The charismatic Fascist leader Mussolini, looking grand and statesmanlike, greeted him in full military dress. Then the two men travelled by motor launch to Venice, cheered on by crowds of Italians.

Once in his hotel suite Hitler complained to Foreign Ministry officials that he had been totally upstaged by the flamboyant Italian dictator. For the rest of the visit, Hitler and Mussolini attended a parade of Fascist troops in the Piazza San Marco and played an embarrassing round of golf at the Lido course. During their brief diplomatic talks, Hitler assured Mussolini that he would not interfere in the independence of Austria. He also added that he had received no support whatsoever from any nation for his rearmament plans. Il Duce refused to bite on either issue. At the official reception to mark the end of the trip, Mussolini left early. Hitler's first major venture on the international stage had been a huge and embarrassing disappointment.[43]

The day after Hitler returned from Italy, the Vice Chancellor Franz von Papen made a dramatic intervention in the dispute between the army and the rabble-rousing SA. Invited to give a speech to students at the prestigious University of Marburg, Papen had decided to use the occasion to warn Hitler's regime about the threat of a 'second revolution'. First he criticized the 'cult of personality' that had grown up around Hitler, then ridiculed Goebbels by stating that 'Great men are not made by propaganda.' Papen then mentioned his hope for a restoration of the monarchy. He defended Christian principles, deprecated the arbitrary violence of the SA, and concluded: 'No nation can live in a continuous state of revolution if it wishes to justify itself before history. Permanent dynamism permits no solid foundations to be laid.'[44]

Papen's highly critical speech was political dynamite. Herbert von Bose, Papen's press secretary, sent three copies to the Ministry of Propaganda days before the speech, requesting it be circulated to the press.[45] Goebbels had either not read this draft or decided not to intervene. A local radio station in Frankfurt am Main made a complete recording of the speech, but it was never broadcast, although edited extracts from Papen's speech were mentioned in a local news bulletin. Only the *Frankfurter Zeitung* was brave enough to publish a very brief extract from the speech in its evening edition.

The international press seized upon Papen's speech as a watershed moment for Hitler's government. *Newsweek* in the United States described it as initiating 'Hitler's first great crisis'. It was generally assumed that Papen's speech represented the views of the army's leaders, as well as the upper-class Junkers and major industrialists.[46] The British *Daily Express* journalist Sefton Delmer shrewdly observed: 'Now we are in the middle of the war for Hindenburg's succession, with Hitler on one side and the Vice Chancellor and his fellow conservatives on the other.'[47]

'I felt an immense sense of relief at having unburdened myself in this way,' Papen later wrote of the speech, 'and was prepared for whatever personal consequences might follow.'[48] His office had increasingly assumed the role of an unofficial complaints department for conservatives disaffected with Hitler's regime. These traditionalists were appalled by Hitler's contempt for the rule of law and they wanted action taken against the thuggish SA. Papen's speechwriter Edgar Jung, his press officer Herbert von Bose and his secretary Fritz Günther von Tschirschky were at the centre of this core dissident inner circle. They wanted Hindenburg to remove Hitler from power and replace him with a new conservative, right-wing government led by Papen and supported by the army.[49]

Goebbels was very angry about the impact of Papen's speech. 'Papen gave a wonderful speech for gripers and critics,' he wrote in his diary. 'Entirely against us, except a few empty phrases. Who wrote it for him? Where is the scoundrel?'[50] Jung, a talented lawyer with a practice in Munich, had co-written the inflammatory speech with Papen. He was arrested by the Gestapo on 25 June. Papen complained to Hitler, but he was told that Jung had developed 'illegal contacts' with foreign countries and would remain in custody pending further investigations. Papen offered his resignation, but Hitler refused to accept it, saying that first he needed to discuss the contents of Papen's speech with Hindenburg. Far from easing tensions, Papen's speech had inflamed them. Goebbels now seemed keener to deal with Papen than with Röhm. 'The Führer must act,' he wrote in his diary. 'Otherwise the reactionaries will get the better of us.'[51]

On 21 June Hitler met Hindenburg, who was very ill and infirm, on his estate at Neudeck. The purpose of the meeting was ostensibly for Hitler to report on his state visit to Italy. Hitler had earlier suddenly withdrawn an invitation for Papen to accompany him. If Hitler wanted to discuss the Papen speech, he soon found out Hindenburg was far more worried about the out of control Brownshirts. Otto Meissner, head of the Office of the President, witnessed Hindenburg telling a shocked Hitler that he must bring Röhm and 'the revolutionary troublemakers finally to reason' or he would introduce martial law.[52] Blomberg, who was also in attendance, gave Hitler a similar stern warning. Hitler was being backed into a corner by the self same conservative elite that had brought him to power.

After this tense meeting with the ailing President, Hitler went to his mountain retreat at Obersalzberg. On 22 July Viktor Lutze noted: 'He [Hitler] led me to his study and, taking me by the hand, swore me to secrecy until the whole matter was settled, but told me Röhm had to be removed.' During this meeting Hitler presented Lutze with details of Röhm's alleged plans for a coup.[53] Was the leader of the SA really planning to overthrow Hitler? In his evidence at the Nuremberg trials Field Marshal Paul von Kleist said that the higher ranks of the army really did expect a coup:

> Around about 24 June 1934, I, as army commander in Silesia, was warned by the Chief of the General Staff that an attack by the SA on the army was imminent and was told that I should unobtrusively keep my troops on the alert. During the tense days following, I received a flood of reports and information which gave a picture of feverish preparations on the part of the SA.[54]

On 25 June a secret order from Röhm calling the SA to take up arms came into the possession of Captain Conrad Patzig, the chief of the *Abwehr*, the counter-intelligence department of the War Ministry.

The order from Röhm was a forgery, but it was sent to Himmler and Heydrich, who told Hitler it was authentic.[55] Colonel-General Werner von Fritsch issued an order placing German troops on full alert with all leave cancelled. Franz von Papen later recalled that most conservatives and army leaders believed that Röhm really was planning a coup and they acted accordingly.[56]

On 27 June Hitler met Blomberg at the Reichswehr Ministry and informed him that he now intended to take action against Röhm and the SA. The next day, in order to maintain an air of normality, Hitler attended the wedding in Essen of local Nazi Gauleiter Josef Terboven. During the wedding reception Hitler was called away from the dinner table to receive an urgent phone call from Berlin. Paul Körner, a close associate of Göring's, told him that Papen was going to meet Hindenburg on 30 June, a meeting the Vice Chancellor had conveniently neglected to tell Hitler about. Lutze noted in his diary that Hitler, on hearing this news, said 'I've had enough' and promptly left the wedding reception. He returned to the nearby Hotel Kaiserhof, accompanied by Göring and Lutze.[57] Hitler then called Röhm and ordered him to gather every senior SA leader at a conference in the Hotel Hanselbauer in Bad Wiessee at 10 a.m. on 30 June.

On 29 June the *Völkischer Beobachter* published an article by Blomberg in which he pledged 'absolute loyalty' to Hitler's government and declared 'The *Wehrmacht* and the state are one.' On that same day Hitler arrived at the picturesque Hotel Dreesen in Bad Godesberg near Bonn. In Berlin, Göring and the SS were ready to suppress not only the SA leadership, but a much wider hit list of conservative targets. Although Goebbels was Berlin Gauleiter he was left out of the loop in the planning of the purge, because Göring wanted to maintain sole control over the Berlin bloodbath. Perhaps it was at Göring's request that Hitler invited Goebbels to Bad Godesberg.[58]

Just before midnight on 29 June Hitler read a message from the Munich Gauleiter Alfred Wagner. He reported that menacing gangs of SA men were roaming around the streets of Munich, shouting: 'The Führer is against us, the *Reichswehr* is against us.'[59] Himmler telephoned Hitler to inform him that the Brownshirts were planning to seize government offices in Berlin at dawn. This was pure scaremongering.[60]

The period from 30 June to 2 July is now known as the infamous 'Night of the Long Knives'.[61] Hitler decided to fly to Munich to deal with Röhm personally. At 1.45 a.m. on 30 June a small group – including

Goebbels, Lutze and Hitler's press chief Otto Dietrich – flew from Bonn to Munich. The plane landed at about 4 a.m. at Oberwiesenfeld. At the airport Hitler was greeted by Alfred Wagner. Two Munich SA leaders – August Schneidhuber and Wilhelm Schmid – had been summoned to the airport. Hitler went up to the men, ripped off the epaulettes from their shoulders and told them bluntly: 'You are under arrest and will be shot.' They were taken away to the nearby Stadelheim Prison.

Next Hitler was driven by his chauffeur Erich Kempka – followed by two back-up cars – to the Hotel Hanselbauer in Bad Wiessee to personally confront Röhm, arriving shortly after 6.30 a.m. Hitler insisted on arresting Röhm himself. There are several colourful accounts of what happened inside the Hotel Hanselbauer. Kempka later recalled that Hitler was accompanied by two armed, plain-clothed police detectives. Hitler entered Röhm's room and told him, 'You are under arrest.' Half-asleep, Röhm looked up and replied, 'Heil, my Führer.' Röhm then got dressed, walked downstairs to the hotel reception area, sat on a comfortable armchair, ordered some coffee and calmly smoked a cigar.[62] Speer later claimed that Hitler had told him that he had been unarmed when he entered Röhm's hotel room, as were the two policemen.[63]

Other SA leaders were being arrested elsewhere in the hotel. Edmund Heines, the Breslau Police President and Röhm's SA deputy, was found naked in bed with an eighteen-year-old man who acted as his chauffeur. Goebbels noted: 'A disgusting scene, which made me feel like vomiting.'[64] All those arrested were driven to Munich's Stadelheim Prison in two commandeered buses.

It was around 10 a.m. when Hitler finally reached the Nazi Party headquarters in Munich. In an impromptu and ranting speech, he accused Röhm and his associates of engineering the 'greatest betrayal in world history'.[65] He claimed that Röhm had been given 12 million Reichsmarks in bribes from the French government and that he planned to assassinate him.[66]

Hitler announced that the new SA leader would be the fiercely loyal Viktor Lutze. He then drew up a list of six SA 'traitors' that he wanted executed immediately, including Heines, Schmid and Schneidhuber. These orders were swiftly carried out. Surprisingly, Röhm's name was not on the list. As Alfred Rosenberg observed in his diary: 'Hitler did not want to have Röhm shot.'[67]

Meanwhile, Goebbels sent the code word 'Hummingbird' (*Kolibri*) to Göring in Berlin. It was the signal to begin the liquidation of opponents. Göring, Heydrich and Himmler were at the heart of this ruthless killing spree in the German capital. It was carried out in true gangster style. Hitler had no prior knowledge of many of the names on the hit list. The focus of these Berlin killings was not on the SA, but on the conservative reactionaries undermining Hitler's government.

Papen, who had been kept completely in the dark about the purge, went to see Göring at his residence in the Air Transport Ministry. He noticed that the whole area was crammed with SS guards. Göring was alone in his study with Himmler. When Papen asked what was going on, Göring informed him that he was dealing with political insurgents in Berlin. Papen angrily pointed out that as Vice Chancellor he had a right to know. Göring then told Papen that 'for his own safety' he should return home immediately. Papen was driven to his home, which was surrounded by SS guards. When he got inside he found that the telephone line had been cut and his radio confiscated. A police captain told him that he could have no contact with the outside world. Papen remained there for three long days, not knowing what had happened to his close colleagues.[68]

Meanwhile, a heavily armed SS unit had arrived at Papen's office. They entered it and shot dead his press officer Herbert von Bose at point-blank range. The post-mortem report noted that Bose had been shot five times. Papen's speechwriter Edgar Jung, who had been in custody since 25 June, was shot at Gestapo headquarters in Berlin. His corpse was dumped in a ditch near the Oranienburg concentration camp and it was not discovered until 1 July. Papen was horrified and later recalled: 'I was shocked and disgusted at the cowardly murder of Bose and Jung.'[69]

Papen had no illusions now. He was firmly out in the cold. A day after the purge was complete, Hitler asked Speer to redesign the Borsig Palace in which Papen's offices as Vice Chancellor were located. Papen's remaining staff were ordered to leave the building immediately. Speer went to inspect the Palace and saw a pool of dried blood on the floor. There, on 30 June, Herbert von Bose had been shot.[70]

Erich Klausener, a senior official in the Ministry of Traffic and Postal Affairs and another close colleague of Papen, was also murdered. His son Erich, who was seventeen at the time, later recalled:

> We received a strange telephone call around 3.30 that afternoon. The person said someone had called and told him something had happened at the ministry. My mother frantically tried to get in touch with my

father's superior, Eltz-Rübenbach, who finally agreed to talk to her. But he was hesitant and intimidated and didn't know any details. We went to the ministry ourselves [...] Two SS men, armed with rifles, stood in front of the office where my father had been shot. They had been ordered to shoot anyone who tried to gain entrance to the room. Towards the middle of the next week, we found that the SS had cremated my father's remains. Even everything concerning the urn burial was hush hush. In the end, we did have a fairly open service.[71]

The former German Chancellor Kurt von Schleicher and his wife were gunned down by SS troops in their home in Berlin. According to the official account, when the SS entered Schleicher's house the former Chancellor drew his pistol and fired just as his wife flung herself in front of him. She was killed in the crossfire. It is often thought that Göring sanctioned Schleicher's murder, but Papen later recalled Göring telling him that it had been a direct order from Hitler.[72] Goebbels was sorry that Schleicher's wife had been killed by accident. 'A shame,' he noted in his diary, 'but there's no changing that.'[73]

General Ferdinand von Bredow, a close associate of Schleicher, living in retirement in Berlin, was arrested at his home, bundled into a police van and beaten to death.[74] Hitler's political critic Gregor Strasser was brutally murdered at Gestapo headquarters in Berlin. He was shot in the head, then left to bleed to death. At Dachau concentration camp Gustav Ritter von Kahr, who had been instrumental in the collapse of the 1923 Beer Hall Putsch in Munich, was brutally killed by SS men with pickaxes. 'Thus, November 9, 1923 was avenged after all,' Alfred Rosenberg recorded in his diary.[75] Otto Ballerstedt, who was responsible for Hitler spending time in prison in 1923, was also murdered in Dachau. Another victim was Fritz Gerlich, a journalist and a long-standing critic of Hitler during the Weimar period. Karl Zehnter, the gay landlord of a large beer hall called the Nürnberger Bratwurstglöckl, near Munich's cathedral, a favourite haunt of Röhm and his homosexual friends, was also killed. Gregor Strasser's lawyer Gert Voss refused to open a safe when the SS called on him and he was promptly shot dead. There were a few cases of mistaken identity. For instance, Wilhelm Schmid, a music critic, was mistaken for someone else and murdered.

A delegation including Frick, Göring, Himmler and Rosenberg met Hitler's flight from Munich at Berlin's Tempelhof airport at 10 p.m. on 30 June. Rosenberg noted in his diary: 'Hitler wore no hat; his face was pale, unshaven, sleepless, at once gaunt and puffed,' but 'it was clear that the murders of his friends had cost no effort at all. He felt nothing.'[76]

In fact, the purge had left Hitler horribly conflicted. In a speech to the Reichstag he described his order to murder the SA leaders as the 'bitterest decision of his life'.[77] He offered Gregor Strasser's widow a generous state pension. Ernst Röhm's mother received a similar offer, but turned it down. She also refused to accept that her son had ever been a homosexual.[78]

On 1 July more blood was shed. Göring and Himmler both advised Hitler that Röhm had to be liquidated. After some deliberation, Hitler finally relented. Two SS officers – Theodor Eicke, the Camp Commandant of Dachau, and his deputy Michael Lippert – were given the task. When they arrived at Stadelheim the governor initially refused them entry, claiming the SS had no legal jurisdiction to enter a state prison without the necessary documentation. An order to the governor was telegraphed from the Reich Chancellery and the two SS officers were finally escorted to cell 474, where Röhm was being held. They entered, placed a Browning revolver on the table and ordered Röhm to shoot himself. When he refused he was promptly shot, first in the neck and then in the head. His last words were reportedly 'My Führer.' It's unclear which SS officer fired the fatal bullet. Eicke later said: 'I am proud I shot this faggot with my own hands.'[79]

On the evening of 1 July Goebbels gave a talk on national radio to explain the purge. He said that a 'small clique of professional saboteurs' had been planning a coup and had to be dealt with. A 'clean sweep is being made', he added, of all the hotbeds of 'corruption and moral degeneration'.[80] Goebbels dwelt on what he called the 'stomach-churning homosexuality of Röhm' and other members of his inner circle, which he claimed had brought the Nazi Party 'under

Kurt von Schleicher with his wife Elisabeth going to vote for the 31 July 1932 National Election.

a suspicion of a contemptible and disgusting sexual abnormality'.[81]

Göring ordered every item of evidence concerning the planning of the Night of the Long Knives to be destroyed. Some documents survived, however, giving an official murder toll of eighty-three; of those, fifty were in the SA.[82] The German historian Rainer Orth has meticulously tried to establish the precise number of deaths. He has identified ninety of those killed by name. The current agreed figure is a hundred, including ten people Orth was unable to identify by name. A total of thirteen Nazi Reichstag members were killed in the purge.[83] A further 1,100 people were detained, but most of them had been released by the autumn. Many victims of the purge were quickly cremated to avoid any awkward questions about how they died.

Hindenburg – no fan of the SA – fully endorsed the purge, sending his good wishes to Hitler in a telegram: 'I note from the reports I have received that through your decisive intervention and your courageous personal commitment you have nipped all the treasonable intrigues in the bud. You have saved the German nation from serious danger and for this I express to you my deeply felt gratitude and my sincere appreciation.'[84]

The international response to this murder spree was surprisingly relaxed. This was due in part to Röhm's well-known reputation as a thug. 'Herr Hitler, the German Chancellor, has saved his country,' declared the *Daily Mail*. 'Swiftly and with inexorable severity Hitler has delivered Germany from men who had become a danger to the unity of the German people and to order in the State.'[85] The Paris-based communist newspaper *Deutsche Volkszeitung* spiced up the story by claiming that Hitler had killed intimates who had become dangerous, because they knew too much about 'the private life of the Führer, who is himself a homosexual'.[86] Germany's strict censorship laws meant that no such accusation was ever made in the German press. In the United States *The Nation* concluded that Hitler had retained power, but that Germany was now destined to become a military dictatorship with Hitler a mere figurehead for the army.[87] Victor Klemperer noted in his diary that his postman, who was not particularly pro-Nazi, said of the purge: 'Well, Hitler simply sentenced them. A chancellor sentences and shoots members of his own private army!'[88]

On 3 July Hitler held a cabinet meeting to discuss the purge. He gave a lengthy account of the origin of what he called the 'high treason plot' led by Röhm and its necessary suppression. He emphasized that if he thought the state was threatened he was permitted to exercise prerogative legal power to order executions. Hitler reminded them of Röhm's stubborn disagreements with the *Wehrmacht* and his refusal to cease this behaviour on Hitler's order. He then informed his colleagues that the clique headed by Röhm had a 'homosexual disposition' and that they had tried to blackmail Röhm.[89] Hitler was also convinced Röhm and Schleicher were planning a coup d'état. He did not order all of the executions during the purge, he said, but he took full responsibility for the bloodshed, because it had 'stabilized the authority of the Reich government for all time'.[90]

Blomberg congratulated Hitler on his decisive action and not a single cabinet minister uttered a word of protest. Franz Gürtner, the Justice Minister, enthusiastically welcomed the bloodbath. The cabinet then approved a law which retrospectively declared that all of the killings had been perfectly lawful and a legitimate act of self-defence in a state emergency.

On 13 July Hitler delivered a lengthy and emotional speech justifying his actions in the Reichstag, which was still in its temporary home in the auditorium of the Kroll Opera House. Göring introduced him and spoke of 'the Führer's terrible hours of sorrow' when he had realized that Röhm, a man he trusted, had betrayed him.[91]

What followed was one of Hitler's most effective speeches but similar in content to what he told the cabinet ten days before. Hitler placed all of the blame for the purge on Röhm's coup attempt. He claimed that Schleicher was deeply involved too. He concluded by saying: 'If anyone reproaches me and asks why I did not turn to the regular courts, then all I can say is this: in that hour I was responsible for the fate of the German people. I gave the order to shoot the ringleaders in this treason.'[92] When he had finished, the Reichstag deputies rubber-stamped the new law to retrospectively legalize the purge.

Hitler received many enthusiastic letters from the German public offering support for his actions. Typical was this one written by Stanislaus Jaros from Lobstädt in Saxony, a party member since 1930 and an active member of the storm troopers:

> I followed your speech from the Reichstag building, sentence for sentence, with a pure heart and deep reflections. It penetrated my heart and soul like a deliverance, a salvation for the whole German people. My heart bled inwardly and tears came into my eyes. I congratulate you, my Leader, on your energy and your prompt decision by which you saved us from this bitterly difficult fate and called to account the mutineers and condemned them to just punishment.[93]

Victor Klemperer made the following observation on Hitler's speech in his diary: 'Hitler does not think he is a murderer. In fact, he presumably did act in self-defence and prevented a substantially worse slaughter. But, after all, he appointed these people to their posts [...] The dreadful thing is that a European nation has delivered itself up to such a gang of lunatics and criminals.'[94]

As a reward for its key role in the purge, Hitler released the SS from the jurisdiction of the SA on 20 July. The *Schutzstaffel* was now independent and accountable only to him. In reality, the incremental growth in power of this Nazi protection squadron was to prove much more of a threat to the German army than the thuggish Brownshirts had ever been. Nevertheless, the purge of the SA continued. All SA special representatives in the federal regional governments were removed. The SA went from being the loud and boorish street movement of the National Socialists to a much more obedient grouping. A hard-core SA supporter offered the following observations on the aftermath of the purge:

> What I can't understand is that after the murders in Wiessee the
> SA let itself be stripped of power so easily. It simply fizzled out.
> But by then most of the SA men had got jobs. The hunt for jobs
> was on: an SA man becomes a gas man, a state employee. One
> got a job with the welfare office, another with the job centre.
> Many had been unemployed and now they had work. Most lost
> much of their revolutionary élan.[95]

The high drama of the Night of the Long Knives had barely subsided when a new political crisis erupted in Austria. On 22 July Goebbels took part in a discussion at the Bayreuth Music Festival alongside Hitler, Theodor Habicht, the superintendent of the Austrian Nazi Party, Hermann Reschny, the head of the Austrian SA, and Franz von Pfeffer, a former SA chief of staff in Berlin. It's clear that a coup attempt to overthrow the Austrian government was discussed and endorsed by Hitler. Goebbels's brief note on this meeting has survived: 'Austrian question. Will it work? I'm sceptical.'[96]

Hitler took it for granted that Germany and his 'beloved Austria' (he was born in what was then Austria-Hungary) would one day be united. Austria had previously been the capital of the multi-ethnic Habsburg Empire, but this had been dissolved in 1919 at the Paris Peace Conference, which also prohibited a union (or *Anschluss*) of Germany with Austria. The newly created First Austrian Republic was tiny, with a population of 7 million German-speakers, most of whom lived in Vienna. Its population of 200,000 Jews was much larger in percentage terms than Germany's.[97]

Hitler's dream of uniting Germany with Austria had one major obstacle: the Austrian Nazi Party was not popular. It polled just 16 per cent in the 1932 elections. The two major political parties in Austria were the conservative Christian Social Party and the left-wing social democrats. Between them, they secured 80 per cent of the votes. In fact, in response to the rise of Nazism in Germany, the Christian Social Party transformed itself into the extreme, right-wing Fatherland Front, led by the diminutive (4' 11") Engelbert Dollfuss. He transformed Austria into an authoritarian state, banned the social democrats and the Nazi Party and ruthlessly put down communist unrest, leaving 1,600 dead in police clashes on the streets. The Fatherland Front resembled a Fascist party with its similar uniforms, a copycat swastika symbol and salutes, but it had no anti-Semitic policies.[98] Above all, Dollfuss and his Fatherland Front wanted to preserve Austria's independence. He developed close relations with Mussolini's Fascist Italy in the hope that this would prevent a Nazi takeover. Britain and France also demanded that Germany must continue to respect Austrian independence.

On 25 July the Austrian Nazi Party launched a bungled coup codenamed Operation Summer Festival. Armed men wearing swastika armbands forced their way into the cabinet room inside the Vienna Chancellery building on the Ballhausplatz. They shot Dollfuss twice and left him lying on the floor of the room with no medical attention for three hours, before he finally expired.[99] The Austrian government suppressed the revolt, fully supported by a loyal police force and army. The Nazi ringleaders were arrested. Dollfuss became a martyr, depicted by his supporters as bravely dying in defence of Austrian freedom.

Dollfuss's murder was condemned around the world. Mussolini was

Austrian Chancellor Engelbert Dollfuss *(left)* with Benito Mussolini *(second left)*, during a visit to Italy in 1934.

particularly outraged, because Dollfuss had become a close friend. Il Duce travelled to Vienna to offer his personal condolences to Dollfuss's family. He told the Austrian Vice Chancellor Prince Ernst Rüdiger von Starhemberg: 'Hitler is the murderer of Dollfuss. Hitler is the guilty man, he is responsible for this.'[100] Hitler had been attending a performance of Wagner's *Das Rheingold* at the Bayreuth Festival on the evening of the Austrian coup. He publicly and vehemently denied any involvement, but nobody believed him.

The cold-blooded murder of Dollfuss seemed to Mussolini a clear case of the Nazi regime exporting abroad the lawlessness of the Night of the Long Knives. To make it abundantly clear he opposed any plans Hitler might have to absorb Austria into Germany, Mussolini sent several army divisions to the Austrian border. In Austria the Nazi murderers of Dollfuss were executed. The new Austrian Chancellor was Kurt von Schuschnigg, who was firmly committed to keeping Austria an independent nation, but the years ahead would be more difficult than he could ever imagine.

Coming so soon after the purge, the Dollfuss Affair was enormously damaging to Hitler's carefully cultivated image as a man of peace on the international stage. Hitler's government agreed a new policy of caution and restraint concerning the Austrian question, at least while Germany remained weak militarily. In an attempt to ease tensions, Hitler appointed Franz von Papen as the German ambassador to Austria. Mussolini's actions, however, had hardened hearts. Hitler told Goebbels that he had 'broken with Rome for good', because of Mussolini's fiercely anti-Nazi speeches during the crisis.[101]

In the meantime, Hindenburg's health seriously declined. On 1 August Hitler visited the dying president, at his Neudeck estate. Hindenburg was delirious and mistook Hitler for Kaiser Wilhelm II, addressing him as 'Your Majesty'. Returning to Berlin later that day, Hitler called a cabinet meeting at which he gained agreement to pass the 'Law on the Head of State of the German Reich'. This stipulated that upon Hindenburg's death the office of president would be abolished and the roles of head of state (Führer) and Reich Chancellor would merge. He would also assume the additional role of the commander-in-chief of the armed forces. The cabinet approved this law, which had no constitutional legality, with no dissensions.

The following day Hindenburg died aged eighty-six. At a meeting of the cabinet Hitler told his colleagues that he had 'lost a personal friend'. He said that another referendum would now follow on 19

August to allow the German public to either accept or reject the amalgamation of the posts of President and Chancellor into the post of Führer.[102] William Shirer noted in his diary: 'Hitler did what no one expected. He made himself President and Chancellor.'[103]

Members of the *Wehrmacht* were now obliged to swear the following personal oath to Hitler: 'I swear by God this holy oath that I will show absolute obedience to the Führer of the German Reich and People, the commander-in-chief of the *Wehrmacht*, and that as a brave soldier I will be willing to sacrifice my life at any time for this oath.'[104] Soon all government and police officials had to take this oath. As Hitler told Rosenberg: 'Over in the Foreign Office they will have their heads in their hands today, for I have Hindenburg's authority. Now the fun has ended.'[105]

On 6 August the *Daily Mail* published another lengthy 'exclusive' interview with Hitler by George Ward Price. Hitler categorically denied any involvement in the abortive Austrian coup and stressed that Germany would go to war only 'in self-defence'. He would never attack Austria, he said, but some Austrians felt a bond with his country: 'We cannot prevent Austrians from seeking to restore their ancient connection with Germany.' Germany would once again join the League of Nations, he said, provided it was granted absolute equality with other nations. He also promised that not a single German soldier would be sacrificed to gain any colony in the world.[106]

On 7 August a lavish state funeral for Paul von Hindenburg was held at Tannenberg, the site of one of his greatest victories in the Great War when he had crushed the Russians in August 1914. In his will Hindenburg asked to be buried next to his wife on his Neudeck estate, but Hitler ignored this. In a brief funeral oration Hitler said that Hindenburg's name would remain immortal and he closed with the pagan words: 'And now enter thou upon Valhalla!'[107]

Hindenburg's political testament was finally opened at the Reich Chancellery on 14 August. There was a private letter to Hitler and a political will. In the letter Hindenburg asked Hitler to restore the German monarchy, but Hitler never made public the letter's contents. Hitler did publish Hindenburg's testament in its entirety, largely because it was full of praise for his achievements. Hitler's Nazi movement, Hindenburg wrote, had created a classless unity among the German people. He ended his political testament with the hope that Hitler's rule would 'ripen into the absolute fulfilment and completion of the historic mission of our people'.[108]

[overleaf] President Hindenburg's funeral cortege travels through Tannenberg, the scene of one of his military victories in the 'Great War'.

On 17 August Hitler delivered his only major speech during the referendum campaign and it was broadcast live on German radio. The German revolution was now at an end, Hitler told his audience at Hamburg City Hall. His new position as Führer would depend upon two things: the Nazi Party and the army. 'I am now responsible for the entire German Volk,' he added. 'And no action will take place for which I will not vouch with my life.' He ended by warning his critics: 'In this state, there will no longer be a right to carp, but only a right to do a better job.'[109]

In the referendum of 19 August the German people overwhelmingly approved of Hitler's abolition of the post of president and his decision to merge the roles of head of state (Führer) and Reich Chancellor. A total of 88.1 per cent (38,394,848) voted in favour of Hitler's actions, with just 9.9 per cent (4,300,370) against. There were 873,000 invalid or spoiled ballot papers. The turnout was high at 95.7 per cent, although 2 million people did not bother to vote at all. Goebbels was disappointed with an 88.1 per cent endorsement. 'I expected more,' he wrote in his diary.[110] In some areas – notably Berlin, Breslau, Hamburg and Leipzig, all areas with previously high numbers of socialist and communist voters – up to 20 per cent voted against the proposition. 'All the voters were intimidated and intoxicated with phrases and festive noise,' Victor Klemperer noted in his diary. 'One third votes Yes out of fear, one third out of intoxication, and one third out of fear and intoxication. And Eva [his wife] and I also simply put a cross at No out of a certain degree of despair, and not without fear. Nevertheless, despite the moral defeat, Hitler is the undisputed victor, and there is no end in sight.'[111]

For much of the year the noisy rebelliousness of the SA and its bloody suppression had dominated German politics, which had been good news for German Jews. In 1933 eighty different regulations against Jews had been introduced into law, but in 1934 this fell to just fifteen.[112] The so-called 'Jewish question' had not been forgotten, but the Nazis had eased off for the time being, because they knew it made Germany unpopular abroad. It was not the West's moral disapproval they feared so much as an economic boycott, which would have a devastating effect on Germany's frail recovery. Accordingly, Hitler adopted a policy of tactical pragmatism on the 'Jewish question', rarely mentioning it in his major speeches during 1934. It almost felt as if things had returned to normal. At a race meeting in Hamburg, for instance, Sir Eric Phipps, the British ambassador, was surprised to see several Jewish racehorse owners mingling with Nazi and government officials.[113] Jews were

Front page of the violently anti-Semitic newspaper *Der Stürmer* (*The Stormer*), which contained the slogan at the bottom of the front page: 'The Jews are our misfortune.'

still being oppressed in other areas of national life, however. On 24 March Jews were excluded from membership of the Reich Chamber of Culture.[114] They were still being encouraged to emigrate, too.

One destination that Hitler's government was very keen for Jews to emigrate to was Palestine. On 25 August 1933 German authorities had signed the ingenious and controversial Haavara Agreement with the German Zionist Federation and a group of Zionist businesses based at the Hanotea plantations in Natanya just outside Tel Aviv. At this time Palestine was a British-controlled mandate under the auspices of the League of Nations. The British restricted immigration to the region by insisting that anyone entering needed a capital of 1,000 Palestinian pounds, the equivalent of £1,000 pounds in 1934 (£50,000 at today's value). This large sum became known as the 'capitalist visa', because only rich people could afford the entry fee.

The scheme operated for German Jews in the following way: Jews purchased German farm equipment to a value of 1,000 Palestinian pounds, which was then exported to companies in Palestine. Upon arrival, the Jews were reimbursed the cost of the goods and they could buy a residency visa. The Haavara Agreement helped Jews to leave Germany, but it also encouraged German exports. Around 50,000 German Jews fled to Palestine between 1933 and 1939 under this agreement, around 10 per cent of all German Jewish emigration. The Haavara Agreement was controversial with Nazis, too, because it involved Nazis and Zionists working together. It would be incorrect to assume, however, that the Haavara Agreement meant that Hitler was in any way pro-Zionist or favoured the establishment of a Jewish state. All he wanted to do was get as many Jews as possible out of Germany.[115]

Rabid anti-Semites like the prominent Nazi Julius Streicher and his newspaper *Der Stürmer* continued to produce vicious anti-Jewish propaganda. On 1 May *Der Stürmer* published a hugely controversial 'special issue' alleging that Jewish ritual murders were taking place, under the headline 'The Jewish Murder Plot Against Humanity Is Uncovered'. Two stereotypical Jews were depicted in a drawing, holding a vessel to collect the blood from the naked bodies of the Aryan Christian children they had supposedly murdered. Needless to say, these outrageous claims were completely fabricated and Hitler publicly distanced himself from the article, which aroused negative publicity abroad.[116]

Undoubtedly some Nazis at a grass-root level were disappointed that the 'Jewish question' no longer seemed to be a priority for Hitler.

Julius Streicher, the editor of *Der Stürmer* (*right*), with Hitler.

The Führer received several letters from German people complaining that Jews continued to prosper in the business world. Early in the year, for instance, a businessman from Chemnitz called Richard Fichte wrote to Hitler complaining about the favourable treatment of Jewish department stores. These stores purchased glass containers 'considerably more cheaply than obtainable by businessmen of German blood', he said. Hitler should 'step in immediately and with the full rigour of National Socialist consistency to forestall the violent reaction that must result in the German-blooded business world when it learns that even in the Third Reich it is beaten down to the advantage of the Jews'.[117] Anger against the Jews had not gone away, even if it was politic for Hitler to ignore it for now. The president of the Kassel district noted in a report on 8 August: 'The attitude of the National Socialist organization in regard to the Jewish question remains unchanged and is often in conflict with the Minister of Economics [Schacht], particularly with regard to the treatment of Jewish businesses. I have repeatedly been compelled, together with the State Police, to cancel boycott initiatives.'[118]

Anti-Semitism was everywhere, it seemed. Jakob Falkenstein, in a letter to Hitler dated 5 February, summarized discontent among farmers in Hüttenfeld in the state of Hesse: 'Dairy farming is the local occupation. And in this area, most cattle-dealers are Jewish. As a result, only the Jews can provide cows to milk.'[119]

The British journalist Philip Pembroke Stephens outlined in graphic detail the continuing persecution of German Jews in rural areas in an article for the *Daily Express*, published on 25 May. In the town of Arnswalde, he noted: 'Jew-baiting has been brought to a fine art and cafés carry the slogan "No Jews allowed here."' In certain parts of Bavaria, Stephens found Jews were banned from swimming baths. Synagogues and Jewish cemeteries were being routinely vandalized, with police turning a blind eye. 'German Jews', he concluded, 'are friendless, persecuted and told by Nazi officials "the best thing you can do is die."' Shortly after this article appeared, Stephens was arrested by the Gestapo and deported.[120]

The annual Nuremberg Rally took place from 4 to 10 September. It was called the Party Rally of Unity and Strength. Hitler chose Albert Speer to stage-manage the event. He designed a 'Cathedral of Light' in the arena, using 130 anti-aircraft search lights shining their beams into the sky on the vast Zeppelin Field. At the head of the stadium a giant painted wooden eagle with a 100-foot wing span was erected. It

Hitler Youth poster called: 'The Hand of the Führer of the Reich.'

diese Hand
führt das Reich

deutsche Jugend folge ihr
in den Reihen der H.J.!

was a tense event, as many Brownshirts were still smarting from the recent blood purge, but it went off without any protests. The American journalist William Shirer noted in his diary: 'Like a Roman emperor Hitler rode into the medieval town at sundown today past solid phalanxes of wildly cheering Nazis who packed the narrow streets.'[121]

The rally was filmed by the talented director Leni Riefenstahl and released in 1935 as the infamous feature film *Triumph des Willens* (*Triumph of the Will*). When Hitler offered her the appointment, Riefenstahl replied: 'I am not a member of the party and I don't even know the difference between the SA and the SS.'[122] Rather than it being a Nazi Party production, she insisted the film's production credit should go to her own company, L. R. Studio-Film GmbH (renamed Rally-Film). The film was distributed in cinemas by the partly state-owned Ufa. *Triumph of the Will* brought Riefenstahl instant fame and later damaged her career after the war. A remarkable exercise in propaganda (the American director Frank Capra called it 'lethal' and 'a psychological weapon aimed at destroying the will to resist') it depicts Hitler as a charismatic demi-god. 'The bond between Führer and the people was of supreme importance,' Riefenstahl said. 'Showing this is one of the tasks I have set myself.'[123] The film had a production staff of 170, including sixteen cameramen, and Riefenstahl drew on footage from the newsreels of the Ufa and Tobias film companies. *Triumph of the Will* won a gold medal at the Venice Biennale in 1935.

On 4 September the Munich Gauleiter Alfred Wagner read out Hitler's proclamation in the Luitpold Hall to open the Nuremberg Rally. It declared that the National Socialist revolution had now come to an end because it had achieved everything that could be expected of it. There would be no state of permanent revolution, because the leadership now had the power to do anything it wanted. This was ex-

emplified by Hitler being the new Führer, supported by an army with the power to 'crush any and all attempts to instigate acts of violence against the leadership of the National Socialist movement'.[124]

Hitler appeared in person before a crowd of 200,000 for the main speech at the Nuremberg Rally on 7 September. William Shirer witnessed the spectacle:

> 'We are strong and will get stronger,' Hitler shouted at them through the microphone, his words echoing across the hushed field from the loudspeakers. And there in the floodlit night, jammed together like sardines, in one mass formation, the little men of Germany, who had made Nazism possible, achieved the highest state of being the Germanic man knows: the shedding of their individual souls and minds – with the personal doubts and problems – until under the mystic lights and at the sound of the magic words of the Austrian [Hitler] they were merged in the Germanic herd.[125]

Women in Hitler's Germany could be in no doubt that Nazism was a male-dominated movement. Hitler opposed any idea of equality of the sexes or equal rights for women, although under his regime they retained the right to vote. The feminist movement of the Weimar era was dismissed as a 'Jewish swindle'. Women were expected to be wives and mothers first and foremost, leaving the men to wear the uniforms, the jackboots and, especially, the trousers. Men and women occupied separate spheres under the Nazis. Motherhood was venerated, as was the family unit. Families were given extra allowances, loans and tax breaks. As an inducement, special medals were awarded to women who chose to stay in the home and bear children.

The Nazi ideal of womanhood was projected through organizations like the National Socialist Women's League (Nationalsozialistische Frauenschaft), which was very popular and boasted 5.8 million members. Each year Hitler spoke to the Women's League at the Nuremberg Rally. In 1934 he began his speech by stating that women had been his most loyal supporters within the National Socialist movement. On the other hand, 'women's liberation', he said, was a phrase invented by 'the Jewish intellect'. He promised to restore the natural state of nature in which men and women had separate but mutually supportive roles: 'If it is said that a man's world is the state, that the man's world is his struggle, his willingness to devote himself to the community, one might perhaps say that a woman's world is a smaller one. For her world is her husband, her family, her children and her home.' These two worlds, according

Propaganda poster for the League of German Girls (*left*).

Nazi propaganda promoting motherhood entitled 'Mother and Child'.

to Hitler, complemented each other: 'It is not right "when a woman forces her way into a man's world". It is more natural for her to stay out of this world and concentrate on the home.'[126]

At the end of the Nuremberg Rally, the journalist William Shirer noted in his diary:

> You have to go through one of these to understand Hitler's
> hold on the people, to feel the dynamic in the movement he's
> unleashed and the sheer disciplined strength the Germans
> possess. And now, as Hitler told correspondents yesterday – in
> explaining his technique – the half million men who've been
> here during the week will go back to their towns and villages and
> preach the new gospel with new fanaticism.[127]

On 14 November Victor Klemperer found that Hitler worship had wormed its way into academia. He and 100 of his university colleagues in Dresden were forced to swear an oath of loyalty to Hitler:

> I was not present at the first oath-taking during the holidays, in
> the hope of avoiding it altogether. It was not to be. The ceremony,
> as cold and formal as possible, lasted less than two minutes.
> We spoke the words in chorus after the rector who had first
> reeled off: 'You swear eternal loyalty. I am duty-bound to draw
> your attention to the sanctity of the oath.' And afterwards: 'You
> are duty-bound to put your signature to the oath on a printed
> form.'[128]

On 19 December Hitler held a lavish party to promote Anglo-German friendship in Berlin. Among the twenty-four specially invited guests was Lord Rothermere, the newspaper magnate and owner of the *Daily Mail*. He was accompanied by his star journalist George Ward Price, whose interviews with the Führer had done so much to improve Hitler's image in Britain. What especially attracted Rothermere to Hitler was his fervent hatred of communism. After dinner Hitler told one of his British guests: 'It's ten years to the day since I was released from Landsberg Prison.'[129] He had come a long way since then. By the end of 1934 Adolf Hitler was the undisputed political master of the Third Reich.

Leni Riefenstahl with the giant eagle
that towered over the Zeppelin Field,
the venue of the Nuremberg Rally.

1935
·
BREAKING FREE OF VERSAILLES
·

In his New Year message Adolf Hitler expressed a strong desire for the Saar to be returned to Germany. Under the terms of the Treaty of Versailles in 1919 this region in southwestern Germany had been placed under international administration for fifteen years. In January 1935 about 540,000 Saarlanders of voting age were asked to decide in a referendum whether they should remain under the administration of the League of Nations or join France or rejoin the German Reich.

The pro-Nazi *Deutsche Front* group engaged in a propaganda battle masterminded by Goebbels, who spent money freely on posters, parades and rallies. Their main campaign slogan was 'Return home to the Reich!' A variety of inducements were offered to the Saarlanders to vote in favour of rejoining Germany, including winter fuel relief payments, better occupational pensions for state employees, and a promise that no concentration camps would be established in the Saar region for at least two years. Jews would be exempt from discriminatory laws for a year. On the opposite side was the 'Defeat Hitler in the Saar' campaign led by social democrats and communists who argued that the Saarlanders should remain under the control of the League of Nations.

There was some pressure and intimidation during the referendum. British journalist Sheila Grant of the *Observer* wrote on 13 January: 'Jewish shopkeepers have been asked to hand over their voting cards to the *Deutsche Front* officials. Brutal attacks on supporters of the status quo continue in isolated places.'[1]

On 15 January the referendum result was declared. A whopping 90.73 per cent (477,089) of Saarlanders voted to rejoin Germany, while just 8.87 per cent (46,613) wanted to retain the status quo and a mere 0.4 per cent (2,124) opted to join democratic France. More people spoiled their ballot papers (2,161) than wanted to join France. At 97.99 per cent the turnout was extraordinarily high. As Klaus Mann, a leading figure in the exiled Social Democrat Party, observed: 'This is our worst political defeat since January 1933. It proves the slogans of the left have no appeal.'[2] Victor Klemperer wrote in his diary: 'The 90 per cent vote in the Saar is really not only a vote for Germany, but literally for Hitler's Germany.'[3]

On the following day a gleeful Hitler was interviewed by the American journalist Pierre Huss of the Hearst Press. 'The results of the plebiscite fill me and every single one of my staff with infinite pride in the German *Volk*,' he said. 'At the same time, this is a condemnation of the Peace Treaty of Versailles of truly historic dimensions.' After the return of the Saar, Hitler claimed to have 'no further territorial demands on France' but warned 'never shall the new German Reich consent to any limitations to the rights of our people'.[4]

On 17 January George Ward Price of the *Daily Mail* was granted yet another interview, during which Hitler made a strong plea for peace, aimed squarely at British public opinion: 'When I talk about peace I am expressing none other than the uttermost desire of the German *Volk*. I know the horrors of war, no gain can compensate for the losses it brings.' In any future European war, Hitler predicted the only winners would be the communists. He made two further promises: (1) 'Germany will never break the peace', and (2) 'If anyone should attack us, they will fall on a hornets' nest – for we love freedom just as much as we love peace.' As for the League of Nations, his message had not changed: 'Whether or not we return to this body depends exclusively upon whether we can belong to it as a completely equal nation.'[5]

The pro-German British peer Lord Lothian met Hitler in Berlin on 29 January. Lothian suggested that a fresh political and armaments agreement was required, offering Germany full equality. Hitler responded with a lengthy monologue which castigated the 'Bolshevik' Soviet Union, ruled out any use of force against Poland or France or the Low Countries, and promised to fully respect Austria's independence. It would be the 'greatest madness' for Britain and Germany to ever go to war with one another again, he added. Lothian was impressed and believed every word. 'I am convinced Germany does not want war and is prepared to renounce it absolutely provided she is given equality,' he wrote in a letter to *The Times*, shortly after returning to Britain.[6]

On 3 February the British and French governments issued a joint communiqué proposing a far-reaching European system of security based on a series of security pacts covering Central and Eastern Europe and dubbed the 'Eastern Locarno'. Of some interest to Hitler was a provision to drop the military clauses in the Treaty of Versailles which limited the size of the German army to 100,000, a clear inducement for Germany to return to the League of Nations. Another pact limiting the extension of air power between France, Britain, Germany, Italy and Belgium was also proposed. Hitler offered a seemingly conciliatory response to these new Anglo-French proposals on 14 February, especially the promise to allow Germany to rearm. However, he refused to restrict his freedom of movement by becoming involved in an Eastern Locarno guarantee system. Instead, he suggested bilateral talks should precede any more general talks and invited British ministers to come to Berlin.[7]

During a meeting of the Ministerial Committee on Disarmament on 19 February the British Prime Minister Ramsay MacDonald said that it would be 'a profound mistake' for a British delegation to go to Germany. Instead, he argued, 'the Germans ought to be made to come here'. Leading Conservative Stanley Baldwin (who would become Prime Minister in June 1935) believed that 'there was no use in talking to anyone except Hitler'. He suggested that Sir John Simon, the Foreign Secretary, accompanied by Anthony Eden, the Lord Privy Seal, should go to Berlin.[8]

On 9 February a tall, blond, blue-eyed, twenty-year-old British upper-class socialite called Unity Mitford met Hitler for the first time at his favourite restaurant, the Osteria Bavaria in the arty Schwabing area of Munich. She had lunched there regularly for several weeks in the hope of attracting Hitler's attention and eventually it worked. Hitler invited her to join him at his table. When she told him her middle name was Valkyrie, Hitler replied: 'You are a Valkyrie? You

choose who shall die in battle and bring the bravest of the warriors to Valhalla, the afterlife hall of the slain, ruled over by the god Odin. You serve them mead and take them as lovers.'[9] Shortly after this brief encounter Mitford wrote to her sister Diana (who would go on to marry Oswald Mosley, the leader of the British Union of Fascists): 'He invited me to his table, paid for lunch. I think I'm the happiest girl in the world.'[10]

Unity Mitford's Nordic good looks clearly appealed to Hitler. Her diary reveals that she met him no less than 140 times between February 1935 and September 1939. This is remarkable given the fact that during this whole period Hitler's romantic partner was Eva Braun. Charlotte Morley, the editor of the Mitford letters, believes it was a close friendship, 'but not a love affair'.[11]

Unity Mitford was an enthusiastic supporter of Hitler's anti-Semitic policies. In a letter to the Jew-baiting *Der Stürmer* newspaper she wrote: 'The English have no notion of the Jewish danger. English Jews are always described as "decent". Perhaps the Jews in England are cleverer in their propaganda than in other countries, I cannot tell, but it is a certain fact that our struggle is extremely hard. Our worst Jews work only behind the scenes.' She even asked Julius Streicher to publish her full name at the bottom of the letter, as 'I want everyone to know that I am a Jew-hater.'[12]

It had long been a dream of Hitler's to produce an affordable car for ordinary *Volk* and on 14 February he delivered a speech at Berlin's International Automobile and Motorcycle Exhibition in which he boasted of the superiority of German cars and motorcycles. 'I am happy to say that a brilliant designer [Ferdinand Porsche] has succeeded, with the cooperation of his staff, in completing the preliminary plans for the German *Volkswagen* [People's Car],' he announced enthusiastically, 'and will finally be able to test the first models beginning mid-year.'[13]

On 24 February, the anniversary of the founding of the Nazi Party, Hitler gave a speech in Munich's Hofbräuhaus to his faithful party followers. In a message that was aimed at world opinion as much as the people in the beer hall, he said:

> The nation is united in a yearning for peace and determined to defend German liberty. We want nothing but to coexist with other peoples in mutual respect. We do not wish to threaten the peace of any people. But we will tell the world that anyone who would rob the German *Volk* of liberty must do so by force and each and every one of us will defend ourselves against force.

Adolf Hitler with Unity Mitford.

[overleaf] Hitler salutes Stormtroopers in Saarbrücken on 4 March 1935, following victory in the territorial referendum in January 1935, which returned the Saar to German control.

> Never will I nor any government after me that is born of the
> spirit of our Movement affix the nation's signature to a document
> signifying a voluntary waiver of Germany's honour and equality
> of rights.[14]

Hitler spoke next at Saarbrücken, the capital of the Saarland, during celebrations to mark the official return of the territory to Germany on 1 March. Hitler saw himself as a liberator seeking to give the Saarlanders national self-determination. It was a great day for Germany, he said, and for Europe, too. It showed how popular National Socialism was. The referendum result had brought 'compensatory justice' to the people of the region and it would help to improve relations with France. Once again he insisted that Germany wanted peace: 'It must be possible for two great peoples to reach out to one another and jointly combat the miseries that threaten to swamp Europe.'[15] In a passionate conclusion, to wild cheering, Hitler declared: 'This day should be a lesson to those who believe that they can rob a nation by terror or force of its character, who believe that they can tear out a piece of a nation and steal its soul. Blood is stronger than any paper documents. By the referendum you have eased my task extremely, which is to make Germany happy.'[16]

On 4 March the British government published a White Paper on defence, outlining its opposition to Germany's 'clandestine air re-armament' and in response proposed a 50 per cent increase in spending on the Royal Air Force over a five-year period. The German press, orchestrated by Goebbels, denounced the British move. Irritated, Hitler promptly withdrew his invitation to meet Sir John Simon and Anthony Eden on 7 March, citing a 'hoarse voice, a sore throat' or, as foreign press correspondents in Berlin put it, 'A diplomatic cold.'[17] Hitler told Rosenberg: 'Those ruling England [*sic*] must get used to dealing with us on an equal footing.'[18]

General Ludwig Beck, the Chief of the General Staff, prepared a top-secret memorandum for Hitler on 6 March outlining the optimum size of a German army in peacetime. Beck predicted Belgium, Czechoslovakia, France and Poland might unite to attack Germany in a pre-emptive war, before Germany had fully regained its military strength. However, he doubted whether Britain or the Soviet Union would join in such a limited European war. Moving on to the key foreign policy objectives in the coming years, he made the following observations: Germany had to achieve full equality in armaments and remove the restrictions imposed by the Treaty of Versailles – including the ban on conscription, the limits upon the size of the German army, and the prohibition of a German air force – as well as ending the demilitarized zone in the Rhineland, the disputed region along the Rhine river. Beck proposed a peacetime army of twenty-three divisions, around 360,000 men, which could be increased to sixty-three divisions by 1939, with a strength, by then, of 1 million men.[19]

On 9 March Göring suddenly announced the existence of the German air force or *Luftwaffe*. This was an outright breach of Article 198 of the Treaty of Versailles. The German government was testing the international mood concerning rearmament, because Hitler was planning an even bolder move. On 13 March he summoned Colonel Friedrich Hossbach, his *Wehrmacht* administrative assistant, to a meeting at the Hotel Jahreszeiten in Munich. Within days, Hitler said, he intended to publicly announce the reintroduction of army conscription. Hossbach suggested that Hitler should announce an ambitious expansion to thirty-six divisions, an army of 550,000 men. Hitler agreed with this figure, which was much higher than Beck had advised in his earlier memorandum, but when Hitler informed his War Minister Werner von Blomberg of his intention, Blomberg was astonished. The announcement that conscription was to be reintroduced was extremely risky, Blomberg warned, because if the French decided to intervene militarily, Germany was still unprepared for war. Konstantin von Neurath, the German Foreign Minister, was also given prior knowledge of Hitler's announcement. In his view, the chance of France taking military action was not very high.[20]

On 16 March Hitler met his cabinet and quickly gained agreement to issue the 'Law for the Build-up of the *Wehrmacht*'.[21] This stated that because Germany had fulfilled its disarmament responsibilities under the Treaty of Versailles – while, incidentally, the victorious Allies had continued to rearm and had stifled all attempts to agree equality for Germany in armaments negations – Hitler's government was now 'compelled to take measures necessary to end the unworthy and dangerous defenceless state of a great people and Reich'.[22] To this end, army conscription would be reintroduced, raising the number of army divisions to thirty-six or 550,000 men. This was well above the 100,000 limit on the German army's strength that had been set by the Treaty of Versailles.

'The Führer laid out the situation,' Goebbels wrote in his diary. 'Extreme solemnity. Then he read out the proclamation, together with the law. Everyone [in the cabinet] was profoundly moved. Blomberg stood up and thanked the Führer. For the first time, there was a salute

[overleaf] Left to right, John Simon, British Foreign Secretary, Anthony Eden, Lord Privy Seal (*both wearing top hats*), the German Foreign Minister Konstantin von Neurath (*holding hat*) and Eric Phipps, the British Ambassador (*also in top hat*), after talks with Hitler.

of "Heil" in the room. Versailles had been erased by law. A historic hour. We are once again a major power.'[23]

This dramatic move in foreign policy illustrates how determined Hitler was to break free of the Treaty of Versailles. It would become a familiar pattern in his foreign policy during the 1930s. He would present the Western Powers with a fait accompli to which they were then invited to respond. The West's half-hearted response to each of Hitler's foreign policy surprises simply encouraged Hitler to keep on unilaterally revising the Treaty of Versailles, step by step. Each revisionist move was presented by Hitler as entirely legitimate and justifiable, and was usually followed by a declaration of his ardent desire for peace. In this way, Hitler went from one effortless foreign policy triumph to another, his opponents scarcely realizing his supreme cunning. The themes Hitler championed – honour, equality of treatment, national self-determination – all seemed perfectly reasonable and justified, even echoing the rhetoric of the League of Nations. Added to this, a clear majority of the German people supported Hitler's flouting of the Treaty of Versailles.

On the following day was Heroes' Remembrance Day (*Helden-gedenktag*), a national public holiday to commemorate Germans who had fallen during the Great War. An enormous military parade in Berlin turned into a huge celebration. Hundreds of thousands of happy Germans thronged the streets. Blomberg announced in a passionate speech at the end of the day: 'Germany will again take the place it deserves among the nations. We pledge ourselves to a Germany which will never surrender and never again sign a treaty that cannot be fulfilled.'[24]

'The German *Volk* does not want war, it wants only the same rights as all others,' Hitler insisted in another interview with the *Daily Mail* journalist George Ward Price. 'The act of restoring German military sovereignty touches upon those points in the Treaty of Versailles that have in any case long since lost their legal validity by virtue of the refusal of other states to perform their respective obligations to reduce arms.'[25]

On 18 March there was feverish diplomatic activity in response to Hitler's public announcement of his intention to expand the German army. The French and Italian governments issued sharply worded official protests against the move. President Franklin D. Roosevelt did not object to Hitler's decision, adding the United States wanted to be a 'good neighbor' to all European nations. The British government sent a meek letter of protest, followed by a grovelling request for Sir John

Simon and Anthony Eden's visit to Germany to be rescheduled. The German government was more than happy to oblige. This was a clear hint that the British government was going its own way in its diplomatic dealings with Germany. For their part, the Polish government raised no objection to Germany's rearmament, although they would come to regret it later. Victor Klemperer was not impressed by the international response, noting in his diary: 'The protests of the foreign powers are weak-kneed, and they accept the fait accompli. Result: Hitler's regime is more stable than ever.'[26]

The diplomatic options were limited for the Western Allies at this time. There was no appetite in Britain, France or Italy for a 'preventative war' to stop Germany. A far more appealing policy, especially for the British government, was to recognize German demands for equality in armaments, but to try and achieve this through peaceful negotiation. Another possibility was to create a strong anti-German bloc in Europe, which the French government appeared to favour, but the British government felt the creation of an antagonistic, anti-German alliance would only worsen relations and lead to war anyway.

On 25 March Eden and Simon finally arrived in Berlin for two days of talks on Anglo-German rearmament. This exchange of views took place in a surprisingly relaxed atmosphere, with Hitler, Neurath and Ribbentrop all present. Eden observed that Hitler 'was definitely more authoritative and less eager to please than a year before'.[27] The Führer led the discussion without notes and dominated the conversation.

On the first day Hitler emphasized to his British guests that the Soviet Union was much more of a threat to the Western Powers than Germany. Eden asked on what basis he made this assertion, to which Hitler replied that during his rise to power the Bolsheviks had tried to undermine Germany. Sir John Simon suggested that Germany should join an Eastern Locarno to protect all of the small nations of Eastern Europe. Hitler refused to join such an arrangement on the grounds that Lithuania – one of the countries Simon had mentioned – contained a German minority in the Memel region, which, Hitler claimed, was being denied national self-determination. Hitler said that he preferred bilateral agreements rather than collective arrangements involving several powers.[28] In the evening a lavish dinner was held in the Reich President's palace. The entire German cabinet attended, along with leading Nazi officials.

The next day the talks moved on to the main issue of German rearmament. Hitler pushed strongly for equality of treatment for

Germany. When the British ministers asked him to justify Germany's unilateral rearmament, Hitler gave his favourite response: 'Did Wellington, when Blücher came to his assistance at Waterloo, first ask the legal experts of the Foreign Office whether the strength of the Prussian army exceeded the limits fixed by treaty?'[29] (Eden found this analogy ridiculous.)[30] When questioned about the current strength of the German air force, Hitler claimed that the *Luftwaffe* had already reached parity with Britain's RAF. Eden and Simon found this quite unbelievable and they were right. Hitler was lying.[31]

As the talks drew to an inconclusive end, Hitler suggested an Anglo-German naval agreement which promised to restrict German naval strength to 35 per cent of the current British total. Eden and Simon did not accept or reject this idea. Their visit culminated with a dinner in the Reich Chancellery on the evening of 26 March. They reached no concrete agreement on any issue during the talks, but the discussions were conducted in a friendly atmosphere. Hitler remained completely inflexible, giving no guarantee that he would join in any collective security arrangements. Eden wrote in his diary: 'Results bad [...] whole tone and temper different from a year ago.' He felt that Hitler, although a skilled negotiator, had been 'shifty and devious' throughout their conversations.[32]

Leni Riefenstahl's hugely anticipated film documentary *Triumph of the Will* premiered at the Ufa-Palast am Zoo movie theatre in Berlin on 28 March. A large crowd gathered outside to greet the arrival of the film's main star, Hitler, accompanied by Hess and Goebbels. *Triumph of the Will* brilliantly captures the fervour of the Nuremberg Rally of 1934. It opens with Hitler's Messiah-like arrival through the clouds by aeroplane. He is seen for the first time as he exits the plane, greeted by cheering crowds. The film then follows his open-topped Mercedes as it drives through the streets of Nuremberg passing cheering crowds. The camera constantly cuts, with clever editing, from Hitler raising his arm in the familiar Nazi salute to the beaming faces of the crowd: men, women and blond-haired children. It is probably the most memorable opening sequence of any Nazi propaganda film. *Triumph of the Will* then covers the various speeches at the Nuremberg Rally, including the opening ceremony, Hitler's address to the Hitler Youth, and his emotional closing speech.

Triumph of the Will was an instant success. A reporter for the magazine *Film-Kurier* observed: 'When the "Horst Wessel Song" strikes up in the closing frames, the audience rises from its seats, deeply moved, and sings along; it sounds like a vow to loyally follow the Führer.'[33] The *Völkischer Beobachter* called it 'the greatest film we have seen'. Goebbels noted: 'Whoever has seen and experienced the face of the Führer will never forget it. It will haunt him through days and dreams, and will, like a quiet flame, burn itself into his soul.'[34]

On 9 April Hitler arrived, without invitation, at the seventieth birthday party of General Erich Ludendorff. As a special surprise, he walked up to Ludendorff and placed a personal letter in his hand, appointing him a Field Marshal. Ludendorff was not impressed. He banged the table with his fist and shouted: 'You cannot nominate any-one Field Marshal, Herr Hitler! An officer is named Field Marshal on the battlefield! Not at a birthday tea party, in the midst of peace!' Outraged, Hitler immediately left the party.[35]

Between 11 and 14 April the leaders of Britain (Ramsay MacDon-ald), France (Pierre-Étienne Flandin) and Italy (Benito Mussolini) met in the Italian resort town of Stresa by Lake Maggiore. They joint-ly issued the strongly worded 'Final Declaration of the Stresa Con-ference'. It condemned Germany's reintroduction of conscription and announced a joint determination to uphold the Locarno Pact of 1925. They also pledged to resist any further unilateral breaches of the Paris Peace Settlement. These were words rather than deeds, however. There was no mention of any concrete military action being taken against Germany via the League of Nations. As Goebbels noted in his diary: 'The same old song. Condemnation of German violation of treaties. That need not interest us if they do not attack us.'[36]

On 17 April the League of Nations condemned Germany's introduction of conscription too, but also put forward no concrete proposals to introduce economic sanctions against Germany. Hitler dismissed the League's rebuke as another attempt to discriminate against Germany, or as *Newsweek* put it: 'Hitler told the League council it could go jump in Lake Geneva.'[37]

On 1 May Hitler delivered the keynote speech at the third National Labour Day rally at Berlin's Tempelhof airfield, before a huge crowd estimated at 1.5 million. Reviewing his achievements over the past year, he declared:

> Great tasks have always been accomplished only by strong
> leaders, but even the strongest leadership must fail if it does
> not have a faithful, inwardly steadfast and truly strong *Volk*
> standing behind it. I ask of you: renew on this day of the
> greatest and most glorious demonstration in the world your

vow to your *Volk*. To our community and to our National Socialist
State. My will – and this must be the vow of each one of us – is
your faith. To me – as to you – my faith is everything I have in
this world.[38]

The next morning a letter arrived at the home of Professor Victor
Klemperer from the Director of the Ministry for Popular Education. It
read: 'On the basis of paragraph 6 of the Law for the Restoration of the
Civil Service I have recommended your dismissal. Notice of dismissal
enclosed.' Klemperer telephoned the university, but no one knew about
his redundancy. 'At first I felt alternately numb and slightly romantic,'
he wrote in his diary, 'now there is only bitterness and wretchedness.
My situation will be very difficult. I shall receive my salary [800
Reichsmarks] until the end of July and after that a pension, which will
amount to approximately 400 [Reichsmarks].'[39]

On that same day the Franco-Soviet Treaty of Mutual Assistance
was signed. Unlike the pre-1914 Franco-Russian Alliance it contained
no specific military agreements, no arrangements for collaboration in
the event of war between the military general staffs, and referred to no
automatic circumstances when it would be triggered. Any 'unprovoked
aggression' against France or the USSR first had to be established
by the League of Nations. As Maxim Litvinov, the Soviet Foreign
Minister, commented: 'One should not place any serious hopes on the
pact, in the sense of military aid in the event of war. Our security
will still remain exclusively in the hands of the Red Army. For us,
the pact has predominantly a political significance.'[40] A fortnight later
the Czechoslovak-Soviet Treaty was signed. This obliged the Soviet
Union to aid Czechoslovakia militarily against any foreign aggression,
provided that the French (Czechoslovakia's main ally) first came to
Czechoslovakia's aid.

These diplomatic moves by France, the Soviet Union and Czechoslovakia prompted Hitler to mount a peace offensive, aiming primarily
at influencing sympathetic sections of British public opinion. To
this end, Hitler wrote a letter in early May to Lord Rothermere, the
owner of the *Daily Mail*, emphasizing his 'unalterable determination
to render a historically great contribution to the restoration of a
good and enduring understanding between both great Germanic
peoples'. Appealing to British upper-class snobbery, he claimed that
an Anglo-German understanding 'would form in Europe a force for
peace and reason of 120 million people of the highest type'. Hitler
hoped Rothermere would circulate his letter widely among the British

Establishment and he did. Even George V read it. It was treated with a little more detachment by the Foreign Office though.[41]

On 10 May in an interview in the *Daily Telegraph* Hitler insisted that he wanted peace. He still accepted the Locarno Pact and the German-Polish Pact in the East. As for the Soviet Union he said that there were no circumstances under which he would sign a treaty with the 'Bolsheviks' – a direct put-down of the recently signed Soviet-French treaty. He would rather hang himself, he added. He also noted that recent events had shown that the League of Nations had ceased to matter as an international peacekeeper.[42]

On 12 May Józef Piłsudski died. Goebbels commented: 'Poland is losing its best man, and we're losing the most important figure in the great game.'[43] Göring went to Piłsudski's state funeral, while in Berlin Hitler attended a Catholic requiem mass in honour of Piłsudski, who had ruled Poland since 1926 and established a virtual dictatorship.

On 21 May the old *Reichswehr*, the central military organization of Germany since 1919, was officially renamed the *Wehrmacht*. At the same time, Hitler issued the secret Reich Defence Law, appointing himself as the *Wehrmacht*'s supreme commander.[44] Later that day, he delivered an important and carefully crafted speech on foreign policy in the Reichstag. It was characteristically duplicitous, full of the soothing language of peace, tolerance and conciliation. The new Germany was misunderstood, Hitler said. War solved nothing. Germany needed peace and wanted peace. He had no desire to conquer or threaten other nations. He would not interfere in the internal affairs of Austria or conclude a union with that country. Germany had been denied equality since 1918 and treated as a second-class nation. Despite all this, Germany was still prepared to cooperate with other nations.

Hitler then made several proposals for maintaining peace in Europe. Germany would not return to the League of Nations until it rid

Eva Braun, aged 19, in 1931.

itself of the Treaty of Versailles. If that happened, Germany would rejoin. However, Germany would continue to 'unconditionally' adhere to the non-military clauses of the Treaty of Versailles and uphold its obligations as set out in the Locarno Treaty. Hitler further promised Germany would abide by the demilitarization of the Rhineland. He even contemplated the prospect of Germany participating at some future point in upholding the collective security and disarmament arrangements of the League of Nations, and declared a willingness to sign non-aggression pacts with all of Germany's neighbours.

As for Eastern Europe, Hitler ruled out taking part in a collective security 'Eastern Locarno' because it included the Soviet Union. The Soviets wanted to destroy the independence of Europe, he said, and he criticized the French government for signing the Franco-Soviet Treaty of Mutual Assistance. In an obvious olive branch to Mussolini, Hitler said he regretted the deterioration of German-Italian relations after the Austria crisis. In a nod to the British, too, he promised to limit the German navy to 35 per cent of the Royal Navy, and said that he wanted only air parity with Britain.[45]

The Times editorial in Britain was positively gushing in its response: 'The speech turns out to be reasonable, straightforward and comprehensive. No one who reads it, with an impartial mind, can doubt that the points of policy laid down by Herr Hitler may fairly constitute the basis of a complete settlement with Germany – a free, equal and strong Germany, instead of the prostrate Germany upon which peace was imposed sixteen years ago.'[46] The American journalist William Shirer noted in his diary: 'I fear the speech will impress world opinion and especially British opinion more than it should.'[47]

At this time Hitler was suffering from a persistent hoarse throat, greatly exacerbated by straining his voice during his emotional speeches. He feared that he might have throat cancer. On 23 May he underwent an operation under local anaesthetic to remove a small, non-cancerous but painful polyp on his vocal chords. The surgery was performed in the Reich Chancellery by Professor Carl von Eicken, a throat-cancer specialist at the University of Berlin's Charité Ear Nose and Throat Hospital. Eicken advised Hitler to rest his voice for a month.

Preoccupied by the major political events of early 1935, as well as his own health, Hitler had completely neglected his young 'mistress' Eva Braun. The lack of contact with Hitler in the first half of 1935 led to her feeling deeply anxious and depressed. On 29 April she wrote: 'Love does not seem to be on the agenda at the moment.' She was worried that Hitler was going to replace her with his new British friend Unity Mitford, who became the chief object of her jealousy: 'She's called Valkyrie and looks the part, including the legs. And he likes such dimensions.'[48]

Eva Braun was born on 6 February 1912, the daughter of Friedrich (Fritz) Braun, a Munich schoolteacher, and his wife Franziska, a seamstress. When Hitler first met her in 1929 she was only seventeen and he was instantly attracted. She commented that at their first meeting Hitler 'devoured her with his eyes'.[49]

It was not until the suicide of his beloved half-niece Geli Raubal in 1931, however, that Hitler's relationship with Eva grew more serious. Frau Winter, Hitler's housekeeper in his Munich apartment, later claimed that he became sexually intimate with Braun sometime during 1932.[50] Yet Braun remained a 'secret lover', rarely accompanying him to social events, except in the company of his official photographer Heinrich Hoffmann, for whom Braun was an assistant. She allegedly attempted suicide in 1932, but there is no firm evidence for this.

Hitler's exact early relationship with Braun remains something of an unsolved mystery. A lack of reliable surviving documents

Adolf Hitler with Eva Braun.

adds to the frustration. In a letter to her sister Gretl, dated 23 April 1945, Braun asked her to destroy all of her private correspondence, especially her personal letters to Hitler.[51] This may explain why every Hitler biography is a let-down, because they lack not only Hitler's personal correspondence, most of which was destroyed, but also his correspondence with Eva Braun.

Our only detailed glimpse into her relationship with Hitler is a twenty-two-page excerpt from a diary she wrote covering the period 6 February to 28 May 1935. It was found by an American soldier after the war, although its authenticity has long been disputed. In 1967 Ilse Braun, Eva's elder sister, confirmed that it was Eva's handwriting. Braun's chief biographer Heike Görtemaker also leans towards the diary excerpts being genuine.

'Yesterday he came quite unexpectedly,' Braun wrote on 18 February, 'and it was a delightful evening. I am so endlessly happy he loves me so much and pray it will always be so.'[52] Other entries show that she often had great difficulty actually meeting with Hitler. On 1 March she describes 'two marvellously beautiful hours with him until midnight' in his apartment in Munich. At the end of March she mentions the frustration of being seated next to him at a formal dinner, but not 'able to say a single word'.[53] Hitler said a very distant goodbye to her at the end of the dinner and handed her an envelope with money inside, 'as he had done before', she noted bitterly.

Albert Speer and other members of Hitler's inner circle often witnessed Hitler handing Braun envelopes containing money at social events. Hitler promised her that he wanted to buy her a 'little house' near to his own apartment and told her that she could give up her job at Hoffmann's photographic studio.[54] This led to the general impression that Hitler was more like a 'sugar daddy', rather than an equal partner. This is perhaps unsurprising, given the age difference between them was twenty-three years.[55]

At the end of May 1935, feeling lonely, hopeless and abandoned, Braun sent Hitler a pleading letter, noting in her diary: 'If I don't have an answer by 10 tonight, I will simply take my 35 pills and gently slumber to the other side. This time it's going to be dead certain.'[56] Hitler never replied. So, in the early hours of 29 May, feeling completely abandoned, Braun seems to have followed through on her ultimatum. Her sister Ilse found her unconscious after taking about twenty-five sleeping tablets. Ilse called a doctor and, ironically, it was a local Jewish physician, Dr Martin Marx, who saved Eva Braun's life.[57]

Whether this was a genuine suicide attempt is not certain, but Hitler's reaction and actions afterwards suggest that he thought it was. Her relationship with Hitler was transformed in the following months. To begin with, Braun moved out of her parents' home on 9 August into a three-bedroom apartment on 42 Widenmayerstraße, Munich. This was rented and elegantly furnished by Hoffmann, with funds provided by Hitler. The flat was a five-minute walk from Hitler's apartment. Eva Braun's sister Gretl moved in with her, along with a Hungarian maidservant.

Hitler allowed Braun much closer contact with him from this point onwards. She was permitted to appear at public events and became a regular visitor at the Berghof, Hitler's mountain retreat, when he was at home. In September she attended the Nuremberg Rally for the first time.[58] All this did not please her parents, who objected to their daughter being openly set up as his 'mistress'. On 7 September her father Fritz wrote a strongly worded letter to Hitler, asking for his daughter to be 'returned to the bosom of her family'. Eva promised her father that she would deliver this letter to Hitler in person, but she never did. Her mother sent a similar letter to Hitler by post, but he never replied.[59]

On 1 June Hitler appointed Joachim von Ribbentrop as Ambassador Extraordinary and Plenipotentiary for Special Missions. Hitler primarily wanted him to negotiate a naval agreement with the British. Ribbentrop spoke fluent English, but unfortunately he was tactless, arrogant and charmless in equal measure, but with a dog-like devotion to Hitler. His diplomatic efforts in London were hampered by his constant trips back and forth to Germany to be closer to his Führer, which prompted the satirical magazine *Punch* to nickname him 'The Wandering Aryan'.[60]

Talks about a naval agreement between Britain and Germany began in the Foreign Office in Whitehall, London, on 4 June. Neither the French nor the Italian government was consulted beforehand. Ribbentrop issued a blunt ultimatum to Sir John Simon, the Foreign Secretary: agree to the German proposal of a 35 per cent naval ratio or the negotiations were at an end. Simon pointed out that such language should be used at the close of negotiations and not at the beginning.

On the following day the British delegation continued with the talks. The venue this time was the Admiralty. Simon began by announcing that the British government, after some discussion, had agreed to accept Hitler's demands. Thus, a pattern of behaviour was established between Britain and Germany during these negotiations: the Germans would make strong demands, the British would raise some technical objection, but then agreed to them in full.[61] The mode operation became known as appeasement.

The Anglo-German Naval Agreement was signed in London on 18 July (ironically, the anniversary of the Battle of Waterloo) by Ribbentrop and Simon. It limited the German navy to 35 per cent of the size of the Royal Navy, but by recognizing Germany's right to a larger navy, it allowed Germany to build five battleships whose tonnage and armaments were greater than anything the British already had at sea. In addition, twenty-one cruisers and sixty-four destroyers were planned. Not all of these vessels were completed by 1939, but enough submarines were built to inflict significant losses on the Royal Navy and merchant ships in the first year of the Second World War.[62]

Hitler described the signing of the naval agreement as 'the happiest day of my life'. He felt Anglo-German naval rivalry had been one of the chief reasons for the antagonism between the two nations prior to the outbreak of the Great War.[63] Goebbels wrote ecstatically in his diary: 'As I arrive at the Führer's office, the Naval Agreement has just been signed. Führer very happy. Big success for Ribbentrop and all of us.'[64]

As a signatory of the Stresa Front Agreement of 1935, Britain was supposed to resist any attempt by Germany to breach the Treaty of Versailles. Instead, operating outside the jurisdiction of the League of Nations, Britain had assisted Germany in doing just that. The agreement illustrated once again that British and French policy was pulling in different directions. As Victor Klemperer shrewdly observed: 'The enormous foreign policy success of the Naval Agreement with England [Britain] consolidates Hitler's power very greatly. Even before that I have recently had the impression that many otherwise well-meaning people, dulled to injustice and in particular not properly appreciating the misfortune of the Jews, have begun to halfway acquiesce to Hitler.'[65]

Throughout the spring and summer months of 1935 anti-Jewish disturbances and demonstrations flared up all over Germany. Offensive slogans were daubed on walls and shop windows. Effigies of Jews were regularly burned in the streets, Jewish cemeteries vandalized and in many cities the statues of famous Jewish personages were defaced by graffiti or pulled down by the local authorities. On 11 April Rudolf Hess, the Deputy Führer, sent a memorandum to Nazi Party members warning them not to 'vent their feelings by acts of terror against individual Jews as this can only result in bringing party members into conflict with the political police'.[66]

There were several reasons for this sudden resurgence of anti-Semitism in Germany. To begin with, Hitler's government had so far failed to deliver the promised upturn in the economy. Unemployment remained at 3.3 million in January 1935. The prices of food and fuel were also rising as wages stagnated due to a government freeze on pay rises. Consumers complained of food shortages and a lack of basic goods in the shops.[67] At the Nuremberg trials Hjalmar Schacht, the Minister of Economics, said he asked Hitler when he had assumed office in August 1934: 'How are the Jews in our national economy to be treated?' and that Hitler had replied: 'The Jews can be active in the domestic economy as before.'[68] In addition to this, there had been no major anti-Semitic legislation since mid-1933, even though Point 4 of the Nazi Party programme had promised Jews in Germany would be stripped of their citizenship. In *Mein Kampf* Hitler had made clear that he opposed sexual relations between Aryans and Jews, but there was still no law preventing German-Jewish marriages or sexual relations in place. All this had led many rank-and-file members of the SA to demand some fresh action on the so-called 'Jewish question'. This fresh outbreak of anti-Semitism received support not just from frustrated storm troopers, but also from senior figures in the Nazi elite at national and regional levels and even in the army. In May the *Wehrmacht* banned marriage between Aryan soldiers and non-Aryan women.

Munich was subjected to large-scale anti-Jewish agitation. In April slogans such as 'Out with Jews' and 'Stinking Jews' were daubed on shop windows. On 25 May gangs of Nazi activists attacked Jewish businesses and shops. In a letter to the Reich Interior Minister Leopold Weinmann a Jewish businessman described 'scenes straight out of the Wild West [of America]' on the streets of Munich.[69] Local Munich police reports of these disturbances in April and May indicate the involvement of three groups: older storm troopers, members of the Hitler Youth and exiled Austrian Nazis.[70] A social democrat agent in Bavaria observed: 'The persecution of the Jews is not meeting with any active support from the [general] population. But on the other hand, it is not failing to make an impact. Unnoticed racial propaganda is leaving its traces. People are losing their impartiality towards the Jews and many are saying to themselves the Nazis are actually right to fight them.'[71]

On 15 May an article entitled 'The Visible Enemy' appeared in the SS periodical *Das Schwarze Korps*. It was written by the high-ranking Nazi official Reinhard Heydrich, who said: 'Every *Volk* that, during times of political and racial weakness, has permitted Jewish immigration and later even racial interbreeding with Jews has been systematically corroded.' According to Heydrich, there were two groups of Jews living in Germany: the Zionists who strove to establish a Jewish state and to encourage emigration; and the 'more dangerous' assimilationists who denied their Jewish heritage by claiming to be German and converting to Christianity: 'It is primarily these assimilationists who, with every imaginable declaration of loyalty and the obtrusiveness that is unique to their race, threaten to sap the foundations from National Socialist principles.' The original anti-Jewish legislation of 1933 had placed severe limits on the influence of the Jews, Heydrich admitted. 'But the Jew in his tenacity and pertinacity only saw in this legislation a limitation. For him, the only questions worth posing were: how can I retain control of my former position, and how can I work to harm Germany?'[72]

The anti-Semitic newspaper *Der Stürmer* ran a campaign against Jewish-Aryan marriage and sexual relations during the summer of 1935. It highlighted sexual abuse cases involving Jews and young German girls. Outrageous false accusations of ritual murder featured regularly, too. The retired Jewish teacher Willy Cohn observed: 'It is no fun going out any more. The repulsive articles in the *Stürmer* are everywhere. It is surprising that more doesn't happen, given how incited the populace is.'[73] In Dresden Victor Klemperer noticed that '*Der Stürmer* was displayed at many street corners on "special noticeboards" with each one bearing the slogan in large letters: "The Jews are our misfortune."'[74]

At the Nuremberg trials, the publisher of the newspaper Julius Streicher denied that it had incited its readers to engage in violence against Jews. 'The content of *Der Stürmer* was not incitation,' he said. 'During the twenty years I edited the newspaper I never wrote in this connection: "Burn Jewish houses down, beat them to death." I did not intend to agitate or inflame, but to enlighten.'[75] The judges saw things differently and found Streicher guilty of incitement. He was hanged in 1946.

'Some people think,' Goebbels told a rally in Berlin on 30 June 1935, 'that we haven't noticed how the Jews are trying once again to spread themselves over all our streets. The Jews ought, please, to observe the laws of hospitality and not behave as if they were the same as us.'[76] There were violent scenes on Berlin's fashionable Kurfürstendamm on

Leading Nazi Joachim von Ribbentrop arrives in London for talks on the 1935 Anglo-German Naval Agreement.

15 July. Jewish-owned shops were vandalized. Jews were chased down the boulevard and many were severely beaten.[77] This violence was a reprisal for a Jewish protest a few days earlier over the screening of *Pettersson & Bendel*, a Swedish anti-Semitic film. Goebbels, who was on holiday with his family in the Baltic Sea resort of Heiligendamm at the time, noted in his diary: 'Telegram from Berlin. Jews demonstrating against an anti-Semitic film. The Führer has had enough. This is truly outlandish. Something will have to be done soon.'[78]

In Breslau during July several Jews were sent to concentration camps. They were accused of 'race defilement' (*Rassenschande*), meaning sexual relations with Aryans, even though this was not yet a criminal offence. As Arnon Tamir, who lived in Germany, puts it: 'Speaking for myself, I can only say at that time – and I was a young lad – the mere idea of becoming friendly or more with a German girl was poisoned right from the start by these horrible cartoons and headlines which claimed that the Jews were contaminating German girls.'[79]

On 11 July a hundred storm troopers descended on the cattle market in Fulda, a city in Hesse, attacking Jewish cattle-dealers and their customers. Cattle were released, running aimlessly and dangerously through the streets. The anti-Jewish agitation in the city continued for several days.[80] According to a report by the Bavarian Gestapo: 'Approximately 15–20 young bathers had demanded the removal of the Jews from the swimming bath by chanting in the park that adjoins the pool. The chant went: "These are German baths, Jews are not allowed in, out with them," and so on. A considerable number of other bathers joined in the chanting, so that the majority were demanding.' After this demonstration, complaints were submitted to the manager and the local lord mayor. A few days later a sign was erected at the swimming bath which read 'Entry Forbidden to Jews.'[81]

Rudi Bamber, a Jew, recalled that 'one had to be more and more careful, because many of the towns and villages had notices, "Jews not wanted", so it was difficult to find where one could go and be accepted as a Jew.'[82] Victor Klemperer had noticed it too: 'The Jew-baiting has become so extreme, far worse than during the first boycott, there are the beginnings of a pogrom here and there, and we [Jews] expect to be beaten to death at any moment.'[83] On 18 August Hitler gave a speech in Königsberg in which he talked of the need to implement the anti-Semitic Points 4 and 5 of the Nazi Party programme, with a new law regulating the status of Jews. Such a law, he added, was in preparation.[84]

The eruption of anti-Jewish violence in Germany was widely re-ported abroad. Worried about a possible foreign boycott of German exports, Schacht called a meeting of key ministers at the Ministry of Economics on 20 August to discuss the treatment of Jews. It was attended by Wilhelm Frick, Minister of the Interior, Franz Gürtner, Minister of Justice, Bernhard von Bülow, Permanent Secretary at the Foreign Ministry, Adolf Wagner, Gauleiter of Munich, and representatives of the Gestapo, the Nazi Party Racial Office and the Sicherheitsdienst des Reichsführers-SS, or SD, the intelligence agency of the SS, represented by Heydrich. Schacht was most concerned about the economic effects of anti-Semitic agitation and violence. Frick pointed out that he had tried to stop local disorder against Jews, but he also outlined the anti-Jewish legislation being prepared by the Ministry of the Interior, including a new citizenship law. Gürtner suggested that nobody would obey the law if they thought it was unfair. Local authorities were already turning a blind eye to anti-Jewish persecution. Bülow was most concerned about the effect on public opinion abroad of further anti-Jewish laws, and he warned that they could lead to an international boycott of the 1936 Olympic Games. Wagner said that the state and Nazi activists were responding differently to the Jewish question. The government, he suggested, had to take into account the 'anti-Semitic' mood of the German public.[85] The minutes of this meeting were forwarded to Hitler on 9 September.

The seventh Nazi Party rally, named the 'Reich Party Congress of Freedom', began in Nuremberg on 10 September.[86] In his opening proclamation Hitler stressed the importance of the fight against 'Jewish Marxism'. The 'inner enemies of the nation' would be confronted by the Nazi Party rather than the state bureaucracy, he said, a clear indication that new legislation against the Jews was about to be implemented.

On 13 September Hitler gave a speech to the NS-Frauenschaft (National Socialist Women's League) in which he praised the contribution of women to the Nazi movement:

> Our opponents deride us as not wanting to give women any other task than giving birth to children, but for a woman that is the utmost elevation [...] With every child to which she gives birth for the nation, she is waging a battle for the nation. The man stands up for the *Volk* just as the woman stands up for the family. A woman's equal rights lie in the fact she is treated with the high regard she deserves in those areas of life assigned by nature.[87]

The following day Hitler spoke to members of the Hitler Youth. The heavy, beer-drinking, hard-living German youth was now a thing of the past, he told them, and a new type of youth was emerging in the new Germany: 'What we want from our German youth is different from what was wanted in the past. In our eyes, the German youth of the future must be slim and slender, swift as a greyhound, tough as leather and hard as Krupp steel.'[88]

At 8 p.m. on 15 September Hitler convened a special session of the Reichstag in the Cultural Association building in Nuremberg. It was the first and last time that a Reichstag session took place outside Berlin. The last time the Reichstag had met in Nuremberg was in 1543. Hitler announced three important new laws, two of which were related to the so-called 'Jewish question'. He believed that this legislation could usher in a new era of toleration between Germans and Jews.

It was originally planned that Hitler would announce only one law at the Nuremberg Rally, which was to make the swastika the new national flag. However, it seems that Hitler felt this was an ideal moment to announce new anti-Jewish measures on German citizenship and marriage between Jews and Aryans. It seems unlikely that Hitler decided on the spur of the moment, after arriving in Nuremberg, to introduce these race laws. A new Reich citizenship had been discussed within the government ever since he came to power. The Ministry of the Interior had convened a committee on Population and Race Policy as long ago as July 1933, and they had discussed a law excluding Jews from full citizenship rights. It seems the recent rise in public anti-Semitism convinced Hitler the timing was now right to push ahead with his long-standing desire to exclude all Jews from Reich citizenship.[89] In this respect, the laws he announced at Nuremberg were not as hastily improvised as is sometimes supposed.

Hitler enjoyed springing big announcements on the public and even on his own cabinet. It was a clever political strategy to wrong-foot opponents, giving them little time to think or object. Hitler could have passed these laws himself, but he wanted a public show at the Nuremberg Rally, which he knew would be publicized worldwide.

In a short speech, Hitler attacked the Jews in Germany and abroad for fomenting disharmony. In effect, he was blaming the victim: the Jews, who he said, had caused the violence that was being done to them by an 'outraged populace'. The only way out of this situation, he explained, was to introduce new laws to create a tolerable relationship between the Jews and the German people.[90] He pre-warned his conservative critics that it would be a grave mistake on their part to believe that their protests would prevent his government from dealing with 'Jewish problems'. The three new laws were read out by Göring, before Hitler said in conclusion:

> My deputies! You have now approved of the laws, the impact
> of which will become evident only in its full scope after many
> centuries have passed. See to it that the nation itself does not
> stray from the straight and narrow path of the law. See to it that
> our own *Volk* adheres to the path of the law. See to it that this
> law is ennobled by the most tremendous discipline of the entire
> German *Volk*, to whom and for whom you are responsible.[91]

Hitler immediately ratified the new laws. The 'Law on the National Flag' made the swastika the official flag of the Reich, replacing the old black, white and red banner of imperial Germany. Hitler had wanted to do this in 1933, but he had waited because of possible opposition from Hindenburg. This new measure was brought forward after a highly publicized incident in July 1935 in New York City when anti-Nazi protestors had boarded the German liner the SS *Bremen* and hauled down the swastika, then thrown it in the river. When Hitler's government protested, the American government responded by stating that it was the Nazi Party swastika flag which had been insulted and not the German flag. This new law changed the status of the Nazi flag so that, as Göring stated, 'He who offends this flag insults the nation.'[92]

The 'Reich Law of Citizenship' declared that only those of 'German or kindred blood' could be full citizens of Germany. The remainder, defined as 'half-breed Jews', were classed as 'state subjects' without full citizenship rights.

The 'Law for the Protection of German Blood and German Honour' prohibited 'racial treason' (*Rassenverrat*), meaning intermarriage, and 'race disgrace' (*Rassenschande*), meaning extramarital sexual intercourse between Jews and Germans. This had been a key demand of the Nazi demonstrations in recent months. In addition, Jews were not allowed to employ Aryan women under the age of forty-five as domestic servants. This was related to the frequent allegation of Nazi anti-Semites that Jewish men sexually exploited their servants. Jews were no longer allowed to raise the Reich flag, either, although they could fly 'Jewish colours'.

These anti-Jewish laws had been drafted quickly and lacked substantive detail. A small team of key administrators was sent to Nuremberg from Berlin late on the evening of 13 September to turn them into legislation. It was led by Bernhard Lösener, head of the 'Jewish question' at the Ministry of the Interior, and his assistant Franz Albrecht Medicus. Both had undertaken preparatory work for at least a month.[93] They were told upon arrival by the state secretaries Hans Pfundtner and Wilhelm Stuckart of Hitler's instruction for them to formulate a Jewish law prohibiting marriage or any sexual relations between Jews and Aryans, as well as the employment of Aryan maids in Jewish households. Also involved in drafting the Nuremberg Laws were Walter Sommer from Hess's staff, who was not a master of detail, and Dr Gerhard Wagner, from Hitler's staff, who was the leader of the National Socialist German Physicians' Association. Wagner was also a key figure in the sterilization programme. A firm supporter of racial laws, ever since 1933 he had advocated a ban on marriages between Aryans and Jews.[94]

Wagner kept putting forward radical drafts which Lösener opposed and then amended. In the end there were four different versions of the anti-Jewish Nuremberg Laws in a sliding scale of severity: A, B, C and D. The main issue of contention was whether the laws should apply only to 'full Jews' or to 'half-breeds' as well. The most extreme and radical version was draft A, which excluded from any civil rights all Jews of mixed descent. The most moderate was draft D, which included them and offered substantial legal protection. Hitler chose draft D, because he wanted to be seen as a moderating influence on the 'Jewish question' both in public and especially abroad.[95]

Hitler then demanded a 'Reich Citizenship Law', which had been under discussion for weeks. The drafting of both anti-Jewish laws was not completed until 2.30 a.m. on 15 September. Despite the Nuremberg Laws, certificates of Reich citizenship were never issued to German citizens. All Germans, except those defined as Jews, remained classified as Reich citizens rather than subjects. The fine detail of the laws would be hammered out later by experienced civil servants.

The Reich Representative Council of Jews in Germany issued the following statement, which was published in the newspaper *C.V.-Zeitung* on 16 September:

> The laws passed by the Reichstag at Nuremberg have most adversely affected Jews in Germany. But they are intended to create the basis on which a tolerable relationship between the German *Volk* and the Jewish *Volk* will be possible. The Jewish Representation in Germany is prepared to commit all its energy to this end. The prerequisite to a tolerable relationship is the hope

that the end of the boycotts and defamation will permit Jews and Jewish communities in Germany to sustain their moral and economic existence.[96]

In the *Völkischer Beobachter* on 17 September Hitler described these new laws as 'the sole means of coming to passable terms with Jews living in Germany', and he renewed the Nazi Party order for members to 'refrain from taking independent action against Jews'.[97] The introduction of the Nuremberg Laws showed how the rank and file of the Nazi Party could still force Hitler into more radical action on the 'Jewish question'.

On 16 September Hitler inaugurated a new aspect of the Nuremberg Rally: *Wehrmacht* Day. All three defence services paraded in front of Hitler and he delivered a lengthy speech to them afterwards. The army was a demonstration of the defensive strength of the German people, he said, and it must always preserve and maintain the organized military might of the Reich and give loyalty and obedience to the Führer. He predicted: 'One day a page in world history will be devoted to us, the men from the National Socialist Party and the German army who joined efforts to build and safeguard the new German Reich. One day we will stand then, side by side, immortalized in the pantheon of history.'[98]

On 25 September a meeting of the Nazi Party's Racial Bureau was chaired by Walter Gross and attended by all the regional leaders of the organization. Gross briefed them on Hitler's position regarding the Nuremberg Laws. Hitler wanted 'half-breed' Jews to be assimilated into German society and for the economic boycott of Jews to end, because it threatened to interfere with rearmament. Gross also told the meeting that Hitler did not want Jews – in their new, impoverished position – to become a burden on public welfare.[99]

There has been heated debate among historians as to how many people were affected by the Nuremberg Laws. A detailed demographic study carried out by the *C.V.-Zeitung*, the newspaper of the Central Association of German Citizens of Jewish Faith, published on 16 May 1935, claimed that there were 450,000 'full Jews' living in Germany at that time. *Mischlinge* (the legal term used in Nazi Germany for those with Aryan and Jewish ancestry) with one to three Jewish grandparents numbered 250,000, but as this figure included 50,000 who had converted to the Jewish religion, that meant 200,000 were in the *Mischlinge* category at the time the laws were introduced. Of these, about

75,000 were 'half-Jews' and approximately 125,000 'quarter-Jews'.[100] Genealogists now became the most sought-after experts in the country as people strove to verify their racial purity.

Hitler believed that the Nuremberg Laws would encourage more Jews to emigrate. They were really a 'get out now' warning. Jews who remained in Germany were now viewed as aliens and were progressively dehumanized and discriminated against by the state. The new laws led moderate Jewish leaders to accept that their efforts to stop Jews being excluded from German society had failed. They now urged younger Jews to leave. Older Jews hoped that they would be left alone, albeit in increasingly impoverished circumstances.

On 3 October an event occurred that was to have huge ramifications for European diplomacy, as well as the credibility of the Stresa Front and the League of Nations. Italy launched an unprovoked military attack on the ancient mountain kingdom of Abyssinia (modern-day Ethiopia) in pursuit of Mussolini's pipe dream of creating a new Roman Empire. Abyssinia had been the object of his imperial ambitions to avenge Italy's unexpected and humiliating defeat at the Battle of Adwa in 1896. It was the only African nation not to be captured by a European power during the late nineteenth-century Scramble for Africa. Mussolini's forces used poison gas and extensive bombing raids, which destroyed whole villages. The poorly equipped armed forces of the Ethiopian Emperor Haile Selassie were no match for a modern, mechanized army.

It seems that Mussolini had decided to conquer Abyssinia in 1934. In January 1935 he received encouragement from Pierre Laval, the French Foreign Minister, on the condition that he took it peacefully. Laval promised Mussolini that he would ensure the League of Nations would not impose economic sanctions, because he wanted to keep Mussolini firmly in the anti-German camp. Added to this, at the Stresa Conference in April Mussolini had wrongly mistaken British indifference to discussing Abyssinia as evidence that they had no objection to his military aims there.[101] On 8 June Robert Vansittart, the Permanent Undersecretary at the Foreign Office, told Sir Samuel Hoare, the new Foreign Secretary: 'Italy will have to be bought off – let us face and use ugly words – in some form or Abyssinia will perish.'[102]

The Italian invasion was condemned most strongly by the British government, led by the new Prime Minister Stanley Baldwin, but especially by Anthony Eden, Minister without Portfolio for League of Nations Affairs. A British general election was called in mid-

October, with the National Government making the central theme of its campaign support for collective security under the League of Nations. It worked and Baldwin's National Government was returned with a huge overall majority. In retrospect, however, taking such a hard line against Mussolini had the effect of moving Italy closer to Hitler's Germany, with disastrous consequences.

The League of Nations unanimously condemned Italy's action and imposed economic sanctions, although they were weakly applied and excluded oil. The French government offered a very restrained response, and the divisions between Britain and France were once again cruelly exposed. Mussolini had plunged Europe into an even bigger crisis than Hitler's announcement of conscription in March.

Hitler was delighted about the schisms developing between Italy, Britain and France. Goebbels, with Hitler's approval, advised the German press to adopt a pro-Italian stance.[103] Shirer noted in his diary on 4 October: 'The Wilhelmstraße [the Reich Chancellery] is delighted. Either Mussolini will stumble and get himself so heavily involved in Africa that he will be greatly weakened in Europe, whereupon Hitler can seize Austria, hitherto protected by the Duce, or he will win, defying France and Britain and thereupon be ripe for a tie-up with Hitler against the Western democracies. Either way Hitler wins.'[104]

News began to filter through British and French diplomatic channels indicating that Mussolini might be willing to accept an Anglo-French plan that would leave him with most of Abyssinia. The new British Foreign Secretary Sir Samuel Hoare hoped that a compromise could be worked out behind the scenes. On 2 December the British cabinet agreed that Hoare should go to Paris to discuss a face-saving formula with Laval. A secret plan was agreed on 8 December, whereby Italy retained 60 per cent of the captured territory, leaving Abyssinia with access to the sea by means of a twelve-mile corridor to a port in British-controlled Somaliland, or, as an editorial headline in *The Times* memorably put it, 'A Corridor for Camels'.[105]

The supposedly top-secret Hoare–Laval Pact was leaked to the French press and published in the *L'Oeuvre* and *L'Echo de Paris* on 9 December. The source of the leak was undoubtedly Alexis St Leger, a diplomat at the French Foreign Office on the Quai d'Orsay, who wanted to sabotage the initiative. British newspapers recoiled from the Hoare–Laval Pact with an explosion of moral indignation. *The Times* claimed that British public opinion would never have supported the plan if it had been made public beforehand.[106] The debacle led George V to make a pun: 'No more coals to Newcastle. No more whores to Paris.'[107] On 18 December Hoare, vilified in the press and abandoned by his cabinet colleagues, was forced to resign. He cited ill health rather than lack of judgement. He was replaced by Anthony Eden, who at thirty-eight was the youngest Foreign Secretary Britain had seen since 1851.

Eden had built up his political reputation as a keen supporter of the League of Nations but the Abyssinian affair had dealt a serious blow to the League's credibility. British foreign policy was deeply damaged, too. The British had been shown to pay lip service to collective security in public, so as to court electoral popularity, while privately engaging in a secretive and cynical abandonment of those principles to buy off a Fascist dictator. Far from being bought off, however, Mussolini now felt betrayed by Britain and France and decided to move closer to Germany.

On 28 November Hitler was interviewed by Hugh Baillie, the President of the United Press of America, who asked him to explain the reasons behind the Nuremberg Laws against Jews. 'This legislation is not anti-Jewish,' Hitler replied, 'but rather pro-German. It was designed to protect the rights of Germans against destructive Jewish influences.' He claimed that since the Nuremberg Laws had been enacted, anti-Jewish feeling had diminished throughout the country.

On the proposed expansion of the German army, Hitler stated: 'The purpose of the build-up of the German *Wehrmacht* is to protect Germany from attacks by alien powers, Germany is a major power of the first rank and has a right to have a first-class army.' Baillie then pressed Hitler on how large he wanted the army to be. Hitler replied: 'A large army of millions which Germany had in the Great War would only happen if there was another major war on that scale.'[108]

Whenever Hitler was in Berlin, he hosted a daily weekday lunch at the Reich Chancellery in Wilhelmstraße. It usually started after 1.30 p.m. and there were mostly twenty or more guests present. Goebbels, Göring and Rosenberg were regulars. Hitler delivered long monologues at these gatherings. Goebbels was noted for his anecdotes and especially his stinging jokes about Hitler's critics. Rosenberg recalled that Hitler once gave a lengthy speech at one of these lunches about his love of vegetarianism, deriding meat-eaters as 'corpse-eaters'. Hitler believed that eating vegetables was healthier. He was also keen on vitamin supplements. 'Once scientists understood the science of vitamins,' he said, 'then man could live to be 250 years old.'[109]

On 13 December Hitler and Neurath, the German Foreign Minister, held a meeting in Berlin with Sir Eric Phipps, the British ambassador, ostensibly to discuss armament limitations. Phipps found Hitler in an extremely confident and belligerent mood. Hitler ridiculed the principle of collective security and said that the Hoare–Laval Pact had severely comprised this principle. He criticized British 'anti-fascist behaviour' throughout the Abyssinian crisis and warned that if Mussolini fell from power chaos would ensue and communism would be the chief beneficiary. Hitler then boasted that Germany could have occupied the Rhineland on the same day that he announced conscription in March. Neurath went even further: he warned Phipps that if the British and French generals engaged in military staff talks over Italy, then this would force German troops to move into the demilitarized Rhineland. Phipps thought that Hitler had revealed his 'real face' at this meeting.[110]

The threat that Germany posed to world peace worried the Conservative MP Winston Churchill, too, although in 1935 he remained a marginal political figure who had been excluded from the British cabinet since 1931. Churchill's continued public support for the balance of power principle added to the impression that he was yesterday's man. Even so, he remained a powerful and feared backbench voice in the House of Commons, consistently urging the government to rearm to meet the German threat.

In November 1935 an article by Churchill called 'The Truth about Hitler' appeared in the *Strand* magazine in which he concluded, prophetically:

> We cannot tell whether Hitler will be the man who will once
> again let loose upon the world another war in which civilization
> will irretrievably succumb, or whether he will go down in history
> as the man who restored honour and peace of mind to the
> great Germanic nation and brought it back serene, helpful and
> strong to the European family circle. It is on this mystery of
> the future that history will pronounce. It is enough to say that
> both possibilities are open at the moment. If, because the story
> is unfinished, because, indeed, its most fateful chapters are yet to
> be written, we are forced to dwell on the dark side of his work
> and creed, we must never forget nor seek to hope for the brighter
> alternative.[111]

1936

·

OLYMPIAN
HEIGHTS

·

Hitler's New Year message was read on German national radio by Joseph Goebbels. It highlighted his determination for Germany to remain a bulwark against Soviet Bolshevism.[1] No mention was made, however, of a question that was uppermost in Hitler's thoughts at this time: should German troops reoccupy the demilitarized Rhineland? This was strictly forbidden under Articles 42 and 43 of the Treaty of Versailles. If German troops entered the Rhineland, the Western Allies would certainly regard it as a hostile act. It would also breach the Locarno Treaty of 1925, signed by Belgium, Britain, France, Germany and Italy.

In February the French Chamber of Deputies was due to ratify the Franco-Soviet Treaty of Mutual Assurance. This would provide Hitler with an obvious pretext to move into the Rhineland. According to Otto Meissner, Hitler's State Secretary, Hitler had wanted to repudiate the Locarno Treaty when the Franco-Soviet Treaty was originally signed in 1935. His Foreign Minister Konstantin von Neurath talked him out of it, fearing a possible French military response.[2]

On 3 January Hitler brought together his Gauleiters (the leaders of a Gau: a region or province) and Reichsleiters (National Leaders) to a meeting in Berlin. He outlined to them his ambitious plans to rearm Germany. He made a passionate plea for their devotion, even threatening to kill himself if this did not happen. Hess later assured Hitler that everyone in the room offered him their unquestioned loyalty.[3] It was a bizarre meeting, but hinted that something was preoccupying his mind.

The well-known French journalist Titaÿna (the pen name of Élisabeth Sauvy-Tisseyre) interviewed Hitler for *Paris Soir* on 19 January. He hoped to use it to influence the upcoming vote by the French parliament on the Franco-Soviet Treaty. Titaÿna described the palace in Wilhelmstraße – where Hitler lived while in Berlin – as characterized by an 'austerity of architectural and interior design reflecting the straight-forward nature of the new Germany'. She was astonished by Hitler's vivid blue eyes. 'At this moment,' she gushed, 'I understand his magical appeal to the masses.'

She asked him if German foreign policy was really based on pacifist principles. Hitler replied: 'The word "pacificism" has two meanings and does not have the same meaning in France as it does for us. We cannot accept a pacifism that means forfeiting our rights. For us pacifism can only become a reality if it is built on the basic premise that each [nation] has the right to live.' He was then asked if a complete revision of the Treaty of Versailles would endanger the interests of other nations, to which he replied: 'The Treaty of Versailles had two consequences. It confirms the fact of territorial conquest and it establishes a moral conquest.' The treaty was 'outrageous', he argued, because it sought to 'humiliate and discriminate against a people'.

He then derided communism for lowering the expectations and standard of living of the Russian people. It would have been a catastrophe if communism had triumphed in Germany, he added. When Titaÿna asked his opinion of a possible union between Austria and Germany, Hitler replied that it was an issue that no one was 'excited about' in Germany, while in Vienna the union was used as a 'bogeyman' to inflame Austrian domestic politics.

He ended the interview by urging French tourists to attend the upcoming Winter and Summer Olympic Games, promising the French could travel around freely: 'We shall not tell them that Germany is a paradise, for there is no such thing in the world.'[4]

On 20 January the British king George V died, aged seventy. He was succeeded by his unpredictable son Edward VIII. It was well known that the new king was pro-German. Hans Luther, the German ambassador to the United States, sent a cable to Berlin reportedly outlining a recent conversation between Edward and a member of the US State Department, during which the king had criticized the French desire to encircle Germany, and expressed sympathy with Hitler's foreign policy position.[5]

Edward VIII's private life was not without controversy, either. He was conducting an affair with an American divorcee, Mrs Wallis Simpson, while she was still married to her second husband. Their romance was kept out of the British newspapers due to a self-imposed news blackout, but it was common knowledge in America.

At a lunch at the Reich Chancellery on 20 January, Hitler informed his close ministerial colleagues of his determination to implement a 'sudden solution' to the question of the Rhineland demilitarized zone, whenever 'an opportune moment' arose.[6]

The state funeral of George V, which took place at St George's

Chapel, Windsor Castle, on 28 January, was attended by dignitaries from around the world, including the German Foreign Minister Neurath. He reassured Eden, the British Foreign Secretary, that Germany was not planning to reoccupy the Rhineland and would uphold the Locarno Treaty.[7] Meanwhile, Hitler attended a special memorial service for George V held at St George's Anglican Church in Berlin.

On 30 January Hitler delivered a speech in Berlin's Lustgarten (Pleasure Garden), a park near the site of the Berlin City Palace, attended by 30,000 storm troopers, to mark the third anniversary of his coming to power. During the past year, he told the audience, Germany had regained its honour but was no longer defenceless. National Socialism was not a doctrine of lethargy, but of fighting, he concluded.[8] In response, the British *Daily Herald* editorial warned 'the abnormal of 1933 had become the normal of 1936'.[9] The *Manchester Guardian*, looking back over the previous three years, concluded that Hitler had transformed Germany into 'an oppressive police state'.[10] In contrast, the pro-Hitler *Daily Mail* adopted a much more positive tone: 'This is a memorable date in the history of Europe,' it said. 'Germany by [Hitler's] magnetic influence [...] has been placed once more at the forefront of nations.'[11]

During the afternoon of 4 February Hitler held a meeting with the British peer Lord Londonderry, who was in Berlin, accompanied by his wife Edith, as part of a three-week unofficial visit designed to improve Anglo-German relations. Hitler, who did most of the talking, highlighted the need to combat Bolshevism, his hope for a return of the German colonies and, more worryingly, his desire for territorial expansion in Eastern Europe. He felt that the League of Nations was becoming increasingly a 'paper illusion', supported by a 'few typewriters'. Germany would make no public statement about its foreign policy aims, but once again he repeated his desire for a 'close, friendly alliance with Britain'.[12]

Returning home, Londonderry said he had found Hitler 'very agreeable' and keen to improve relations with Britain, but a little bit obsessed with the Soviet threat. Lady Londonderry sent a letter to Hitler, thanking him warmly for his hospitality and praising him personally: 'To say that I was deeply impressed is not adequate,' she wrote. 'I am amazed. You and Germany remind me of the Book of Genesis in the Bible. Nothing else describes the position accurately.'[13]

On the evening of 4 February Wilhelm Gustloff, the 41-year-old founder and leader of the Swiss Nazi Party, was assassinated. He had played a key role in distributing anti-Semitic Nazi propaganda in Switzerland. David Frankfurter, a Croatian Jewish medical student, whose father was a rabbi, had been so incensed by this he looked up Gustloff's address which was in the local phone book in Davos. He then went to Gustloff's home and knocked on the front door. It was opened by his wife. Frankfurter told her he had come to see her husband. She invited him in, asking him to wait in the study. When Gustloff entered the room, Frankfurter pulled out a gun and shot him five times. He calmly left the house, with the screams of Gustloff's wife ringing in his ears, and handed himself in at the local police station. Goebbels wrote in his diary: 'The Jews are going to pay a high price for this.'[14] Immediate retaliation was ruled out, however, due to the need to project a friendly image to the world during the Olympic year.

The Winter Olympics opened on 6 February in Garmisch-Partenkirchen. This picture-postcard Bavarian market town was decked out with swastikas and Olympic flags. A new ski jump with a 142-foot tower, an outdoor stadium holding 15,000, and a 10,000-seater indoor ice stadium had been built at huge expense. There were twenty-eight participating countries and a total of 646 athletes.

The opening ceremony of the ten-day event began at 11 a.m. in blizzard conditions, before a crowd estimated at 60,000. Hitler's arrival was greeted by ecstatic cheers and a band played 'Deutschland über alles' and the 'Horst Wessel Song'. The Greek team was the first to enter the stadium. Every team lowered their national flags as they passed by Hitler, with the sole exception of the American team. Most nations gave the Olympic salute, which sent the crowd wild, because it was mistaken for a Nazi salute. When the British team entered, they were shocked to hear the stadium announcer say: 'The British greet the Führer with the German salute.' Goebbels also misinterpreted the Olympic gesture: 'Almost all foreign athletes performed the Hitler

David Frankfurter on trial for the assassination of the founder the Swiss Nazi Party Wilhelm Gustloff.

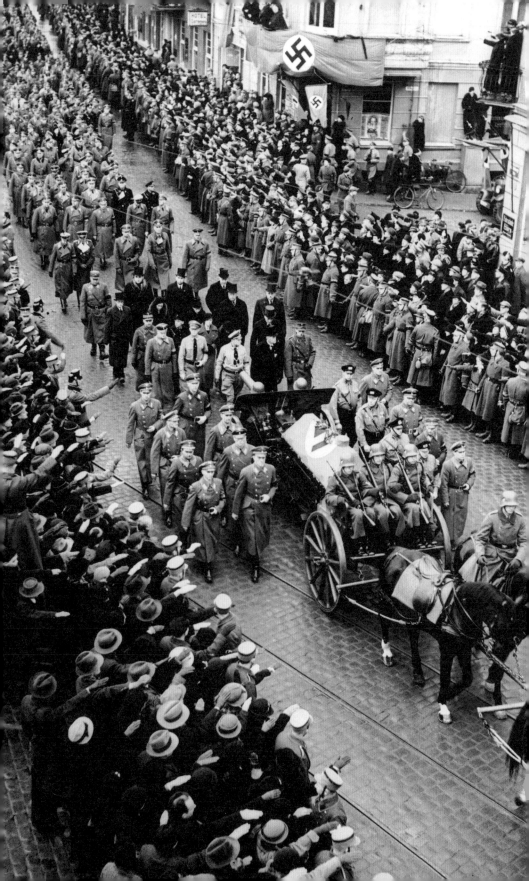

salute when they marched past the Führer.'[15] The American team had anticipated this possibility and did not raise their arms at all. In contrast, the Austrian team gave enthusiastic Hitler salutes. Once the procession had ended, Hitler declared the Winter Olympics open.

The undoubted star of the Winter Games was the elegant Norwegian figure skater Sonja Henie, known as the 'Ice Queen'. She dominated women's figure skating since winning Olympic gold at St Moritz in 1928, but she saved her best performance for Garmisch-Partenkirchen, winning her third gold medal in a row. Hitler viewed Henie's Nordic good looks as the epitome of Aryan womanhood.

Norway topped the medal table with seven gold medals, five silver and three bronze. Germany, with three gold and three silver, came in second. However, the biggest winner of the 1936 Winter Olympics was undoubtedly Hitler himself. He was on a charm offensive throughout the Games and even managed to congratulate the gold medallists who had defeated German opponents.[16] 'Everyone is praising our organization,' Goebbels noted. 'And it certainly was brilliant'.[17] As Shirer observed: 'They've greatly impressed most of the visiting foreigners with the lavish but smooth way in which they've run the Games and with their kind manners.'[18]

On 12 February Hitler travelled from Garmisch-Partenkirchen in a special train, accompanied by Goebbels and other leading Nazis to attend the funeral service of Wilhelm Gustloff in Schwerin, his home town in the north German state of Mecklenburg-Vorpommern. Hitler delivered a sombre eulogy, blaming 'our Jewish foe' for Gustloff's murder. At the reception afterwards, Hitler told Colonel Friedrich Hossbach that soon he intended to order the military reoccupation of the Rhineland. He had intended to wait until 1937, he added, but the row between Britain, France and Italy over Abyssinia had left him convinced that the Western Allies were in disarray and the time to act was now.[19]

On 14 February Hitler delivered a speech at the International Automobile Exhibition in the Exhibition Halls on the Kaiserdamm in Berlin. A car should no longer be considered a luxury item, he argued, and he wanted to produce an affordable 'people's car' (*Volkswagen*) costing 5,000 Reichsmarks. 'I am so ruthlessly determined', he said, 'to have the preliminary work for producing the German Volkswagen carried on and brought to a conclusion.' He felt a target of 2 to 3 million sales was possible because of the improving living standards of the German people.[20]

Funeral procession of
Wilhelm Gustloff, 12 February 1936.

[overleaf] Hitler at the opening
ceremony of the Winter Olympics in
Garmisch-Partenkirchen on 6 February
1936.

On that same day, Hitler asked Ulrich von Hassell, the German ambassador to Italy, how Mussolini would react if Germany denounced the Locarno Treaty and moved troops into the Rhineland. Hassell replied that Mussolini thought the Stresa Front was already dead and that because Il Duce wanted to improve German-Italian relations he would not oppose Hitler's remilitarization of the Rhineland. It was Anglo-French opposition to Mussolini's actions in Abyssinia that made Mussolini less opposed to German revisionism. Mussolini was not prepared to publicly endorse Hitler's repudiation of the Locarno Treaty, however, but he would oppose any resulting Anglo-French military action or economic sanctions against Germany. Hassell's views gave Hitler the green light to reoccupy the Rhineland.[21]

Hitler was interviewed for *Paris-Midi* by French journalist Bertrand de Jouvenel on 21 February. The Führer's theme was Franco-German friendship. He began by stating, 'It is extraordinary that you [the French] should still consider German aggression possible.' Asked why he had never amended the stridently anti-French passages of *Mein Kampf*, Hitler replied: 'I am no writer. I am a politician. How am I going to rectify it? I am doing it every day in my foreign policy directed towards friendship with France. My corrections will be in the great book of history.'

He then advised the French parliament not to ratify the treaty with the Soviet Union: 'Do you realize what you are doing? You let yourselves become involved in a diplomatic game of power, which has only one desire and this is to create disorder among nations.' Hitler ended on a warning note: 'I am offering you an agreement that will be approved by 90 per cent of the German nation, 90 per cent which follow me. Here is your chance, if you don't take it, think of the responsibility towards your children. You are confronting a Germany where nine-tenths show confidence in their leader, and this leader is telling you: "Let's be friends."'[22]

Goebbels noted in his diary: 'He's still brooding. Should he remilitarize the Rhineland? Difficult question. The Führer is going to forge ahead. He thinks and ponders and then suddenly acts.'[23]

On 27 February the Franco-Soviet Treaty of Mutual Assistance was ratified in the French Chamber of Deputies by 353 to 164 votes. Under orders from Goebbels, the German press offered a restrained response. On the same day, the French cabinet met and agreed that in the event of German troops moving into the Rhineland, France would not take isolated military action but would sound out the League of

Nations and the other signatories to the Locarno Treaty: Belgium, Britain and Italy to discuss the issue.[24]

According to Goebbels, on 1 March Hitler finally made up his mind to reoccupy the Rhineland: 'He's now completely determined. His face projected calm and resolve. Once again a critical moment has come that calls for action.'[25]

On 2 March Hitler held a secret meeting in Berlin with his key military commanders: General Werner von Blomberg, the Minister of War, General Werner von Fritsch, the head of the army, Admiral Erich Raeder, head of the navy, and three leading members of the Nazi elite: Göring, Goebbels and Ribbentrop. (Not in attendance was Neurath, the Foreign Minister.) Hitler told them he intended to reoccupy the demilitarized Rhineland under the code name 'Winter Exercise' on Saturday, 7 March, and asked them to make all necessary arrangements. Blomberg's immediate directive for the military reoccupation of the Rhineland is dated 2 March.[26]

It was not until 6 March when Hitler informed the cabinet of his decision to militarily reoccupy the Rhineland. Goebbels noted that those cabinet members not in the loop were 'immensely astonished'.[27] When the news was announced, every foreign diplomat and press correspondent in Berlin was taken by surprise. Even the soldiers involved in Winter Exercise were only told of the nature of their mission shortly before it began.[28]

On 7 March German troops marched into the Rhineland. Along the route they were greeted by delirious, cheering crowds, throwing flowers at their feet. It was another of what became known as 'Hitler's Saturday Surprises'. The ambassadors of Britain, France and Italy were summoned to Wilhelmstraße at 10 a.m. to be informed of another fait accompli. They were issued with a lengthy memorandum justifying the move on the grounds that the Franco-Soviet Treaty had rendered the Locarno Treaty null and void.

A wide-ranging, seven-point peace proposal was added, offering a twenty-five-year non-aggression pact between Germany, France and Belgium, with Britain and Italy as the guarantors. Long-term non-aggression pacts with Germany's vulnerable Eastern European neighbours were also on offer. Germany even promised to return to the League of Nations. Once again, a flagrant unilateral breach of international treaties was presented as entirely justified and accompanied by ambitious peace proposals. In his diary, Shirer described Hitler's peace proposals as 'pure fraud and if I had any guts,

[overleaf] Three commanders –
left to right: army figures Werner von
Blomberg, Werner von Fritsch, with Navy
chief Erich Raeder.

or American journalism had any, I would have said so in my dispatch tonight'.[29]

Leopold von Hoesch, the German ambassador to Britain, called on Eden at 10 a.m. to inform him. He also outlined Hitler's offer of several non-aggression pacts. Eden expressed regret over Germany's action, but promised to consider these fresh proposals. When Eden telephoned the Prime Minister Stanley Baldwin, who was at Chequers, his country retreat, Baldwin told him there was no support in Britain for military action.[30] Eden considered the Rhineland coup to be 'the most carefully prepared example of Hitler's brazen but skilful methods. The illegal deed was abundantly wrapped up with assurances for the present and promises for the future. The appeal was nicely judged. The timing was perfect, including the choice of a weekend.'[31]

At noon on 7 March Hitler addressed the Reichstag, which was still in its temporary home in the Kroll Opera House. He began by outlining the inequalities of the Treaty of Versailles once again and the 'consistent failure' of the Western Allies to grant Germany equal status. He then warned of the danger of Bolshevism: 'I will not have the gruesome communist international dictatorship of hate descend upon the German people.' Due to the ratification of the Franco-Soviet Treaty, he added, 'Germany no longer feels bound by the Locarno Treaty.' He then announced: 'In the interest of the most basic right of a people to secure its borders and maintain its ability to defend itself, the government of the German Reich has today restored its full and unlimited sovereignty in the demilitarized zone of the Rhineland.' Nazi Reichstag deputies rose to their feet, their arms raised aloft, and shouted 'Sieg Heil!' Once the cheering had died down, Hitler mentioned the peace proposals he had already presented to the Western Allies. Finally, he announced new elections on 29 March.[32]

Hitler later described the forty-eight hours following the German remilitarization of the Rhineland as 'the most nerve-racking of my life. If the French had retaliated, we would have had to withdraw with our tails between our legs, for the military resources at our disposal would have been wholly inadequate for even a moderate resistance.'[33]

This was untrue. *Wehrmacht* generals sent in nineteen infantry battalions to reoccupy the Rhineland, a total of 22,000 men. These were supplemented by a police force (*Landespolizei*), numbering 14,500 men, making a total of 36,500 men. These forces were supported by 156 artillery guns and 54 fighter planes. No bomber aircraft or tanks were included, to emphasize the defensive nature of the operation.[34] The German units were given orders to fight should the French army invade, and there were no orders to immediately withdraw, as Hitler later suggested.[35]

It's often assumed the French missed a golden opportunity to march its troops into the Rhineland to expel the German forces. This is another fallacy. The French military high command had ruled out any offensive action against Germany as long ago as 1930, when French occupying forces had left the Rhineland.[36] Under the command of General Maurice Gamelin, France adopted a defensive, 'long-war strategy'. The fear was that another war with Germany would be a repeat of the Great War, although instead of muddy, rat-infested trenches, French troops would occupy the newly built underground trenches of the Maginot Line.[37] The chief French aim in a future war was to first hold back a German attack, then mount a naval blockade with the help of Britain, which would damage the German economy, and only then moving to offensive warfare much later in the conflict.

So there was no French plan to attack Germany, either in a preventive war or to reverse a German reoccupation of the Rhineland. In truth, in March 1936 the French army had no strike force capable of dealing with even the small German force deployed in the Rhineland. Not a single French army combat unit was ready for action at the time of the German remilitarization. The French did not even have a minimal expeditionary force ready to move into the Rhineland in such an emergency either.[38]

On 8 March, when the French cabinet met, only a minority of ministers demanded an immediate military response. Instead, Albert Sarraut, the caretaker French Prime Minister, told the French people in a national radio broadcast that he would not negotiate with Germany while German troops were in the Rhineland. He called on the remaining Locarno signatories – Belgium, Britain and Italy – to fulfil their obligations should the French decide to take military action. This was pure bluff. Pierre-Étienne Flandin, the French Foreign Minister, hoped to sound out the British government about taking a strong stand over the remilitarization, by insisting that German troops withdraw from the Rhineland, pending negotiations. Most of all, Flandin wanted a strong Anglo-French declaration of unity in the face of the growing German threat.

The Polish government made it clear to the German Foreign Ministry that it wanted nothing to do with problems arising from the breakdown of the first Locarno Treaty. Józef Beck, the Polish Foreign Minister, stressed Poland's continuing commitment to the 1934

[overleaf] German troops march into the Rhineland, 7 March 1936.

German-Polish Non-Aggression Pact. When Beck's pledge to offer full support to France was leaked by the French press on 10 March, Hitler came to the conclusion that the Polish government could not be trusted in future.[39]

In a cabinet paper dated 8 March the British Foreign Secretary Anthony Eden dismissed the idea that France would take military action. After a period of 'sulking and passive obstruction', he wrote, the French would agree to negotiations with the German government on its peace proposals, which Eden later described as the 'most important document since the end of the Great War'. It did not occur to Eden that Hitler's peace proposals were not genuine at all.[40] Meanwhile, in a telegram to Eden, Eric Phipps, the British ambassador to Germany, observed: 'Herr von Ribbentrop I believe strongly supported the occupation of Rhineland and even told Chancellor [Hitler] it would be warmly welcomed in Britain. He is convinced the vast majority of British people are pro-German.'[41]

It was on Monday 9 March when British politicians and the press finally responded fully to Hitler's actions. The remilitarization of the Rhineland had 'profoundly shaken confidence in any engagement into which the government of Germany may in future enter', Eden told a packed House of Commons, but there was 'no reason to suppose that the present German action implies a threat of hostilities'. Eden said he would consider Hitler's peace proposals carefully and objectively with a view to rebuilding the foundations of peace in Europe.[42] The British government never contemplated acting militarily over Germany's reoccupation of the Rhineland or encouraging the French to do so either. The general British attitude was summed up by Lord Lothian's famous comment: 'The Germans are only going into their own back garden.'[43]

An editorial in *The Times* entitled 'A Chance to Rebuild' dismissed the idea that the remilitarization of the Rhineland was an act of aggression at all, observing that 'there is still a distinction to be drawn between the march of detachments of German troops, sent to reoccupy territory indisputably under German sovereignty, and an act which carries fire and sword into a neighbour's territory'. Admittedly there were 'gaps and obscurities' in Hitler's peace proposals, the newspaper conceded, but they were in no way a camouflage for an unfolding plan of aggression. In conclusion: 'The old structure of European peace, one-sided and unbalanced, is nearly in ruins. It is a moment, not to despair, but to rebuild.'[44]

On the same day Hitler gave a two-hour interview to George Ward Price of the British *Daily Mail*, published on 11 March. In answer to a question on the remilitarization of the Rhineland, Hitler commented: 'We have restored sovereign rights to the German Reich and have brought ancient Reich territory back under the protection of the entire nation.' It was not an aggressive act, he added, and in no way a threat to French security. Because the Franco-Soviet Treaty of 2 May 1935 had compromised and violated the Locarno Treaty, he argued, Germany could no longer leave a vital border economic region 'defenceless and without protection'.

Asked why he had once again chosen to act unilaterally rather than engage in a process of negotiation in international affairs, Hitler suggested that he had done so because the other signatories to the Locarno Treaty would have probably rejected the reoccupation of the Rhineland, just as they had blocked previous efforts to secure equal rights for Germany.[45]

In a letter published in *The Times* on 12 March Lord Londonderry argued in very similar terms, depicting the remilitarization as a 'direct and understandable result of the Franco-Soviet Treaty and the French failure to acknowledge German demands for equality of treatment'. Casting Germany's conduct as merely a logical consequence of past Allied mistakes, Londonderry also took seriously Hitler's peace proposals.[46]

In a public speech in Karlsruhe that evening, Hitler justified his actions once more:

What I have done, I did according to my conscience and to
the best of my knowledge, realizing the necessity of protecting
Germany's honour, in order to lead Germany again to a position
of honour in this world. And should unnecessary sorrow or
suffering ever come to my people because of my associations, then
I beseech the Almighty God to punish me.[47]

In Munich on 14 March Hitler gave one of his most famous speeches on foreign policy: 'Neither threats nor warnings will move me from my path. I go with the certainty of a sleepwalker along the path laid out for me by Providence. My aim is peace founded on equality.'[48]

The Council of the League of Nations met in St James's Palace, London, on 19 March, to discuss its formal response to Hitler's Rhineland coup. In defence of the German government, Ribbentrop argued that Germany's remilitarization of the Rhineland had ended 'a sad chapter of discrimination, misunderstanding and hatred towards

Germany'.[49] His plea for the Council to delay a vote and consider Germany's peace plan fell on deaf ears. After a brief adjournment, the League passed a resolution criticizing Germany's actions as a violation of international law and condemning Germany as a breaker of treaties. (Only Chile abstained.) Despite these strong words, however, no course of action was suggested.

In the evening Eden handed Ribbentrop a letter, the text of which had been agreed beforehand by Britain, France and Belgium. 'The Text of Proposals', as it became known, was subsequently published as a British government White Paper. It called upon the German government to cease further military action in the Rhineland. Furthermore, as a conciliatory gesture to restore confidence, Germany should allow an international force to operate on both sides of the German border area, and agree to refer the matter to the arbitration court of the Hague Tribunal, pending further negotiations. After further discussions between the British, French and Belgian military staff, the British government agreed to come to the aid of France and Belgium should either face unprovoked aggression. Given Eden's initial complacency, 'The Text of Proposals' shows just how far the French government had pushed him towards taking a firmer public stance against Germany.[50] The Italian government refused to endorse it.

The German press, orchestrated by Goebbels, reacted to Eden's letter with furious indignation, describing it in headlines as 'Collective Shamelessness' and 'Shylock's Pound of Flesh'. The *Völkischer Beobachter* called it 'nothing less than a new crime against Europe'.[51] In a damage limitation exercise, aimed to dampen German anger, Eden suggested the White Paper was merely a discussion document and not a set of concrete demands.

In reply the German government made it 'unmistakably clear' that it categorically rejected the proposals outlined in the White Paper, but promised that in a week's time Hitler would submit his own detailed set of counterproposals.[52]

By now the German referendum campaign was in full swing. Hitler delivered speeches in eleven German cities. 'I do not intend to draw up secret documents or conclude any secret alliances,' he declared in a speech in Ludwigshafen on 25 March. 'I assure you, my fellow countrymen, I will never pledge Germany to anything without informing the whole German people. Now they say we must go down on our knees again. What is the world thinking of? We are not a tribe of negroes [*sic*] but a highly civilized people.'[53]

On 27 March Hitler told workers in Essen:

I have not upheld the rearming of the German people because I am
a shareholder. I am perhaps the only statesman in the world who has
no bank account. You yourselves know how often I have held out the
hand to the other powers, always I met only with rebuffs. I proposed,
in order that no one could feel threatened, that all should disarm
completely. We are prepared to disarm, if the others will do the
same. The proposal was rejected. I declared my readiness to accept an
army of 200,000 men. That was also rejected. I then declared that I
would be content with an army of 300,000 men. That was rejected,
too. Finally, I declared myself ready for an agreement on an air force
on equal conditions. Once again that was rejected. The German
people desires peace, desires understanding, desires calm. It wishes to
work to earn its daily bread and live decently.[54]

On 29 March Hitler's remilitarization of the Rhineland was
endorsed by a whopping 44,500,000 German voters (98.8 per cent),
with only 540,244 (1.2 per cent) voting against or spoiling their ballot
paper. The turnout was 99 per cent. No head of state had ever received
such an overwhelming endorsement from voters. It stiffened Hitler's
resolve not to yield to Anglo-French pressure. Shirer noted in his
diary: 'There's no doubt, I think, that a substantial majority of the
German people applaud the Rhineland coup regardless of whether
they're Nazis or not.'[55]

When the German government unveiled yet another 'constructive
peace plan' on 1 April it was a rehash of the previous proposals outlined
by Hitler in his speech to the Reichstag on 7 March. Hitler set 1 August
as the deadline for achieving some initial progress.[56] All of Germany's
neighbours were offered twenty-five-year non-aggression pacts once
more, plus disarmament agreements, and a promise that Germany
would return to the League of Nations once these agreements were
concluded. In short, it was a comforting fairy tale, directed primarily
at British public opinion.

Leopold von Hoesch, the German ambassador to Britain, had never
been sympathetic to Hitler's government. Writing to the German
Foreign Minister Neurath, he had denounced the remilitarization
of the Rhineland, believing it would only serve to bring Britain and
France closer together. On 10 April Hoesch died suddenly of a heart
attack in his bedroom at the German Embassy in London.

On 6 May Eden welcomed Hitler's new peace proposals though
added a note of caution: 'His Majesty's government regrets that the
German Government have not been able to make a more substantial

contribution towards the re-establishment of the confidence, which is such an essential preliminary to the wide negotiations we both have in view.'[57]

On 7 May the British and French governments submitted a foreign policy questionnaire to the German government. One question asked whether Germany intended to annul any undertakings it had already made in the future. Another wanted the German government to state that it would respect the existing territorial and political status of European nations. The aim of these questions was to draw out Hitler's real intentions. In reply, Hitler mocked the whole tone of the questionnaire as being like something a schoolmaster at a British public school might submit to an errant pupil, by demanding assurances of future good behaviour. The German press joined in this criticism, with the *Frankfurter Zeitung*, in a typical response, describing the questionnaire as 'not even honourable'.[58] Hitler refused to answer any of the questions contained in the questionnaire.

Despite this breakdown of trust, informal initiatives continued to try and improve Anglo-German relations. Many of these were conducted outside the formal diplomatic channels. Thomas Jones, a retired Welsh Liberal civil servant and a close friend of Prime Minister Baldwin, visited Germany in May 1936 at the invitation of Ribbentrop, who hoped that Jones might act as an unofficial diplomatic go-between between the German government and Baldwin.

When Jones arrived at Ribbentrop's plush Berlin villa on 16 May he told him that although he was friendly with Baldwin, he was really 'a person of no importance'. 'I want Mr Baldwin to meet Hitler,' Ribbentrop replied. 'He is not a dictator in conversation. He is like Mr Baldwin.'[59] On the following day Jones met Hitler in his Munich apartment, which he described as 'solid and Victorian in décor and furnishings'. He was very impressed by Hitler's good manners and polite, reasonable manner. When he explained that Baldwin was keen to improve Anglo-German relations, Hitler suggested a personal meeting in Germany.[60]

Back in Britain, Jones conveyed Hitler's offer to Baldwin at 10 Downing Street. Baldwin did not want to go to Germany, but he was not averse to inviting Hitler to a meeting at Chequers. Eden disliked the idea of Baldwin going to Germany, but he also saw that inviting Hitler to Britain would be very controversial too and would antagonize the French government during a time of great international tension. Baldwin told Jones that he would consider making an official visit to Germany, but only if accompanied by Eden.

Ribbentrop was extremely dismayed when Jones told him of Baldwin's position on the idea of a visit. Later he claimed that Hitler had been reduced to tears when he heard that Baldwin had rejected his offer of a face-to-face meeting. This seems doubtful, but Hitler certainly regarded it as a snub.[61]

On 17 June Hitler appointed Heinrich Himmler as chief of the police, thereby uniting the ordinary uniformed police force (Orpo), the Gestapo, and the criminal investigation police (Kripo) to form the Security Police (Sipo). Himmler was already in control of two key Nazi security forces, the SS and the SD, as well as overseeing the concentration camps. The result of this reorganization was to greatly enhance the power of the SS within the Nazi state.

As well as curbing crime and repressing political opponents, the SS had a new mission: to purge 'racially weak' and 'asocial' elements from the National Community. The concentration camps were now expanded to accommodate alcoholics, Gypsies, homosexuals, the long-term unemployed, prostitutes, repeat criminal offenders, and those of mixed black and German parentage. These 'asocial' groups joined political and religious dissidents and Jews.

On 19 June German boxer Max Schmeling, a former world heavyweight champion, met the previously unbeaten black heavyweight Joe Louis in a highly publicized fight before a recorded crowd of 38,878 at the Yankee Stadium in the Bronx, New York. Louis was regarded as a champion in waiting, destined to take on the current world heavyweight champion James Braddock. Louis was regarded as unbeatable. Schmeling was the 10–1 underdog. Polite and softly spoken, Louis was not a popular figure in white America. He often taunted white opponents in the ring. His marriage to a white woman was also viewed unfavourably, especially in the segregated South. Schmeling was a sporting hero in Germany. Though not a Nazi Party member, he was a firm supporter of Hitler. For his part, Hitler turned a blind eye to the fact that Joe Jacobs, Schmeling's flamboyant, cigar-smoking, fedora-wearing New York manager was Jewish.

The build-up to the fight saw an escalation in Nazi racist rhetoric, although Schmeling refused to join in. The boxing match was to be broadcast live on the radio all around the world and on the eve of the fight one German advert announced: 'It is every German's obligation to stay up tonight. Max will fight overseas with a Negro [sic] for the hegemony of the white race.'

The fight began at 10.06 p.m. New York time: 4 a.m. in Germany. From the opening bell, Schmeling's heavy and well-timed right-hand punches thundered home to the head and body of Louis. He had never faced such power-punching before. In the twelfth round, Schmeling launched a flurry of unreturned punches before Louis was knocked down to the canvas and sensationally counted out in one of the biggest upsets in boxing history.

The contest was portrayed in Germany as a victory for the 'racially superior Aryan'. Goebbels wrote in his diary: 'In the twelfth round, Schmeling knocks out the Negro [*sic*]. Wonderful. A dramatic, exciting fight. The white man over the black man and the white man is a German [...] Didn't get to bed until 5 a.m. I'm very happy.' He sent a telegram to Schmeling: 'For your victory, which we have experienced on the radio, my most heartfelt congratulations. I know that you have fought for Germany. Your victory is a German victory. We are proud of you, best wishes and Heil Hitler.'

Hitler sent flowers to Schmeling's wife Anny Ondra, a popular Czech film star, with a card stating: 'For the wonderful victory of your husband, our greatest German boxer, I must congratulate you with all my heart.' Schmeling told a reporter from the *Berliner Lokal-Anzeiger*: 'Please tell my countrymen at home that this is the happiest day of my life. I have to report to the Führer in particular that the thoughts of all my countrymen were with me in this fight; that the Führer and his faithful people were thinking of me.'

Now a national hero, when Schmeling returned to Germany aboard the *Hindenburg* passenger airship on 26 June a cheering crowd of more than 10,000 people turned out to greet him at Frankfurt Airport. He received an even bigger welcome when his plane landed at Berlin's Tempelhof Airport later on the same day. The anti-Semitic publisher Julius Streicher described Schmeling as the symbol of 'a New

German heavyweight boxer Max Schmeling hits American Joe Louis with a devastating right hand en route to victory in their fight at the Yankee Stadium, New York on 19 June 1936."

Germany, a Germany that has faith again'. The official SS newspaper *Das Schwarze Korps* claimed Schmeling had 'saved the reputation of the white race'.

On 27 June, accompanied by his mother, Schmeling met Hitler for coffee and cake at the Reich Chancellery. He took with him the official film of the fight to be shown in Hitler's personal cinema. As Hitler watched, he gave a running commentary, slapping his thigh with delight every time Schmeling landed a punch on Louis. Goebbels, also present at the screening, wrote: 'Dramatic and thrilling. The last round was quite wonderful. He really knocks out the Negro [*sic*].'

The feature film of the Schmeling v Louis fight premiered in Berlin on 8 July and then played to huge cinema audiences around the country. Schmeling became a Nazi sporting superstar, which greatly embarrassed the boxing authorities in the United States. Despite losing the match, Louis was granted a world title fight against the world heavyweight champion James Braddock. He defeated Braddock by a knockout, but said: 'I ain't no champion until I beat Schmeling.'[62]

On 11 July the Austro-German Agreement was signed after being brokered in Vienna by Franz von Papen, the German ambassador to Austria. Under its terms, Germany promised to recognize Austrian sovereignty, to refrain from interfering in the country's internal affairs, and to respect Austria's special relationships with Hungary and Italy. Membership of the Nazi Party continued to be prohibited in Austria, although Kurt Schuschnigg, the Chancellor of Austria, allowed moderate Nazis to hold administrative posts within the government and civil service. This offered Nazis the opportunity to undermine the authority of the Austrian government. Even more significant was Austria's agreement to define itself as a 'German state' and also to follow Germany's lead on foreign affairs. Hitler told Goebbels: 'We must maintain tension in Austria and Czechoslovakia. Never let things settle down.'[63]

Hitler attended the Bayreuth Festival in Germany in late July, which featured performances of operas by Richard Wagner. On 25 July two Nazi functionaries arrived in Bayreuth from Morocco. They were accompanied by a Spanish army officer with a personal letter from the Spanish Nationalist leader General Francisco Franco. He was asking for *Luftwaffe* planes to help carry troops from Morocco into Spain to attack Madrid and overthrow the left-wing Popular Front government, which had been democratically elected earlier that year. Hitler asked members of his inner circle whether he should come to

Franco's aid. Neurath and Ribbentrop were opposed. Blomberg, for the army, and Admiral Wilhelm Canaris expressed similar reservations. Initially, Göring was hesitant about getting involved, until he realized that the Spanish Civil War might prove a useful testing ground for the *Luftwaffe*.

Spain's Popular Front government requested military support from France, where a Popular Front government led by Léon Blum had taken office a month earlier. The British government, meanwhile, opted for a policy of strict neutrality.

On 25 July, the same day on which Franco sought Hitler's support, Blum announced that France, too, would remain neutral. Indeed, the British and the French established a Non-Intervention Committee, and a Non-Intervention Agreement was signed in August by all European governments, including Britain, France, Germany, Italy and the Soviet Union. If the outbreak of the Spanish Civil War suggested that the coming world struggle would be between communism and fascism, the Western democracies were content to remain spectators.

As a committed anti-communist, Hitler decided it was his duty to support Franco. He ordered the immediate dispatch of twenty Junkers-Ju-52 transport planes and six fighter planes. Two clandestine trading companies were set up (Hisma in Spain and Rowak in Germany) to channel military supplies and raw materials to Franco, as well as troops and aircraft.

For the next three years until Franco's victory in 1939 Germany provided him with the Condor Legion with an average strength of 6,500 airmen to fight the Republicans in Spain. In comparison, Mussolini deployed 80,000 troops during the civil war to aid Franco. By November, both Hitler and Mussolini had publicly recognized Franco and the Nationalists as the legitimate Spanish government.

It was assumed that Franco's victory would be swift, but his failure to capture the government in Madrid ensured that the civil war dragged on. This suited Hitler, because the war in Spain diverted international attention from his own plans. Hitler did not want Franco to lose, but he was content to leave the major burden of military support to Mussolini.

The Soviet Union now faced a real dilemma. The Communist International or Comintern, the international organization for the propagation of communist ideas, which was funded by Stalin's government, portrayed the Spanish Civil War as a struggle between the reactionary force of fascism and the progressive ideals of communism.

However, Stalin wanted to keep out of the war, so in August the USSR signed a Non-Intervention Agreement proposed by Britain and France.

Stalin insisted that if the Republican government wanted Soviet military support it must first transfer a significant portion of the gold reserves of the Bank of Spain (valued at $500 million) to the Soviet Union. Only then would any military assistance be provided. The so-called 'Moscow Gold' was duly handed over, but even then direct Soviet military involvement in the Spanish Civil War remained more limited than is often supposed. It never rose to more than 2,000 soldiers on the ground at any time. The International Brigades numbered around 36,000. Of these, the French contingent of about 10,000 fighters was the largest. Around 5,000 exiled German and Austrian communists also fought against the Nationalists. It was thanks to this Soviet and Comintern support that Franco was prevented from winning a swift victory in 1936.[64]

During late July the world's greatest athletes were gathered in Berlin for the Summer Olympic Games. Anti-Semitic posters and newspapers had been removed from public places. Banned books suddenly reappeared and jazz was played in night clubs.[65] The International Olympic Committee (IOC) awarded the Games to Germany in 1931, when Germany was still a democratic nation. Some people had called for a boycott, but only the Soviet Union refused to send a team. Spain was absent too due to the start of the civil war. The IOC insisted that no Jews should be excluded from the German team. In 1934 the German Olympic Committee had selected twenty-one Jewish athletes to attend a training camp. In the end, however, just one 'half-Jew', the fencer Helene Mayer, competed for Germany, and because she was Jewish she had been forced to leave Germany and settle in the United States beforehand. She won a silver medal.[66]

For the first time in Olympic history, a purpose-built, men-only Olympic Village was constructed west of Berlin. It resembled an enormous motel with extensive leisure and canteen facilities. The female athletes were less fortunate. They were housed near the stadium in a large, austere, red-brick house, which lacked the same facilities as the Olympic Village.[67]

More than 1,800 foreign journalists covered the Berlin Olympics, accompanied by a retinue of photographers, and newsreel cameramen. Radio commentaries broadcast events around the world. Leni Riefenstahl was commissioned to make the official documentary

[overleaf] The German team enter the stadium during the opening ceremony of the 1936 German Olympic Summer Games.

film entitled *Olympia* which was released in two parts: *Fest der Völker* (*Festival of Nations*) and *Fest der Schönheit* (*Festival of Beauty*). Both films premiered in Berlin on 20 April 1938.[68]

Each sporting fixture at the Games was attended by leading members of the Nazi elite. To impress foreign visitors lavish social events were organized by Goebbels, Göring and Ribbentrop. Goebbels entertained 3,000 guests on an island on the River Havel; Ribbentrop held a garden party in the grounds of his villa in Dahlem attended by 600 people. The most spectacular of all was hosted by Göring with around 800 guests. It was held on the manicured lawns behind the brand-new Air Ministry, where a mock eighteenth-century illuminated village was created, complete with folk dancers, donkeys, a bakery, and several fairground rides. Waitresses in period costumes carried huge trays of pretzels, beer and champagne. As the British Conservative MP Henry 'Chips' Channon observed, 'nothing had been seen on this scale since the days of the Emperor Nero'.[69]

The opening ceremony took place on Saturday 1 August at the newly built Olympic Stadium: the Reich Sports Field. At 3.18 p.m. Hitler left the Reich Chancellery to make the nine-mile journey to the stadium in an open-topped Mercedes. An estimated 1 million Germans and tourists lined the route. When Hitler entered the stadium at around 4 p.m. a huge cheer went up from the 100,000 spectators.

Once Hitler had taken his seat in the VIP box, an orchestra played '*Deutschland über alles*' and the 'Horst Wessel Song'. At 4.15 p.m. the traditional parade of the athletes began. In keeping with Olympic tradition, the Greek team entered first. There were huge cheers for the French team, because the crowd thought they gave a Nazi salute. The British team did not give the Olympic salute in case it was confused with a Nazi salute. The crowd saw this as disrespectful and remained silent. As the US team marched past Hitler they removed their hats, but did not salute either. American athlete Marty Glickman said many of the US team could be heard saying of Hitler, 'Hey, he looks like Charlie Chaplin.'[70] The last team to enter was the host nation. Dressed all in white and wearing caps, they gave a Nazi salute and most enthusiastically.

The five-ringed Olympic flag was raised, accompanied by an Olympic hymn specially composed by world-famous German composer Richard Strauss. It was performed by the Berlin Philharmonic Orchestra, accompanied by a 1,000-strong choir. Then 20,000 pigeons (not doves, as was reported in the press) were released into the sky. In the most dramatic moment of the ceremony, a solitary German athlete, Siegfried Eifrig, entered the stadium carrying the Olympic torch, which had travelled 1,910 miles in a relay of runners from Athens to Berlin. He handed it to Fritz Schligen who took it up the steps of the Marathon Gate to light the Olympic flame. Finally, the German weightlifter Rudolf Ismayr took the Olympic oath while holding a swastika flag and not, as was traditional, the Olympic flag. 'We swear,' he said, 'that we will take part in the Olympic Games in loyal competition, respecting the regulations which govern them for the honour of our country and the glory of sport.'[71] The opening ceremony of the Berlin Olympics was more elaborate than any other since the modern Olympic Games began in 1896. The Nazis had a talent for spectacle and many of the innovations of the 1936 Games have been followed ever since.

The star athlete of the Berlin Olympics was the black American sprinter Jesse Owens, who won four gold medals, including the Men's 100 metres. This neatly punctured the Nazi idea that Aryans were the master race. It has long been argued that Hitler refused to shake Owens's hand after his victories, but in fact Hitler did not congratulate any of the athletes in the stadium after the first day of the Games. Then he had shaken hands with the Finnish and German medal winners, but the Belgian IOC President Henri de Ballet Latour had told him to stop this, unless he was prepared to do the same for every winner. Perhaps fearing an Owens win, Hitler dropped the idea.

Other credible witnesses suggest that Hitler was greatly incensed by Owens's victories. Hitler Youth leader Baldur von Schirach recalled that when he suggested to Hitler that he should invite Owens to the Reich Chancellery, Hitler angrily replied: 'Do you truly believe that I will allow myself to be photographed shaking hands with a Negro [*sic*]?'[72] Albert Speer also noted in his memoirs that Hitler 'was highly annoyed by the series of triumphs by the marvellous coloured [*sic*] runner Jesse Owens'.[73]

The German athlete Siegfried Eifrig enters the Berlin stadium with the Olympic torch which had been carried by relay runners all the way from Greece.

Goebbels described the victory of Owens in the 100 metres as 'a disgrace. The white race should be ashamed of itself'.[74] Ironically, some African-American athletes felt they were treated better in Germany than in the segregated parts of the United States. 'When I came home,' observed Archie Williams, winner of the 400 metres, 'somebody asked me, "How did those dirty Nazis treat you?" I replied I had not seen any dirty Nazis, just a lot of nice German people. And I didn't have to ride at the back of the bus over there.'[75]

Germany topped the medal table with 89 medals in all: 33 gold, 26 silver and 30 bronze. The United States came second with 56 medals of which 24 were gold. The British team came tenth, with 14 medals, just four of which were gold.

Overall, the 1936 Olympic Games were a huge propaganda triumph for Adolf Hitler and his regime. Foreign reporters and tourists praised the slick organization and friendly atmosphere. Frederick Birchall, for instance, in a piece for the *New York Times* headlined 'Olympics Leave a Glow of Pride in Reich', wrote that:

The superstar of the 1936 Berlin Olympics
US athlete Jesse Owens on his way to
victory in the 200 metres.

Foreigners who know Germany only from what they have
seen during this pleasant fortnight can carry home only one
impression. It is that this is a nation happy and prosperous
beyond belief; that Hitler is one of the greatest political leaders
in the world today, and that Germans themselves are a much
maligned, hospitable, wholly peaceful people who deserve the
best the world can give them.[76]

On 11 August Hitler announced the appointment of 43-year-old
Joachim von Ribbentrop as the German ambassador to Britain.[77] *The
Times* thought it was 'a good choice'.[78] The *Daily Telegraph* concluded
that, because Ribbentrop was very close to Hitler, 'a phase of closer
diplomatic activity between the two capitals is bound to follow'.[79] The
Daily Mail headline described Ribbentrop as 'A Welcome Ambassador',
whose 'moderation and tact have been greatly appreciated in Britain'.[80]

Many others were much less enthusiastic about him. Unity
Mitford told Hitler that Ribbentrop was something of a joke figure
in London high society. Henry 'Chips' Channon described the new
ambassador as 'like the captain of someone's yacht, not quite without
charm. But shakes hands in an over-hearty way.'[81] Göring thought
that Ribbentrop understood little of foreign countries and especially
the British mindset. Ribbentrop's knowledge of Britain, he added,
was confined to whisky. Hitler responded by saying that Ribbentrop
knew many influential members of the British political elite, to which
Göring replied: 'The trouble is they know him.'[82] This would seem to
be borne out by the remarks of Eric Phipps, the British ambassador in
Berlin, who described Ribbentrop as 'lightweight, irritating, ignorant
and boundlessly conceited'.[83]

On 22 August Admiral Miklós Horthy, the elected regent of
Hungary, became the first foreign leader to visit Hitler's newly
refurbished and expanded residence the Berghof (meaning 'Mountain
Court') at Obersalzberg, near Berchtesgaden.[84] This huge complex was
built around his previous modest two-storey, four-bedroomed Alpine
chalet home Haus Wachenfeld, which Hitler previously rented and
bought in 1933.

Hitler drew up his own initial sketches for the expansion of the
Berghof and from these the architect Alois Degano created detailed
plans. Interior design was under the supervision of the German architect
Gerdy Troost, the widow of architect Paul Troost. Construction work
was completed in the summer of 1936 and an inauguration ceremony
took place on 8 July.

The financing of the Berghof's huge expansion remains shrouded in mystery. Hitler claimed he financed it from a huge advance on future royalties of *Mein Kampf*. However, the surviving royalty records and bank account statements suggest this was not true. The Berghof project was overseen by Martin Bormann, chief of staff to the Deputy Führer Rudolf Hess. Bormann was in charge of the Adolf Hitler Fund, which collected 'voluntary' financial donations from big business. Between 1933 and 1945 deposits to this fund amounted to some 700 million Reichsmarks (equivalent to $3 billion today). The Berghof expansion project brought Bormann into much closer proximity to Hitler and he became not just a colleague but a valued friend and even something of a political guru. Hitler met Bormann regularly for coffee and cake on most weekday afternoons. As Goebbels noted in his diary: 'The Führer is very satisfied with Bormann. He possesses energy and discretion.'[85]

Hitler's Berghof residence had spectacular views of the Berchtesgaden Alps, straddling the border between Berchtesgaden in Bavaria and Salzburg in Austria. It had thirty rooms spread over three floors, including the imposing rectangular Great Hall on the ground floor, which contained a huge red marble fireplace. Opposite was a large panoramic window, overlooking the mountains, which was twenty-eight feet wide and twelve feet high. Unity Mitford was impressed: 'The effect is highly extraordinary. The window – the largest piece of glass ever made – can be wound down like it was yesterday, leaving it quite open.'[86]

A nineteen-feet long marble table dominated the room, near to which was a huge globe of the world. There were two Gobelin tapestries and some large bookcases. Art adorned the walls, including works by major Italian and German artists. Separated only by a large curtain was a more modest living room. It was here Hitler spent most of his time. Connected to this room was a grand dining room, with a table large enough to sit twenty-four guests.

The Berghof became the focal point of Hitler's life as Führer, especially before the beginning of the Second World War. It's possible to determine Hitler's closest friends by examining the most frequently invited guests to the Berghof. Hitler never viewed work as a friendship club. He made a clear division between work colleagues and friends. He liked to surround himself with people he felt at ease with. He rarely discussed politics or military matters with his friends. Göring, for instance, a man Hitler clearly valued and trusted as a political colleague, and who lived nearby, was not part of the Berghof in-crowd. Nor was

Himmler, who was the organizer of the SS and the most able Nazi bureaucrat. Himmler's right-hand man, Heydrich, was not a Berghof regular either. Hitler valued Ribbentrop's views on foreign policy, but he, too, was not a regular visitor. Goebbels and his wife Magda were central figures in Hitler's Berlin circle, but although they were frequently invited to the Berghof, their visits were brief and they stayed in a nearby villa. On the other hand, Baldur von Schirach, head of the Hitler Youth, was invited quite regularly. However, because Hitler was irritated by the forthright opinions of Schirach's wife Henriette (the daughter of Heinrich Hoffmann, Hitler's official photographer) the invitations to the couple gradually dwindled. Albert Speer and his wife Margarete were regularly guests and Hitler regarded them both as friends. Speer, for his part, was a little less enthusiastic, observing in his memoirs that Hitler was not only his social inferior, but also rather boring and repetitive in conversation. Speer introduced Hitler to his own friends Karl and Anni Brandt, who also joined the Berghof inner circle. Karl, an eminent doctor and surgeon, and Anni, the most famous German swimmer of the 1920s, joined the Nazi Party in 1933. They became devoted to Hitler and were keen supporters of his racial policies.

Hitler's private rooms on the first floor consisted of an office, a bath-room and a bedroom, next to which, separated by two interconnecting doors, was Eva Braun's apartment with a living room, a bedroom and a bathroom. Angela Raubal, Hitler's straight-talking, often rude, half-sister, who acted as his housekeeper, had become progressively estranged from him during 1935 because she strongly disapproved of his relationship with Eva. She left the Berghof and married the architect Professor Martin Hammitzsch on 18 February 1936.

The precise nature of Hitler and Eva's relationship at the Berghof has never been fully resolved. For the benefit of the domestic staff, Eva was given the official-sounding title of 'private secretary'. Whenever staff or guests were present, Hitler avoided open displays of intimacy, treating her as if she were a work colleague. Eva addressed Hitler as 'my Führer' and he addressed her as 'Fräulein Braun'.

Historians have long speculated about their sex life. Domestic staff often heard him call her his *Tschapperl*, a diminutive meaning a 'naive or clumsy child'. Speer thought that Hitler was very close to Eva and fond of her, but he was less sure whether their relationship was sexual. The domestic staff at the Berghof are probably more reliable witnesses. A housekeeper, Herbert Döhring, said at a post-war trial that he and his wife doubted there was a sexual relationship between the couple.

[overleaf]   Soldiers gather at the
1936 Nuremberg Rally to celebrate
the remilitarization of the Rhineland.

However, Heinz Linge, Hitler's closest assistant at the Berghof, had no doubt that they were sexually intimate. Gretel Mittelstrasser, the wife of Döhring's successor as housekeeper, was also certain that Hitler and Eva Braun slept together regularly. There is also evidence from Hitler's personal doctor that Hitler sought medication to improve his sexual performance.[87]

Throughout the summer of 1936 it was not just the Olympic Games and the refurbished Berghof that was occupying Hitler's mind. A major debate among leading figures in the armed forces concerning rearmament, the future of the German economy and foreign policy was underway.[88] In 1933 the army had given itself four years to build up a defensive force able to withstand a French attack. From 1936 to 1940 the aim of rearmament spending was to build up an offensive force capable of gaining new territory. The *Luftwaffe* planned to raise its strength from 48 squadrons in 1936 to 200 by 1938, with an emphasis on improving its bomber capacity. The army's expansion plans for 1936 to 1940 were even more ambitious: to expand to 102 divisions, fully equipped, numbering 3.6 million men by 1940.

It's often thought the German army was planning to create a fully motorized army capable of rapid offensive '*Blitzkrieg*' operations by 1940. The real plans were much less ambitious. The intention was for seven tank (*Panzer*) divisions to be ready for action by 1940. There would be around 1,000 vehicles per army division of 17,700 men, but the bulk of army transport for each division would be horses. The *Wehrmacht* planned to have 630,700 horses supporting the infantry. The total cost of this army expansion was budgeted at a total of 35.6 billion Reichsmarks, which would stretch the German economy to its limit. As a result, the economy would need to be geared towards rearmament at the expense of domestic consumption.[89]

Towards the end of August 1936 Hitler drafted a memorandum so top secret it was typed in triplicate, with just one copy each for Blomberg and Göring. No one else was given the full text, which later became known as the 'Four-Year Plan'. In it Hitler explained that he wanted the German army and the economy to be fully prepared for war by 1940.

In public, this memorandum was presented as being purely about economics. In the full secret version, however, Hitler stated bluntly that politics was the struggle of nations for survival. The new danger to Germany was Soviet Bolshevism, he said, which was intent on spreading communism worldwide, supported by world Jewry. A victory for the Soviet Union in this ideological war, Hitler declared, would lead to the annihilation of the German people. This was the major threat that German rearmament intended to prevent. If the German army did not become the strongest in the world in the next four years it would be on the losing side in this apocalyptic conflict with Bolshevism and Jewry.

Hitler felt Germany faced stark economic choices. It could not improve its export trade or devalue the mark or build up its foreign currency reserves. The German economy was not large enough to support massive rearmament and at the same time improve the standard of living for the general public. Imports were rising, but Germany's foreign currency reserves were falling at an alarming rate. Germany was overpopulated, Hitler said, and the German people required new 'living space' (*Lebensraum*). This could only be achieved through territorial conquest. After its victory in the coming war, Hitler predicted, Germany would emerge as a superpower. Only then would wages and living standards improve.

Hitler's Four-Year Plan made it clear the Germans would gain *Lebensraum* chiefly at the expense of the Soviet Union. German industry would be encouraged to support the plan or face increased state control. In the meantime, the German economy would have to become as self-sufficient as possible in the years between 1936 and 1940. Hitler concluded his memorandum by setting out two key aims: (1) the German army must be operational within four years; and (2) the German economy must be fit for war within four years.[90]

At a secret meeting of the Prussian ministerial council on 4 September Göring read out a summary of Hitler's secret memorandum, adding his own views, and observed: 'It starts with the assumption that war with Russia is unavoidable.' Nobody could predict when the war would begin, Göring added, but in preparation for this showdown with Russia, Germany had to mobilize its economy and society. Synthetic products would be developed in order to reduce the nation's reliance on imports. Two new laws would also be issued to support the Four-Year Plan: (1) 'A law making economic sabotage punishable by death', and (2) 'Make all Jews responsible for all damages inflicted by individual specimens of this community of criminals upon the German economy and thus upon the German people.'[91]

While this secret German war-planning continued, Ribbentrop managed to persuade David Lloyd George to visit Germany. Lloyd George, who had been the British Prime Minister from 1916 to 1922, hoped that his high-profile visit might help improve Anglo-German relations. He arrived at the Vier Jahreszeiten Hotel in Munich on 3 September, accompanied by his son Gwilym and daughter Megan, who were both MPs, as well as Thomas Jones, who had been deputy secretary to the cabinet during Lloyd George's coalition government; Philip Conwell-Evans, the pro-German academic; A.J. Sylvester, Lloyd George's private secretary; and his doctor Lord Bertrand Dawson.[92]

When Lloyd George's team dined with Ribbentrop on the first evening, Dawson thought Ribbentrop was too 'obsessed by the Bolshevik danger' and told him not to push this theme too strongly when dealing with British diplomats.[93] Lloyd George was not impressed by Ribbentrop at all and commented in private: 'That man could never hold his own in any political conversation and as for representing his country at an international conference, he would be at the mercy of any intelligent opponent.'[94]

On 4 September Lloyd George, accompanied by Conwell-Evans, met Hitler for coffee at the Berghof. In fact Hitler was there to greet him in person as his limousine arrived, around 4 p.m. Once seated inside the Great Hall, Hitler and Lloyd George instantly hit it off; the former British Prime Minister said of the panoramic window: 'The dramatic beauty of the spectacle almost took one's breath away.'[95]

Their talk covered several issues: the communist threat, the Spanish Civil War and Germany's need for 'living space' (*Lebensraum*). Lloyd George praised the peace proposals Hitler had offered after the remilitarization of the Rhineland and he criticized the British decision to hold talks with the French military at that time.

Hitler enjoyed the meeting so much that he invited Lloyd George to come again the following day. This time all of Lloyd George's visiting party came with him. Hitler went on a charm offensive. 'If the war had been won by the Allies in the Great War,' Hitler said, 'it was not in the first place the soldiers to whom victory was due, but to one great statesman, and that is yourself, Mr Lloyd George.' Deeply moved, Lloyd George responded by saying that Hitler was the 'greatest living German of the age', and went on to suggest that if Hitler had been in power in 1918 then Germany would not have collapsed.[96] Hitler said that he was very keen to encourage further Anglo-German understanding, while Lloyd George, more in a spirit of goodwill rather than truthfulness, observed that the appointment of Ribbentrop as German ambassador was welcomed in Britain.[97]

On his return to Britain Lloyd George wrote an article for the *Daily Express*, published on 17 September, entitled 'I Talked to Hitler'.

It bordered on hero worship. Lloyd George felt Hitler was 'a born leader of men', possessed of a 'magnetic, dynamic personality with a single-minded purpose, a resolute will and a dauntless heart'. As for his popularity among the German people, 'the old trust him, the young idolize him. It is not the admiration accorded to a popular leader, it is the worship of a national hero, who has saved his country after despondency and degradation.'

Hitler, Lloyd George argued, was 'the George Washington of Germany' and in no way a threat to world peace: 'The idea of a Germany intimidating Europe with a threat that its irresistible army might march across frontiers forms no part of the new vision.' He suggested Hitler had heeded the lessons of the Great War and he was confident that 'The establishment of a German hegemony in Europe, which was the aim of the old pre-war militarism, is not even on the horizon of Nazism.'[98]

Lloyd George repeated his enthusiasm for Hitler in a private letter to Ribbentrop in which he described his trip as 'memorable' and noted that his admiration for Hitler had in fact intensified due to his personal contact: 'He is the greatest piece of luck that has come to your country since Bismarck and personally I would say since Frederick the Great.'[99]

Between 8 and 16 September the eighth Nazi Party Congress was held at Nuremberg, with the usual parades, torchlit processions and speeches. It was called the 'Rally of Honour' to celebrate the remilitarization of the Rhineland, but the key theme of every major speech was anti-Bolshevism. In his opening proclamation on 9 September Hitler mentioned his Four-Year Plan, but couched it in purely economic terms as a way of reducing Germany's reliance on imports. The following day, in a speech entitled 'Bolshevism: the World Enemy', Goebbels promised a renewed programme of anti-communist propaganda.

Meanwhile, the British Foreign Secretary Anthony Eden tried to revive the idea of a new Western Pact to replace the Treaty of Locarno. In a memorandum of 17 September circulated to the governments of Belgium, France, Germany and Italy he suggested negotiating a new diplomatic agreement in which all signatories agreed not to attack each other by land, sea or air, or to resort to war with one another, but instead would guarantee to observe all non-aggression pacts agreed between Belgium, France and Germany regarding attacks on each other. It was suggested the jurisdiction of this new agreement should be adjudicated by the League of Nations and would not cover other agreements made by the signatories with powers not party to the agreement.[100] According to Ribbentrop, Hitler was not at all pleased by the contents of Eden's memorandum, especially the suggestion that the League of Nations should be allowed to judge what constituted a breach of the agreement.[101]

On 4 October Hitler gave a speech at the annual harvest festival celebration on the Bückeberg, a hill near the town of Hamelin. Hitler concentrated on the economy, asserting his determination to resist any calls from 'Anglo-Saxon' world markets for Germany to devalue its currency and improve its exports. Devaluation, he said, would lead to a rise in import prices and drive up inflation. He also pledged to continue with price and wage controls. For Hitler, the only answer to Germany's economic problems was self-sufficiency (*autarchy*).[102]

In response to the remilitarization of the Rhineland, King Leopold III announced on 14 October that Belgium was reverting to the policy of neutrality that had existed before the Great War. Belgium would accept guarantees from its former Locarno partners, but it would no longer offer them military aid should they be invaded. Germany's growing military strength had clearly demonstrated to a frightened Belgian government that being obligated to defend France against German aggression was now potentially hazardous.[103]

This Belgian diplomatic move infuriated the French government and took the British completely by surprise. Hitler was delighted. France was now deprived of a direct route to attack Germany through Belgium. Germany could now concentrate building up its western frontier fortifications along the 213-mile stretch of territory bordering France. The French, who had not continued the Maginot Line along the Belgian border, were now faced with extending these fortifications some 250 miles to Dunkirk. This was not possible in the short term.[104]

Hitler signed the official directive for his Four-Year Plan on 18 October. Göring, who was in charge of its implementation, issued several decrees that gave him supreme responsibility over economic policy, thereby completely undermining Hjalmar Schacht, the Economics Minister. The Four-Year Plan cemented Göring's position as the second most powerful figure in Hitler's government. Not only did he oversee the *Luftwaffe*, but he was Minister-President of Prussia and still nominally controlled the Gestapo.

At a meeting of the armed forces on 5 December Göring announced that he was now in charge of the German military. On 17

December he told key industrialists in a speech: 'No end of the rearmament is in sight. The struggle which we are approaching demands a colossal measure of productive ability. The only deciding point in this case is victory or destruction. If we win, then business will be sufficiently compensated [...] We are now playing for the highest stakes.'[105]

Towards the end of the year, Hitler sought a much closer friendship with Mussolini's Italy.[106] On 21 October Mussolini sent Count Galeazzo Ciano, the new Italian Foreign Minister, and his son-in-law for diplomatic talks in Germany. Meeting Neurath, Ciano ridiculed Ribbentrop's efforts to bring about a meaningful Anglo-German friendship. Furthermore, he said that Italy would stay in the League of Nations solely to sabotage it from within.

On 24 September Hitler had met Ciano at the Berghof and told him that Mussolini was 'the first statesman in the world with whom no one else has the right even remotely to compare himself'. Germany and Italy, he said, should unite in an invincible coalition against the Soviet Union and the Western democracies. For his part, Ciano was keen to sour relations between Germany and Britain and showed Hitler a copy of a telegram from Eric Phipps, the British ambassador in Berlin, describing Hitler as 'dangerous adventurer'. The British had built up an empire by being adventurers, Hitler replied, but they were now 'governed merely by incompetents'.[107]

On the following day, Germany and Italy agreed to a secret, informal alliance soon to be known as the Rome–Berlin Axis. It was in a speech delivered in Milan's beautiful Piazza del Duomo on 1 November that Mussolini first described the close relationship between Italy and Germany as an 'axis'. It was founded, Il Duce said, on collaboration and peace.[108] What strengthened the Rome–Berlin Axis was the mutual respect and friendship between Hitler and Mussolini despite their very different personalities. Mussolini was confident, gregarious, extrovert and sociable. Hitler was far more solemn and restrained. Hitler's admiration extended as far as keeping a heavy bronze bust of Mussolini in his study at the Brown House, the Nazi headquarters in Munich.[109]

In the meantime, Ribbentrop had taken up his post as German ambassador to Britain. He arrived at Victoria Station in London on 26 October. He greeted waiting journalists with a Nazi salute and the following statement: 'Germany wants to be friends with Great Britain. I think the British people also wish for British friendship. The Führer is convinced that there is only one real danger to Europe and to the British Empire and that is the spreading of communism, this most terrible of diseases.'[110] The *Daily Telegraph* thought it unfortunate that 'the new envoy could suggest no better grounds for Anglo-German friendship than common hostility to a third country [the Soviet Union].'[111] On 30 October Ribbentrop met with Edward VIII, who later recalled: 'The occasion was not without strain. The appointment of this polished but bombastic opportunist was not calculated to ease British apprehensions.'[112]

At the Berlin Sport Palace on 28 October Göring delivered a rousing speech before a huge crowd in which he outlined the importance of the Four-Year Plan. However, the American ambassador William Dodd noted that Göring also attacked Britain in his speech, even though Lord Londonderry was present as an invited guest. This was a sure sign, Dodd concluded, that passions had cooled within the Nazi elite for any kind of Anglo-German understanding.[113]

On 25 November Germany and Japan signed the Anti-Comintern Pact, an agreement intended to run for at least five years to collaborate against international communism (the Communist International) as well as Soviet propaganda. In two secret protocols, Germany and Japan agreed to consult on what measures to take 'to safeguard their common interests' should either nation be attacked by the Soviet Union, and not to sign any treaty contrary to the spirit of the pact. The Japanese government agreed to this under pressure from hardline elements within Japan's military. Ribbentrop described the pact as 'an epoch-making event, a turning point in the defensive struggle of all nations loving order and civilization against the forces of subversion'. The agreement seemed of little practical value, beyond expressing opposition to communism.[114] William Shirer, who was present at the signing of the agreement, observed:

> Ribbentrop, who signed for Germany, strutted in and harangued
> us for a quarter of an hour about the pact's meaning, if any.
> He said it meant, among other things, that Germany and Japan
> had joined together to defend 'Western Civilization'. This was
> such a novel idea, for Japan at least, that at the end of his talk
> one of the British correspondents asked him if he had understood
> him correctly. Ribbentrop, who has no sense of humor, then
> repeated the silly statement without batting an eye.[115]

The British government was puzzled by the Anti-Comintern Pact. Robert Vansittart, a leading Foreign Office diplomat, told the

Japanese ambassador in London that he thought it was 'ill staged and ridiculous'.[116]

At a cabinet meeting on 1 December Hitler spoke for three hours on foreign policy. He said that Europe was now divided into two camps: pro-communist and anti-communist. If communist regimes came to power in France and Spain it would lead to a Europe-wide crisis. In the long run, he said, the small authoritarian states – Austria, Hungary, Poland and Yugoslavia – could not be relied upon to keep the threat of communism at bay. Germany needed to move closer to the anti-communist states of Italy and Japan.

In early December the British press finally broke the story of Edward VIII's romantic relationship with the American divorcee Mrs Simpson. The king wanted to marry her, but his role as the nominal head of the Church of England made this impossible, so it was fiercely opposed by Cosmo Lang, the Archbishop of Canterbury, and other leading figures in the Church. Edward had some powerful supporters, notably the influential press baron Lord Beaverbrook, Winston Churchill, but he also had some powerful enemies, especially the Prime Minister. Baldwin told Edward VIII that his proposed marriage to Mrs Simpson was unacceptable on religious, constitutional and moral grounds, and he gave the king a stark choice: choose the throne or Mrs Simpson. The king asked if parliament could pass a law allowing Mrs Simpson to become a princess but not queen (a morganatic marriage), but Baldwin rejected the idea.[117] After weighing up his options, the king decided love came before his loyalty to the constitution. He signed the legal instruments of abdication on 10 December and on the following day, introduced as His Royal Highness Prince Edward, he explained his decision to abdicate on BBC radio. Edward's brief reign was over and the following day he left Britain for Austria. Prince Albert, Duke of York, took the title of George VI and replaced his brother on the throne.[118]

Edward VIII's abdication was regarded as a disaster by Hitler, who believed that the king could have been helpful in brokering the Anglo-German alliance he so desired. Ribbentrop convinced Hitler that Edward had been deposed by a Jewish plot within the British Establishment.[119] In a telegram to Neurath, Ribbentrop complained that a 'systematic agitation has been fomented in Britain against the king', and that his 'friendly attitude towards Germany had undoubtedly gained the king powerful enemies'.[120]

On Christmas Day 1935, Hitler had selected Dr Theodor Morell as his personal physician. Morell was an unattractive character: bald, overweight with ill-fitting, horn-rimmed spectacles. He graduated from medical school in Munich in 1912, then became an army medic during the Great War. After the war, he set up a private practice specializing in dermatology and venereal diseases in a building on the fashionable Kurfürstendamm in Berlin. He was very successful and included among his clients members of the political elite, businessmen and film and sports stars.[121]

Morell was something of a German pioneer in homeopathic medicine. He mainly treated patients with natural extracts and vitamins, often injecting them directly into the bloodstream. For stomach complaints Morell used Mutaflor, which contains a strain of *E. coli* isolated in 1917 from the faeces of a soldier seemingly immune to dysentery and other intestinal diseases. This treatment was viewed with scepticism by the other medical professionals, but Morell used it

The Berghof, Hitler's mountain retreat.

extensively and it seemed to produce improvements in minor stomach ailments.[122]

Heinrich Hoffmann, Hitler's official photographer, was convinced that Morell had cured him of a minor sexually transmitted condition. It was at a dinner party in Hoffmann's Munich house that Hitler first met with Morell in the summer of 1936. A lifelong hypochondriac, Hitler loved talking about his various real and imagined ailments. He told Morell that he was suffering from a constant lack of energy, migraines, indigestion, crippling stomach pains, flatulence and insomnia. The most persistent problem of all was severe stomach pain after every meal. Doctors who have studied Hitler's medical records cannot agree on what exactly caused this. One possibility is gallstones. Another is viral hepatitis – a common condition that causes inflammation of the liver. The fact that Hitler sometimes had jaundice suggests this might be the case.

Hitler had excluded from his diet certain foods that made his stomach hurt, including cakes, bread, meat and milk. He became almost completely vegetarian, eating honey, mushrooms, cheese and yoghurt. To lessen the pain, he mainly took over-the-counter painkillers from a local chemist. These were much stronger than those available nowadays. Hitler thought that his constant stomach pain meant that he would die young. 'I shall not live much longer,' he confided to Albert Speer. 'I must carry out my aims as long as I can hold up, for my health is getting worse all the time.'[123]

Invited to the Berghof to give the Führer a thorough medical examination, Morell noted that Hitler had dietary complications, a gastrointestinal upset, an enlarged liver, swelling in his central abdomen and eczema on his shins. He recommended Mutaflor capsules and shortly afterwards Hitler's stomach problems dramatically improved. At this point Hitler began to think of Morell as something of a miracle worker. Morell then gave Hitler glucose and vitamin injections, which gave Hitler huge energy rushes, leading him to comment: 'Nobody has ever before told me so clearly and precisely what is wrong with me. His method of cure is so logical that I have the greatest confidence in him. I shall follow his prescription to the letter.'[124] Once Hitler had appointed him as his personal physician, Morell became a permanent fixture in the Führer's entourage at the Reich Chancellery and at the Berghof. Morell saw Hitler on most days, right up until a fortnight before Hitler's death.

Morell's arrival had a profound impact on Hitler's personality, not least because he encouraged Hitler's drug dependency, but it would be wrong to attribute Hitler's horrific actions in the years ahead to the arrival of this unorthodox physician. As Albert Speer put it: 'Hitler's aims and plans never changed [...] Power itself was the main drug underlying his activity.'[125]

When the initial effect of Mutaflor wore off and Hitler's stomach pain returned, Morell tried new treatments and administered what he called 'power injections'. These mainly consisted of glucose and vitamins to which he added an opioid painkiller called Eukodal, a close relative of heroin. Was Hitler addicted to this drug? It is difficult to say, based on the surviving evidence. As well as the sleeping pills he took for his insomnia, Hitler was prescribed the stimulant Optalidon and the sedative Brom-Nervacit, which are both highly addictive. He also regularly took an even more addictive drug: methamphetamine, diluted with a glucose solution. This isn't mentioned in Morell's records, but Heinz Linge, Hitler's valet, witnessed the administration of this injection each morning, after which Hitler became alert and full of energy, as well as being more cheerful, talkative and physically active.

Hitler also had injections of something called Pervitin in Germany, which was modelled upon the American drug Benzedrine, which was freely available in tablet form from local chemists. Athletes took Benzedrine in the days before drug-testing, truck drivers used it to stay awake on long journeys, and housewives took it too. There was even a popular song that contained the line 'Who put the Benzedrine in Mrs Murphy's Ovaltine?' The negative side effects of continued amphetamine use are now well documented: suspiciousness, agitation, loss of emotional control, impulsiveness, irritability, anger and impaired judgement. Some of these traits were certainly present in Hitler's personality but most had been present before Hitler took any drugs.[126]

Hitler rewarded Morell handsomely. The doctor bought an elegant villa costing 338,000 Reichsmarks – of which Hitler provided a 200,000 Reichsmarks interest-free loan, which was converted into a cumulative fee for his medical treatment. Morell became a celebrity doctor, which brought many new patients, including Eva Braun, although she complained to Hitler that Morell had body odour. In 1938 Hitler awarded Morell an honorary professorship.[127]

In many ways 1936 was the high point of the peacetime years of Hitler's Germany. The bold military move into the Rhineland was an extraordinary gamble, but it paid off spectacularly. No military retaliation by France or Britain was ever seriously expected. The Olympic Games were not only a major feat of organization but also a global propaganda success for the Nazi regime. A new axis was evolving with Italy and Japan, while Austria was gradually becoming a German satellite state. All this helped to raise Hitler's personal standing within Germany to new heights.

The outbreak of the Spanish Civil War also offered the *Luftwaffe* a valuable new training ground and gave Hitler an opportunity to further his anti-communism. It also usefully diverted the world's attention away from Germany's rearmament and Hitler's long-term foreign policy objectives.

Beyond Germany there was a growing pessimism about the international situation. A defiant Germany, Italy and Japan had all rejected international law, in response to which President Roosevelt's strong words meant very little for as long as America remained neutral and preferred not to get involved in European security.

By the end of 1936 the world order that had been established in 1919 with the Treaty of Versailles was on the verge of collapse. Britain and France were losing faith in yet more treaties and alliances designed to deter Germany, Italy and Japan from military action. Was this not just a return to the failings of the past which had brought about the Great War? The diplomatic dilemma facing Britain and France was becoming stark: either passively accept international treaties being revised or even torn up, or take a stand and try to halt by force any further military aggression.

1937

·

DECEPTIVE
CALM

·

Adolf Hitler told Göring's wife Emmy that his Christmas holiday had been 'the first happy one in long years'.[1] Hitler was feeling much healthier. Goebbels noted in his diary that Hitler was 'developing fantastic prospects for the future. Germany will either triumph in the coming battle or cease to exist'.[2] Hitler decided to use 1937 to pause and take stock, after the dramatic and nerve-racking military surprises of the previous two years. To outside observers it seemed that Hitler was settling down to consolidate his power inside Germany.

On 2 January Britain and Italy signed the so-called 'gentleman's agreement', which pledged to respect the rights and interests of the two nations in the Mediterranean and to uphold Spain's independence. This annoyed Hitler, because it suggested that Mussolini was keeping his foreign policy options open.

On 5 January the British Foreign Secretary Anthony Eden received a letter of protest from Ribbentrop, the German ambassador, which claimed a Polish news agency had leaked details of their private meeting on 17 December 1936. Eden assured Ribbentrop this leak had not come from the British Foreign Office, and he suggested the German Foreign Ministry contained the whistle-blower.[3]

On the same day, Hans-Adolf von Moltke, the German ambassador to Poland, sent a telegram to Neurath, the German Foreign Minister, giving details of his recent conversation with Józef Beck, the Polish Foreign Minister, concerning the Danzig question. Danzig (Gdańsk) was a largely German city in the disputed region between Poland and Germany. Beck had complained to Moltke about the increasing restrictions on the rights of the Polish minority which had been introduced by Arthur Greiser, the Nazi Senate President of Danzig. Under new rules, some Polish workers had even lost their jobs. Moltke told Beck these claims were exaggerated and gave his assurance that any flagrant cases of discrimination would be investigated by Greiser. Moltke told Beck Polish-German negotiations should be confined to Danzig's relations with the League of Nations, not such minor domestic issues.[4]

Meanwhile, Göring was sent out to Fascist Italy on 14 January to maintain good relations. He spoke candidly to the Italian diplomat

Massimo Magistrati about Germany's foreign policy aims, telling him that Germany would not be ready for war until January 1940. Göring also held talks at the Palazzo Venezia, the Italian Chancellery in Rome, with Benito Mussolini and his Foreign Minister Count Ciano. It wasn't long before the talk turned to Austria. Göring said that a union between Germany and Austria was 'inevitable' and 'must come without delay', but he promised that Germany would not launch a 'surprise attack'. The German interpreter Paul Schmidt noted that as he translated these words, Mussolini shook his head in disagreement.[5]

Göring then said that Germany would not tolerate a restoration of the Habsburg monarchy. This idea had recently been suggested by the Austrian Chancellor Kurt Schuschnigg. Mussolini made clear he opposed this. Göring asked Mussolini to put pressure on Schuschnigg to adopt a more conciliatory attitude towards local Nazi Party leaders. In reply, Mussolini pointed out that he was now very unpopular in Austria and needed to proceed with great caution in any discussions with the Austrian government. Ciano, adding weight to this point, mentioned the frosty reception he had received from the Austrian public on a recent diplomatic visit to Vienna. Mussolini ended the discussion by stating that he wanted Austria to remain independent.

The Italian diplomat Massimo Magistrati, who was also present at the meeting, noted that Mussolini thought the meeting had gone very badly and had increased his fear that Germany was determined to unite Germany and Austria by force.[6]

In a telegram to Neurath, Ulrich von Hassell, the German ambassador to Italy, put a completely different spin on the meeting. He reported there was harmony between Mussolini and Göring on all the key issues. Mussolini seemingly felt the visit had enhanced German-Italian collaboration and told Göring his public engagements during his time in Italy had earned him 'the liking of the Italian people'.[7]

On 19 January Eden delivered a major speech on the international situation in the House of Commons. 'If 1937 must be a year of acutely different international problems,' he began, 'and of that there can be no doubt, it is also a year of international opportunities.' He advised against British intervention in the Spanish Civil War and expressed continued support for the League of Nations. Then he turned his attention to German foreign policy:

> The future of Germany and the part she is to play in Europe
> is today the main preoccupation of all Europe. Here is a great
> nation of 65 million people, in the very centre of our Continent,

which has exalted race and nationalism into a creed which is practised with the same fervour as it is preached. All the world is asking at this present time whither these doctrines are to lead Germany, whither are they to lead all of us? [...] Europe cannot go on drifting to a more and more uncertain future. She cannot be torn between acute national rivalries and violently opposed ideologies, and hope to survive, without bearing scars that will last for a generation. Germany has it in her power to influence a choice which will decide not only her fate, but that of Europe. If she chooses cooperation with other nations, full and equal cooperation, there is nobody in this country who will not assist wholeheartedly to remove misunderstandings and to make the way smooth to peace and prosperity.[8]

On the following day Beck, the Polish Foreign Minister, met Neurath in Berlin. Beck told him that Poland did not seek any further rights over Danzig, but that the rights of Polish nationals living in the city had to be protected. Neurath promised to examine this issue, but observed that the 'very unfriendly attitude of the Polish press' towards Germany was not helping matters. When he asked Beck to urge restraint on the Polish press when reporting on Danzig and German affairs, Beck replied that his control over the free press was extremely limited.[9]

At this time, Czech-German relations were also becoming strained. On 21 January Dr Vojtěch Mastný, the Czechoslovak Minister to Germany, met Ernst von Weizsäcker, the Director of the Policy Department at the German Foreign Ministry. Mastný drew attention to the continuing hostility towards Czechoslovakia in the German press. Weizsäcker replied that the people of Czechoslovakia were living in 'unjustified fear' of Germany, but as they had unwisely sought the protection of France and the Soviet Union they 'must now face the consequences'. When Mastný denied that any secret military agreement existed between Czechoslovakia and the Soviet Union, Weizsäcker informed him that 'Russian officers had been seen in Czechoslovakia and vice versa'.[10]

Hitler addressed the Reichstag on 30 January on the fourth anniversary of his coming to power. This speech had now become an annual event in the Nazi calendar. As Hitler walked to the podium, the familiar chant of 'Sieg Heil!' rang out. He began by saying that 'nobody could doubt that during the last four years a revolution of the most momentous character has passed like a storm over Germany'. The Nazi revolution, he maintained, had been accompanied by 'an absence of bloodshed and destruction'. Surely it was the first revolution in history when 'not a single window pane was broken'. Nazism was not about destroying human life or property, he said, but determined to build a new and better life for the German people. This had been largely achieved, he claimed, through a massive reduction in unemployment from 6 million in 1933 to 600,000 today. At the same time, the nation's cultural life had been purged of Jewish influence. As for the concentration camps, only 'hardened criminals' now remained in them. The National Socialist revolution came to an end, Hitler added, when the SA rebels had been crushed with an 'iron hand' during the Night of the Long Knives.

Hitler then moved on to his foreign policy achievements, high-lighting the restoration of military service, the creation of a new air force, the reconstruction of the German navy and the rearming of the army, which was made possible by the remilitarization of the Rhineland: 'I regret to say that it was not possible to carry through all the necessary measures by way of negotiation. But at the same time, it must be remembered that the honour of a people cannot be bartered away, it can only be taken away.' He then declared to loud cheers that there would be no more foreign policy surprises: 'Peace is now our highest priority.'

Hitler next responded to Anthony Eden's speech of 19 January. 'I think I read those statements carefully and have understood them,' he said. Eden was wrong in saying that Germany wanted to isolate itself from the problems of the world, pointing out that Germany had entered into several political agreements since 1933, including with Austria, Italy, Japan and Poland, improved relations with Bulgaria, Greece, Hungary, Portugal and Yugoslavia, and was willing to guarantee the safety of Belgium and the Netherlands.

If there was division in Europe it was not Germany's fault, Hitler added. Europe had been divided by the injustice of the Treaty of Versailles. Added to this was a second source of international disunity: the Soviet Union's determination to export Bolshevism. Hitler advised Britain to join Germany in its crusade to halt the intolerable 'pestilence' of Bolshevism: 'We use every means in our power to keep this peril away.' It was unimaginable that a National Socialist Germany would 'ever be bound to protect Bolshevism or that we, on our side, should ever agree to accept the assistance of a Bolshevik state'.[11]

In Britain the *Daily Telegraph*'s diplomatic correspondent concluded that Hitler's speech had been influenced by moderates in the German army, who had advised him against embarking on any further foreign policy adventures.[12] The *News Chronicle* thought that Hitler's promise of no further foreign policy surprises seemed hollow, because he made no effort to seek a peaceful European settlement.[13]

In Brussels, however, Hitler's offer to guarantee Belgian neutrality was warmly welcomed. On 3 February Herbert von Richthofen, the German ambassador in Belgium, was summoned to meet Leopold III. The king said that he had listened to the Führer's speech with great interest and had felt an 'especial satisfaction about the statements concerning guaranteeing Belgium neutrality'.[14] In Berlin on the same day Weizsäcker was visited at the German Foreign Ministry by Jacques Davignon, the Belgian ambassador. Davignon wanted to know whether Hitler was really offering a firm and binding guarantee of Belgian neutrality. Weizsäcker's response was much more guarded than Hitler's speech, stressing: (1) this offer would only take effect if the negotiations for a new Western Pact – in which Belgium would be included – should break down, and (2) Hitler's statement was not a unilateral German guarantee of Belgium's neutrality.[15]

Meanwhile, Germany's ambassador in Rome Ulrich von Hassell informed the German Foreign Minister Neurath that Mussolini had been disappointed that Hitler had not mentioned in his speech either the Rome–Berlin Axis or Göring's recent successful visit to Italy.[16]

On 4 February a strange incident occurred at Buckingham Palace. During a formal ceremony at which foreign ambassadors, accompanied by leading officials, presented their credentials to the British monarch, the German ambassador Ribbentrop greeted George VI with a Nazi salute. The startled king nearly fell over as Ribbentrop violently raised his hand.[17] The British press responded with outrage. Hitler demanded a written explanation from his gaffe-prone ambassador. 'I presented my credentials to the king and conveyed the greetings of the Führer and chancellor,' Ribbentrop reported. 'I added that the Führer, since the beginning of his political career, had pursued the aim of British-German understanding. The king received my statements in a very friendly way. He reciprocated the greetings and said that he shared the view that German-British understanding was a necessity.'[18] The king was not surprised or offended by his use of the salute. The reports in the British press were 'distorted and mistaken'.[19] Neurath felt that Ribbentrop had caused Germany deep embarrassment and drafted a report to Hitler recommending that in the future Ribbentrop should conform to normal British customs.[20]

Meanwhile, German relations with the French were unravelling. On 8 February André François-Poncet, the French ambassador to Germany, met diplomat Hans-Heinrich Dieckhoff at the German Foreign Ministry to complain about a speech Goebbels had given in Hamburg on 4 February. Goebbels, the Nazi Propaganda Minister, had criticized what he called the 'cunning Popular Front government' in France. On top of this, the French ambassador was upset that during his speech on 30 January Hitler had made no mention of France and had been very negative about the prospects for a new Western Pact to replace the Locarno Treaty.[21]

Back in London on 14 February Ribbentrop met Lord Halifax, who was acting as Foreign Secretary while Eden was away on leave. Ribbentrop told Halifax that the hostile attitude of the British press towards Germany was hampering Anglo-German relations. He complained that his recent meeting with George VI had been grossly distorted by the media. Halifax expressed some sympathy with these remarks, but explained that the freedom of the press limited the government's power to do anything. Ribbentrop then told Halifax that Germany demanded the return of its colonies, which had been confiscated under the terms of the Treaty of Versailles. British public opinion opposed this, Halifax warned, because there was still considerable mistrust as to Germany's ultimate intentions.[22]

In February there was a heated debate in Berlin as to who should represent the German government at the forthcoming coronation of George VI in London. Hitler had originally chosen Göring, but there was outrage when this news was leaked to the British press, particularly from the opposition Labour Party and Jewish organizations. In turn, Göring was greatly angered by these British objections to his presence. In the end Neurath persuaded Göring to step aside. It was decided that Field Marshal Werner von Blomberg, the Minister of War, would go instead.[23]

On 23 February Himmler ordered the Prussian State Criminal Police Department to conduct a series of raids against 'professional and habitual criminals'. When these raids went ahead on 8 March, 2,000 people were taken into custody and sent straight to concentration camps. Almost all of the prisoners were men. Himmler's aim was to wipe out Germany's criminal sub-culture, especially in the working-class areas of big cities, but there was an economic motive, too. Germany was suffering from labour shortages as unemployment fell. Industries involved in armament production needed workers.

Himmler saw his raids as a means of providing businesses with cheap labour. At a meeting of government officials on 11 February Himmler floated the idea of adding the 'work-shy' – defined as the long-term unemployed – to his list of anti-social individuals who should now be sent to the concentration camps. In March the first raids on the long-term unemployed took place. The number of 'criminal' and 'asocial' prisoners grew rapidly in the camps. In 1937 most of them ended up in Sachsenhausen and Buchenwald, thereby changing the composition of the prisoner population.

A political prisoner in Dachau witnessed a speech given by SS compound leader Hermann Baranowski to a group of 'habitual criminals' in spring 1937: 'Listen up, you filth! Do you know where you are? […] I'll explain it to you. You are not in a prison and you are not in a penitentiary either. No, you are in a concentration camp. That means you are in an educational camp. You are to be educated here – and we'll educate you all right. You may rely on that, you stinking swine.'[24] By the end of 1938 these so-called 'asocial' inmates made up around 70 per cent of the concentration camp population.

In February Hitler told his inner circle that the continuing struggle between Nazism and the Christian churches had to come to an end.[25] The spiritual allegiance of German Catholics to the Vatican in Rome was supposed to have been protected by the 1933 Concordat, yet a third of the 25,500 Catholic priests in Germany were subjected to some form of harassment by the Gestapo. Some monasteries, convents of nuns and youth organizations had also been closed down. The Hitler Youth often disrupted Catholic church services and some Catholic publications had already been banned. Many priests and monks faced false sexual abuse allegations. In 1937 Catholic priests and theological students were banned from joining the Nazi Party. In January a delegation of German Catholic bishops travelled to Rome to outline a mounting list of complaints about the treatment of Catholics in Germany.[26] On 25 February the Vatican complained to the German government about the proposed abolition of Catholic private schools. It was yet another violation of the Concordat. The Vatican warned that if such persecution continued it would publish its private correspondence with the German government and cause acute international embarrassment to Hitler's Germany.[27] Relations did not improve. On 3 March the German Foreign Ministry concluded that the decision to abolish Catholic private schools did not breach the terms of the 1933 Concordat.[28] The Vatican was informed of this decision on 11 March.[29]

After the Great War a horseshoe-shaped area on the frontier of Germany and Austria called the Sudetenland was allocated to Czechoslovakia, despite the fact that it was home to 3.5 million German-speakers. Now their demands for 'national self-determination' became a source of disagreement between Germany and Czechoslovakia. The German diplomat Otto von Erdmannsdorff noted in a memorandum, dated 2 March, that Konrad Henlein, a Sudeten German and founder of the Sudeten German Home Front, had delivered a speech four days earlier in which he made two key demands to the Czech government: (1) the introduction of self-administration, which would not infringe on the unity and frontiers of the Czechoslovakian state; and (2) the citizens of Czechoslovakia should be grouped into national corporate bodies and endowed with true equality of rights, which should be enshrined in law. Erdmannsdorff recommended to Neurath that the German government should support Henlein's demands for greater autonomy for the German minority in the Sudetenland.[30]

On 3 March the Mayor of New York City Fiorello La Guardia, an outspoken critic of Hitler and an ardent defender of Jewish rights, gave a speech to the Women's Division of the American Jewish Congress. At the upcoming New York World's Fair, he said, there ought to be a 'Chamber of Horrors' dedicated to 'that brown-shirted fanatic', meaning Hitler. Two days later the German newspaper *Der Angriff* responded angrily to his speech, calling La Guardia a 'shameless Jew lout'.[31] Soon there was a full-blown diplomatic row between Germany and the United States. William Dodd, the US ambassador to Germany, visited Neurath at the Foreign Ministry. He told Dodd that La Guardia's insulting remarks about Hitler had caused 'general indignation in Germany'. La Guardia was of passionate 'Italian extraction', Dodd replied by way of explanation, but added that in his opinion the US press was hostile towards Germany largely because of its anti-Jewish policies. An irritated Neurath told Dodd that his opinion 'constituted interference in German affairs' and promptly ended the conversation.[32]

In the States, Hans Luther, the German ambassador to Washington, lodged an official complaint about La Guardia's speech. Cordell Hull, the US Secretary of State, told Luther that President Roosevelt was very unhappy about the mayor's remarks. La Guardia had been told to stop being rude about Hitler in the future. Such insults did not represent the views of the United States government, and they should not be taken seriously. In a democratic society it is impossible to restrain the free speech of individual citizens, Hull concluded.[33]

[overleaf] The aftermath of the bombing of the Basque city of Guernica by the German Condor Legion on 26 April 1937, during the Spanish Civil War.

Meanwhile, the diplomatic relations between Germany and the Vatican had worsened. On 10 March Pope Pius XI issued an encyclical entitled 'With Burning Concern' to every Catholic bishop in Germany in which he was highly critical of Hitler's treatment of Catholics.[34] He outlined the many difficulties Catholics endured, highlighting several breaches of the Concordat. The Pope wrote: 'We have been observing for some time now the cross carried by the church in Germany and the increasingly difficult situation of these men and women who have kept the faith and remained true to her in thought and deed.' He condemned those in Germany who made 'race, nation and state the supreme norm of all value and suggested a destructive religious war was underway'. He also protested about interference in Catholic youth organizations and schools.[35] Around 300,000 copies of the Pope's encyclical were printed and smuggled into Germany. Most Catholic priests in Germany read out the Pope's encyclical at the pulpit on 21 March which was Palm Sunday.

Hitler was outraged that the Catholic clergy, supported by the Pope, should openly criticize his religious policy in Catholic churches. Copies of the letter were seized by the Gestapo and its publication was expressly forbidden. The German Foreign Ministry made a formal protest to the Vatican against the Pope's 'interference in German domestic affairs', and on 6 April Hitler ordered the Minister of Justice Franz Gürtner to recommence sexual abuse trials involving Catholic priests and monks, which had been suspended in 1936.[36] In a speech on 28 May Goebbels depicted the Catholic church as riddled with financial and sexual corruption. In his diary he admitted that Hitler had sat beside him as he wrote his speech, 'dictating my declaration of war against the clergy' and offering him many lines to include which were 'Very stinging and drastic, I would not have gone that far.'[37]

On 10 March the German government finally submitted a memorandum outlining its position on a proposed Western Pact. This new proposed security agreement between Belgium, Britain, France, Germany and Italy was intended to replace the Treaty of Locarno, but the German proposals were really a list of objections to the whole idea. The German government opposed offering territorial guarantees to all the signatories in all circumstances. It also rejected the idea that in the event of military aggression the League of Nations should decide which nation had violated the agreement. Germany wanted all existing diplomatic agreements signed by any of the signatories to be kept outside the terms of this new pact. The German government even suggested that a non-aggression pact was meaningless when any one state retained the right to intervene if it was involved in a war with a third state. There should be no exceptions, Germany said. Only countries inside the new pact who were not directly involved in any conflict between any of the signatories should be able to adjudicate on which nation had violated the agreement. In short, the Germans rejected the Western Pact.[38]

On the following day the Italian memorandum was circulated, which raised similar concerns about the Western Pact's viability. The Treaty of Locarno had a clear purpose, the Italian government said. It had helped to maintain the territories belonging to Belgium and Germany, and France and Germany along the Rhineland. Belgium, France and Germany had all pledged not to attack each other, under the Locarno accords, while Britain and Italy acted as guarantors of this straightforward arrangement. According to the Italian government, the intention of the French government regarding this new agreement was to create a collective non-aggression pact between all five signatories to provide a security guarantee to all. Each signatory would pledge to commit no aggression or invasion on the other by land, sea or air. It was no longer a limited guarantee, but a much wider obligation for each of the signatories to offer military assistance to the others, potentially even beyond Western Europe.

The Italian government could see no advantage in signing up to such a wide-ranging agreement. Any new treaty should be specific and simple. The key issues, as they saw it, were to guarantee Belgium protection from attack and to arbitrate over any breaches of the peace between France and Germany. Jointly with the British, the Italians were prepared to guarantee Belgium's safety and to maintain the territorial status quo between Germany and France, but they would go no further than this.[39]

At this time, the Czechoslovakian government was becoming increasingly anxious about Germany's intentions in the Sudetenland. Meeting Neurath on 20 March, Vojtěch Mastný, the Czechoslovak Minister to Germany, explained that his government proposed a diplomatic agreement under which Germany would guarantee the territorial integrity of Czechoslovakia. Neurath was in no mood to compromise with the Czechs. He bluntly told Mastný that any such agreement was out of the question until the Czechoslovakian government cut all of its current ties with the Soviet Union and the treatment of the Sudeten German minority had greatly improved.[40]

On 12 April Hassell, the German ambassador to Italy, reported on the current state of the Berlin–Rome Axis. The Italian public, he said, were beginning to appreciate the political importance of German-Italian collaboration, but serious concerns remained over Germany's treatment of Catholics, especially any infringements of the Concordat. The Pope's recent encyclical had only magnified these fears.

Hassell was still not convinced that Germany could rely on Italy's friendship if it came to war. For this reason, he argued that the British government remained an extremely desirable ally in terms of the future aims of German foreign policy. Should there be any conflict between the British and the Italians in the Mediterranean it would be sensible for Germany not to commit to either side in advance.[41]

On 15 April Edvard Beneš, the President of Czechoslovakia, told Ernst Eisenlohr, the German ambassador to Czechoslovakia, that while his country wanted to come to an understanding with Germany, it still needed support from other nations to maintain its independence, otherwise it would become a mere vassal of Germany. Beneš added that he was trying to do all he could to solve the problems experienced by the Sudeten German minority.[42]

Józef Lipski, the Polish ambassador to Germany, met Neurath at the Foreign Ministry on 17 April. Lipski wanted to know if any progress had been made on the Western Pact following the recent memoranda circulated by Germany and Italy. Neurath told Lipski that the British government seemed in no hurry to move things forward. Lipski then turned to recent press speculation abroad that Germany and the Soviet Union were about to come to some kind of agreement. There was no truth in these rumours whatsoever, Neurath said, and they were probably invented by the Czechoslovakian government.[43]

On that same day Neurath circulated advice to German diplomats about the 'use of the German salute abroad'. This was clearly in response to Ribbentrop's gaffe earlier in the year. The instruction advised that provided the salute could 'be given without causing offence, it is to be used on official occasions by representatives of the Reich and [diplomatic] missions abroad'. In each country, however, use of the Hitler salute was to be settled 'in accordance with existing regulations and customs'. Henceforth, Ribbentrop ceased to use the Nazi salute in front of the British king and bowed instead.[44]

On 19 April Hitler had a meeting at the Reich Chancellery with George Lansbury, the former leader of the British Labour Party. Lansbury, a Christian pacifist, wanted Hitler to attend a peace conference involving all the major world powers, including the United States. Hitler's interpreter Paul Schmidt observed of Lansbury: 'One could tell from his eloquent exposition how enthusiastic he was, but most of the time I noticed Hitler's thoughts were elsewhere.'[45] Hitler gave no indication that he would attend such a conference and saw Lansbury as of little political importance. Lansbury commented of his meeting with Hitler:

> He is simple and clear cut, as was Lenin, and sure he is right, as was Lenin, and as determined to stand by German independence. He is ruthless and quite cynical, with everything that seems to stand in his way. He will not go to war unless pushed into it by others. He is a good conversationalist and did not monopolize more time than I did.[46]

Lansbury's visit became a source of satire. Hugh Kingsmill's end-of-year satirical book *1938: A Pre-View of Next Year's News* imagined a meeting between Lansbury and 'Migs Carlo', an American serial killer, after which Lansbury says: 'I think that talk has cleared the air. There is a long way to go, but Mr Carlo and I found ourselves in substantial agreement on a number of topics.'[47]

During his state visit to Italy Kurt Schuschnigg, the Chancellor of Austria, met Mussolini on 22 April. He asked him about reports in the British and French press stating Italy was weighing up its options between supporting Hitler's desire for an *Anschluss* (the union of Austria and Germany) or the restoration of the Habsburg monarchy, which was Schuschnigg's preference. Mussolini dismissed these reports and tried to reassure Schuschnigg that although the Rome–Berlin Axis was important to him, he would support Austrian independence should Austrian Nazis try to mount another coup, just as he had when they had assassinated Dollfuss in 1934.[48]

On 24 April the British and French issued a joint communiqué to the Belgian government promising to 'defend the frontiers of Belgium [...] against any aggression or invasion and to prevent Belgian territory from being used, for the purposes of aggression against another state'. Belgium was also released from any obligations under the Locarno Treaty.[49]

On the following day the *Luftwaffe* Condor League, supported by the Italian Legionary Air Force, bombed and destroyed much of the Basque city of Guernica in northern Spain. This shocking event showed the world what civilian populations could expect if there were another war. Initially, the Basque government estimated the death toll as being 1,654, although more recent studies suggest a more realistic figure of 153. The German government denied that the *Luftwaffe* had carried out the attack and tried to pin the blame on Basque nationalists, but there is little doubt that the *Luftwaffe* played a key role in the air raid, deploying forty-three bombers.[50] On 28 May *The Times* directly implicated the *Luftwaffe* in the attack in a report entitled 'The Tragedy of Guernica' by the war correspondent George Steer.[51] The Germans reacted angrily. 'The German Press has been savage about *The Times*, in fact, worse than at any period I can remember,' said H. G. Daniels, a *Times* correspondent in Berlin. 'The latest discovery is that if you spell it backwards it spells SEMIT, which leads them to deduce we are a Jewish-Marxist organization.'[52]

On 29 April Hitler gave a speech to 3,000 specially selected future Nazi leaders at the opening of an elite political education academy at Vogelsang Castle in the Rhineland. Speaking more frankly than he did in his public addresses, he said that he would not tolerate any authority above the nation, not even the church. Democratic countries produced 'soft' and 'worthless' individuals all pulling in different directions: 'Only the Jew could have thought up and introduced such idiocy.' As for the Nazi leaders of the future, Hitler wanted them to be appointed solely on merit: 'It matters not who their fathers are, what their mothers were.' On his own style of leadership, he commented: 'I always go to the very brink of boldness, but never beyond it.'[53]

The new British ambassador Sir Nevile Henderson arrived at the British Embassy in Wilhelmstraße in Berlin on 30 April, replacing Sir Eric Phipps, who became the British ambassador to France. Henderson's previous diplomatic posting was British ambassador to Argentina. Robert Vansittart, the anti-Nazi Permanent Undersecretary for Foreign Affairs, had proposed Henderson for the job and Anthony Eden had approved the appointment, without either looking very closely into Henderson's political views.[54]

Ribbentrop told Hitler that Henderson was a close friend of the Rothschild banking family and probably 'an agent of World Jewry'.[55] This was nonsense, although some in the British government were worried about Henderson's appointment for a very different reason. 'I hope we are not sending another Ribbentrop to Berlin,' Eden's Private Secretary Oliver Harvey wrote in his diary.[56] He was right to be concerned, as Eden later recalled: 'It was an international misfortune that we should have been represented in Berlin at this time by a man who, so far from warning the Nazis, was constantly making excuses for them, often in their company.'[57]

Hitler spoke, as usual, at the huge May Day celebrations in Berlin. He said the chief aim of the Four-Year Plan was to ensure that the German people had the necessities of life in the future. 'I am, after all, a child of the people,' he continued, 'and I do not come from some castle but from a working-class family.' At the same time, however, the German people 'must be prepared to obey orders'. He warned church leaders to limit themselves to religious matters. If they wrote letters and 'encyclicals' claiming rights that trespassed upon those of the state, 'we shall force them to return to the realm of spiritual and pastoral activities where they belong'. Nor was it appropriate 'for them to criticize the morality of the state when they have more than enough reason to worry about their own morals'.[58]

Neurath, the German Foreign Minister, made an official visit to Rome between 3 and 6 May. He learned that Mussolini was of the opinion that Italy and Germany had already made enough sacrifices in the ongoing Spanish Civil War. Unless Franco tackled the war much more vigorously, Mussolini planned to withdraw Italy's support.

The conversation then turned to Austria and the recent visit to Italy of Kurt Schuschnigg, the Austrian Chancellor. When Mussolini mentioned that Schuschnigg had favoured restoring the Habsburg monarchy, Neurath rejected the idea as 'totally unacceptable'. Mussolini agreed such a move would spell the end of Austria, but he failed to mention promising Schuschnigg that Italy would help protect Austrian independence in the event of a German attack. Mussolini assured Neurath he had told Schuschnigg to drop his hostility towards Austrian Nazis, but once again this was a lie. Neurath wanted to know if Mussolini had been consulted about the Anglo-French declaration to uphold Belgian neutrality. Mussolini said he had not been consulted. Neurath noted that Mussolini had 'spoken bitterly' of British Foreign Secretary Anthony Eden's determination to sideline Italy in any discussions with France and Belgium on matters of European security.[59]

Meanwhile, some influential British appeasers continued to portray Hitler's foreign policy aims in a favourable light. In January 1935, for instance, the British Liberal peer Lord Lothian had written a letter to *The Times* observing that 'The central fact in Europe today is that Germany does not want war.'[60] Now, on 4 May 1937, Lothian visited Hitler in Berlin, where he found the Führer in a very angry mood. The British are incapable of recognizing the communist peril, Hitler said.

He told Lothian he remained pro-British and thought a war between the two countries would be useless, but he was becoming increasingly disheartened by the negative attitude of the British government and the press towards Germany.[61]

Upon his return to Britain Lord Lothian avoided mentioning Hitler's anti-British rant. Instead, he put a positive spin on Anglo-German relations, arguing in the May edition of *Nineteenth Century and After* that 'Germany's demands were not unreasonable and there were possibilities for a settlement in Eastern Europe with an *Anschluss* of Austria, and with special rights for German minorities in Poland and Czechoslovakia'.[62]

The German rigid airship the *Hindenburg* was a beacon of German aeronautical technology. Not only could it cross the Atlantic in half the time of the fastest ocean liner, but it offered luxury travel in comfortable cabins, a first-class restaurant and a cocktail and piano bar. After a flight from Frankfurt on 6 May, however, while attempting to dock with its mooring mast at Naval Air Station Lakehurst in New Jersey, the *Hindenburg* burst into flames and crashed. The probable cause of the huge fireball was a hydrogen leak. The disaster killed 35 people (13 passengers and 22 crew), but 62 of the 97 on board miraculously survived. One worker on the ground was also killed. The victims were given the sort of lavish, high-profile funerals more usually reserved for fallen war heroes. The German press suspected sabotage, but there is no evidence for this claim. An eyewitness claims to have heard a gunshot before the airship exploded, and in *Who Destroyed the Hindenburg?* (1962) Adolph A. Hoehling suggests that Eric Spehl, a German crew member who died in the fire, was the culprit. Spehl is supposed to have opposed Hitler's regime and had a communist girlfriend, but the evidence remains doubtful.[63]

The second anniversary of the signing of the Franco-Soviet Treaty of Mutual Assistance came around and the Soviet press expressed its disappointment with the current state of relations between the two countries. As Friedrich von Schulenburg, the German ambassador to the Soviet Union, made clear in a memorandum to Neurath on 10 May, the Soviets were annoyed about the failure of the French government to move towards greater military collaboration. According to the Soviet newspaper *Pravda*, France and Britain seemed more willing to negotiate with the aggressor powers (meaning Germany and Italy) rather than upholding the principles of collective security. The mood in the Soviet Union was that the USSR was strong enough to defend its own frontiers without the aid of France, and that in the event of war the Franco-Soviet Treaty was of more use to France than the Soviet Union.[64]

The new British ambassador Sir Nevile Henderson presented his official seals of office to Hitler in the Reich Chancellery on 11 May. He found Hitler in a very sullen mood. After reading out a prepared speech of friendship, Henderson offered his personal condolences for the loss of the *Hindenburg*. Hitler told him that he suspected sabotage, because 'there had been several warning letters before the departure of the *Hindenburg*'.[65]

In Britain the Coronation of George VI took place at Westminster Abbey on 12 May. Field Marshal Werner von Blomberg was Germany's representative. On the following day he met the Prime Minister at 10 Downing Street. Baldwin told Blomberg that he had always been fond of Germany and even studied German at school. He wanted a close friendship between their two nations and said that it would be a catastrophe if they went to war again. Blomberg responded by saying that Hitler also desired friendly relations with Britain.[66]

Later that day Blomberg met Eden at the Foreign Office. Eden was dismayed that the negotiations on the Western Pact had stalled. He felt that even if Germany could not accept the League of Nations as an arbitrator, it would also not be satisfactory to leave it to either Britain or Italy to decide whether or not to intervene in the event of an aggression. Blomberg replied that he was certain a Western Pact could be concluded despite these points of disagreement. He then raised the question of the German colonies, suggesting that their return was a matter of economic necessity. Eden avoided answering this question.[67]

On 14 May Blomberg met the Chancellor of the Exchequer (and soon to be the Prime Minister) Neville Chamberlain, who, although friendly, adopted a rather cool and reserved attitude during their conversation. Chamberlain reiterated the very strong desire in Britain for improved Anglo-German relations. Blomberg felt that the atmosphere between the two nations would be greatly improved if certain sections of British public opinion abandoned the notion that Germany was cold-bloodedly planning war. Similarly, he said, there was no need for Germany and France to be at odds, except over the Franco-Soviet Treaty. Chamberlain agreed that the treaty was an 'unnecessary complication to the European situation', but he also noted that France 'needed to be convinced it had nothing to fear from Germany'.[68]

[overleaf] The German airship *Hindenburg* catching fire and exploding just before landing at Lakenhurst, New Jersey USA on 6 May 1937."

In a speech before 500 priests at the Quigley Seminary in Chicago on 18 May Cardinal George Mundelein criticized Nazi propaganda against the Catholic Church and denounced the show trials in Germany of priests, monks and teachers on what he called 'trumped-up' sex charges. Mundelein then called Goebbels 'crooked' and described Hitler as 'an Austrian [wall]paper-hanger and a poor one I'm told'. He concluded that Hitler's rise to power could only mean that the 'brains of 60 million Germans had been removed without them knowing it'.[69]

Hitler was deeply outraged by the cardinal's speech, which was widely reported in the German press and abroad. On 29 May he instructed the German chargé d'affaires in Rome to present a note of protest to the Vatican Holy See, describing the speech as deeply insulting. The Vatican was urged to publicly 'distance itself from the unfortunate remarks of the cardinal, correct these and express regret over the incident'. Since no such statement had yet been issued, the German government concluded that the Vatican approved of his derogatory comments.[70]

On 21 May Ribbentrop sent a report to Neurath on the Coronation of George VI. During his conversations with Eden, Ribbentrop felt that the British Foreign Secretary had maintained his generally negative attitude towards Germany, but talks between Blomberg and Chamberlain left the impression that Chamberlain would lead on foreign policy much more than Baldwin ever had.[71] By now, Ribbentrop began to realize he had failed as German ambassador to Britain, both politically and socially. His time in London convinced him an Anglo-German alliance would never happen because British policy was too closely allied to France.[72] 'Ribbentrop talked of England,' Goebbels noted in his diary. 'There is not much to be done with the English right now. England does not share our position and we do not share hers. So be it.'[73]

On 22 May *Le Journal de Paris* published an interview with Adolf Hitler by the French poet, novelist and politician Abel Bonnard, a member of the Académie française. The discussion focused on Nazi policies aimed at improving the lives of German workers. Hitler spoke of the importance of his labour organization 'Strength through Joy' (*Kraft durch Freude* or the KdF). 'All in all, I say, a human being ought to be understood in his soul, as in his profession,' Hitler told Bonnard, 'so that he can arrive at a better understanding of his essence, as reflected in his work and his personality. It is not merely a question of building each citizen a house, one also needs a light to shine inside of it.' It was

The coffins of the German victims of the *Hindenburg* disaster lying in state in New York.

wrong to suggest that the German people lived under a dictatorship, he said. 'A government like ours could never stay in power without the will of the people to support it. The German *Volk* stands behind me because it knows that I truly care about its spiritual problems and advocate its concerns.'[74]

In Britain soon after the Coronation of George VI, Stanley Baldwin resigned and Neville Chamberlain became the new Prime Minister, at the age of sixty-eight, on 27 May. He was born in Birmingham on 18 March 1869, the eldest son of Joseph Chamberlain, the famous Liberal-Conservative radical and imperialist. His half-brother Austen was the British Foreign Secretary who had helped to negotiate the Locarno Treaty. Neville became Lord Mayor of Birmingham in 1915, but his career in national politics began in 1918 when he was elected as Conservative MP for Birmingham Ladywood.

Chamberlain's career was helped by the fall of Prime Minister David Lloyd George in 1922, because Lloyd George had disliked him (he once begrudgingly described Chamberlain as 'Not a bad Lord Mayor of Birmingham in a bad year'). It was Stanley Baldwin who aided Chamberlain's rapid rise from the backbenches. He appointed him to the cabinet as Minister of Health between 1924 and 1929, then as Chancellor of the Exchequer from 1931 to 1937. In fact, Chamberlain was credited with dragging the British economy out of the economic depression of the 1930s.

Chamberlain was thin with greying hair and a thick moustache. He wore tailored suits and starched collars and always carried an umbrella outdoors. In person, he was shy and serious, seldom flippant or light-hearted. His nickname, although nobody said it to his face, was 'The Coroner'. He chose his friends and political allies with care. His hobbies were solitary ones: walking his dog, angling and birdwatching.

Chamberlain is remembered as a weak and cowardly politician, but in fact he was strong-willed, intelligent and extremely determined. Few British prime ministers have dominated their cabinets with such supreme managerial skill. The minutes of the British cabinet from 1937 to 1939 reveal how persuasive Chamberlain could be when it came to convincing ministers to follow his lead. Furthermore, Chamberlain always based his foreign policy on detailed reports produced by the chiefs of national defence and various defence committees. He believed international differences could be solved through face-to-face negotiations. Above all, he believed that 'war wins nothing, cures nothing and ends nothing'. He considered the French government and

Poster offering leisure trips with the Labour Front organization 'Strength Through Joy' (*Kraft Durch Freude*).

Wandere mit Kraft durch Freude

Auskunft gibt dir:

FISCHER
-RHEIN

military chiefs to be unreliable and the United States government as hopelessly wedded to isolationism. As a firm anti-communist, he ruled out any British alliance with the Soviet Union. At the same time, he could see that the League of Nations had failed in the past to prevent war and to protect the victims of war. His ideal was for Britain to act as a mediator between nations in order to create a new system of non-aggression pacts which would replace the Locarno Treaty.

On 29 May the German heavy cruiser *Deutschland* was attacked by Spanish Republican and Soviet bombers, while anchored off Ibiza: thirty-one sailors were killed. At the time the *Deutschland* had been engaged in patrols around the Republican-held coast of Spain, as agreed by the Non-Intervention Committee. Two days later Hitler held a meeting with the naval leader Erich Raeder, as well as Minister of War Blomberg, with Göring and Neurath also present. It was agreed that in retaliation for the bombing of the *Deutschland*, the German heavy cruiser *Admiral Scheer* would shell the Republican-held city of Almería. Twenty-one civilians died and thirty-nine houses were destroyed in this incident.[75] In a further protest at the attack on the *Deutschland*, Germany walked out of the Non-Intervention Committee.

On 1 June the British ambassador to Germany Henderson made what was described at the time as a 'diplomatic gaffe', but which he later referred to as a 'calculated indiscretion'. As the guest of honour at a dinner of the *Deutsch-Englische Gesellschaft* – the German equivalent of the Anglo-German Fellowship, a membership organization designed to improve relations between Britain and Germany – Henderson gave a speech in which he said that were it not for their misconception of the Nazi regime, the British people 'would lay much less stress on Nazi dictatorship and much more emphasis on the great social experiment which is being carried out in the country. Not only would they criticize less, but they might learn some useful lessons.' His high praise for Hitler's social reforms provoked outrage in the British press, with Henderson earning the nickname 'Our Nazi ambassador at Berlin'.[76]

Blomberg began a three-day visit to Italy on 2 June to discuss German-Italian military ties. Mussolini's government, keen to impress the famous German Field Marshal, put on a lavish pageant of Italian military history. On a boat trip to Capri, Blomberg's enthusiastic praise for George VI's lavish coronation greatly annoyed Mussolini. Italian feathers were also ruffled when Blomberg said that he had no wish to comment on the quality of the Italian army. 'No one asked him to make such a judgement,' Ciano later observed. 'We have proved ourselves on too many battlefields to have need of approval and recommendation even from Marshal Blomberg.'[77]

On 6 June in a speech to 200,000 party members at a rally in Regensburg, Hitler emphasized his firm belief in God, but also promised that 'I will never allow anyone to tear this *Volk* asunder, to reduce it to a heap of religious camps.' Germany would go into the future with 'the deepest belief in God'. His political achievements would not have been possible without God's help: 'I know the fruits of human labour are hard won and transitory if not blessed by the Almighty. Work such as ours which has received the blessing of the Almighty can never be undone by mere mortals.'[78]

The French government finally produced a memorandum on the proposal for a new Western Pact on 10 June. It began by stating that the Locarno Treaty guaranteed the frontiers between France and Germany, and Germany and Belgium, giving special status to the demilitarized Rhineland, a zone which had now disappeared. The French government did not think it would be right for any of the signatories to a new pact to give up their right to act against aggression under the Covenant of the League of Nations. It was agreed that the Treaty of Locarno was a simple guarantee system. The French government proposed that any new pact should be just as straightforward. What was needed was a new Locarno for Western Europe, but the Council of the League of Nations should be the arbitrator of any new agreement.[79]

The German government felt that the French memorandum showed they wanted a revised Locarno Pact, with the League of Nations acting as arbitrator, but retaining the right to act on its own if it felt there was a flagrant case of aggression by any one of the signatories. In other words, the French government wanted to be able to meet any act of aggression without being hampered by any of the terms of a new treaty.[80] All of these various memoranda produced by Britain, France, Germany and Italy concerning a new security pact had revealed one thing: how widely different were their aims and intentions and the extreme difficulty of coming to any new arrangement on the security of Europe.

Relations between Germany and Britain had cooled by now. On 19 June a letter from Neurath informed Henderson, the British ambassador, that he would not be accepting his invitation of an official visit to London. Two days later, Henderson met Hitler, who was 'still in an emotional state over the dead German sailors' on the *Deutschland*, whose funeral he had recently attended at Wilhelmshaven. Henderson pleaded with Hitler to allow Neurath's visit to London to go ahead, but the Führer 'refused to listen to any of my logical arguments', Henderson later recalled, 'and persisted in the standpoint that he could not for a moment permit his Foreign Minister to leave Germany'. Henderson was convinced that a jealous Ribbentrop had persuaded Hitler to veto Neurath's visit, because he regarded it as 'detrimental to his own prestige and wounding to his personal vanity'.[81]

At this time the German army was considering the 'possibility' of military aggression against Austria and Czechoslovakia. On 24 June Blomberg drew up a 'top secret' memorandum entitled: 'Directive for the Unified Preparation of the Armed Forces for War'. Only five copies of this document were typed. Blomberg stated that Germany could rule out the possibility of a pre-emptive attack by the Western Powers or the Soviet Union, because they had no desire for war and were not prepared for it. Germany had no intention of launching a war either, he added. Nevertheless, Blomberg went on to argue that in the period 1937–8 the German armed forces must be ready to exploit any 'favourable opportunities' that arose and also to plan for all eventualities. Germany was assumed to have no definite allies in any of these scenarios.

Blomberg then outlined two possible future wars: (1) war in Europe on two fronts, with the main struggle in the West (Case Red) or (2) war on two fronts, but the main conflict located in Southeast Europe (Case Green). In the first scenario it was suggested that France might stage a surprise attack in the West. The second possibility was a war in Eastern Europe, beginning with a surprise German attack on Czechoslovakia. In this Case Green scenario a pretext was required to justify such an attack. Any Czechoslovakian resistance would be eliminated quickly and the country occupied.

Blomberg outlined three other possible situations which required 'special preparation' by the German armed forces: (1) Case Otto: a German armed intervention in Austria should the Austrian government seek a restoration of the Habsburg monarchy. (2) Case Richard: war in Spain should the Republicans defeat General Franco. It was suggested that only the German navy would be heavily involved in such a conflict. (3) Case Red/Green: Britain, Lithuania and Poland join a war against Germany. In Blomberg's view, every effort should be made to prevent Britain from joining or forming a coalition against Germany.[82]

At a rally in Würzburg on 27 June Hitler delivered another surprisingly religious speech, again stressing the divine nature of National Socialism: 'And when I look back on the five years behind us, I cannot help but say: this has not been the work of man alone.' Had Providence not guided the German people, he added, 'I surely would often have been unable to follow these dizzying paths. That is something our critics above all should know. At the bottom of our hearts, we National Socialists are devout! We have no choice; no one can make national and world history if his deeds are not blessed by Providence.'[83]

In reality, however, the Catholic Church remained an irritant for Hitler and he was also losing patience with the rebel clerics of the Protestant Confessing Church. One of his most vocal critics was the high-profile Lutheran pastor Martin Niemöller. Niemöller was an unlikely and largely accidental Nazi opponent. In the 1920s he had strong nationalist leanings and even welcomed Hitler's coming to power, because of his strong anti-communist stance. However, when the fiercely pro-Nazi German Christian movement tried to Nazify the Protestant Church, Niemöller formed the Pastors' Emergency League in September 1933. In May 1934 these rebellious pastors issued a declaration of principles at Barmen rejecting any attempt to merge Nazism with existing Lutheran religious practices.

Hitler soon came to the conclusion that Nazifying the Protestant Church was politically unworkable. He fell out with and sidelined the Reich Bishop of the German Evangelical Church, Ludwig Müller, and in 1935 he appointed the Nazi lawyer Hanns Kerrl as Reichsminister of Church Affairs, in order to win the loyalty of Protestant clerics and bring an end to the 'Church Conflict', which was now being widely reported in the foreign

Martin Niemöller, the Lutheran pastor who opposed Hitler's church policy.

press. Kerrl established local committees to mediate in conflicts within the Protestant Church, but he also ordered the Gestapo to keep under close surveillance the remaining rebel pastors.

During the summer of 1937 there was a Gestapo crack down on the Confessing church and around 700 pastors were taken into custody. Undeterred, Niemöller made ever more critical speeches about the Nazification of church policy. During a sermon on 19 June he read out the names of the pastors who had been forbidden to speak or removed from their parishes or placed under arrest, and he said defiantly: 'The Gospel must remain the Gospel; the Church must remain the Church. The creed must remain the creed. Protestant Christianity must remain Protestant Christianity.'[84]

Hitler was no longer willing to tolerate such outspoken comments. Niemöller was arrested at his home on the morning of 1 July, then sent to Moabit Prison and kept in solitary confinement. He was later transferred to the Sachsenhausen concentration camp. 'I was not pleased with being cut off in this way,' he later recalled, 'and suddenly not knowing any more what was happening with the Church.'[85]

The pastor's arrest made headlines around the world, but it was downplayed in Germany. 'Pastor Niemöller finally arrested,' Goebbels noted in his diary. 'Small mention of this in the [German] press. The thing is now to break him, so he can't believe his eyes and ears. We must never let up.'[86] In spite of Hitler's long-standing animosity towards the Christian churches, they remained the only domestic institutions in Germany to escape deep penetration by Nazi ideology. Hitler decided that the subjugation of the church would have to follow a major victory in war.

British Foreign Secretary Anthony Eden produced yet another memorandum on the faltering idea of a new Western Pact on 16 July. It attempted to draw together the various suggestions expressed in previous memoranda by Belgium, France, Germany and Italy. Eden suggested a five-power conference was required to conclude any final agreement. Despite considerable differences of opinion, in his view there were enough 'elements of agreement' to suggest that the following principles should underpin the new security agreement: (1) undertakings of non-aggression. (2) promises to come to the assistance of others in the event of violation. (3) a clear definition of what cases of aggression constituted violation, which should be a matter for impartial international judgement. (4) the provision that signatories could go to the immediate assistance of a signatory subjected to aggression where immediate action was necessary. Until a new agreement was reached it would be best to adhere to the existing Locarno Treaty.[87]

On 19 July Hitler opened the new House of German Art (Haus der Deutschen Kunst) in the Prinzregentenstraße in Munich. This impressive gallery was constructed following the plans of Hitler's favourite architect Paul Ludwig Troost (who had died in 1934) and was financed by public donations. The grand opening was preceded by a huge parade through the streets of the city, with floats depicting 2,000 years of German culture. The new gallery housed 'Blood and Soil' Nazi art depicting scenes of peasant life, breast-feeding mothers, square-jawed peasants and Teutonic warriors on horseback.

Hitler used the occasion to deliver one of his longest speeches on the role of art in Nazi Germany. He denounced modern art as 'un-German' and 'degenerate'. Modernism had flourished during the Weimar years, but Hitler would stamp it out, he promised. His House of German Art would display only 'classic' German art and it would encourage new art that reflected upon what it meant 'to be German'. The art of the new Reich, Hitler said, was neither ancient nor modern, but simply German: 'Just as the essence and blood of our *Volk* does not change, so must art too dispose of its transient character.' There would be no place in German art galleries for 'international art', which he described as 'decadent, Bolshevik and Jewish art, full of distortion and ugliness'. Above all, it was Hitler's 'inalterable decision' to wipe out from the discourse of German art all those modish catchwords such as 'inner experience', 'strong cast of mind' and 'primal crudeness', which he dismissed as 'stupid, false excuses, phrases and prattles'.[88]

In parallel with the Great German Art exhibition at the House of German Art, a second state-sponsored exhibition entitled 'Degenerate Art' (*Entartete Kunst*) opened nearby, on the Hofgarten parade. The intention was to hold up modern art to public ridicule. More than 650 modern paintings and sculptures – all of them banned from exhibition since 1933 – were gathered together from the storage rooms of German art galleries. There were works by, among others, Henri Matisse, Paul Klee, Pablo Picasso, Marc Chagall and Otto Dix. The exhibition was divided into nine sections, with derogatory subtitles poking fun at the paintings.

Much to the embarrassment of the Nazi organizers, the Degenerate Art exhibition drew three times as many people as the Great German Art exhibition. Goebbels even tried to suggest that the exhibition's popularity was in fact an expression of the loyal German public's

[*overleaf*]   Hitler visiting the opening of the House of German Art (*Haus Der Deutschen Kunst*).

outrage towards modern art. In the autumn the Degenerate Art exhibition went on a nationwide tour of twelve German cities.[89]

On 20 July Eden asked Henderson to seek an interview with Göring to ask him to explain why in a recent speech he had said that he now regarded Britain 'as an enemy in Germany's path'. Göring agreed to meet Henderson at his country estate just outside Berlin, but he was unable to provide Henderson with any specific examples of how Britain was acting in a hostile manner towards Germany.

The discussion quickly moved on to the current international scene. Göring complained that Britain's allegiance to the League of Nations made it oblivious to the real difficulties that Germany had in finding new outlets for the expansion of its food supplies and its growing population.

Their conversation turned to Austria. Göring insisted that the *Anschluss* was 'inevitable' and if a referendum were held tomorrow, more than 80 per cent of Austrians would vote for union with Germany. In

Hitler visiting the exhibition of Degenerative Art with Joseph Goebbels *(front)*.

fact, he admitted he had recently told Guido Schmidt, the Austrian Foreign Minister, that the sooner the Austrian government accepted the *Anschluss*, the better. Göring felt the complaints of the ethnic Germans in the Sudetenland could not be ignored either. If Britain truly wanted an Anglo-German understanding it had to recognize Germany's territorial claims in Austria and Czechoslovakia. If it did not, Germany would continue to advance its claim for a return of the colonies. The British public seemed to support improved Anglo-German relations, Göring noted, but British politicians were 'generally hostile'.[90]

Hitler began taking up the cause of ethnic Germans in his speeches. On 31 July Hitler addressed a crowd of 500,000 at a traditional German singing and music festival in Breslau. German-speakers from abroad were also in attendance. Hitler told the audience there were 95 million German-speakers in Europe and 33 per cent of them did not enjoy the privilege of living within the current borders of the German Reich. The German anthem *'Deutschland über alles'* was a rallying cry for ethnic Germans throughout Europe, he said. They all sought 'a connection to the Reich' and this anthem helped to establish this bond: 'We who are gathered here today from all the German lands, from many territories outside the Reich, we all perceive ourselves as one community. You are the singers and thus the spokesmen of the German nation.'[91]

On that same day back in Berlin Neurath sent a circular to the German embassies in Belgium, Britain, France, Italy and the Netherlands, as well as to the German consul in Geneva, outlining the official German government view of Eden's memorandum of 16 July. It stated Eden had wrongly assumed there was 'far-reaching agreement' on matters of principle related to the Western Pact. There was, Neurath argued, no unity at all, as was clear from the contents of all the other memoranda on the issue. The French government had not modified its position at all. There was no agreement either on which impartial, international decision-making body would arbitrate in the event of aggression by any of the signatories. The German and Italian governments had firmly rejected the idea that the League of Nations should have any involvement in a new Western Pact. The British government was therefore proceeding from the erroneous assumption that the basic principles outlined by Eden in his memorandum represented any commonly agreed view.[92]

Meanwhile there was growing dissatisfaction with how Hitler's government was being portrayed in the British press. *The Times*'s coverage of the destruction of Guernica by German bombers and the Nazification of the church were underlying factors in the decision to expel Norman Ebbutt, the newspaper's Berlin correspondent, on 9 August, although the official justification was that this was retaliation for the deportation from Britain of three German journalists suspected of espionage. Ebbutt was an old-fashioned liberal and convinced anti-Nazi, which made him a thorn in the side of the German government.

On 4 September the *Daily Mail* published a letter from Hitler to the newspaper's owner Lord Rothermere. 'I am no new advocate of Anglo-German understanding,' Hitler wrote in a fresh attempt to woo the British public. 'I have made between four and five thousand speeches, yet there is no single speech of mine, nor any line I have written, in which I have expressed anything contrary to this concept or against an Anglo-German understanding. Such an agreement between England and Germany would represent the weight and influence for peace and common sense of 120 million of the most valuable people in the world.'[93]

Between 6 and 13 September the Nazi Party's annual Nuremberg Rally took place. This year it was called the 'Rally of Labour' to celebrate the reduction of unemployment from 6 million in 1933 to less than 1 million in 1937. Hitler's opening proclamation highlighted the social achievements of his rule: 'The way in which we in National Socialist Germany direct all our efforts towards the solution of social problems is a contribution towards the education of our individual fellow countrymen into a consciousness of social duty which at its final result will also produce the community of the people in the noblest sense of the word.'[94]

On 7 September, in a speech on 'culture', Hitler once again made a vehement attack on modern art, which he claimed had only flourished through 'clever and cunning Jewish cultural propaganda', supported by 'so-called art experts'. The Degenerate Art exhibition had shown the German public that there was nothing original in Weimar modern art: 'On the contrary,' he concluded, 'all of these so-called modern artists are the most pathetic and inept copyists of all time. Naturally, not copyists of what is decent, but of nonsense.'[95]

Hitler addressed Nazi Party leaders on 10 September. Present at this event was Nevile Henderson, the British ambassador, who later recalled:

[overleaf] The amazing Cathedral of Light, designed by Albert Speer, which featured at the Nuremberg rallies from 1934 to 1938.

Hitler himself arrived at the far entrance of the stadium, some 400 yards from the platform, accompanied by several hundred of his followers, marched on foot up the central passage to his appointed place. His arrival was theatrically notified by the sudden turning into the air of 300 or more searchlights with which the stadium was surrounded. The blue-tinged light from these met thousands of feet up in the sky at the top to make a kind of square roof, to which the chance cloud added realism. The effect, which was both solemn and beautiful, was like being inside a cathedral of ice.[96]

In the speech which followed Hitler said that the Nuremberg Rally was still the most splendid and emotional event of the year. It reminded him of his struggle as he rose to power: 'I am so pleased to have my old fighters before me again once a year. I always have the feeling that, as long as the human being has the gift of life, he should yearn for those with whom he has shaped his life.'[97]

In his closing address to the rally on 13 September Hitler concentrated on the international danger posed by Soviet Communism. Bolshevism, he said, was 'the brain-child of the Jews'. Western democracies would not accept the threat of Bolshevism despite it being the greatest menace the world had faced since the collapse of nations in antiquity. 'When I quite intentionally present this problem as Jewish,' he added, 'then you, my party comrades, know this is not an unverified assumption, but a fact proven by irrefutable evidence.' He went on to claim that the Soviet Union was a brutal dictatorship in which '80 per cent of the leading positions are held by Jews'.[98]

On the following day Franz von Papen, the German ambassador in Vienna, reported to Hitler about a recent meeting he had with Schuschnigg, the Austrian Chancellor. After noting that Schuschnigg continued to be extremely hostile towards National Socialism, Papen suggested that the possibility was 'open to us of forcing the resignation of the Schuschnigg government'. He also asked Hitler to discuss the current Austrian situation with Mussolini 'with complete frankness'.[99]

Mussolini and Hitler during an open topped limousine tour through Berlin.

Between 25 and 29 September Mussolini made his first official visit to Germany. His special train arrived at Munich's central station at 10 a.m. As Mussolini stepped on to the red-carpeted platform dressed in his newly tailored Fascist militia uniform, he was met by Hitler, dressed more simply in the military version of the Nazi Party uniform: brown peaked cap, brown tunic, white shirt and black trousers.

Mussolini was driven to Hitler's private Munich apartment, where the two leaders had a friendly, informal talk for an hour. Paul Schmidt, Hitler's interpreter, observed the two leaders at close quarters:

> Hitler did not sit upright at the table but leaned forward.
> When he became worked up the much-caricatured lock of
> long black hair fell over his receding forehead, giving him an
> untidy, Bohemian appearance. I noticed his coarse nose and
> undistinguished mouth, with its little moustache […] Mussolini
> was of a wholly different type. He stood firmly erect, swaying
> from the hips as he talked. His Caesarean head, with its powerful
> forehead and broad square chin thrust forward under a wide
> mouth, might easily have been modelled from the Romans of old.

His face bore a much more animated expression than Hitler's, when his turn came to thunder against the League of Nations. Indignation, contempt, determination, cunning lit up his highly mobile face.[100]

On the evening of 27 September, in a pre-rehearsed demonstration of Nazi efficiency, Hitler and Mussolini's special trains arrived simultaneously on opposite platforms at the Heerstraße Station in Berlin. Hitler's train was slightly speeded up to ensure that he arrived first to greet Mussolini. A grand dinner in the Reich Chancellery followed, then Hitler gave a speech, praising Mussolini as 'the brilliant creator of Fascist Italy'. In return, Il Duce described Hitler as a 'warrior' who had 'restored the German people to a consciousness of their own greatness'.[101]

The culmination of Il Duce's visit was a huge evening rally held at Berlin's Maifeld near the Olympic Stadium on 28 September. An estimated 1 million spectators were present. Mussolini delivered his speech in German, which was broadcast live simultaneously on German and Italian national radio. Halfway through, a torrential rainstorm soaked the microphones. Mussolini had difficulty reading the notes of his speech which were soaked in rain. The audience had little idea what he was saying, but one sentence was clear enough: 'The strength of our two countries constitutes the strongest guarantee for the preservation of a civilized Europe, true to its cultural mission and armed against destructive forces.'[102] Afterwards, Mussolini, now drenched to the skin, went on a motorcade through Berlin before cheering crowds.

Victor Klemperer saw a newsreel of Mussolini's visit at his local cinema:

> Mussolini's gesticulation and facial expressions [during his speech at the Maifeld] and his broken, barely comprehensible German were very amusing. The spectacular staging was terrific – but in the end it is exactly the same staging again and again: militarized masses and goose-stepping and laying wreaths and war games in support of peace. In the end, the effect is deadening – provided one is not aroused by it.[103]

Mussolini departed from Berlin's Lehrte Station on the afternoon of 29 September. He had been deeply impressed by the German efficiency and military power he had witnessed. As he watched Hitler wave goodbye to his guest, Goebbels observed: 'These two great men belong at each other's side.'[104] For his part, Hitler had been won over by

Mussolini, deciding that he was second only to himself as the greatest leader of the age. His admiration for Mussolini was now joined by a genuine warmth and affection for him.

Ulrich von Hassell prepared a memorandum detailing his conversations with Mussolini during his visit. Mussolini told the ambassador that he was now in agreement with Hitler on all subjects. Austria was a German country, Mussolini said, and it could never have a policy different from Germany, even though he wished to see Austrian independence maintained. He felt that Schuschnigg would be sensible enough to be guided by Germany. In reply, Hassell said that he doubted this and pointed out the fact that Schuschnigg was still refusing to include National Socialists in his government.[105]

Hitler attended the annual Reich Harvest Festival celebration in Bückeberg on 3 October. Once again, he invoked God as his guide:

> If we adhere to this path, decent, industrious and honest, if we
> do our duty bravely and loyally, it is my belief that the Lord
> will help us again and again in the future. He does not abandon
> decent people for any length of time. While He may sometimes
> put them to the test or send them trials, in the long run He will
> always allow His sun to shine upon them and ultimately give
> them His blessing.[106]

The former King Edward VIII, now the Duke of Windsor, began a controversial twelve-day 'private visit' to Germany on 11 October, accompanied by his new American wife, now a duchess. Still angry about his forced abdication in 1936, the royal duke wanted to publicly demonstrate his admiration for Hitler's regime and he refused to be prevented from doing so by the British Establishment. The Duke visited factories, as well as housing and public works projects, in the company of Robert Ley, the leader of the German Labour Front. He visited a German beer hall, drank with workers and joined in a singalong. Crowds cheered him wherever he went, as if he were still king. The visit of the Duke and Duchess of Windsor created a blaze of publicity inside Germany and around the world. They met key Nazi figures such as Göring, Goebbels, Hess and Himmler, and at a training school in Pomerania a reporter for the *New York Times* observed the Duke giving the Nazi salute, although the Duke later denied this.[107]

The Duke and Duchess of Windsor met Hitler at the Berghof on 22 October. The Duke expressed his admiration for the industrial, housing and social welfare arrangements he had seen during his visit. Paul Schmidt, who acted as interpreter, observed: 'In the conversa-

[overleaf] Hitler standing on the
train platform in Berlin before Mussolini
departs at the end of his state visit in
September 1937.

tion there was, so far as I could see, nothing to indicate whether the Duke of Windsor really sympathized with the ideology and practices of the Third Reich, as Hitler seemed to assume. After they left Hitler commented of the Duchess: "She would certainly have made a good Queen."'[108]

While this royal visit took place, the German government released a statement on 13 October making the following surprising promise: 'The German government considers that the inviolability and integrity of Belgium are common interests of the Western Powers. It confirms its determination that in no circumstances will it impair this inviolability and integrity, and that it will at all times respect Belgian territory.'[109] Once again, Hitler wanted the world to think that his intentions were peaceful.

On 5 November Kurt von Kamphoevener, a diplomat at the German Foreign Ministry, offered Neurath advice as to how best to deal with Eden's memorandum of 16 July. He reported that no further progress had been made on the Western Pact negotiations since then and that Belgium, France and Italy had no interest in adopting Eden's proposals. Kamphoevener felt that it was advisable to ask Ribbentrop to inform the British Foreign Office that the German government was holding back on replying to the memorandum, because it did not think the current discussions on the Western Pact would succeed while there was still conflict in the Far East and Spain.[110]

At 4.15 p.m. on that same day Hitler began a secret meeting with his leading military officers. Minister of War Werner von Blomberg was there; as well as Werner von Fritsch, commander-in-chief of the army; Hermann Göring, head of the *Luftwaffe* and overseer of the Four-Year Plan; and Erich Raeder, commander-in-chief of the navy. Foreign Secretary Konstantin von Neurath was also in attendance, along with Hitler's military assistant Friedrich Hossbach, who wrote up the minutes of the meeting, which then became a memorandum, dated 10 November 1937. The 'Hossbach Memorandum' would be a key document at the Nuremberg war trials, which aimed to prove that Hitler had a cold-blooded plan for an offensive and to escalate the war in Europe.[111]

The meeting, which lasted until 8.30 p.m., was ostensibly called to discuss problems of rearmament, because Germany's productive capacity was being overstretched with shortages of skilled labour and key raw materials, notably aluminium, iron, oil, rubber and steel. However, instead of discussing the allocation of raw materials between the different branches of the armed forces, Hitler delivered an extensive monologue on the future of German foreign policy.

He began by reaffirming his determination to acquire 'living space' (*Lebensraum*) in Eastern Europe. Everything else was subordinate to solving this problem. This differed little from Hitler's territorial aims as laid out in *Mein Kampf.* Achieving this had always been the key aim of his foreign policy. Hitler wanted everyone present to unite behind his vision of the future.

Only very limited self-sufficiency could be expected from the Four-Year Plan, Hitler told them. A re-engagement with the world economy was neither a viable solution nor an alternative, because it would restrain Germany's freedom of action. This was an attack on the Economic Minister Hjalmar Schacht's continuing desire to improve German exports. The return of the German colonies would be possible only when Germany was more powerful. Living space that could be developed for agricultural production was available only on the continent of Europe. The main question to be decided in Hitler's view was when and how Germany would apply military force to achieve this central foreign policy goal.

There were three possible scenarios that Hitler could foresee. It was his 'unalterable decision' to solve the problem of 'living space' in the period from 1943 to 1945 (Case 1), but if the opportunity arose beforehand – possibly because of a political crisis in France – then Germany should move to invade Austria and Czechoslovakia as early as 1938 (Case 2), or, if France became involved in war, most probably with Italy (Case 3). In all of these cases, the next German foreign policy moves would be against Austria and Czechoslovakia. The incorporation of Austria and Czechoslovakia into the Reich by military force would strengthen Germany's borders, he said, but it would also improve food supplies for 5 or 6 million Germans.

Hitler predicted that France and Britain – which he described as Germany's 'two worst enemies' – would naturally oppose his programme of territorial expansion. He was not frightened by either of them. The British Empire was 'rotting away', he said, while France had been weakened by internal division and political instability. He doubted whether Britain or France would do anything to prevent a German takeover in Austria or Czechoslovakia. He was certain that France would not act in either case without British support.

This was an important meeting. It was significant because Hitler had now put before his top military staff his immediate goal of territorial

[overleaf] The Duke and Duchess of Windsor standing with Hitler outside the Berghof on 11 October 1937.

expansion. He had also made clear that in order to achieve this aim he was ready and willing to engage in a war with Britain and France.[112]

A lengthy discussion followed. Blomberg, Fritsch and Neurath were taken aback by what amounted to a plan for a European war. It was not the long-term prospect of German aggression in Europe, at a time when Germany was fully ready, that bothered them, but they were not convinced that Germany would be militarily prepared to take on France and Britain as soon as 1938. Fritsch was so shocked that he asked Hitler if he should postpone a long-planned extended holiday to Egypt. Hitler said there was no need, because war was not imminent. Blomberg pointed out that the western fortifications designed to protect Germany from a French attack were not yet complete. Blomberg was a loyal admirer of Hitler, so his opposition was unusual. After all, as Henderson, the British ambassador, later recalled: 'Blomberg once said to me that if Hitler were to order him and his army to march the next day to the North Pole they would do it without a moment's hesitation.'[113] In his memoirs Hossbach noted that 'the discussions became quite heated' and it was obvious that Hitler was angry about the vehemence of the opposition.[114] Neurath later remembered that after the meeting he went to his office in the Foreign Ministry, where he became physically sick and called a doctor. It may have been the first of several mild heart attacks which he endured in the coming weeks.

Two days later Neurath ignored the oath of secrecy that Hitler had demanded and told Colonel Ludwig Beck about Hitler's plans for war.[115] Beck worried that attempting to annexe Austria and Czechoslovakia by force before rearmament was complete ran the risk of Germany ending up in a potentially catastrophic war with Britain and France.[116]

After being less than enthusiastic in the secret meeting, Blomberg quickly fell into line. On 7 December he issued the 'First Supplement on Unified Preparations for War of the *Wehrmacht* of 24 June 1937'. The original Case Red plan, which envisaged a pre-emptive, defensive strike against Czechoslovakia, was changed to Case Green and it stated that 'Once Germany has attained full war preparedness in all spheres, the military basis will have been created to conduct an offensive war against Czechoslovakia and thereby carry the German space problem [*Lebensraum*] to a triumphant conclusion, even if one or other great power intervenes against us.'[117]

Meanwhile, Ribbentrop, who had been sidelined during Mussolini's visit to Germany, but was head of the Ribbentrop Bureau, which Hitler often sanctioned to undertake diplomatic discussions independent of the German Foreign Ministry, opened talks with the Italian government in the hope that Italy might join the Anti-Comintern Pact concluded between Germany and Japan. When Neurath heard about this, he immediately contacted the Italian Foreign Minister Ciano (via Bernardo Attolico, the Italian ambassador in Berlin) to inform him that it would be unwise for Italy to join the pact, because it might have negative repercussions, especially from the British government. When Ribbentrop contacted Hitler, the Führer was supportive of his initiative, but he wanted Ribbentrop to keep Neurath informed of developments.

Ribbentrop arrived in Rome on 22 October. He met Ciano, who sought clarification as to whether a 'confidential' clause existed in Germany's agreement with Japan. Ribbentrop refused to admit to any secret protocols, respecting the Japanese government's insistence upon confidentiality. In the evening Ribbentrop met Mussolini, who confirmed that he was willing to join the agreement with Germany and Japan to protect their nations from attack by the Soviet Union. On 6 November Italy formally signed the Anti-Comintern Pact and Hitler sent Mussolini a letter congratulating him on his decision. As Ciano noted in his diary, although the Anti-Comintern Pact was 'anti-communist in theory' it was 'in fact unmistakably anti-British'.[118]

On 8 November Ribbentrop met Hitler in Munich during the annual commemoration of the Beer Hall Putsch of 1923. Ribbentrop expected to be congratulated on brokering Italy's entry into the Anti-Comintern Pact, but instead Hitler was furious with him. Ribbentrop had not kept Neurath fully informed of his discussions with the Italian government over the pact. Hitler had also heard rumours Ribbentrop was telling people that he was about to replace Neurath as his Foreign Minister. 'What do you think you are doing?' Hitler shouted. 'I will not tolerate such behaviour.' Ribbentrop was so upset by this response that he offered to resign. Hitler refused to accept his resignation and told him to return to his post in London.[119]

Lord Halifax, Lord President of the Council, a former Viceroy of India, and the Conservative Leader in the House of Lords, made a five-day visit to Germany in late November, primarily to attend a hunting exhibition in Berlin, which Halifax later described as 'a gruesomely Teutonic affair'. Before the trip, Prime Minister Chamberlain, aware the negotiations for a new Western Pact had stalled, asked Halifax to sound out Hitler on possible talks towards a general settlement of

[overleaf] The huge crowd gathered for Hitler's speech at Reich Harvest Thanksgiving Festival in Bückberg, near the ancient town of Hamelin, in 1937.

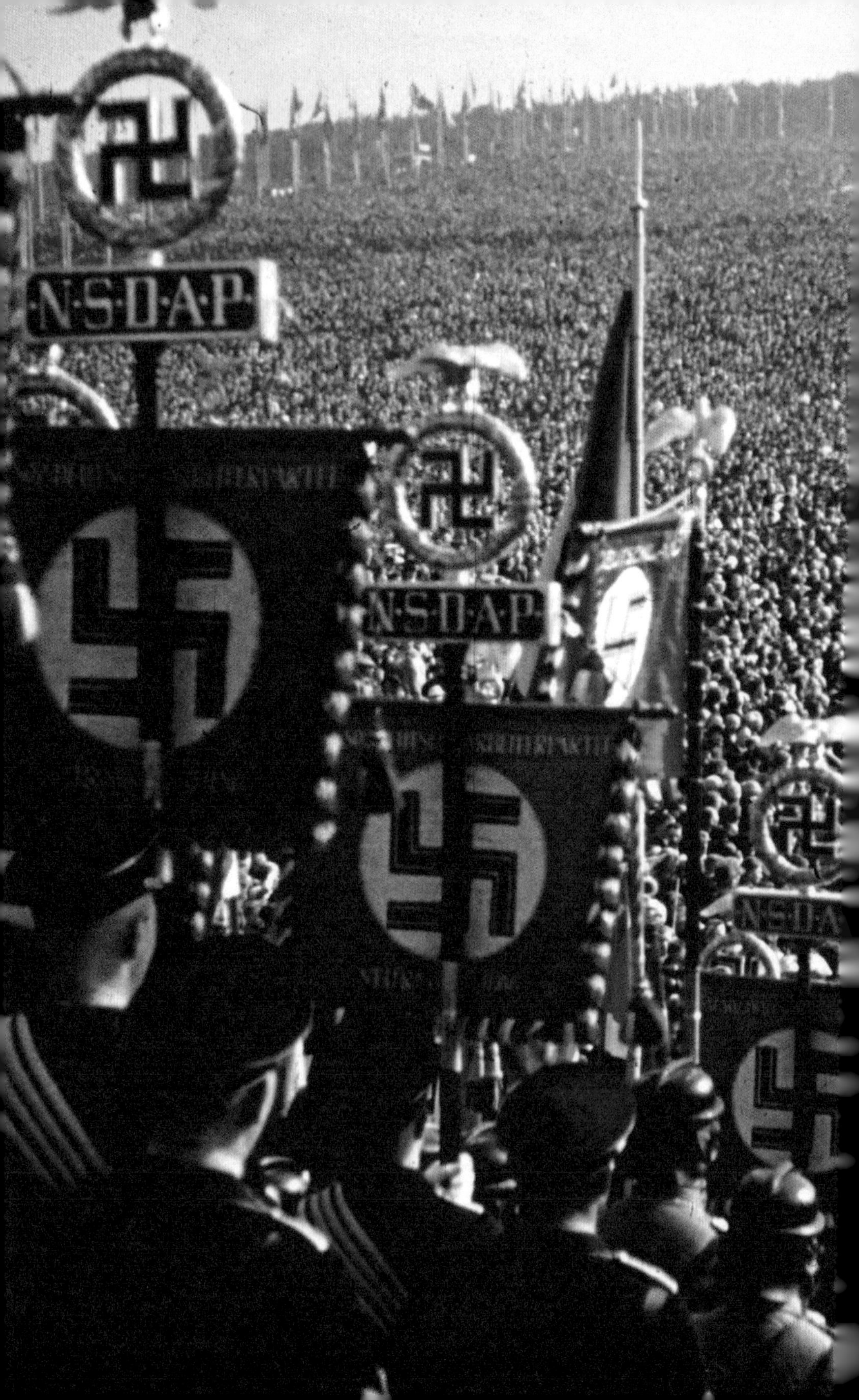
N·S·D·A·P
N·S·D·A·P

European problems. Eden was sceptical about the wisdom of the visit.

Halifax – very tall and humourless, with a lisping voice – arrived in Berlin on 17 November. He met Hitler on 19 November after an overnight journey from Berlin on Hitler's special train. There was an initial faux pas, when, as Hitler greeted him outside the Berghof, Halifax briefly mistook him for a footman. Once inside, Halifax said to Hitler: 'I have brought no new proposals from London. I have chiefly come to ascertain the German government's views on the existing political situation and to see what possibilities of a solution there might be.' Hitler, already in an angry mood, was furious about this comment. He felt it sounded very much like Eden's patronizing questionnaire, which Hitler had refused to answer a year before.

Things then went from bad to worse as the afternoon wore on. After what Halifax described as a 'rather indifferent meat lunch', Hitler launched into a list of high-handed demands. The British press must stop making negative comments about him. He wanted a close union with Austria, a solution to the Sudeten German problem in Czechoslovakia, and the freedom to extend German economic influence throughout Eastern Europe. 'Obstacles are being put in my way repeatedly in Southeast Europe by the Western powers!' he shouted. Hitler then suggested that the best way to stop the growth of Indian nationalism was 'to shoot Gandhi'. Halifax who had developed respect for Gandhi during his time as Viceroy of India was astonished by this outburst.

In an attempt to diffuse this increasingly uncomfortable situation, Halifax promised to discuss Hitler's concerns with the editors of Britain's newspapers. He went on to praise the Führer for eradicating communism in Germany. Then, instead of avoiding all mention of Austria and Czechoslovakia, as he had been advised to before his visit by Eden, he said that the British government would not oppose negotiated solutions in both cases, provided no military force was used.

Hitler showed no interest during the meeting about engaging in further talks on a negotiated settlement of European problems. On the train back to Berlin, Neurath told Halifax that Hitler's angry and sullen mood was attributable to extreme tiredness due to overwork.[120] Hitler's interpreter Paul Schmidt told Göring 'how badly things had gone' during the meeting at the Berghof and 'expressed the fear that Halifax would return to London with a very poor opinion of the chances of reaching an agreement with Germany'. Göring tried to repair the damage by explaining to Halifax that Germany was interested in some kind of Anglo-German understanding.[121] In his diary Halifax noted: 'He [Hitler] gave me the impression of feeling that, whilst he had attained to power only after a hard struggle with present-day realities, the British government was still living comfortably in a world of its own making, a fairyland of strange, if respectable illusions.'[122]

At Augsburg in a speech to a local Nazi Party group on 21 November, Hitler publicly asserted the right of Germany to *Lebensraum*. His carefully calculated public mask of peace was beginning to slip:

> Having built a new and strong life for the German people.
> Today we are facing new tasks. For the living space of our *Volk*
> is too confined. The world is attempting to disassociate itself
> from dealing with this problem and answering this question.
> But it will not succeed. One day the world will be forced to take
> our demands into consideration. I do not doubt for a second that
> we will procure for ourselves the same vital rights as other people
> outside the country in exactly the same way as we were able to
> lead it onwards within.[123]

Two days later Hitler attended the official opening ceremony of the 3rd National Socialist Order Castles (NS-Ordensburgen) in Allgäu. These were elite military schools for the training of top Nazi SA and SS leaders, as well as adult Hitler Youth leaders. At this gathering Hitler gave a significant 'secret speech', its contents never made public. The new German state, he said, was not based on Christian principles or even on the concept of a nation state. It was a self-contained National Community, a Germanic Empire of the German Nation, which would be 'merciless against all adversaries'. It opposed 'religious fragmentation' and the democratic party system. This new nation, he continued, had the 'moral justification to step before the world with vital demands'. What Hitler had given Germany, he argued, was strong leadership committed to the German people. What he now demanded from the party, the people, the church and the army was 'absolute obedience' in the coming struggle in which the 'New Germany will be victorious'.[124]

On 26 November the conservative Reich Minister of Economics Hjalmar Schacht resigned after his repeated warnings to Hitler of the danger of all-out rearmament had been ignored. He predicted the German economy would collapse under the weight of the massive public spending on rearmament. The creation of the Four-Year Plan, led by Göring, had severely undermined his authority. Hitler grew tired of listening to Schacht's warnings of economic doom and gloom.

He insisted that Schacht should remain in the cabinet as a Minister without Portfolio and even persuaded him to stay on as President of the Reichsbank to reassure the financial markets.[125] Göring took over as interim Minister of Economics before the Nazi loyalist Walther Funk became Schacht's permanent successor on 5 February 1938. After reading that Schacht had given up the Economics Ministry in his daily newspaper, Victor Klemperer noted: 'It is nevertheless possible that future historians will describe this little point as the beginning of the end. Only: How many years separate this beginning from the final end?'[126]

On Christmas Eve Hitler attended the traditional festive party for Nazi veterans in Munich. Afterwards, he was driven home to his apartment by Karl Krause, his 26-year-old personal bodyguard and valet. As the two men opened Christmas presents in the living room, Krause thought Hitler was in an unusually ebullient mood. He suggested they get a taxi and go for a walk around town. They ended up in Königsplatz in Munich's crowded city centre. When Krause expressed concern for the Führer's safety, Hitler turned to him and said: 'Don't be afraid. No one would ever believe Adolf Hitler would be walking home alone in Munich.' When they returned to the apartment, Hitler seemed delighted by this escapade. However, when Himmler heard about it on the next day he severely reprimanded Krause.[127]

On 28 December Ribbentrop completed a twenty-three-page report on the current state of Anglo-German relations.[128] He had spent most of the month working on it. He noted that while some British individuals welcomed friendly relations, others within the British government were deeply hostile towards Germany, most notably, Foreign Secretary Anthony Eden, Permanent Undersecretary for Foreign Affairs Robert Vansittart, Duff Cooper, the Secretary of State for War, and most Foreign Office officials. This latter group, he thought, were now in the ascendancy and had helped to bring about the abdication of Edward VIII.

Ribbentrop was deeply sceptical about Lord Halifax's recent visit to Germany, regarding it as an attempt to hold up German military action in Austria and Czechoslovakia. Ribbentrop also viewed Chamberlain's desire for negotiation with Germany as an obvious delaying tactic, while all the time British rearmament gathered pace.

Ribbentrop thought that Britain and France would soon offer up the German colonies, in return for Germany maintaining the territorial status quo in Europe. Britain 'might' even accept the union of Germany and Austria, but he predicted that an armed assault on Czechoslovakia would mean war with Britain and France.

In a brief separate document entitled 'Personal Conclusions', Ribbentrop finally admitted that his attempt to forge an alliance with the British had failed: 'I no longer have any faith in any [Anglo-German] understanding,' he concluded. 'Britain does not desire in close proximity a paramount Germany, which would be a constant menace to the British Isles.'[129]

As 1937 came to an end, Germany was moving firmly in the direction of war, just as Neville Chamberlain was moving firmly in the opposition direction.

1938
·
HIGH
ANXIETY
·

In his traditional New Year's Day message Hitler claimed that his main aim in 1938 was to upgrade the *Wehrmacht*, 'for we believe that only as a strong state can we, at such a tumultuous time, obtain for our people that good which seems most delightful: peace'. There seemed nothing in these soothing words to worry the international community.[1]

On 12 January Hitler and Göring acted as witnesses at the civil wedding of the 59-year-old Minister of War Werner von Blomberg. His bride was Luise Margarethe Gruhn, twenty-five years his junior, and employed as a stenographer. He met her while out for a walk in Berlin's Tiergarten in September 1937. Blomberg's first wife Charlotte Hellmich, the daughter of a high-ranking army officer, had died prematurely in 1932, leaving him to bring up their children alone. On 22 December 1937, after attending the state funeral of General Erich Ludendorff, Blomberg told Hitler that he intended to marry his new love, whom he described as coming from 'lowly circumstances'. Hitler raised no objection. The only person to suspect there might be a problem concerning Blomberg's remarriage was Colonel Alfred Jodl, who noted in his diary on 15 December 1937 that Blomberg seemed 'in a high state of excitement. Reason not known. Apparently, a personal matter.'[2]

Blomberg had a good reason to be anxious. On 22 January, just ten days after his marriage, the Berlin police – acting on a tip-off from a member of the public – found an official file revealing Luise Gruhn to have been registered as a prostitute by the police in 1932. Pornographic photos of her, dating from 1931, were also in the file, along with details of a 1934 criminal conviction for stealing a gold watch from a wealthy client. Wolf-Heinrich Graf von Helldorff, chief of the Berlin police, decided not to send the file to his superior Heinrich Himmler, but forwarded it instead to General Wilhelm Keitel at the War Ministry. Keitel sent the file straight back to Helldorff rather than dealing with the matter himself. Helldorff next sent the file to Göring, who, after reading it, said: 'This is a catastrophe.'[3]

When Göring showed Hitler the police file at the Reich Chancellery on 24 January the Führer was stunned. Fritz Wiedemann, Hitler's personal assistant, recalled: 'He paced up and down in his room, a broken man, his hands behind his back, shaking his head and muttering, "If a German field marshal can marry a whore then anything is possible in this world."'[4]

Göring showed Blomberg the police file and advised him to annul his marriage if he wanted to keep his job. Blomberg refused. On 27 January Hitler met with Blomberg, who agreed to resign. Hitler offered him a generous retirement pension plus 50,000 Reichsmarks towards an extended holiday. Hitler was convinced that Blomberg had known about his new wife's criminal past before the marriage and had hoped the details would never come to light.[5]

The obvious candidate to be Blomberg's successor as Minister of War was 57-year-old Werner von Fritsch, the commander-in-chief of the army. However, Hitler had reservations about him. He had not forgotten that at the Hossbach Memorandum meeting of 5 November 1937 Fritsch had been vehemently opposed to his plans for military aggression against Austria and Czechoslovakia. It was well known that Fritsch was unsympathetic to Nazism and had resisted efforts by Himmler to allow the SS to indoctrinate German army officers with Nazi ideas.

While pondering Fritsch's appointment, Hitler suddenly remembered an incident in the summer of 1936, when Himmler had presented him with a police file containing homosexual allegations made against Fritsch. Otto Schmidt, a Berlin rent boy, blackmailer and petty criminal, had claimed that he saw Fritsch engaging in a homosexual act in a dark alley near Potsdam railway station. Schmidt claimed he had then blackmailed Fritsch. In 1936 Hitler had dismissed this claim, even ordering the police file to be destroyed, but the file still existed – the director of the SD Reinhard Heydrich had defied Hitler's order and kept it.

On 25 January Hitler told Friedrich Hossbach about this potentially damaging allegation against Fritsch. Hossbach was convinced of Fritsch's innocence and wanted to question him personally, but Hitler refused. On the following evening Hossbach ignored Hitler's order and put the allegations directly to Fritsch, who described them as 'A pack of stinking lies'.[6]

On 27 January Hossbach told Hitler about this act of disobedience. He was summarily dismissed by Hitler on the following day. Goebbels described the Blomberg–Fritsch scandal as 'The worst crisis since the Röhm affair [in 1934]. I'm completely shattered. The Führer looks like

a corpse. I find Blomberg's behaviour incomprehensible [...] And now Fritsch is a 175 case [meaning a homosexual – under Paragraph 175 of the German criminal code sex between men aged twenty-one and over was punishable by a prison sentence]. He gave me his word of honour it's not true. But who can believe it?'[7] Blomberg made matters worse by describing Fritsch as 'a confirmed bachelor' who was 'no woman's man'.[8]

Hitler told Fritsch that if he admitted his guilt the matter would be hushed up,[9] but Fritsch continued to deny the allegations. Otto Schmidt was brought from the Börgermoor penal camp to the opulent Reich Chancellery library on 26 January to confront Fritsch face to face. Fritsch claimed to have never met the man before in his life, but Schmidt doggedly stood by his story. On the next day Fritsch was interrogated by the Gestapo and once again confronted by his accuser. Schmidt's testimony contained intimate details that seemed compelling, but some obvious mistakes were missed by the Gestapo officers handling the case. For instance, Schmidt had described Fritsch as a smoker, but Fritsch had quit smoking in 1925. He said Fritsch had worn a fur coat whenever he met him, but Fritsch didn't own such a coat. He claimed that Fritsch called himself a 'General of Artillery', which was not his army title.[10] Nevertheless, the official report on the case, written by Franz Gürtner, the Minister of Justice, concluded that the allegations against Fritsch had not been 'conclusively refuted'.[11] On 3 February Fritsch was asked to submit his resignation. He refused to do so, unless he was offered a chance to clear his name at a trial in the Reich Court Martial (*Reichskriegsgericht*), the highest German military court. This request was granted but he still reluctantly resigned.

Fritsch's trial began in secret at the Reich Court Martial in Berlin on 10 March. Göring acted as the chairman, supported by two leading armed forces figures: General Walther von Brauchitsch and Admiral Erich Raeder. During the hearing serious flaws in the Gestapo's investigation were brought to light. Under cross-examination, Schmidt told the court that he had been threatened with violence by the Gestapo unless he incriminated Fritsch. He now felt it was all a case of mistaken identity. Schmidt said that the person he had seen engaging in a homosexual act was not Fritsch but a wealthy retired cavalry officer with a similar but differently spelled name called Frisch. It was this man that Schmidt had blackmailed.

On 18 March Fritsch was acquitted,[12] but he was now convinced that Göring and Himmler had conspired to end his military career.

Werner von Blomberg (*left*) and Werner von Fritsch, Supreme Commander of the German Army (1935–8).

To Himmler, Fritsch said in court: 'Your whole attitude in this case shows that you were determined, in a biased manner, to portray me as the guilty one.'[13] In December 1938 he told the German diplomat Ulrich von Hassell that Göring had been the key instigator of his downfall. Fritsch felt that Göring had made sure that Schmidt had denounced him in front of Hitler and then had conveniently changed his story at the later military trial.[14] However, there is no convincing evidence to suggest that Göring or Himmler plotted the downfall of either Blomberg or Fritsch.

The scandalous Blomberg–Fritsch affair rocked Hitler's government to its foundations, although no details were ever made public. Hitler was so destabilized by the crisis that he even postponed his traditional 30 January speech to the Reichstag. Naturally the international press began to speculate as to the reason for this unusual delay. *The Times* hinted at unspecified 'domestic problems', while the *News Chronicle* suggested that there had been disagreements over Jewish policy and trouble with the industrialists over the pace of rearmament.[15]

On 3 February Hitler had a two-hour meeting with Goebbels to discuss the Blomberg–Fritsch crisis. Hitler had been foolish to trust Blomberg, he said, and did not believe Fritsch's denial of being a homosexual, observing that 'those sorts of people always do that'. Hitler told Goebbels that he had decided to take over complete control of the *Wehrmacht*.[16]

On 4 February Hitler met his cabinet for what proved to be the last time. 'As he speaks, he sometimes chokes back tears,' Goebbels noted. 'He was [he said] too ashamed to step out on to the balcony on 30 January.'[17] Hitler gave the cabinet a detailed account of the two sex scandals, reading out excerpts from the police files. He then explained his plans for wide-ranging changes at the top of the *Wehrmacht*, the Foreign Ministry and the Economics Ministry in the hope that this would provide a smokescreen around the Blomberg–Fritsch crisis.

Hitler was already the Supreme Commander of the Armed Forces, but now he abolished the War Ministry and appointed himself as the head of a new body – the High Command of the Armed Forces (Oberkommando der *Wehrmacht* or OKW) – to which all three defence services – the army, navy and air force – would now be subordinated. General Wilhelm Keitel, a Hitler loyalist, was appointed first chief of the OKW.[18] Walther von Brauchitsch replaced Fritsch as commander-in-chief, but before accepting the post he revealed that he was in the midst of divorce proceedings himself and revealed his estranged wife was demanding a considerable financial settlement. Hitler gave Brauchitsch 80,000 Reichsmarks to pay her off, leaving the general immediately indebted to the Führer.[19] Once in place, Brauchitsch proved just as willing to carry out Hitler's orders as Blomberg had been and he promised Hitler that he would bring the *Wehrmacht* closer to National Socialist ideology.[20] Göring was given the grand title of General Field Marshal in the army, giving him seniority over all the other commanders-in-chief except Hitler. Twelve other generals who were no longer required were offered early retirement.

'The Führer wants to divert the spotlight from the *Wehrmacht*,' Jodl noted in his diary. 'Keep Europe gasping and by replacements in various posts not awaken the impression of an element of weakness but of a concentration of forces.'[21] Now that the obstacles to Hitler's full command of the army had been removed, everything was now in place for a transition towards a much more aggressive foreign policy.

Neurath was replaced as Foreign Minister by Ribbentrop, who would observe some years later as a war criminal at the Nuremberg trials: 'It was clear to me at the beginning that I would be working in the shadow of a titan and that I would have to impose on myself certain limitations. I would not be in a position to conduct foreign policy as it is done by other foreign ministers. The commanding personality of the Führer dominated foreign policy.'[22] Although Neurath appeared to have been promoted to President of the Privy Cabinet Council, a new body tasked with advising Hitler on diplomatic matters, the council never met and he had been quietly sidelined. He, too, had been opposed to Hitler's aggressive war plans. By contrast, Ribbentrop was a committed Nazi and it was widely expected that he would now begin an extensive purge of conservatives from the Foreign Ministry. However, the existing personnel and structure remained largely unchanged. New appointments were made in the diplomatic service. Several high-profile ambassadors were dismissed: Herbert von

Hitler greets British Prime Minister Neville Chamberlain on the steps of the Berghof, 15 September 1938.

Dirksen in Tokyo, Ulrich von Hassell in Rome and Franz von Papen in Vienna. Dirksen subsequently became Ribbentrop's replacement as the German ambassador to Britain.

The Blomberg–Fritsch crisis was effectively a bloodless Night of the Long Knives. Hitler had managed to respond to unforeseen events in such a way as to emerge even more powerful than before. As the scandal unfolded it had provided him with an opportunity to remove conservatives in the military to place more power in his own hands. Hitler had not planned the removal of Blomberg or Fritsch but as the two men had been critics of a more aggressive foreign policy their departure was welcome.

The international reaction to these changes was one of profound shock. Ivan Maisky, the Soviet Union's ambassador to Britain, noted in his diary on 7 February: 'In general, the army was a restraining factor in German policy: it opposed the occupation of the Rhineland and it was very unenthusiastic about the Spanish adventure. The army believed Germany was not ready for a big war.' Maisky felt that Hitler's military and diplomatic reshuffle would lead to a more aggressive German foreign policy and he predicted that 'forceful attempts to seize Austria and, perhaps, Czechoslovakia are also more probable'.[23]

In Vienna, the German ambassador Franz von Papen was 'almost speechless with astonishment' when he received news of his own dismissal. He rushed to see Hitler at the Berghof on 5 February, but Hitler refused to explain in any detail why he had sacked him. Papen then revealed to Hitler that in December 1937 Kurt Schuschnigg, the Austrian Chancellor, had requested a meeting with Hitler to discuss problems related to the Austro-German Agreement of 1936. Papen suggested that Hitler make a definite date to meet him. 'That is an excellent idea,' Hitler replied, 'please go back to Vienna immediately and arrange for us to meet.' Papen reminded the Führer that he was no longer ambassador to the German Reich in Vienna. 'That makes no difference,' Hitler said. 'I beg you, Herr von Papen, to take over the affairs of the Legation again, until the meeting with Schuschnigg has been arranged.'

Years later, at the Nuremberg trials, it was alleged by the prosecution that Papen had persuaded Schuschnigg to meet Hitler in the full knowledge that Hitler would present him with a series of bullying demands which threatened Austrian independence. Papen vehemently denied this,[24] but there remain serious doubts about his version of events. For instance, Goebbels recalled a lunch in Berlin in December

Kurt Schuschnigg (1897–1977),
15th Chancellor of Austria between
1934 and 1938.

1937 at which Papen had 'mentioned a plan he had devised to bring down Schuschnigg'.[25]

At any rate, Papen relayed Hitler's invitation to the Austrian Chancellor. Schuschnigg accepted, but not without seeking an assurance beforehand that Hitler would respect Austria's independence. Hitler readily agreed to this request. Schuschnigg intended to offer concessions to Hitler at the meeting, including allowing moderate Nazis into his government. Wilhelm Keppler, one of Hitler's advisers in Austrian affairs, recommended a softly-softly approach. He told Ribbentrop that if Germany tried to solve the Austrian problem by 'peaceful evolution', then 'I believe the present moment offers good prospects for substantial progress, and I am convinced that we shall slowly gain political ascendancy over Schuschnigg.'[26]

Hitler met Schuschnigg, who was accompanied by Guido Schmidt, his State Secretary for Foreign Affairs, on 12 February. It was a bitterly cold winter day. Papen greeted the Austrian visitors at the border and drove with them to the Berghof. Also at the Berghof on that day were Wilhelm Keitel, new chief of the OKW, Walther von Reichenau, the commander of German forces on the Austria–Germany border, and Hugo Sperrie, the commander of the *Luftwaffe* in the area. It is unclear whether this was a mere coincidence or whether Hitler had invited them to make the atmosphere more intimidating for his Austrian guests. When Ribbentrop, the new Foreign Minister, suddenly arrived it became clear to Schuschnigg that this meeting was not going to be the friendly ice-breaker that Papen had promised him.

Hitler greeted the Austrian Chancellor at the bottom of the steps leading up to the Berghof. Once indoors, Schuschnigg was alone with the Führer in his spacious second-floor study. The only account of what happened next comes from Schuschnigg. He described it at length in his testimony at the Nuremberg trials, then expanded upon it in his post-war memoirs. In an attempt to lighten the mood, Schuschnigg began by admiring the view from the window. Hitler snapped back: 'We are not here to discuss the beautiful view and the weather.' He then gave a lengthy anti-Austrian rant: 'The whole history of Austria is just one uninterrupted act of high treason [against Germany]. This was so in the past and is no better today. This historical nonsense must now come to a long overdue end.'

Hitler continued in this aggressive manner for about an hour, while Schuschnigg struggled to get a word in edgeways. When Schuschnigg said that all he wanted was a 'better understanding' between Germany and Austria, Hitler shot back: 'I am telling you that I am going to solve the so-called Austrian problem one way or another.' Schuschnigg pointed out that Austria was not alone in the world, but Hitler poured scorn on the idea any military support from Britain, France or Italy would be forthcoming. He ended with a stark ultimatum: 'I give you once more, and for the last time, the opportunity to come to terms. Either we find a solution now or events will take their course.'[27]

Over lunch, Hitler transformed from being an intimidating bully into a charming host. He told Schuschnigg about his love of cars and his grandiose building plans. However, after lunch things became serious again. Ribbentrop presented Schuschnigg with a two-page written 'agreement'. Giving evidence at the Nuremberg trials, Ribbentrop said that by this stage Schuschnigg looked 'obviously shattered by Hitler's harangue' and he had offered the Austrian Chancellor a cigarette to calm his nerves.[28]

The harsh terms presented to Schuschnigg in the 'agreement' included demands to lift the ban on the Austrian Nazi Party and to implement an amnesty for all imprisoned Nazis. It was further demanded that the pro-Nazi politician Dr Arthur Seyss-Inquart should be appointed as Austrian Minister of the Interior with command over the police; and that Edmund Glaise-Horstenau, another pro-Nazi, should be offered the post of Minister of War, with orders to bring into closer union the Austrian and German armies. Preparations would begin to incorporate Austria into the German economy. To aid this process, the Austrian banker Hans Fischböck would become Minister of Finance. In his testimony at the Nuremberg trials, Seyss-Inquart commented: 'The agreement at Berchtesgaden on 12 February contained a definite stipulation to the effect I was to be the liaison man between the Austrian government and the Austrian National Socialists on the one side and the German Reich on the other.'[29] Papen later claimed to have known nothing about these further demands being made upon Austria, describing them as 'an unwarrantable interference in Austrian sovereignty'.[30]

If Schuschnigg bowed to Hitler's demands it would mean the end of Austrian independence. 'Ribbentrop advised me to accept the demands at once,' Schuschnigg later recalled. 'I protested and referred him to my previous agreement with von Papen, made prior to coming to Berchtesgaden, and made clear that I was not prepared to be confronted with such unreasonable demands.'[31] The Austrian Chancellor was invited to join Hitler in his study in the Berghof, where

[overleaf] Hitler is greeted by huge cheering crowds as the drives through Vienna after the Anschluss

he explained that he was minded to sign the 'agreement'. However, he explained to Hitler that according to the Austrian constitution only Wilhelm Miklas, the President of Austria, could make a final decision on the matter. At this point Hitler completely lost his temper and asked Schuschnigg to leave the room. Hitler then loudly shouted down the corridor for Wilhelm Keitel to come to his study, but as Keitel entered the room Hitler just smiled at him. It was all an act. The whole scene had been designed to further intimidate Schuschnigg. After a short while, the Austrian Chancellor was allowed back into the Führer's study. 'I have decided to change my mind for the first time in my life,' Hitler told him. 'But I warn you this is your last chance. I have given you three additional days to carry out the agreement.'

Under extreme duress, Schuschnigg signed the draft agreement. He declined Hitler's invitation to stay for dinner and decided instead to depart for Vienna with Guido Schmidt. Papen accompanied them in the car back to the Austrian frontier. They sat in complete silence, until Papen said: 'Now you have some idea, Herr *Bundeskanzler* [Chancellor], how difficult it is to deal with such an unstable person.'[32]

Back in Vienna, Schuschnigg implemented all of the governmental changes that Hitler had demanded. A road map had seemingly been established for a swift union of Austria and Germany. Soon the international press began to speculate as to what really happened when Schuschnigg met Hitler at the Berghof. No reports of the encounter had yet appeared in either the Austrian or the German press. Initially, British newspapers came to the conclusion that the meeting must have gone well for the Austrian Chancellor.[33] Then on 16 February the British press revealed details of Hitler's bullying of Schuschnigg. This leak clearly came from the Austrian Chancellor. The *News Chronicle* reported: 'From the very start of the interview Chancellor Schuschnigg found himself subjected to great pressure.'[34] *The Times* revealed that Schuschnigg 'underwent a trying ordeal. Herr Hitler used the plainest language in stating his demands and it is understood that he indicated grave consequences if they were not accepted.'[35] There was, however, little enthusiasm – in the press or in parliament – for Britain to oppose the incorporation of Austria into the German Reich. A *Sunday Times* editorial was typical: 'No rational man proposes that this country should go to war to save Austria.'[36]

In Berlin, Arthur Seyss-Inquart met Hitler on 17 February to discuss the Austrian question. He greeted Hitler with a Nazi salute (years later, at the Nuremberg trials, this would be used against him

Hitler with the last Chancellor of Austria Arthur Seyss-Inquart, who served for just two days.

by the prosecution in support of their claim that he had acted as a Nazi puppet throughout the Austrian crisis). Seyss-Inquart told Hitler that Schuschnigg had advised him to adhere to the notion of an independent Austria and to emphasize the fact that the *Anschluss* – the annexation of Austria by Nazi Germany – could be achieved only within the framework of the Austrian constitution. National Socialist principles were not to be imposed on the Austrian public by force. He felt public opinion in Austria had not yet evolved towards supporting the *Anschluss*. Hitler replied: 'This is not a question of the 25 points.* One cannot proclaim a dogma; one must arrive from the pan-German and the national German conception to a National Socialist one.' In other words, he was willing to accept, at this stage at least, that the *Anschluss* should evolve gradually and not be suddenly imposed upon the Austrians by a military occupation.[37]

While the precise character of the *Anschluss* was being negotiated in Germany, a political crisis was brewing in Britain. On 18 February Prime Minister Chamberlain, accompanied by Eden, his Foreign Secretary, met the recently ennobled Count Dino Grandi, the Italian ambassador, to discuss the unfolding events in Austria. Chamberlain hoped that the Austrian crisis might help to bring Mussolini back into the Anglo-French camp, given his past opposition to the *Anschluss*. Eden was rightly not so sure. Grandi refused to discuss the Italian government's view on Austria, but he conveyed the news that Mussolini was willing to open fresh talks with Britain.

The meeting was briefly adjourned. During this interval Grandi overheard a furious row between Eden and Chamberlain, ending with Chamberlain shouting: 'Anthony, you have missed chance after chance. You simply cannot go on like this.' Grandi observed: 'Chamberlain and Eden were not a Prime Minister discussing with the ambassador of a foreign country a delicate matter, but two enemies confronting each other in true fighting posture.'[38] Over the next few days there were heated Cabinet discussions which only emphasized the differences between Eden and Chamberlain. Eden had already expressed concerns about his deteriorating relationship with Chamberlain to Ivan Maisky, the Soviet ambassador, on 11 February.[39] Eden's disenchantment had increased because Chamberlain had set up what amounted to a parallel Foreign Office of trusted advisers, most notably the senior

---

* The 25 Points outlined the political platform of the Nazi Party. Composed by Hitler in 1920, they remained largely unchanged until his death in 1945.

Pro-Hitler poster encouraging Austrians to vote Yes in the 1938 Anchluss Referendum.

official Sir Horace Wilson, who had become a sort of personal envoy to Chamberlain, as well as Lord Halifax. Eden hated being sidelined, controlled and directed. On 20 February he resigned.

It is tempting to view the falling out of Chamberlain and Eden as a clash of personalities: Chamberlain, the clear-sighted bureaucrat, versus Eden, the temperamental and egotistical rising star. In his resignation speech Eden claimed that there had been 'fundamental differences' over policy, but Chamberlain denied this. Eden wanted to widen Britain's diplomatic links to include the Soviet Union and the United States while Chamberlain wanted to reduce the number of Britain's potential enemies by improving relations with Germany and Italy.

Eden was replaced by Lord Halifax, who initially at least supported Chamberlain's policy. Chamberlain admitted he was far happier having a Foreign Secretary who 'never causes me any worry'.[40] Maisky, the Soviet ambassador, noted in his diary that he did not like the idea of an all-powerful Chamberlain in charge of British foreign policy. In his view, the British Prime Minister was 'very obstinate and insistent and once an idea has lodged in his mind he will defend it until he is blue in the face – a rather dangerous quality.'[41]

The talks with Italy began and on 16 April Britain and Italy signed an agreement under which Britain recognized Italian control of Abyssinia in return for a pledge that Italian troops would withdraw from Spain at the conclusion of the Spanish Civil War.

On the same day as Eden resigned, Hitler delivered a three-hour speech to the Reichstag. It was broadcast live on German radio and, for the first time, on Austrian national radio. In his speech Hitler gave a highly sanitized version of recent events. Blomberg's resignation was presented as a 'retirement on health grounds' to spare him further 'aggravations in his private life' (Hitler gave no details as to what these might be). He praised Fritsch, explaining that he had stepped aside in a 'noble spirit' to make way for a younger man. Did these changes at the top represent a 'Nazification of the army'? How could they, Hitler said, when 'the German *Wehrmacht*' was already 'dedicated to the National Socialist State'? As for the Foreign Ministry, it, too, had already embraced Nazi ideals.

Hitler next gave a highly distorted version of his meeting with Schuschnigg. A further settlement had been reached with the Austrian government, he said, to remove any further 'misunderstandings and obstacles' in the way of the political union of Austria with Germany.

This reciprocal arrangement with Austria, he added, would help to 'bring about a gradual lessening of tension in Europe'. The discrimination against the 10 million German-speaking people in Austria and Czechoslovakia must cease, Hitler added, and in the long term he could not stand by and do nothing while people were suffering greatly because of their affection for and loyalty to Germany.[42]

On 24 February Hitler spoke at Munich's Hofbräuhaus beer hall on the eighteenth anniversary of the founding of the National Socialist German Workers' Party in 1920. He criticized what he called 'the smear campaign in the international press' against him and ridiculed a recent article in the British *News Chronicle* which had suggested that German troops were preparing an attack on Czechoslovakia. This story and others in the British press were 'filthy lies', he said, engineered by 'Jewish international poisoners', and he promised:

> We shall move against the Jewish agitators in Germany
> unrelentingly. We know that they are representatives of an
> international anti-German movement and we shall treat them all
> accordingly. They can but lie, defame and slander, while we know
> very well that not one of these Jewish agitators would ever join
> the fight in a war, even though they are the ones who profit from
> these wars.[43]

In Vienna on the same evening Schuschnigg delivered a passionate address to the Austrian Federal Parliament, during which he stressed that Austria had gone to the very limit of its concessions to Germany: 'This far and no further,' he said. Austria would never, he promised, voluntarily give up its independence. He ended with the defiant phrase 'Red-white-red* till we are dead!' (*Bis in den Tod, Rot-Weiss-Rot*). Schuschnigg clearly still hoped that he could rally the Austrian public to uphold Austria's independence.[44]

On 2 March the judges in the Berlin trial of the dissident Lutheran cleric Martin Niemöller delivered their surprise verdict: Niemöller was acquitted of causing a rebellion against Hitler's church policy, but found guilty of making critical comments in his sermons. He was sentenced to seven months imprisonment and fined 1,500 Reichsmarks, but as he had already served eight months in Berlin's Moabit Prison he was immediately released.

The trial had been held in secret. Tickets to the public gallery excluded correspondents from the foreign press. Dr Horst Holstein,

---

* The Austrian national flag colours.

Niemöller's defence lawyer, emphasized his client's patriotism and loyalty to the German state, as well as his war service. In his own testimony, Niemöller told the court that he held no animosity towards National Socialists. His objections to the church policy were solely related to religious observance. Hitler was furious when he learned about Niemöller's release. Ignoring the court's decision, he made the Lutheran pastor his 'personal prisoner', to be held in indefinite 'protective custody'. Later that day two Gestapo officers drove Niemöller to Sachsenhausen concentration camp, where he would remain until 1945.[45]

The British ambassador to Germany Nevile Henderson met Hitler and Ribbentrop on 3 March. He had an offer to make to the Führer, which he hoped would ensure peace in Europe. Britain was prepared to return its former German colonies in Africa, but only on the condition that Hitler promised not to attempt to change Germany's frontiers in Europe. In his reply, a deeply agitated Hitler began by criticizing the anti-German tone of the British press in recent weeks, and ended by dismissing the colonial question as something 'not ripe for settlement as yet'. Hitler then moved on to the Austrian crisis, stressing his support for national self-determination. The British government, he said, needed to understand that Schuschnigg had the support of less than 15 per cent of the Austrian population. If Hitler decided to intervene militarily in Austria, he explained, he would do so with 'lightning speed', but for now he preferred a 'peaceful evolution' of the union between Austria and Germany.[46]

In a bold and unexpected move that took Hitler completely by surprise, Schuschnigg announced in a speech in Innsbruck on 9 March that he was calling a national referendum on Austrian independence. It would be held in just four days' time under the slogan: 'For a free, German, independent, social, Christian and unified Austria!' Posters announcing the vote went up on billboards in Vienna on the following day. Hitler had been arguing for such a referendum for years, but he was furious that Schuschnigg had dared to challenge him in such a public manner. What angered Hitler the most, however, was Schuschnigg's decision to call the vote at such short notice and restricting it to voters over twenty-four, because he knew the strongest support for the Anschluss was among younger Austrians, who would be denied a vote.

Schuschnigg was trying to prevent the Anschluss, but in fact his referendum decision gave Hitler the ideal opportunity to speed it up. By now Hitler was a master at exploiting unforeseen events to his own advantage. Schuschnigg knew the risks he ran by calling the referendum, as he later explained: 'I felt that the moment for a clear decision had come. It seemed impossible to wait with fettered hands until, in the course of some weeks, we should be gagged as well. The gamble was for stakes which demanded the ultimate and supreme effort.'[47]

The duplicitous Austrian Nazi Seyss-Inquart, who was already acting independently from Schuschnigg, warned the Austrian Chancellor in a letter that the decision to call a referendum was a huge mistake because it did not conform to current electoral law, nor had it been agreed beforehand with the ruling Fatherland Front, and besides, there was no certainty it would produce a vote in favour of Austrian independence. Seyss-Inquart urged Schuschnigg to postpone the referendum and instead to call a general election, forming beforehand a coalition government that would include National Socialists.[48]

Hitler was uncertain about how to respond to Schuschnigg's referendum, which was a clear challenge to his authority. 'Schuschnigg is trying a dirty trick,' Goebbels noted in his diary. 'He's making fools of us.'[49] Ribbentrop, who was in London, winding up his affairs as German ambassador, would take no part in the unfolding Austrian crisis. After a conversation with Halifax, the new British Foreign Secretary, he sent a telegram to the German Foreign Ministry, predicting that 'Britain will do nothing in regard to Austria.'[50]

The *Wehrmacht* had not yet drawn up plans for a military invasion of Austria, except for the early draft of Operation Otto, which was rather vague and was intended to be a response to any sudden restoration of the Habsburg monarchy. Hitler ordered Operation Otto to be swiftly updated for immediate military action. The name of the operation was never changed. Informed of Hitler's order to invade Austria, a shocked Colonel Ludwig Beck responded: 'We have prepared nothing.'[51]

Hitler issued Directive Number 1 for Operation Otto at 2 a.m. on 11 March. Events now moved swiftly as German political and military leaders gathered in the Reich Chancellery to discuss the unfolding crisis. They set the date for the invasion of Austria: 12 March. Operation Otto would be directed by the Führer himself. At 10 a.m. an ultimatum from Hitler had been delivered to Schuschnigg personally by Seyss-Inquart. It told the Austrian Chancellor to cancel his referendum by 12 noon or face the military consequences.

It was Göring – in a series of heated telephone calls, which were recorded and transcribed – who directed German policy towards Austria. Hitler later gave him full credit: 'In times of crises you cannot have a better adviser than the Reich Marshal. The Reich Marshal is brutal and ice-cold in crises. I've always noticed when it's a question of facing up to a decision he is ruthless and hard as iron, you'll get nobody better than him and you couldn't find anyone better.'[52]

At 2.45 p.m., after consulting with the President of Austria Wilhelm Miklas, a clearly rattled Schuschnigg telephoned Seyss-Inquart to inform him that he would be calling off the referendum. Loudspeaker vans drove through Vienna blurting out the news. In London Chamberlain was holding a farewell lunch for Ribbentrop at 10 Downing Street when the news came through on Austria. Halifax told Ribbentrop the pressure being placed on Schuschnigg was 'intolerable', but Ribbentrop said he had no idea what was going on. He was not lying. Göring had kept Ribbentrop completely in the dark. This only confirmed the British government's suspicion that Ribbentrop had no real power or influence over German foreign policy.[53]

At 3.30 p.m. Schuschnigg informed Seyss-Inquart of his intention to resign. Seyss-Inquart then telephoned Göring at 3.45 p.m. to tell him that the referendum was off and that Schuschnigg was submitting his resignation to President Miklas. Göring told him that the Austrian President needed to go further and appoint him, Seyss-Inquart, as the new Chancellor of Austria. Once Seyss-Inquart had taken power, Göring wanted him to send a telegram to Germany, which he dictated to him over the phone: it was a request for German troops to enter Austria and restore order. This telegram was designed to justify to the rest of the world the German occupation of Austria. Seyss-Inquart readily agreed. A copy of this telegram was found among seized German documents at the end of the Second World War, but in fact it was never sent.[54]

President Miklas reluctantly accepted Schuschnigg's resignation at 5 p.m. but he stubbornly refused to make Seyss-Inquart Austria's next Chancellor, much to the consternation of Göring. At 5.30 p.m. Seyss-Inquart was back on the phone to Göring, telling him that Miklas wanted Otto Ender, who had briefly been Austrian Chancellor from 1930 to 1931, to take up the post of Chancellor. 'Well that won't do!' Göring shouted down the phone. 'Under no circumstances! The President has to be informed that he has to turn the powers of the Federal Chancellor over to you.'

Later that day, at 7.50 p.m., Schuschnigg made a farewell address on Austrian national radio. He began by telling the world that the German government had given President Miklas an ultimatum, ordering him to nominate as Schuschnigg's replacement a man chosen by the German government or else German troops would invade. 'President Miklas has asked me to tell the people of Austria that we have yielded to force,' he added. 'Since we are not prepared even in this terrible hour to shed blood, we have decided to order the troops to offer no resistance. So, I take leave of the Austrian people with a German word of farewell uttered from the depth of my heart. God protect Austria!'[55]

After the speech, Seyss-Inquart gave Schuschnigg a lift home, because, in his own words, 'I was afraid something might happen to him at the hands of provocateurs.'[56] At midnight, under immense pressure, President Miklas finally gave in and appointed Seyss-Inquart as the new Chancellor of Austria. Every demand in the original German ultimatum had now been met. Miklas resigned on the following day.

Hitler believed, correctly as it turned out, that Britain and France would not lift a finger to defend Austria. He was far more concerned about how Mussolini would react. He sent Prince Philipp of Hesse to Italy by plane to deliver a personal letter to the Italian dictator, informing him of the military action that Hitler was now contemplating. Hitler placed the blame for the turn of events on Schuschnigg. At 10.25 p.m. Prince Philipp called Hitler to inform him that Mussolini would not oppose his plan to occupy Austria. 'I shall never forget him for this,' Hitler replied. 'If he should ever need any help or be in any danger, he can be convinced that I shall stick to him whatever may happen, even if the whole world gangs up on him.'[57]

German troops crossed the Austrian border at 5.30 a.m. on 12 March. They met with no resistance from the Austrian army. Austrians greeted the German soldiers as heroes. 'One cannot call it an invasion,' Seyss-Inquart later observed. 'It was a stormy, loudly cheered entry of German troops.'[58] At noon German radio announced: 'The Führer has decided to liberate Austria and come to the help of those brother Germans in distress.'[59]

At 4 p.m. Hitler crossed the Austrian border near the town of Braunau am Inn, his birthplace. His motorcade was greeted by flowers, cheers and the ringing of church bells. Hitler then motored 74 miles east to Linz, where he had lived as a teenager. He was greeted there by a crowd of 100,000 gathered in the central market place. On the balcony of Linz's Old Town Hall located in the city centre Hitler gave a brief speech, with tears in his eyes, before a cheering, jubilant crowd. Providence, he said, must have singled him out to return his homeland to the Reich. Hitler had planned to go straight to Vienna, but now decided to stay overnight in Linz at the Hotel Weizinger. The huge welcome he had received in Linz, which he regarded as his home town, convinced him, on the spur of the moment, to push ahead with the immediate union (*Anschluss*) of Austria with Germany.

At 3 p.m. on 13 March Hitler announced the hastily drafted 'Law for the Unification of Austria with the German Reich'. Hitler set the date of 10 April for a national referendum in Austria to let the people determine their own future. Elections to the Reichstag would also be held on the same day.

Hitler arrived in Vienna late in the afternoon of 14 March. He had suffered many lonely days in the Austrian capital as a struggling artist from 1907 to 1913. Now he was greeted by a wildly cheering crowd as a new national saviour. This really was a dream come true.

On the next day Hitler delivered a euphoric and emotional speech in the Heldenplatz [Heroes' Square] before a crowd estimated in local newspapers at 200,000. With the *Anschluss*, he said, a 'Greater Germany' (*Großdeutschland*) had come into being. 'I now proclaim for this land its new mission,' he continued. 'The oldest eastern province of the German people shall be from now on the youngest bulwark of the German nation. I can in this hour report before history the conclusion of the greatest aim of my life: the entry of my homeland into the German Reich.'[60] Hitler appointed Gauleiter Josef Bürckel as the Reich Commissioner for the Reunification of Austria. Austria itself was renamed Ostmark ('Eastern March'), a medieval title, the idea being that Austria was now the eastern arm of the Reich.

At 5 p.m. on 15 March Hitler flew back to Munich after his greatest foreign policy triumph to date. His instinctive ability to turn a crisis into a political opportunity was once again on display as he exploited the unforeseen chain of events that led to the *Anschluss*. Emil Myles, from Bad Schmiedeberg, a young soldier in the *Wehrmacht* at the time, felt that the *Anschluss* was a deeply emotional moment for all German soldiers: 'The annexation of Austria, creating Greater Germany, was positive for the people. I heard older people saying, "The Führer won't make war."' It was largely believed that Hitler merely 'wanted to protect German rights and return all territory that belonged to us'.[61]

The international reaction to the *Anschluss* was initially one of profound shock. *The Times* famously summed up the German occupation with the headline 'The Rape of Austria'.[62] 'This is an invasion of an independent state as brutal as that of Japan's into China or Italy's into Abyssinia,' the *Manchester Guardian* declared. 'If it is not also war, it is only because Dr Schuschnigg preferred surrender. This, then, is Hitler's policy, this is the naked fist.'[63]

The reaction of most Austrians was very different. Ferdinand Krones, who lived in Vienna at the time, later recalled: 'Today, people claim Austria was the first victim of Hitler's politics, that Austria was raped by Germany. That's not true. The majority of patriotic Austrians welcomed the union with often tearful joy. And the youth organizations in Austria, including the Catholic ones, were for the *Anschluss*.'[64]

The absorption of Austria into the Reich without a single shot being fired brought some benefits to the German economy, adding 8 per cent to industrial output. In 1937 Austria had produced 600,000 tons of steel, but this was only 4 per cent of overall German production. The addition of 400,000 unemployed workers was a welcome boost to the rearmament programme. The addition of foreign exchange and gold holdings of 1.4 billion Reichsmarks proved useful as a means of purchasing raw materials abroad. It also doubled Germany's dwindling foreign currency reserves.[65]

For Austria's Jewish population the *Anschluss* had very real consequences and a brutal reign of terror began. Much of the violence was inflicted on the 176,000 Jews who lived in Vienna and made up 90 per cent of Austria's Jewish community. Government policy against Jews in Austria was much more radical than it had ever been in Germany. George Gedye, the Vienna correspondent of the *Daily Telegraph*, reported on the vicious wave of anti-Semitic violence that accompanied the German occupation. He saw SA and SS men roaming around Jewish areas, smashing the windows of Jewish-owned shops, wrecking cars and beating up Jews. The Austrian police did nothing to stop this violence.[66] US journalist William Shirer, who was also in Vienna at this time, noted in his diary: 'On the streets today gangs of Jews, on their hands and knees scrubbing the Schuschnigg signs off the sidewalks, with jeering stormtroopers standing over them and taunting crowds around them.'[67]

Nazi laws against Jews were swiftly applied in Austria. By April 7,000 Jewish-owned businesses had been forcibly transferred into Aryan ownership. Jews were summarily dismissed from the civil service, local government, schools, universities, the media, cultural industries and the legal and medical professions.[68] A Central Office for Jewish Emigration was established under the leadership of Adolf Eichmann. He would later become a leading member of the Jewish Office in Himmler's Reich Security Main Office in Berlin, which controlled all of Germany's police and security forces. By May 1939, 100,000 Austrian Jews had left Austria.

In the House of Lords, Halifax delivered a sober speech on the Austrian crisis on 17 March. He said that the British government had never thought the status quo in Austria could be maintained, but it felt that Germany's actions had administered 'a most grave shock to European confidence'. There was no point in bringing the Austrian question before the League of Nations, because 'only war could bring about a change in the situation'.[69] The general British government view was that the *Anschluss* was bound to have occurred at some point and it was generally welcomed by the Austrian people.

It was obvious the next item on Hitler's list of foreign policy objectives was Czechoslovakia, a nation created from the ruins of the multi-ethnic Habsburg Empire by the peacemakers at Versailles. Czechoslovakia was a democracy, but its non-Czech citizens – including Germans, Hungarians, Poles, Ruthenians and Slovaks – were not comfortable in this new state dominated by its 7.5 million Czechs. This diverse melting pot was something Hitler found easy to exploit for his own purposes. He cast himself as the champion of the right to 'national self-determination' of the 3.5 million Germans who were living in the Sudeten areas.[70]

In the aftermath of the *Anschluss*, the British cabinet met several times to discuss Britain's policy on Czechoslovakia. The chiefs of staff sub-committee prepared a detailed report entitled 'Military Implications of German Aggression Against Czechoslovakia'. It concluded that German forces would defeat Czechoslovakia within weeks and that the country could be liberated only after a long and bloody European war – and there was no guarantee that Czechoslovakia would return to being a democracy afterwards. Allowing matters to take their own course was not an option for the British government primarily because two important alliances seemingly protected Czechoslovakian independence. The first was the Franco-Czech alliance of 1925. The second – and more worrying to the British – was a complex pact of mutual assistance between Czechoslovakia, France and the Soviet Union, which had been signed in 1935.

In this context, Chamberlain had already decided that Czechoslovakia's independence would have to be sacrificed to Germany in order to avoid a wider war in Europe. At a cabinet meeting on 22 March he summed up the agreed policy of the British government towards Czechoslovakia: 'We should endeavour to induce the government of

Czechoslovakia to apply themselves to producing a direct settlement with the Sudeten Deutsch. We should persuade the French to use their influence to secure such an agreement.'[71] The cabinet overwhelmingly supported this policy.

On the following day Ivan Maisky, the Soviet Union's ambassador to Britain, met Churchill, then a backbench MP who was disliked by Chamberlain and excluded from his cabinet. As the international crisis had developed Churchill had become the strongest supporter of taking a firm stand against Hitler. 'You know my general standpoint,' Churchill told Maisky. 'I deeply detest Nazi Germany. I believe it to be an enemy not only of peace and democracy but of the British Empire too. I think the only reliable means to restrain this beast could be a "grand alliance" of all the peace-loving states within the framework of the League of Nations. Russia would occupy one of the most prominent positions in this alliance.'[72]

Chamberlain gave a speech in the House of Commons on 24 March which concentrated on the fragile position of Czechoslovakia. The British government, he said, was willing to do everything it could to help in a negotiated settlement between Germany and the Czechoslovakian government over the Sudeten German question. However, if Germany attacked Czechoslovakia, he added, then France was obligated to fulfil its treaty obligations, and if war broke out 'it would be impossible to say where it would end and what governments might become involved'. It was an ambiguous statement but left the impression that Britain would join the French government if it decided to go to war to save Czechoslovakia. This was certainly how Chamberlain's speech was interpreted by German diplomats. Ernst Woermann, the German chargé d'affaires in Britain, viewed Chamberlain's speech as 'a kind of warning to Germany and an emphatic offer of help to France'.[73]

Hitler held a three-hour meeting with Konrad Henlein, the Sudeten German Party leader, on 28 March and told him that he intended to settle the Sudeten German problem 'in the near future' and was no longer prepared to tolerate the German minority being oppressed in Czechoslovakia. He promised Henlein: 'I stand with you, from tomorrow you will be my Viceroy [*Statthalter*].' He instructed Henlein to make demands which were quite clearly unacceptable to the Czechoslovakian government. Henlein summed up Hitler's approach to negotiations in his own words as: 'We must always demand so much that we can never be satisfied.'[74]

On 3 April Hitler gave a passionate speech at a mass rally in Graz, the second largest city in Austria, urging everyone to vote in the elections on 10 April:

> For the first time in the history of our people, a Reich is being constructed in accordance with the will of the people, and I desire to be nothing other than what I have been in the past: the warner of my people, the instructor of my people, the Führer of my people. In the future as well, I will bow to one single commandment, only a commandment that has compelled me ever since I was born: Germany.[75]

The Austrian journalist Erich Kern, who was young and unemployed, witnessed Hitler's speech that evening:

> At this time, the city of Graz had approximately 250,000 inhabitants. It seemed as if every one of them was out to greet the Führer. We stood on the street for seven hours until Hitler finally arrived. He was greeted with tumultuous jubilation. The rejoicing went on into the night. Hitler stayed at the Park Hotel, and thousands swamped the place and cheered all day and night. We young people were full of hope and believed that a new time was coming, that there would be work and bread for all.[76]

Hitler further boosted his election campaign with another speech in Vienna on 9 April. The union of Austria with Germany had not happened by design, he admitted, but was a reaction to Schuschnigg's ill-advised decision to call a referendum. The Austrian government had agreed to come to a negotiated settlement, but Schuschnigg had broken his word and that was why Hitler decided to occupy Austria immediately. Once again, Hitler adopted a messianic tone to justify his actions: 'I believe that it was also God's will that from here a boy was to be sent into the Reich, allowed to mature, and elevated to become the nation's Führer, thus enabling him to reintegrate his homeland into the Reich. There is divine will, and we are its instruments.' Hitler said that coming generations would look back with pride upon the union of Austria with Germany, concluding in a passionate tone: 'May every German realize the importance of this hour tomorrow, assess it, and then bow his head in reverence before the will of the Almighty, who has wrought this miracle in all of us within the past few weeks.'[77]

On 10 April, 99.75 per cent of Austrian voters endorsed the union of Austria with Germany. In Germany, which was now referred to as the Old Reich (*Altreich*), it was 99.08 per cent. Even taking into account a certain amount of ballot-rigging and intimidation, the

Austrian referendum was a huge expression of support for Hitler's actions.[78]

On that same day in France the centre-left politician Édouard Daladier became Prime Minister. As a veteran of the Great War Daladier did not want to see another conflict in Europe and he hoped to resolve German grievances through negotiation. However, Daladier also reluctantly conceded that France, as a matter of honour, would have to go to war with Germany should Hitler resort to military force to achieve his aims, particularly over Czechoslovakia. The new French premier appointed Georges Bonnet, an ambitious and unscrupulous schemer, as his Foreign Minister. Bonnet was a pacifist by conviction and as keen a supporter of the policy of appeasement as Neville Chamberlain.

On 21 April Hitler discussed the situation in Czechoslovakia with Wilhelm Keitel, the chief of the OKW. He ordered Keitel to prepare an updated version of Case Green (*Fall Grün*), the still rather vague plan for a German army to attack Czechoslovakia. Hitler said the ill treatment of the German minority by the Czechoslovakian government meant that the matter had to be settled by force, but he would not order a sudden attack without first inventing a legal justification. Hitler felt that military action should follow a period of diplomatic discussions, which would then gradually escalate into a crisis and then into a war. German military action needed to be 'lightning quick', Hitler told Keitel. The frightening speed of the attack would make foreign powers realize the hopelessness of any intervention.[79]

On 24 April Henlein issued his 8-Point Programme for the settlement of the Sudeten German problem during a speech in Karlsbad, Czechoslovakia (now Karlovy Vary in the Czech Republic). Henlein demanded complete equality for the Sudeten Germans and their recognition as a separate legal entity; also for a Sudeten settlement area to be clearly established, plus measures to be put in place for Sudeten self-government; as well as compensation to Sudeten Germans who had faced discrimination since 1918; and finally for Sudeten Germans to be allowed to freely profess their adherence to the ideology of Nazi Germany. In sum, Henlein wanted the Sudeten Germans to have full autonomy and self-government.[80]

Theodor Kordt, the German chargé d'affaires in Britain, sent the German Foreign Ministry a report on 28 April of his meeting with the French Prime Minister, who was in London having talks with the British government during which he made clear that France would not

[overleaf] Hitler tours Rome with Mussolini during a state visit, 4 May 1938.

permit the destruction of Czechoslovakia. Daladier told Kordt that he was convinced that Henlein's Karlsbad demands had been endorsed by Berlin and he feared that the situation in Czechoslovakia could lead to war. Germany, he warned Kordt, might believe that it was militarily stronger than its probable opponents, but this would be a mistake.[81]

At the annual May Day celebrations in Berlin Hitler addressed members of the Hitler Youth in the Olympic Stadium. The youth of Germany lived in a golden age, he told them. The victory of the Nazi Movement in 1933 had ended divisions and led to the unification of the German people, culminating in the union with Austria. 'Our youth is the building block of our Reich,' he added. 'You are the Greater Germany. It is for you that the German National Community reconstructed itself [...] So on this May Day I greet you in our new Greater Germany. For you are our springtime.'[82]

In Paris, on the same day, Johannes von Welczeck, the German ambassador to France, met with Georges Bonnet, the new French Foreign Minister. Bonnet explained that the recent Anglo-French talks in London were about closer military cooperation between Britain and France, but that this was not directed against Germany. In fact, Bonnet expressed great admiration for the achievements of the new Germany. France now accepted the *Anschluss* as an accomplished fact but Germany's position towards Czechoslovakia differed greatly from that of the French government. Bonnet warned Welczeck that any German military action against Czechoslovakia would trigger the Treaty of Alliance and Friendship, which had been agreed between Czechoslovakia and France in 1924 (indeed, France had been the first nation to recognize Czechoslovakia in 1918). Bonnet also mentioned Britain had agreed to act as a mediator in the crisis, primarily to induce the Czechoslovakian government to be more accommodating to the demands of the Sudeten Germans. Bonnet told Welczeck that if Germany could solve this matter amicably, then Britain and France would seek a broader understanding with Germany in order to ensure the peace of Europe.[83]

On 2 May Hitler left Berlin's Anhalter Station – in a fleet of three special chartered trains – for a week-long official visit to Italy. The 500-strong German party included cabinet ministers, senior diplomats, hand-picked journalists, generals and the wives of Nazi VIPs. Eva Braun travelled, too, but was kept discreetly in the background.

On his arrival in Rome on 3 May Hitler was greeted by the diminutive King Victor Emmanuel III, Mussolini, Ciano and a retinue of other important figures in the Italian government. Horse-drawn carriages waited in front of the specially constructed San Paolo railway station to take the guests on a parade through Rome. The crowd lining the city's streets was estimated at 1 million.

Hitler was accompanied in his carriage not by Mussolini but by the King of Italy himself. He was granted the honour of staying at the grand Quirinal Palace, the king's official residence, surrounded by royalty and courtiers. Hitler was sullen and often rude for most of the visit. He hated being forced into situations over which he had little control. He found the Italian royal family irritating and overly formal. The remaining German visitors stayed at the Grand Hotel Plaza, while a smaller party, including Eva Braun, resided at the Hotel Excelsior.[84]

The following day Victor Emmanuel III held a lavish state banquet. Hitler was seated to the left of the extremely tall Queen Elena of Italy, but the two did not say a single word to each other over dinner. The king later claimed that Hitler had asked for a woman to be sent up to his room on his first night at the palace, but not for the reason one might expect. Ciano tried to make sense of Hitler's request in his diary: 'The explanation it seems is he cannot go to sleep unless a woman turns down the bed before his eyes. It was difficult to find one, but the problem was solved by recruiting a chambermaid from a local hotel.'[85]

Over the next two days Hitler attended Italian navy manoeuvres at Naples and a military parade in Rome. He watched a naval ceremony while on board the battleship the *Conte di Cavour*. The dramatic highlight of the naval exercise was when 100 Italian submarines simultaneously surfaced.

On 7 May Hitler and Mussolini visited an archaeological exhibition about Augustus, the first emperor of the Roman Empire. In the evening, Hitler was the guest of honour at a gala dinner hosted by Il Duce at the Palazzo Venezia, where Mussolini had his main office and from the balcony of which he delivered his bombastic speeches to cheering crowds below. Both men declared their mutual respect for one another during their time together and Hitler took this opportunity to promise that the natural border of the Alps between their two countries was inviolable.

On 9 May, the last day of Hitler's visit, the two dictators travelled together by train to Florence, where they visited the beautiful Uffizi Gallery. Hitler, who had been an artist in his youth, enjoyed this part of the trip most of all, saying later: 'How I would love to travel around like an unknown painter in Italy.'[86] His special train left Rome at midnight.

From the brief political conversations he had during his stay, Hitler had gathered that Italy would grant Germany a free hand in its dealings with Czechoslovakia, although Mussolini had avoided any serious discussion of a possible military alliance between Germany and Italy.

While Hitler was away, General Ludwig Beck, Chief of the General Staff, submitted to Hitler the first in a series of critical and well-argued memoranda opposing Case Green. The first, dated 5 May, argued that Germany was not prepared for a long world war with Britain and France, which was bound to be the result of any unprovoked attack on Czechoslovakia.[87]

On 12 May Ernst von Weizsäcker, the State Secretary in the Foreign Ministry, reported the details of a meeting with Konrad Henlein, the Sudeten German leader. Weizsäcker had given Henlein instructions on how best to approach his two-day visit to London, which was due to begin on the following day. Weizsäcker told him to emphasize to the British the fact that his 8-Point Karlsbad Programme had to be fulfilled, but also to deny that he was acting on instructions from the German government, which, of course, he was.[88]

The British government warmly welcomed Henlein's visit. He met a number of leading British politicians including Churchill, Vansittart and several MPs from across the political spectrum. Henlein's carefully contrived calm and reasonable manner made a very good impression. He presented the Sudeten German problem in Czechoslovakia as a matter of national self-determination. The British press covered Henlein's visit extensively and extremely favourably.[89]

On 20 May the Czechoslovakian government became deeply concerned about reports of a concentration of German troops on its border, which suggested an imminent German invasion. Thus began the so-called 'May Crisis', which lasted until 22 May. The Czechoslovakian government immediately ordered a partial mobilization of its armed forces, which only served to raise international tensions. The Czech Minister Vojtěch Mastný met Weizsäcker at the Foreign Ministry in Berlin to discuss Czechoslovakia's concerns about German troop movements on the border. Weizsäcker told him that these reports were fabricated and completely false, but Mastný pointed out that German troops had been seen on the Czechoslovakian frontier in northern Austria and in Silesia, too.[90]

On that same day the British ambassador Nevile Henderson visited Weizsäcker to ask about the reported rumours of German troop movements in Saxony. 'I told the ambassador that the report was pure nonsense,' Weizsäcker noted.[91] No documents have ever been found in the German archives to indicate that German armed forces were preparing to invade Czechoslovakia at this time.

By mere coincidence, Wilhelm Keitel, on behalf of the OKW, submitted to Hitler at the Berghof a new much more detailed draft of Case Green on 20 May. It had been prepared by Lieutenant Colonel Kurt Zeitzler in consultation with the Führer. It began with a famous quote from Hitler: 'It is *not* my intention to smash Czechoslovakia by military action in the near future without provocation, unless an unavoidable development of the political conditions within Czechoslovakia forces the issue or political events in Europe create a particularly favourable opportunity which may perhaps never recur.'

At this point Hitler ruled out ordering a sudden attack on Czechoslovakia. His preference was to exploit diplomatic tensions to his own ends. The text of Case Green argued that preparations to attack Czechoslovakia would have to be based on the following principles: (1) the whole weight of all forces must be employed in the invasion of Czechoslovakia; (2) in the west, a minimum strength would offer rear cover, which might possibly become necessary; (3) the army formations capable of rapid deployment must force the frontier fortifications with speed and energy; and must break boldly into Czechoslovakia in the certainty that the bulk of the mobile army would be brought up with all possible speed.[92]

On 21 May Henderson met Ribbentrop in the German Foreign Ministry. Ribbentrop complained about the leaking of a private conversation between Ivone Kirkpatrick, the First Secretary at the British Embassy, and Weizsäcker to the Reuters press agency. It reported that Weizsäcker had denied Czech reports about German troop movements. Henderson claimed he had only sanctioned the press release on the Kirkpatrick-Weizsäcker conversation to try and calm the situation.

Henderson then read out a message to Ribbentrop from Lord Halifax, which asked the German government to exert its influence on Henlein to persuade him to enter into negotiations with the Czechoslovakian government. Halifax went on to spell out the dire consequences of German military intervention. If war broke out, he wrote, France would be compelled to intervene and, even though Britain had no treaty commitments, it might be drawn into the conflict in order to assist France.

Ribbentrop was not impressed and immediately gave an angry response: If Halifax's statement was intended as a threat, he said, then

'I must reject such a threat.' It did not induce fear in him at all, but left him 'completely cold'. Such a threat, Ribbentrop added, put simply, meant that Britain and France intended to declare war on Germany if it should go to the assistance of the oppressed Sudeten Germans in Czechoslovakia. Halifax, he said, should be making such threats to the Czechoslovakian government. If France intervened then it would suffer the greatest military defeat in its history.[93]

On 23 May Ribbentrop told Bernardo Attolico, the Italian ambassador, to inform Mussolini, in confidence, that there was in fact no concentration of German troops on the Czechoslovakian frontier. It was the Czech government spreading these false rumours.[94] In Paris on the same day the German ambassador Johannes von Welczeck had a meeting at Daladier's house. Daladier, who regarded the recent developments on the Czech crisis with grave anxiety, said that because of the Treaty of Alliance and Friendship between France and Czechoslovakia, France would go to war if Czechoslovakia was attacked, because above all France valued its honour.[95]

Nobody knows for sure who began the rumour that German troops were massing on the Czechoslovakian border. Ernst Eisenlohr, the German Foreign Minister in Prague, claimed to have evidence from what he called 'a reliable source' in the Czechoslovakian government that Noel Mason-MacFarlane, the British military attaché in Berlin, had been the chief source of the rumour. After receiving reports of German troop concentrations near the Czechoslovakian border, Mason-MacFarlane had apparently conveyed these fears to the British government and the danger of war spread from there.[96]

On 26 May Hitler laid the foundation stone for the new Volkswagen car plant at Fallersleben (renamed Wolfsburg in 1945). In his speech Hitler announced that the new People's Car would be called the 'Strength through Joy' car – *Kraft durch Freude* being the Nazis' state tourism arm, tasked with bringing leisure activities to the masses. Hitler claimed one of his central domestic policy aims was to increase car ownership in Germany. After solving the unemployment problem, he added, he was now determined to push ahead with his plans for producing a car at a price affordable to the ordinary worker: 'The automobile must become THE means of transportation for the *Volk*.'[97]

One of the most persistent myths about Hitler's regime is that it increased the standard of living of the German people. From 1932 to 1938 the amount of food consumed in Germany went up by 18 per cent, clothing sales increased by 25 per cent, and the purchase of household

Hitler attends the foundation stone laying ceremony on 26 May 1938 at the Fallersleben Wolfsburg Volkswagen factory which heralds his determination to mass produce a People's Car (later known as the Beetle).

furniture and household goods rose by 50 per cent. Yet Germany under Hitler cannot be described as an affluent society. In 'The International Comparison of National Income' (1938) the Australian economist Colin Clark estimated that Germans in 1938 enjoyed a standard of living 50 per cent below the United States and 33 per cent lower than in Britain.

Under Hitler the economic position of industrial and agricultural workers was not greatly improved. In many cases, their position was worse than in the Weimar period. From 1932 to 1938 hourly wages for unskilled workers fell by 3 per cent, while the number of hours worked each week went up by 15.2 per cent. Most German workers put in longer hours for less pay. In the Nazi period, wages were paid hourly in pfennigs, one pfennig being equal to one hundredth of a Reichsmark. Only the highest paid skilled workers received 1 Reichsmark per hour. The lowest paid factory workers received 59 pfennigs on average. In 1936, 62 per cent of workers earned less than 1,500 Reichsmarks per year, which was 125 Reichsmarks per month. A further 21 per cent of mainly white-collar workers, but also some skilled blue-collar workers, had annual incomes between 1,500 to 2,400 Reichsmarks. Only 17 per cent enjoyed incomes above 2,400 Reichsmarks per annum.

What did Germans in Hitler's Germany spend their wages on? Most of it went on food. A loaf of bread cost 31 pfennigs, five kilos of potatoes 50 pfennigs and a litre of milk 23 pfennigs. Germans ate four times more bread per week than the average American. Milk consumption was at the same level as the British. Germans ate twice as many potatoes as Americans and Britons. Pork amounted to more than half of German weekly meat consumption. A kilo of bacon at 2.14 Reichsmarks was not cheap. Butter at 3.10 Reichsmarks was very much a luxury item. Eggs cost 1.44 Reichsmarks for a dozen. Beer cost 88 pfennigs per litre. At only 30 pfennigs for ten, cigarettes were much cheaper.

The staples of the German diet during the Nazi era were bread, home-made jam, potatoes, cabbage, pork, with smaller amounts of milk and beer and cigarettes. Expenditure on food and tobacco amounted to between 43 and 50 per cent of weekly working-class household spending. Most Germans lived in rented apartments, which accounted for around 12 per cent of their income every month. A further 5 per cent went on gas and electricity. This left 32 per cent of income to cover clothing, shoes, transport, health care, insurance, household equipment and leisure activities.

The greatest symbol of consumer affluence in the 1930s was ownership of a car. In 1932 there were only 486,001 car owners in Germany. In the United States, by contrast, 23 million people owned a car. In Britain, around 1 million owned a car. Hitler wanted to see German car ownership increase. It did, but not very dramatically. By 1938 there were 1,271,000 German car owners. They were mostly the highest wage earners. The running costs for a car were an enormous 67.65 Reichsmarks per month. The price of the much-vaunted Volkswagen in 1936 was 1,600 Reichsmarks. A savings scheme was introduced, so that people could save 20 Reichsmarks per month towards buying one. In theory, when the fund reached 750 Reichsmarks a car would be delivered and the remaining balance would be paid off through further hire-purchase payments. It took three years to receive a Volkswagen. Only 270,000 people signed up for the scheme, however, and few cars were ever delivered. From September 1939 the 275 million Reichsmarks that had been deposited by savers towards a Volkswagen of their own was diverted to help the war effort.

Overall, there was a slight increase in living standards of people in Hitler's Germany when compared to the period of the Great Depression in the early 1930s, but people in Britain and the United States were much better off. However, Nazi propaganda was extremely effective in persuading the German people that life had improved under the Third Reich more than it actually had. It's now called the 'feel good factor'.[98]

On 26 May Herbert von Dirksen, the German ambassador to Britain, reported to the German Foreign Ministry that Henderson, the British ambassador to Germany, had been the chief architect of the panic known as the 'May Crisis' because he advised British Embassy officials to send their wives and children home to Britain. It was Henderson's pessimistic reports on supposed German troop movements that were the main reason Chamberlain called an emergency cabinet meeting on Sunday, 22 May. However, the British government quickly realized that there was no foundation to his reports. Dirksen noted Henderson was now being mocked in the British press as 'The boy who cried wolf.'[99]

Hitler held a military conference in Berlin on 28 May. He was furious about stories in the international press suggesting he had backed down in May because the Allies had presented a united front in defence of Czechoslovakia. With a map of Europe in front of him, Hitler told his generals that he had made an 'irrevocable decision' to break up Czechoslovakia. He ordered the construction of new fortifications in the west to deal with any possible French military intervention, and he requested a new version of Case Green to be drafted. Hitler had not yet decided what precise action to take, but his wounded pride had persuaded him that action was necessary. 'He's brooding about what decision to make,' Goebbels noted in his diary. 'That usually goes on for a while. But once he's made up his mind, he'll make sure his will is carried out.'[100]

On 30 May Hitler signed the order to begin Case Green. The basic outline of the plan was largely unchanged, but Hitler had written a decisive new opening sentence: 'It *is* my unalterable decision to smash Czechoslovakia by military action in the near future.' The emphasis now was on making immediate plans for the attack. The German government required a 'convenient apparent excuse' and an 'adequate political justification'. No exact date for the attack was included in the revised document, but Keitel's covering note insisted that all necessary preparations had to be completed by 1 October, a date that would prove to be deeply significant as the Czech crisis unfolded.[101]

On 2 June the Supreme Headquarters of the *Oberkommando der Wehrmacht* (OKW) prepared the outline of Operation Red, concerning German combat in Western Europe. It assumed that France would start hostilities, but included no plan to attack France. The entry of the British on the side of France was also assumed to be a certain eventuality, but in the beginning it was predicted Britain would only offer its French ally only air and naval support. The *Wehrmacht* intended to do nothing in Western Europe unless the French army attacked.[102]

Hitler signed another top-secret memorandum on the Czechoslovakian crisis on 18 June. In it he described the settlement of the Czech question as his 'immediate aim' and that it was to be resolved from 1 October 1938 onwards. Action would be taken, he added, only if he was absolutely certain that France and Britain would not intervene. Hitler suspected that the only actual military aid that would be given to Czechoslovakia would be very limited air support from the Soviet Union.[103]

The German Foreign Ministry official Ernst von Weizsäcker prepared a critical memorandum on the current aims of German foreign policy on 20 June. He began by stating that Britain and France stood in the way of Germany's further territorial expansion. In the event of war, he said, it was likely that the Soviet Union and the United States would associate themselves with the Western democracies. The German drive for expansion in Eastern Europe was only possible if

Britain and France tolerated it, without resorting to war. Germany had no viable plan to defeat Britain and France in a long war. In these circumstances, Weizsäcker recommended that Germany should adopt the stance of supporting a negotiated settlement of 'self-determination for the Sudeten Germans', as this was the most likely way to appeal to world opinion, rather than mounting an invasion of Czechoslovakia.[104]

The eagerly awaited rematch between the two rival boxers – the German Max Schmeling and the American Joe Louis – took place on 22 June 1938 before a crowd of 66,277 at the Yankee Stadium in New York City. It was billed as the 'Battle of the Century'. By now sport and politics had become interlinked with the international crisis. After his victory in the first fight in 1936 Schmeling had become a key symbol of Aryan supremacy, a living, breathing, specimen of the master race.

On his arrival in New York City, Schmeling told reporters: 'In Germany, they call me the champion.' In spite of vocal protests from Jewish and anti-Nazi organizations in the United States, the bout went ahead. The *New York Times* commented: 'Schmeling may be a Nazi. He probably is, but over here Schmeling is just a prize fighter when in the ring and a quiet, inoffensive foreigner when out of it.' On the day of the fight, Schmeling received a single sentence telegram from Hitler: 'Wishing you every success.'

As the bell rang for round one Louis bounded out of his corner and hit Schmeling with a flurry of devastating punches. Schmeling only stayed on his feet courtesy of the ropes, but not for long. A vicious right-hand punch sent him to the canvas. He was up again on the count of four, but when another blow made him drop to his knees his cornerman threw in the towel. However, this gesture of defeat was not recognized in the New York State boxing code, so the referee allowed the fight to continue. Louis delivered more unanswered blows. Schmeling hit the canvas once again. The referee counted to eight, then stopped the fight before reaching ten. An African American had beaten Nazi Germany's Aryan superman on a technical knockout in round one. Lasting a mere two minutes and four seconds, it is one of the most famous and important boxing matches of all time.

The fight had been broadcast live on German national radio at 3 a.m., but the programme ended abruptly. 'A terrible defeat,' Goebbels wrote in his diary. 'Our newspapers had reckoned too much on victory. Now the entire nation is depressed. I'll send an encouraging telegram to Schmeling and flowers to [his actress wife] Anni Ondra.' Hitler had not listened to the fight, but he was 'extremely depressed' when

[overleaf] American heavyweight Joe Louis knocks out Max Schmeling in the first round of their eagerly awaited rematch at New York's Yankee Stadium, 22 June 1938.

he heard the result on the next morning. The Ministry of Propaganda immediately went into a damage limitation exercise. On 29 June Goebbels sent a secret directive to all German newspaper editors, ordering them to stop carrying reports and photos of the boxing match. He banned the screening of the fight in cinemas. Hitler made it clear to Schmeling that he did not want to see him fight Louis ever again and risk another humiliating defeat. When war broke out, Schmeling was drafted into the armed forces and served as a paratrooper.[105]

On 5 July Kurt von Tippelskirch, a diplomat at the German Embassy in the Soviet Union, sent a memorandum to Ribbentrop on the attitude of the USSR to recent developments in the Czechoslovakian crisis. Rumours were circulating in Moscow, indicating that the Soviet Union had promised Czechoslovakia extensive military help in the event of war with Germany.

In a speech on 23 June in Leningrad Maxim Litvinov, the Soviet Foreign Minister, said it was the Czechoslovak-Soviet Treaty of Alliance of 1935 that had prevented war during the May crisis. However, Tippelskirch noted that the mood in the Soviet Union towards the pact with Czechoslovakia – and also to a similar pact with France – had now turned extremely negative. It was felt that these treaties were no longer an advantage and Joseph Stalin, the General Secretary of the Communist Party of the USSR, was very reluctant to turn the 1935 Franco-Soviet Treaty of Mutual Assistance into a full-blown military alliance.[106]

The Évian Conference on refugees was held in the Hotel Royal in the French resort town of Évian-les-Bains from 6 to 14 July. Representatives from thirty-two nations attended, although nobody from the German government turned up. After the *Anschluss* the Jewish refugee problem had become a pressing international issue. It was the US President Franklin D. Roosevelt who came up with the idea of this conference in Évian. Unable to attend it himself, Roosevelt chose the Quaker steel magnate and diplomat Myron Taylor to lead the US delegation and chair the meetings.

Taylor made it clear that strict US immigration laws made it impossible for the United States to take in more Jews. The French delegate told the conference that his country had already done much to solve the refugee problem, but could do no more. The British delegates were equally reluctant to adopt an open-door policy to Jews, nor would they support increased Jewish emigration to the British Mandate of Palestine. The Australian delegate argued that Jewish emigration to his country would 'endanger his own race'. For his part, the rabbi and Zionist Stephen Wise, speaking on behalf of the World Jewish Congress, pleaded with the international community to face up to the challenge of rescuing Jews in Europe and to protest against Jewish persecution.

Évian was not a success. No nation – with the exception of the tiny Dominican Republic – agreed to accept Jewish refugees. Shirer, who had attended the proceedings, noted that 'The British, French and Americans seem too anxious not to do anything to offend Hitler. It's an absurd situation. They want to appease the man who is responsible for their problem.'[107] The only concrete outcome of the Évian Conference was the creation of the Intergovernmental Committee for Refugees. It had no funds and no powers. The Nazi *Völkischer Beobachter* newspaper summed up the international community's attitude to Jews as follows: 'No one wants them.'[108]

In a deeply pessimistic memorandum, dated 16 July, Ludwig Beck, Chief of the General Staff, made a last-ditch attempt to persuade Brauchitsch, the army's commander-in-chief, of Germany's unpreparedness for war against Britain and France. A desperate Beck went even further, threatening the collective resignation of the army's high command if Hitler pressed ahead with his plan to attack Czechoslovakia. It was the duty of German officers, Beck added, not to carry out an order that they believed to be wrong. He ended his memorandum with these words: 'Extraordinary times demand extraordinary measures.'[109]

Meanwhile, Hitler had dispatched his loyal personal assistant Captain Fritz Wiedemann to London in mid-July to discuss the possibility of a state visit to Britain by Hermann Göring. However, the underlying purpose of Wiedemann's trip was to engage in informal talks with Lord Halifax on the Czechoslovakian crisis. Wiedemann told Halifax that Hitler would not settle the Czech crisis by force provided a satisfactory settlement was agreed. In reply, Halifax said that the British government would do all it could to bring about a negotiated settlement. Halifax also agreed to a state visit by Göring, once the Czech question was cleared up, although Hitler did not want any such visit to take place.[110]

With the negotiations between the Czechoslovakian government and the Sudeten Germans deadlocked, Halifax suggested on 16 July that a 'distinguished mediator' should be recruited in order to investigate the Sudeten Germans' claims to self-determination. This idea was accepted by Chamberlain, who chose Walter Runciman to undertake this task. Lord Runciman was a respected Liberal peer, a shipping magnate and former president of the Board of Trade, but he had no experience of high-level diplomatic negotiation. In Berlin on 25 July Henderson told Weizsäcker that Chamberlain wanted to send Runciman to Czechoslovakia to act as an unofficial mediator in the Czech crisis. He hoped that the German government would support this initiative. Weizsäcker, who assumed that the French must have approved of this idea already, advised Ribbentrop not to oppose it and this advice was accepted.[111]

Lord Runciman duly arrived in Prague on 3 August. 'Runciman's whole mission stinks,' Shirer noted in his diary. 'Henlein [the Sudeten German leader] is not a free agent. He cannot negotiate. He is completely under the orders of Hitler.'[112] However, Runciman's intervention was useful in other ways. For instance, on 10 August Lancelot Oliphant, Deputy Undersecretary of State at the Foreign Office, told Maisky, the Soviet ambassador to Britain: 'If Runciman succeeds in reconciling the Czechs with the Germans, then wonderful. If he fails, that's also no reason to cry; at least we'll have gained some time.'[113]

On 4 August Walther von Brauchitsch chaired a meeting of Germany's key military leaders, during which General Beck's 16 July memorandum was read out. Most of those present thought that Beck was correct to argue that Germany should not risk a European war over Czechoslovakia, and that it would probably lose if France and Britain were drawn into such a struggle. However, the generals strongly opposed any suggestion of a coup to halt Hitler's plans.

General Walther von Reichenau advised those present not to submit Beck's memorandum to the Führer, but news soon leaked to him of what was discussed between the generals. Hitler summoned Brauchitsch to the Berghof, where, during a tense meeting, Hitler was shown Beck's memorandum.[114] Brauchitsch described Hitler's reaction in his diary: 'He said people were trying to sabotage his work. Instead of the general staff being glad it could work in line with his own way of thinking, it refused any thought of war. It was high time for the chief of staff [Beck] to disappear.'[115]

At a military conference in the Berghof on 10 August Hitler delivered a three-hour speech to a group of younger generals. He outlined his plans to defeat Czechoslovakia, while keeping at bay any French military response through the use of improved western fortifications. In the discussion which followed, several generals expressed reservations about his plans and a disappointed Hitler felt that the group's response had been 'lukewarm'.[116]

On 15 August Hitler attended a demonstration of artillery bombardment at Jüterbog, about 40 miles southwest of Berlin. The idea was to show the doubting generals just how easily modern weapons could breach Czechoslovakia's border fortifications. Afterwards, Hitler gave a speech once again stressing Germany's need for *Lebensraum*, but he could not dispel his audience's fear that the Western democracies would go to war against Germany to defend Czechoslovakia.

On 18 August Beck resigned as Chief of the General Staff, because of his opposition to Case Green. Hitler accepted his resignation three days later, but insisted that it should be kept secret for the time being. Had Beck's decision to go been made public, it would have been deeply damaging to Hitler's plans. Beck's replacement, 54-year-old Franz Halder, was appointed on 1 September. He was the first Catholic and the first Bavarian to hold the post of Chief of the General Staff. Privately, Halder also rejected Hitler's war plans, often denouncing the Führer as 'a criminal, a madman and a bloodsucker'.

On 18 August the German conservative politician and staunch opponent of Nazism Ewald von Kleist-Schmenzin arrived in London at the request of the anti-war head of German military intelligence (*Abwehr*) Admiral Wilhelm Canaris to warn Chamberlain of Hitler's firm plan to invade Czechoslovakia. Kleist-Schmenzin believed that a strong Anglo-French line on Czechoslovakia would force Hitler to back down, but Chamberlain refused to even see him and felt his warnings should be discounted. Churchill did agree to meet him and he came away believing that Kleist-Schmenzin's advice should be heeded by the British government.

Kleist-Schmenzin was not alone in thinking Hitler had to be stopped. Several military officers were also involved in a clandestine opposition group that wished to overthrow Hitler. They not just included Canaris, and his deputy General Hans Oster, but also Ludwig Beck, Carl Goerdeler, a former mayor of Leipzig and Price Commissioner in Hitler's government, General Erwin von Witzleben, commander of the Berlin army defence district, and Ulrich von Hassell, the former German ambassador to Italy. The plan of this group, as it was discussed in August 1938, was to seize Hitler once he had issued the final order to attack Czechoslovakia and to bring him before a court.

On 19 August Ribbentrop told Weizsäcker that 'the Führer was firmly resolved to settle the Czech affair by force of arms'. Ribbentrop was convinced that the Western Powers would not intervene. When Weizsäcker disagreed, Ribbentrop told him that he should 'believe in the genius of the Führer'.[117]

A couple of days later Ribbentrop sent a stern letter to Halifax concerning the lack of progress of Runciman's mission to Czechoslovakia. In Ribbentrop's view, Runciman's intervention had been counterproductive so far, because it had actually encouraged the 'insurgence' of the Prague government.[118]

The following day in Moscow Friedrich-Werner von der Schulenburg, the German ambassador to the Soviet Union, held talks with Maxim Litvinov, the People's Commissar of Foreign Affairs. Schulenburg wanted to find out what assistance the Soviet Union would give Czechoslovakia in the event of a German attack. Litvinov refused to answer this, but he did say: 'You [Germany] desire the destruction of Czechoslovakia, you want to conquer the country.' Litvinov also emphasized that the Soviet government felt the Sudeten German question was a domestic concern for Czechoslovakia and that foreign powers should not interfere.[119]

Between 27 and 29 August Hitler inspected the fortifications on the western border. During the visit General Wilhelm Adam told him that only a third of the fortifications would be complete by the end of October. When Adam then expressed doubts about the wisdom of attacking Czechoslovakia, Hitler replied angrily: 'We have no time to listen any longer to this stuff. You don't understand that we produce in Germany 23 million tons of steel a year, the French only 6 millions and the English only 16 millions. The English have no reserves and the French have the greatest internal difficulties. They'll beware of declaring war on us.'[120]

The prize-winning French author Alphonse de Châteaubriant was granted an interview with Hitler at the Berghof on 31 August. It was widely reported in the French press. The greatest threat to European peace was Bolshevism, Hitler said, and he denied that Germany was retreating into isolationism. It was the collapse of the international economy which forced Germany to seek self-sufficiency through its Four-Year Plan, but he made sure to end the interview on a friendly note: 'In the course of our history we have fought many a battle with France: nonetheless, we remain people of one family. I turn to all of Germany to say: bonds exist between us, bonds we cannot simply erase from our country [...] Let us be honest: we have little reason to hate each other and all the more reason to admire one another.'[121]

On 3 September Hitler held a military conference at the Berghof with Keitel, chief of the OKW, and Brauchitsch, commander-in-chief of the German army, to discuss the progress of their preparations for Case Green. Hitler ordered them to move troops up to the Czechoslovakian border on 28 September. From that date onwards, he said, the German army needed to be 'ready for action' at two days' notice. The provisional date set for the German attack on Czechoslovakia was set as 1 October.[122]

On 5 September Edvard Beneš, the President of Czechoslovakia, informed the leaders of the Sudeten German Party that he would accept any proposals they made, provided they agreed to the Sudetenland remaining a part of Czechoslovakia. He had called their bluff. 'My God,' said Karl Frank, the Sudeten German Party's deputy leader, 'they have given us everything.'[123] However, on 7 September the party's leader Konrad Henlein, under instructions from Hitler, broke off negotiations with the Czechoslovak government following a riot in Moravská Ostrava when a Sudeten German deputy was reportedly punched by a Czech policeman.

The annual Nazi Party Nuremberg Rally had begun a day earlier with the post-*Anschluss* title 'Rally of the Greater Germany'. For all its triumphalism, this would be the last rally of the Nazi era. In his opening proclamation Hitler concentrated on Austria and on domestic economic progress. He promised to solve the unemployment problem in Austria within one year. On the Four-Year Plan, he commented: 'We are building up Germany's economy in such a fashion that it can, at any given time, function independently of other countries and stand on its own two feet.' He even predicted that Germany could withstand a blockade should it be drawn into war.[124]

On that same day Ribbentrop produced a detailed memorandum outlining what he saw as the current policy positions of the major powers involved in the Czechoslovakian crisis. The French government, he wrote, was reluctant to run the risk of war, but still intended to stand by Czechoslovakia should it be attacked. If war broke out, it also seemed highly likely that Britain would stand by France. The Soviet Union would almost certainly intervene if Czechoslovakia was attacked, but Italy would remain neutral. Poland and Romania were unlikely to intervene directly, as were the Hungarians, even though they supported the German position.[125]

An editorial in *The Times* on 7 September suggested that the best solution to the crisis was for Czechoslovakia to cede the Sudetenland to Germany. This possibility had not been publicly discussed until now though in private Chamberlain had been moving to this conclusion during August. Nevertheless, the British government issued a stern statement distancing itself from *The Times* editorial, but the damage had been done. A gleeful German government believed the editorial had been ordered by Chamberlain himself though there is no evidence that he did.[126] Curt Bräuer, the German chargé d'affaires in Paris, met the French Prime Minister Daladier on the same day. Daladier stressed the 'calamitous consequences of a European war' growing out of the Czech crisis, stressing that any European war would only further the spread of communism. There was 'complete understanding' of the German demands in the French government, Daladier added, and there would be no opposition in France if these demands were achieved by peaceful means. However, if there was an armed intervention by German forces then a European war would almost certainly begin.[127]

On the evening of 9 September Hitler held a secret military conference on Case Green in the Deutsche Hof, his favourite hotel in Nuremberg. With him were six leading German generals, including Brauchitsch, Halder and Keitel. Hitler stressed the need for rapid action by strong German armoured divisions to speedily defeat the Czechoslovakian forces before the Western Allies had a chance to respond. He had some doubts about the detailed army plan, which had proposed attacking in northern Moravia, where the Czech fortifications were strongest. Hitler suggested trying to break through in a direction that led to Prague was a much better alternative. This idea was now incorporated into the *Wehrmacht*'s plans.[128]

In his much-anticipated closing speech to the Nuremberg Rally on 12 September, Hitler threw down the gauntlet at his enemies. He spoke of the 'terrorist blackmail' and 'criminal aims of the Czech government', and boasted about the strength of Germany's western defence fortifications. Only then did he move on to discuss the 'unbearable fate of the Sudeten Germans'. The German Reich could no longer accept the persecution of this minority, he said, and he warned the Czechoslovakian president Edvard Beneš: 'The Germans in Czechoslovakia are neither defenceless nor alone. Let this be noted.'[129]

The next day there was a dramatic and unexpected development. British Prime Minister Neville Chamberlain sent the following communication to Hitler: 'In view of the increasingly critical situation I propose to come over at once to see you [in Germany], with a view to trying to find a peaceful solution. I propose to come over by air and I'm ready to come tomorrow.' Chamberlain called this Plan Z. Chamberlain had decided in late August that he would personally visit Hitler should Runciman's mission end in failure. The plan was reserved to just a few close intimates: Horace Wilson, his personal envoy, Nevile Henderson and Lord Halifax. The cabinet was kept in the dark. Hitler was 'thunderstruck' when he heard the news of Chamberlain's offer, but he readily agreed to meet him at the Berghof. In reality, Hitler had little choice. He would have looked like a warmonger if he had rejected Chamberlain's request. Hitler needed to persuade the Western Powers that he was a reasonable man, perhaps even a peacemaker at this stage of the Czech crisis.[130]

On 15 September Chamberlain left Britain for Germany from Heston airfield in west London. Contrary to popular belief, it was not Chamberlain's first time in an aeroplane. In 1923 he had accompanied the Duke of York, the future King George VI, on an internal flight to an industrial fair in Birmingham. With him on this trip were his close diplomatic adviser Horace Wilson and William Strang, the director of the Central Europe division of the Foreign Office. Lord Halifax, the Foreign Secretary, stayed in London. After landing at Munich's Oberwiesenfeld airfield, Chamberlain was greeted by Ribbentrop, Weizsäcker, Henderson and Herbert von Dirksen, the German ambassador to Britain. The party drove in a motorcade to Munich's central station, where they boarded Hitler's own luxurious special train to Berchtesgaden in the Bavarian Alps.

Hitler greeted Chamberlain, who was carrying an umbrella, at the foot of the steps leading to the Berghof around 5 p.m. It was raining heavily. Chamberlain was impressed by the mountain grandeur of the Berghof, but not by Hitler himself, who he thought had the type of undistinguished looks that would not stand out in a crowd. The two leaders then took tea and cake in the Great Hall, before going upstairs to Hitler's office for a one-to-one conversation. The only other person present was Paul Schmidt, who acted as interpreter and took detailed notes. Ribbentrop, much to his great annoyance, was kept outside.

The first conversation between Chamberlain and Hitler amounted to an exchange of ideas. Chamberlain said that he had always desired an Anglo-German understanding. He welcomed the visit of the Prime Minister and emphasized that the chief matter to be resolved between them was the Sudeten German question. Hitler was determined to unite the 10 million Germans who lived in Austria and Czechoslovakia. The Austrians had already achieved their return to the Reich, but now it was also time for the return of the 3.5 million Sudeten Germans in Czechoslovakia. Was he willing to risk war to bring this about? Yes he was, he told Chamberlain.

People in Britain wanted to know whether the incorporation of the Sudeten Germans into the Greater German Reich was all that he was demanding, Chamberlain replied, or whether his real aim was really the violent dismemberment of the Czechoslovakian state. 'Violence?' Hitler said. 'Who's talking about violence here? Herr Beneš uses violence against my countrymen in the Sudetenland.' Hitler made it clear to Chamberlain that he was determined to settle the Czechoslovakian problem one way or another.

Chamberlain thanked Hitler for his clear expression of the German position, but he also pointed out that if Hitler had already decided to move militarily against Czechoslovakia then he had wasted his time coming on such a long journey to meet him. What he was interested in, above all, was the maintenance of peace. In Chamberlain's view, what needed to be agreed was how the inclusion of the Sudeten Germans in the Reich could be carried out in an orderly manner. Chamberlain told Hitler he found the detachment of the Sudeten areas to Germany perfectly acceptable.

Hitler, adopting a much friendlier tone, assured Chamberlain that he would allow him time to consult on the matter and then to come back to Germany for a second meeting. He promised not to set the wheels of his military machine in motion while negotiations continued. Chamberlain admitted he detected a certain 'ruthlessness' in some of Hitler's comments but felt a certain rapport had been established during their conversation. A joint press statement was agreed by the two leaders: 'The Führer and Reich Chancellor had a conversation with Mr Chamberlain, the British Prime Minister, on the Obersalzberg today, during which there was a frank exchange of views on the present situation. The British Prime Minister is returning to England tomorrow to confer with the British cabinet. In a few days a new conversation will take place.'[131]

Henderson asked Ribbentrop for a copy of Schmidt's minutes, but the German Foreign Minister avoided responding to this request. After the British delegation had gone, Ribbentrop told Schmidt: 'The report is intended for the Führer alone. Please note that.' Schmidt felt that this was 'a pure act of spite by Ribbentrop, who wanted revenge for being excluded from the conversation with Chamberlain'.[132] For his part, Chamberlain was extremely concerned and annoyed about the

Germans' refusal to supply him with a copy of the minutes. Without it, he felt that he would not be able to give the cabinet an exact report of his meeting with Hitler. He complained to the Germans that he could not be expected to keep details of a lengthy conversation in his head. The minutes were never provided by Ribbentrop.[133]

On that same day Henlein, leader of the Sudeten German Party, wrote a letter to Hitler, stating: 'I informed the British delegation yesterday that the basis for further negotiations could no longer be the 8 Karlsbad points, but only the achievement of a union with the Reich.' Henlein had predicted that Chamberlain would propose the acceptance of the 8-Point Karlsbad Programme during his meeting with Hitler. Henlein rejected the idea of a referendum and suggested the much more radical step of Germany occupying all regions with more than a 50 per cent German population 'within 24 hours'.[134]

On 16 September Hitler once again granted an interview to George Ward Price of the British *Daily Mail*. He denied that he was planning a war against the Western Powers. It would be 'insane' for such a war to break out, he said. He was 'convinced of the honesty and good will of Mr Chamberlain', but he spoke bitterly about Czechoslovakian intransigence. If President Beneš was a great statesman he would have already agreed to the Sudeten Germans being reunited with the Reich.

Hitler also said during the interview that he could not understand why the French government was so reluctant to allow the Sudeten Germans national self-determination when it had accepted that principle in relation to the Saarland, which had been returned to Nazi Germany in 1935. The creation of Czechoslovakia in 1919 had been 'complete insanity', he added. The moment Germany regained its strength, the Sudeten Germans began to speak out for unification. It was the Czechoslovakian government that was now pitting the European superpowers against each other 'through political and diplomatic trickery'.[135]

Back in London, Chamberlain held a cabinet meeting on 17 September in order to give details of his encounter with Hitler from memory. He gave only a partial account of what had transpired during his meeting. Hitler wanted the transfer of all German-speaking districts of the Sudetenland. As far as he could tell, Hitler was telling the truth when he said his aims were strictly limited to this single demand. What Chamberlain failed to mention was Hitler's uncompromising and bullying tone during their talks or his promise to settle the matter by force unless his demands were met. Lord Runciman, back from his

[overleaf] The four European leaders pictured after the signing of the Munich agreement *(left to right)*, Chamberlain (Britain), Daladier (France), Hitler (Germany) and Mussolini (Italy).

failed mission in Czechoslovakia, advised the cabinet to agree to the transfer to Germany of the predominantly Sudeten German areas of Czechoslovakia without recourse to a referendum. To general assent, this now became agreed British policy.[136]

The next day Daladier, the French Prime Minister, and his Foreign Minister Georges Bonnet arrived in London. Chamberlain told him that Hitler had agreed to carry out the transfer in an 'orderly fashion', knowing he had given no such assurance. In other words, he lied to Britain's key ally at a critical moment. It was soon agreed between the British and French leaders that all the Czechoslovakian territory that was inhabited by more than 50 per cent of Sudeten Germans should be transferred to Germany. In return, Britain and France would join an international grouping to guarantee the safety of the new Czechoslovakian border against any unprovoked aggression. This change in the collective security arrangements would replace the pacts of mutual assistance that France and Czechoslovakia had with the Soviet Union currently in existence. This became known as the Anglo-French Plan. The Czechoslovakian government would be told that if it did not agree to the plan, it would have to face Hitler's Germany alone.

On the following day, identical British and French letters were sent to President Beneš outlining the Anglo-French Plan. At first, the Czechoslovakian government bravely refused to agree to it, but three days later they finally yielded to British and French diplomatic pressure. Beneš issued a brave and solemn statement on Czech national radio:

> We relied upon the help that our friends might have given us, but when the question of reducing us by force arose it became evident that the European crisis was taking on too serious a character. Our friends therefore advised us to buy freedom and peace by our sacrifice, and this in proportion to their own inability to help us. The President of the Republic and our government had no other choice, for we find ourselves alone.[137]

On 20 September Hitler met a Hungarian delegation, which included the Prime Minister Béla Imrédy, the Foreign Minister Kálmán Kánya, plus the chief of the army general staff. Hitler told them that he was determined to settle the Sudeten question, even at the risk of starting a world war, but he was convinced that Britain and France would not intervene. He urged the Hungarian government to demand the Czech government hold a referendum, so that the Hungarian-speaking people of Czechoslovakia could determine their own future, and the Hungarians agreed to do this.[138]

Chamberlain flew to Germany for a second visit on 22 September, firmly convinced that all of Hitler's demands had been fulfilled. At 12.36 p.m. his plane landed at Cologne Airport, where he was greeted by an SS *Leibstandarte* Adolf Hitler military band playing 'God Save the King'. It was a beautiful autumn day and Chamberlain's delegation was driven on the short journey to the picturesque Hotel Petersburg, set on a hill on the right bank in the Rhineland spa town of Bad Godesberg. This time Chamberlain brought with him Ivone Kirkpatrick from the British Embassy in Berlin to act as his own interpreter in order to ensure he had his own written record. Paul Schmidt once again acted as Hitler's interpreter and produced by far the more detailed version of what transpired.

Hitler met Chamberlain at the entrance to the plush Hotel Dreesen, also located on the Rhine. It was one of Hitler's favourite hotels. He stayed there over seventy times. Chamberlain entered the hotel lobby in a confident, positive mood. The two men shook hands then went upstairs to a conference room. Chamberlain spoke first, summarizing the protracted negotiations of the previous week, outlining the details of the Anglo-French Plan. Everything that Hitler had demanded during their encounter at the Berghof had now been accepted, Chamberlain said. Now they only needed to agree to a timetable to implement these demands, including a referendum. The British government was willing to enter into an international guarantee against any unprovoked attack on the remainder of Czechoslovakia. With that, a rather self-satisfied Chamberlain sat back in his chair, with a satisfied expression as if to say – as Schmidt put it – 'haven't I worked splendidly [on your behalf] in the past five days'.

Adolf Hitler expressed his sincere thanks for all of Chamberlain's efforts, but told him the Anglo-French Plan was unacceptable. Furthermore, the matter would have to be solved in the next few days. He upped his demands by presenting Chamberlain with a map outlining the Sudetenland areas he wanted transferred, granting Germany even more territory than he had originally demanded at their first meeting. Hitler also refused to guarantee the border of what remained of Czechoslovakia until after the Hungarian and Polish demands for self-determination had been settled. To add insult to injury Hitler further demanded that any Czech citizen refusing to accept the transfer would be relieved of all property and allowed just a suitcase full of belongings and moved eastwards as a refugee in what remained of Czechoslovakia.

[overleaf]   Cheering crowds greet
Hitler in the annexed Sudetenland,
4 October 1938.

In reply, Chamberlain said he was disappointed and somewhat puzzled by the attitude taken by the Führer. The British Prime Minister pointed out that he had risked his entire political career on gaining Hitler's acceptance for the Anglo-French Plan which gave Hitler everything he had demanded 'without the expenditure of a single drop of German blood'. He added that he was already being accused of having betrayed Czechoslovakia. After two hours of further haggling, Chamberlain, realizing that Hitler's new much harsher terms were unlikely to be accepted by the cabinet, the French or the Czechs, decided to break off talks and left Hitler's hotel to spend a gloomy night in his suite at the Hotel Petersburg.[139]

Chamberlain decided not to meet Hitler on the following day, but instead sent him a letter rejecting his demands. The difficulty, he said, was the suggestion that the Sudeten area should be occupied immediately by German troops before a referendum was held: 'This would be condemned as an unnecessary display of force.'[140]

In his reply, Hitler saw no reason why the territories could not be transferred immediately, because the Czech government had already accepted the principle of national self-determination for the Sudeten Germans in the Anglo-French Plan. If the matter could not be resolved through negotiation, then, Hitler warned, 'Germany is determined to exhaust the other possibilities which then alone remain open to her'.[141]

Chamberlain replied to Hitler's letter in a friendly manner by requesting that he put his proposals in a memorandum and add a map showing the areas of Czechoslovakia that were to be transferred. If he received this, Chamberlain promised to forward it to the Czechoslovakian government. After this memorandum was in his hands, Chamberlain would return to London as there was now little point in him remaining in Germany.[142]

Hitler invited Chamberlain to resume talks at the Hotel Dreesen in order to receive a written copy of his memorandum. It was around 9.30 p.m. on 23 September when Hitler and Chamberlain sat down to talk again. A wide circle of witnesses was present this time, most notably Ribbentrop, Weizsäcker and Friedrich Gaus, the director of the Foreign Ministry's Legal Department, as well as, accompanying Chamberlain, Horace Wilson and Nevile Henderson, plus Ivone Kirkpatrick acting as interpreter.

Hitler thanked Chamberlain for his efforts to find a peaceful solution. A summary of the German memorandum was then read out in English by Schmidt. It stated that it was essential that the separation of the Sudetenland from Czechoslovakia be carried out without delay. There followed the outlining of several German demands: (1) the withdrawal of the Czechoslovakian armed forces, police and customs officials. (2) the areas outlined on a map to be handed over to Germany by 1 October. (3) the Czechoslovakian government was to agree to send home all military forces in the Czech state territory. (4) the Czechoslovakian government was to liberate all political prisoners of the German race. (5) the evacuated territory was to be handed over without any destruction of property. In addition to these key demands, all commercial and transport materials, such as motor vehicles and railway rolling stock, were to be handed over to German officials. Public utilities – gas and electrical plants – would be taken over. No foodstuff, raw materials or livestock were to be removed by Czechs as they left the area. In return, the German government would permit a referendum in the affected areas and alterations to any territory would be agreed by an international commission and a German-Czech commission.[143]

After hearing this, Chamberlain was completely horrified but remained calm and stood his ground stoically. He told Hitler the German memorandum was 'an ultimatum and not a document of negotiation'. It would have a terrible impact on British public opinion. Hitler's memorandum was couched in the language of the conqueror, he added, and laid down everything in non-negotiable terms that left no time for discussion or even the orderly execution of plans. Indeed, the worst aspect of all, as far as Chamberlain was concerned, was the short time span given for its implementation. In response, Hitler claimed that the suggestions in the memorandum were nothing new and had been discussed in their previous conversations. 'With the most profound regret and disappointment,' an obviously frustrated Chamberlain replied, 'I have to state that you have made no effort to assist my attempts to secure peace.'[144]

At 10.30 p.m., in the middle of this highly emotive conversation between Hitler and Chamberlain, a message was handed to Hitler by an aide that relayed news that Edvard Beneš, the President of Czechoslovakia, had just announced the mobilization of the army on Czech national radio. The matter had now been settled, Hitler said, viewing this as an aggressive move. Chamberlain disagreed, arguing that mobilization was simply an understandable defensive measure by the Czechoslovakian government. Hitler responded by saying that there was no chance now of the Czechs agreeing to a transfer of territory.

A solution based on force would result in a huge loss of life, Chamberlain shot back. Hitler was unmoved and quoted an old German proverb in response: 'Better an end to terror than terror without end.' Chamberlain then asked if the German memorandum was the last word on the matter. Hitler said that it was. Then there was really no point continuing the conversation, Chamberlain replied. As far as he was concerned the talks were over. He was going away with a heavy heart, because all of his hopes for peace had been destroyed. Just as the meeting began to descend into a bitter war of words between Hitler and Chamberlain, Ribbentrop suddenly interrupted the conversation. Chamberlain, he pointed out, had not really understood the German memorandum if he thought of it as an ultimatum.

The British delegation called for a break in order to have the English translation of the memorandum read out to them once more. This time Schmidt read it out much more slowly, word for word. When the talks finally resumed, Hitler said that he would give the Czech government until 1 October to surrender the areas that had been marked on the map. Impressed by what seemed a concession by Hitler, Chamberlain agreed to present what would become known as the 'Godesberg Memorandum' to the Czechoslovakian government. The long and heated discussion ended at 1.45 a.m. on 24 September. As he left Hitler's hotel for his own, Chamberlain smiled and gave Hitler a friendly handshake.[145] He had finally stood up to Hitler with passion and in a principled manner.

A very tired and disheartened Chamberlain flew back to Britain on the same day. At 10 Downing Street the British cabinet met three times to discuss the infamous Godesberg Memorandum. Chamberlain told his ministers that he did not believe Hitler intended to 'crush Czechoslovakia and dominate Europe' and tried to suggest there was little 'substantive difference' between the Anglo-French Plan and Hitler's Godesberg proposals. Quite astonishingly he advised his cabinet colleagues that Hitler's demands should be accepted. Some ministers felt the price for peace being demanded by Hitler was now too high. Lord Halifax thought it extremely unlikely that the Czechoslovakian government would accept the Godesberg Memorandum anyway. The cabinet failed to reach any agreement and decided to meet on the following day to finalize its position. It was obvious as the debate dragged on during the three meetings that opposition to accepting Hitler's fresh demands was growing.[146]

Back in Germany, while walking in the garden of the Reich Chancellery with Goebbels on 25 September, Hitler told him that he didn't think President Beneš would accept his memorandum. Even if he did, Hitler was still determined to destroy the whole of Czechoslovakia by force.[147]

In London on the same day the British cabinet met twice more. Halifax, who had endured a 'sleepless night', and was deeply troubled, dropped a bombshell by telling his colleagues that he could not accept the Godesberg Memorandum. A week before he had believed the demands made by Hitler at Berchtesgaden were the only logical way to avoid war, but the events at Godesberg had now convinced him of the 'immorality of yielding to force'. 'I cannot rid my mind of the fact that Herr Hitler has given us nothing and that he is dictating terms', said Halifax, 'just as though he had won a war without having to fight.' There was a difference in principle, he added, between the orderly transfer of territory laid out in the Anglo-French Plan and the 'disorderly transfer' outlined in Hitler's memorandum. Halifax felt the British government should now put the facts before the Czechoslovakian government and if the French government decided to fight against Germany in defence of Czechoslovakia, Britain should offer its full support. With a few exceptions, the cabinet agreed with the assessment of Halifax. Chamberlain, who had privately informed Halifax that his change of mind was 'a horrible blow to me', had been defeated by his own cabinet ministers.[148]

Later that same day, the French Prime Minister and his team arrived in London for talks with British ministers. Daladier was adamant that Hitler should accept the Anglo-French Plan or face war. When Chamberlain asked him if the French were prepared to fight Germany without a firm offer of British support, Daladier simply replied: 'Each of us will do his duty.' No British military support was offered at this stage, but there was now considerable public pressure for Britain to follow France into war.

Jan Masaryk, the Czech ambassador to Britain, next arrived at 10 Downing Street to inform Chamberlain that the Czechoslovakian government had been amazed by the Godesberg Memorandum, because it deprived Czechoslovakia of every safeguard of its right to exist as an independent nation and amounted to a de facto ultimatum usually presented to a defeated nation after a war.[149]

The British cabinet meeting resumed late in the evening. Chamberlain relayed the strong objections of the French and the Czechs to Hitler's memorandum. Nevertheless, Chamberlain still wanted to find a way through to a peaceful settlement. He told the cabinet that he would send a private letter to Hitler, delivered in person by his close adviser Sir Horace Wilson, proposing a conference between Germany and Czechoslovakia and any other interested parties in order to reach a negotiated settlement. The cabinet insisted that if Hitler rejected this proposal, Wilson should tell Hitler bluntly that the Czechs would fight, France would join in and Britain would stand by the French.[150]

On the following day Wilson duly delivered Chamberlain's letter to Hitler in Berlin at 5 p.m. A swift translation was read out to Hitler by Schmidt. In the letter, Chamberlain gave details of the Czechoslovakian government's rejection of the Godesberg Memorandum, especially its insistence upon the immediate evacuation of Czech troops and the occupation of the Sudeten areas by German troops. Nevertheless, Chamberlain wrote, 'a settlement by negotiation still seems possible at an international conference'.[151]

After hearing the contents of the letter, Hitler jumped up from his chair, shouting: 'There is no point in going on with negotiations!' He walked to the door of his office, but then, according to Schmidt, calmly returned to his chair and controlled his anger. Wilson tried to persuade him to behave reasonably, but Hitler continued with another angry tirade against what he saw as the intransigence of the Czechoslovakian government.[152] Wilson should now have issued the stern warning to Hitler that the British cabinet had agreed upon the night before, but the meeting ended without him doing so. Why? Because Chamberlain had advised him to delay the warning to the next day.

In the evening Hitler gave one of his most passionate speeches before a crowd of 20,000 at the Berlin Sport Palace at 8 p.m. It included a lengthy summary of recent events. He then emphasized how conciliatory he had been in his relations with other nations ever since 1933, and offered several examples of this. There was the German-Polish Non-Aggression Pact, the Anglo-German Naval Agreement, guarantees of neutrality to Belgium and the Netherlands, and a 'friendship from the heart' with Italy. He denied wanting to go to war with France: 'We want nothing of France! Nothing at all!' He then praised Chamberlain's efforts to bring about a peaceful solution.

Hitler then said that there were 10 million Germans who wished to return to the Reich. The Austrian referendum had proved that the majority of Austrians wanted to be part of a Greater German Reich. This left the Sudeten German question, which required an immediate solution. In conclusion, he said that he had made Beneš an offer to settle the matter peacefully in the Godesberg Memorandum, which demanded nothing more than what Beneš had already agreed to. Hitler ended with a stark warning: 'War or peace. Either he [Beneš] can accept this offer and give Germans their freedom or we will take this freedom ourselves. We are determined. Herr Beneš now has the choice. He will need to give over the territory by 1 October. He can accept my offer or we Germans will get it for ourselves.'[153] A storm of applause followed and an exhausted Hitler slumped into his chair.

At this point Goebbels theatrically jumped to his feet, took the microphone and exclaimed: 'One thing is for sure: 1918 will never be repeated!'[154] Shirer, who witnessed Hitler's speech that night, noted in his diary: 'Hitler looked at Goebbels as if those were the words he had been searching for all evening and hadn't quite found. He leaped to his feet and with a fanatical fire in his eyes that I shall never forget brought his right hand, after a grand sweep, pounding down on the table and yelled with all the power of his lungs: *Ja!* [Yes!].'[155]

After news of Hitler's speech had reached him, Chamberlain issued a public statement, acknowledging Hitler's friendly comments towards him, and stressing once again that he had still not abandoned his efforts to find peace, 'since it seems incredible to me that the peoples of Europe, who do not want war with each other, should be plunged into a bloody struggle over a question on which agreement has already been largely obtained'.[156]

The US President Franklin D. Roosevelt sent a letter to Hitler, urging him to come to a peaceful settlement:

> So long as these negotiations continue, so long will there remain
> the hope that reason and the spirit of equity may prevail and
> that the world may therefore escape the madness of a new resort
> to war. On behalf of the 130 million people of the United States
> of America and for the sake of humanity everywhere, I most
> earnestly appeal to you not to break off negotiations, looking to a
> fair and constructive settlement of the questions at issue.[157]

Hitler's reply to Roosevelt was uncompromising. He acknowledged the worries of the president, but stated bluntly: 'It is not Germany who is to blame for the fact there is a Sudeten German problem at all and that the present untenable conditions have arisen from it.' The chances of a negotiated settlement, Hitler added, had been exhausted when his Godesberg Memorandum was roundly rejected: 'It now rests not with the German government, but with the Czechoslovak government alone, to decide if they want peace or war.'[158]

What was the attitude of the Soviet Union to all of this frantic diplomacy? Friedrich-Werner Graf von der Schulenburg, the German ambassador to the USSR, reported on 26 September that the French government, for the first time, had asked Litvinov, the People's Commissar of Foreign Affairs, what the Soviets would do if Germany attacked Czechoslovakia. The Soviet government would fulfil its treaty obligations, Litvinov said, and together with France they would offer assistance to Czechoslovakia 'in the ways available to us'. The Soviet High Command was prepared to engage in military staff talks with Czechoslovakia and France, but Litvinov made it clear that the French must act first in defence of Czechoslovakia in order to trigger Soviet involvement.[159]

On 27 September Sir Horace Wilson met Hitler at 12.15 p.m. He read out Chamberlain's friendly statement, issued the night before. Hitler insisted that his terms remained unchanged and non-negotiable: if the Czech government did not accept the terms of his Godesberg Memorandum by 2 p.m. on 28 September, then on 1 October German troops would march into the Sudetenland.

Wilson then informed Hitler that he had been instructed to deliver a further message from Chamberlain. If Germany attacked Czechoslovakia, Britain and France would come to Czechoslovakia's aid, Wilson said. After Schmidt had translated this message for Hitler, the Führer angrily replied that in that case, it was most probable that war would break out in six days. If Czechoslovakia rejected his memorandum, he was 'firmly resolved to smash that country'. The Czechs would most probably reject his terms because they knew that they could count on the support of France and Britain, he added. Wilson had nothing more to say. Just as he was leaving the room, Wilson promised Hitler: 'I will try and make those Czechs sensible.' This comment showed where Wilson's own sympathies lay during the Czech crisis.[160]

Later on the same day Hitler sent Chamberlain a letter expressing his willingness to give a free vote to people in those areas of Czechoslovakia that had been marked for transfer, but only if the Czech government accepted his memorandum in full. If it did not, then Germany would invade Czechoslovakia. He ended his letter by urging Chamberlain to continue with his peace efforts.[161]

War was now expected in Britain and that evening Chamberlain gave a speech live on BBC radio at 8 p.m. in which he famously stated in a defeatist tone:

How horrible, fantastic, incredible it is, that we should be digging
trenches and trying on gas masks here, because of a quarrel in
a faraway country between people of whom we know nothing
[…] However much we may sympathize with a small nation
confronted by a big and powerful neighbour, we cannot in all
circumstances undertake to involve the whole British Empire
in war, simply on her account. If we have to fight, it must be on
larger issues than that.[162]

At 11 a.m. on 28 September Hitler met with the French ambassador
to Germany André François-Poncet, who told him bluntly that an
attack on Czechoslovakia would lead to a European war: 'You deceive
yourself, Chancellor,' he said, 'if you believe you can confine the conflict
to Czechoslovakia.' François-Poncet then produced a detailed map
showing the separate areas to be evacuated in the Sudeten zone. After
the Frenchman had gone, Hitler told Schmidt, who was present at the
meeting, that François-Poncet was the only Western diplomat to make
a sensible proposal: 'I could see at once from his map that it was the
work of military men who knew their job.'[163]

In the end, the most decisive intervention in the Czech crisis
came from Benito Mussolini. Hans von Mackensen, the German
ambassador to Italy, reported that the British government had asked
Mussolini to intervene to bring about a negotiated solution through a
conference of four major powers: Britain, France, Germany and Italy.
Mussolini drafted a personal message to Hitler, emphasizing that he 'as
always stood with the Führer', but on this occasion he gave the British
proposal his firm support.[164]

Mussolini conveyed Chamberlain's idea to Hitler who agreed to
settle the matter at a four-way conference in Munich on 29 September.
The Czech government would not be invited, nor any representative
from the Soviet Union. The German Foreign Ministry press statement
emphasized the need for an 'immediate solution' to the crisis, and it
was hoped that the Munich Conference would 'lead to an agreement
on the measures to be put into effect immediately for the transfer of
the Sudeten territory promised by Czechoslovakia'.[165]

Vladimir Potemkin, the chief of the Soviet Foreign Ministry,
objected bitterly that it was 'really impossible to hold a conference on
the fate of a country without that country being represented'. What
was happening, he added, was the rebirth of the 'notorious' Four-Power
Pact, which only sought to force its will on the rest of Europe. Instead,
the Soviet Union wanted the crisis to be resolved at a European general

conference. In the end, Potemkin predicted, those taking part in the destruction of Czechoslovakia would 'bitterly regret their submission to militant nationalism'.[166]

Mussolini arrived by train at Kufstein in Austria on 29 September in order to attend the Munich Conference. Hitler met him at the railway station beforehand and revealed his plan for a sudden attack – a *Blitzkrieg* or 'lightning war' – on Czechoslovakia. He also admitted that he was still uncertain whether to accept the bloodless victory that was being offered to him by the British and French governments.

The Munich Conference began at 12.45 p.m. at the Führerbau, the administrative headquarters of the Nazi Party. Hitler gave a brief summary of the evolution of the Czechoslovakian question. The talks proceeded smoothly, because the four powers had agreed beforehand the Sudeten German territory that should be ceded to Germany. The conference had given Europe a breathing space, Chamberlain said. Mussolini presented delegates with a draft agreement, which had been prepared the night before by Göring, Neurath and Weizsäcker.

Chamberlain asked for a Czechoslovakian representative to be present during further negotiations on the fine details of the transfer of territory. Hitler said that if the consent of the Czechoslovakian government was required on every point under discussion, then the conference could drag on 'before a fortnight had passed'. Daladier said that he would not accept any protests from the Czech government. Mussolini agreed. By now, Hitler was irritated by Chamberlain raising what he saw as legalistic points and told the British Prime Minister bluntly: 'Our time is too valuable to be wasted on such trivialities.'[167] During the first break in the proceedings, Hitler confided to Mussolini: 'I can get on very well with Daladier; he's been at the front, like we have, and so I can talk sense to him.' This was an obvious reference to the fact that Chamberlain had not fought in the Great War.[168]

The conference resumed at 4.30 p.m. and the discussion concentrated on the timetable for the transfer of Czech territory. No agreement was reached on any boundary 'guarantee' for what would be left of Czechoslovakia. Hitler and Mussolini said that all of the other issues around national self-determination needed to be resolved first. A lengthy discussion followed as to which parts of Czechoslovakia would be transferred to Nazi Germany. It was finally decided that the fine details could be hammered out at a later date.[169]

The Munich Conference ended at 2.00 a.m. on 30 September with Britain, France, Germany and Italy each signing a joint declaration stipulating the timetable for the evacuation of the Czech Sudetenland by non-German Czechs, which was to begin on 1 October and end on 10 October. In fact, the Munich Agreement was really the Godesberg Memorandum with a few minor amendments. The full conditions of the handover would be resolved in more detail by an international commission, composed of representatives of each of the four nations, plus Czechoslovakia.

The final settlement, which was dated 20 November, forced Czechoslovakia to cede to Germany 11,000 square miles of territory in which 2.8 million Sudeten Germans and 800,000 Czechoslovakians were living. Within this area were all the vital Czech military fortifications. In an annexe to the main agreement, Britain and France agreed to guarantee the new boundaries of the Czechoslovakian state against any unprovoked aggression. Germany and Italy gave no such guarantee.[170]

Göring described the Munich Conference as a 'cut-and-dried affair'. In his view, 'Neither Chamberlain nor Daladier was the least bit interested in sacrificing or risking anything to save Czechoslovakia. That was clear as day to me. The fate of Czechoslovakia was effectively settled in three hours.'[171] Goebbels noted in his diary: 'Everybody is relieved that peace has been preserved. We must be clear this applies to us, too. That's how it is throughout the world. The nations do not want another world war.'[172]

The mood was less upbeat in other quarters. Even the British ambassador Nevile Henderson, who had previously been quite admiring of Hitler, admitted to having the 'utmost misgivings' as to whether Hitler would honour the Munich Agreement. Henderson returned to Britain in mid-October, 'thoroughly disheartened and if I had been a free agent I would never have returned to Berlin. The Hitlerian methods had been too much in evidence at Godesberg and Munich as well as in Berlin for me to feel otherwise than disgusted.'[173]

Hitler met Chamberlain on the morning of 30 September in his private apartment in Munich. Chamberlain suggested that they should issue a joint declaration, promising that Britain and Germany would never again go to war with each other, but would henceforth always settle their differences through negotiation. 'My own feeling was that he [Hitler] agreed to the wording with a certain reluctance,' Paul Schmidt observed, 'and I believe only appended his signature to please Chamberlain.'[174]

Hitler had been worried by the cheering crowds that greeted Chamberlain on the streets of Munich. The German people seemed to love the peacemaker, not the warmonger. This led Hitler to conclude his own modus operandi of presenting himself as a man of peace in public, while secretly planning for a war, had been a huge political error. It seemed to him that the German people were not psychologically ready for war. Henceforth, Hitler decided to adopt a much more uncompromising public persona, more closely aligned with his real personality and his true foreign policy aims.

After Munich, Hitler felt that he had allowed Chamberlain and the others to talk him out of doing what he really wanted. As late as 1945 he still looked back on the Munich Agreement as a monumental tactical error: 'We should have started the war in 1938. That was the last chance to keep it localized. But they yielded to us everywhere. Like cowards they gave in to all our demands. That actually made it difficult to seize the initiative for hostilities. We missed a unique opportunity.' [175] Schmidt later recalled: 'At that time I heard much in the Reich Chancellery of Hitler's indignation at the severe criticism of the Munich Agreement in Britain and France and at the British drive to increase its armaments. Hitler did not seem to understand what a severe reverse he had inflicted on Britain and France.' [176]

In fact, Hitler was wrong to think if he had started the war in 1938 he would have triumphed. The military forces available to Germany in 1938 were never as favourable as British ministers and their bungling military and intelligence advisers predicted. The German Chiefs of Staff were as deeply pessimistic as their British counterparts. Hitler's supreme ability to talk a good fight spread the alarm but he was bluffing all along. Only twenty-four fully equipped German divisions were ready for the attack on Czechoslovakia, with only eight divisions left to defend the western front. The *Luftwaffe* was in no way ready to mount a bomber offensive against France or Britain. German naval preparations were practically non-existent. The Western Allies enjoyed naval supremacy. What is more, the German army only had a four-week supply of petrol to sustain its forces during an attack on Czechoslovakia. Chamberlain's mad dash to avoid war led him to bargain away a modern Czech army of thirty-seven divisions and to hand over to the German armed forces 1.5 million rifles, 750 aircraft, 600 tanks and 2,000 artillery guns. In addition, Chamberlain sacrificed the huge Czech Maginot-style fortifications and the Škoda armaments factory complex. In 1938 the output of the Škoda Works equalled all of Britain's armament production.

On a diplomatic level Chamberlain had alienated the Soviet Union and turned its agreement to defend Czechoslovakia into a dead letter. This would have a deep impact on how the Soviet Union government behaved in 1939. The economic position of the Western Allies in 1938 was far stronger than in 1939. Britain and France had large dollar deposits in the USA, whereas Germany's foreign currency and gold reserves were running out. In sum, Chamberlain totally misread how much the balance of power was loaded in favour of Hitler's potential enemies in 1938 than it was in 1939.

Clutching his famous 'piece of paper' signed by Hitler and himself, Chamberlain then waved it above his head shortly after his plane landed on 30 September at Heston airfield around 5.30 p.m. and read out its contents to the waiting newspaper, newsreel and radio reporters. Cheers erupted even from these seasoned journalists. In the previous fortnight Chamberlain had single-handedly invented shuttle diplomacy and he now ushered in the age of the political photo opportunity.

Crowds lined the Great West Road as his motorcade made its way to Buckingham Palace for an audience with King George VI, who brought him to the balcony of the royal residence to receive the cheers of the crowd outside. From there he went to 10 Downing Street, famously but perhaps unwisely declaring from the first-floor window to the crowd below, 'My good friends, this is the second time in our history that there has come back from Germany to Downing Street peace with honour. I believe it is peace for our time.'

Chamberlain received 20,000 letters of praise and numerous gifts from people at home and abroad including umbrellas, fishing tackle, chocolates, cigars, champagne, spirits, biscuits, cake, meat and much else. 'No conqueror returned from victory on the battlefield had come adorned with greater laurels,' said *The Times*.[177] There was an overwhelming sense of relief among the British public, but it was not to last very long. In a famous debate in the House of Commons a few days later, the Conservative MP Winston Churchill described the Munich Agreement as a 'shameful betrayal'.

Lord Halifax also regarded Munich as deeply humiliating, but still preferable to war with Germany. He now saw Hitler as a 'criminal lunatic' and found Nazism utterly repellent. This pessimism led him to ask Chamberlain to form an all-party government of national unity, bringing in Churchill and Eden and even members of the Labour Party.

Chamberlain rejected this idea. In a letter to his sister Ida he wrote: 'A lot of people seem to be losing their heads and talking and thinking as though Munich made war more instead of less imminent.'[178]

German troops marched into the Sudetenland on 1 October. Peter Schober, a Sudeten German, recalled: 'The troops were welcomed and greeted as Germans and that was a big thing for us. We felt that we belonged more to a German-speaking country than to one where the national tongue was Czech. We thought that this was the right solution.'[179] Siegfried Fischer, who also lived in the Sudetenland, remembered: 'The German occupation in 1938 was not seen to be an occupation at all. Rather we waited in happy anticipation for the German troops finally to liberate us. The soldiers were greeted with flowers and great hospitality. This was, then as now, the greatest day of my life. It made me a German citizen.'[180]

On 2 October Hitler spent the evening with Goebbels, telling him of his firm determination to destroy what remained of Czechoslovakia. 'This dead, amorphous state must go,' he said. 'Would France or Britain have gone to war to save Czechoslovakia?' Goebbels thought they would, but Hitler replied: 'I'm sticking with my opinion.'[181]

Edvard Beneš resigned as the President of Czechoslovakia on 5 October. Deeply depressed, he was suffering from mental and physical exhaustion after the trauma of the Czech crisis. He later recalled that he had considered three options during September 1938: risk war and die amid the rubble of his mobilized troops; commit suicide; or go into exile and hopefully return to Czechoslovakia after the country's liberation. In the end he took the third option: leaving Czechoslovakia for Britain on 22 October. He lived at first in Putney. In 1940 the British government recognized the Czechoslovak government-in-exile, and from November 1940 Edvard Beneš, the President of Czechoslovakia in exile, lived in Aylesbury.[182]

On 6 October the German government cancelled all passports held by German Jews in preparation for their being stamped with a large red 'J'. This measure had been insisted upon by the Swiss government as a means of keeping track and restricting the immigration of Jews from Germany and Austria, without needing to introduce visa requirements. The stamp also proved useful to track the movements of Jews not only in Germany but around the world.

Anyone who thought that the Munich Agreement would lead to an easing of international tension was soon to be disappointed. In a speech in Saarbrücken, the capital of Saarland, on 9 October Hitler delivered a blistering attack on the British government. Chamberlain might want peace, he said, but he could be replaced at any moment by Duff Cooper or Anthony Eden or Winston Churchill, and 'the aim of these men would be to start war'. It would be good if the British government ended its 'governess-like guardianship of Germany', he added. The British should stop meddling in the internal affairs of other countries. He promised that the construction of Germany's western fortifications would be speeded up: a clear indication that war with the Western democracies remained a strong possibility.[183]

Czechoslovakia underwent a radical change following the Munich Agreement. Everything was done to accommodate Hitler's demands. František Chvalovský, the new Czech Foreign Minister, arrived in Berlin on 13 October to meet Ribbentrop. He admitted that Edvard Beneš had unwisely guided Czechoslovakia along an anti-German path, but he pointed out that this was not the true feeling of the majority of the Czech people. In future the new Czech government would pursue a policy of the closest cooperation with Germany. Czechoslovakia, he said, would now 'make an honest attempt to comply with Germany's wishes in every respect'.[184]

On the following day Hitler met Chvalovský in Munich. He told him that Czechoslovakia now had two choices. First, to arrive at a friendly settlement with the German Reich. Second, to realize that Czechoslovakia was now in the German sphere of influence and it must adapt itself to these new conditions. If Czechoslovakia ceased to be an enemy, accepted the fact that British and French guarantees were worthless, broke off relations with the Soviet Union, and bowed to the territorial demands of the Hungarians, then he would allow the Czechs to organize their country as they desired. If this did not happen, calamity would follow.[185]

On 16 October Göring met Vojtěch Mastný, the Czech Minister in Berlin, who promised the new Czech government would move sharply to the right: communism would be suppressed, and the 'Jewish problem' tackled. Göring made the following notes after this meeting: (1) the Führer can make any demand on Czechoslovakia; (2) the new Czech Foreign Minister is viewed favourably; (3) after a customs union is formed, currency union is possible.[186]

On the following day, Göring had a meeting with Dr Ferdinand Ďurčanský, the Slovak Minister, who thanked the German government for supporting self-determination for Slovaks. Ďurčanský wanted Slovakia to gain full independence from Czechoslovakia. He also promised to ban the Communist Party and to do something about the 'Jewish problem'. Göring advised Hitler that Slovak demands for independence should be supported, cynically observing that 'A Czech state minus Slovakia is even more completely at our mercy.'[187]

Hitler issued a fresh directive to the *Wehrmacht* on 21 October, in which he outlined three key foreign policy priorities: (1) protect the Reich frontiers against attack; (2) liquidate the remainder of the Czech state; and (3) seize Memel (another disputed territory, this time in Lithuania, which Hitler believed belonged to Germany). It would be possible 'at any time', Hitler added, to smash the remainder of Czechoslovakia. Preparations for this attack would not need to be on anything like the same scale as Case Green. The aim would be to occupy Bohemia and Moravia and to cut off Slovakia.[188]

The Czech crisis had drawn international attention away from the plight of the Jews during the latter part of 1938. Jews who wanted to leave Germany or Austria had to pay an exorbitant 'atonement tax', which left them with hardly any money. All Jews had to use the name 'Israel' if male and 'Sara' if female on all official documents. Every Jew was required to draw up an inventory of all the property they owned to a value of more than 5,000 Reichsmarks. They were now prohibited from practising law and medicine, with Jewish doctors allowed to treat only Jewish patients. Jews were also summarily dismissed from teaching, lecturing and civil service posts. Jewish students were barred from attending universities. Jews were no longer allowed to be cattle-dealers or travelling salesmen. Jewish businesses were being closed down or 'Aryanized' at a rapid rate. Between January and November 1938, 800 Jewish-owned firms, including 340 factories, were transferred into German ownership.

In the aftermath of the Czech crisis, a wave of Jewish deportations and expulsions began. On 18 October Hitler issued an order expelling from Germany all Polish-born Jews who had previously been living there legally. They were ordered to leave their homes and allowed to take only a suitcase with them. On 27 October the Gestapo began to deport 18,000 Polish Jews. They were brutally manhandled on to trains and transported to the Polish border. The Polish authorities agreed to admit them only after pressure from the German government. They housed the deportees in makeshift camps in terrible conditions.

Among these deported Polish-Jewish families were the Grynszpans from Hanover. Their seventeen-year-old son Herschel was living as an illegal immigrant in Paris with his uncle when he heard the news of

Ernst vom Rath, the German diplomat whose assassination by Jewish teenager Herschel Grynszpan triggered off Kristallnacht.

his family's forcible deportation from Germany. On 7 November he bought a revolver, loaded it with five bullets and went to the German Embassy intent upon assassinating Johannes von Welczeck, the German ambassador to France. Instead he was given directions to the office of a much more junior diplomat, Ernst vom Rath, ostensibly to discuss a passport issue.

Grynszpan fired five times at Rath, but only two bullets hit him. He was rushed by ambulance to a nearby Paris hospital in a critical condition, but still alive. 'Being a Jew is not a crime,' Grynszpan told the French policeman who arrested him. 'I am not a dog. I have a right to live and the Jewish people have a right to live on this earth.'[189]

The shooting of a German diplomat by a Jew was portrayed in the German press as an 'act of war by international Jewry'. The *Völkischer Beobachter* urged all Germans to take strong action against Jews. Goebbels announced that all Jewish newspapers and magazines must immediately cease publication. The shooting came a day before the fifteenth anniversary of the failed Beer Hall Putsch in 1923. Hitler delivered his traditional speech to a packed Bürgerbräukeller in Munich on 8 November, but he did not mention the Paris attack.

At 4.30 p.m. on 9 November Ernst vom Rath died of his injuries in hospital. Hitler was informed of his death around 9 p.m., during a dinner reception in Munich's Old Town Hall. Goebbels noted in his diary: 'I describe the situation to the Führer. He decides to let the demonstrations continue. Withdraw the police. For once the Jews should feel the rage of the people.'[190] At 9.30 p.m. Goebbels gave a speech at the dinner, expressing his outrage at a Jew murdering a German and outlining his support for violent action against all Jews.[191]

What followed on the night of 9–10 November became known as *Kristallnacht* ('Crystal Night' or the 'Night of Broken Glass'). Goebbels issued instructions – not to the police, but to party officials – to carry out 'spontaneous demonstrations'.[192] Himmler and Heydrich were also in Munich, attending the annual swearing-in of new SS recruits at the Feldherrnhalle in the city centre. They heard about the start of the pogrom just before midnight and they were both furious that Goebbels had acted without first consulting them.

The first official police order relating to this anti-Jewish violence was issued by Heinrich Müller, the head of the Gestapo, at 12.05 a.m. on 10 November. He explained that arson attacks by Germans on Jews were already underway, primarily against synagogues. He asked Gestapo officers to prepare for the arrest of between 20,000 and 30,000

Polish-Jewish refugee Herschel Grynszpan who shot and killed German diplomat Ernst vom Rath in Paris.

[overleaf] Ordinary Germans walk past shattered Jewish shops the day after Kristallnacht.

Jews, who would be taken into 'protective custody'. Around 30,000 of them ended up in concentration camps. A First World War veteran, Hans Frankenberger, was taken to Sachsenhausen concentration camp. 'Nothing will harm us,' he said, 'because we fought in the war.' He was very badly treated, before his release on 28 November. His family said that he was a 'broken man' and when they asked him about his ordeal, his only reply was: 'I am not allowed to tell you, and I won't tell you, as I'm sworn to secrecy.' A friend later heard details of the savage beatings that Frankenberger had endured, commenting: 'I would never have believed what the Germans are able to do in these camps.'[193]

At 1.20 a.m. on 10 November Heydrich issued an order via a telex message to the state police and the SD officers. They were told to prevent looting, but not to hinder demonstrations or arson attacks on synagogues, provided their destruction did not affect any adjoining German-owned property.

The scenes of destruction on *Kristallnacht* were truly shocking. Around 1,000 synagogues were set on fire by Nazi mobs and approximately 267 were destroyed. Around 7,500 of the remaining 9,000 Jewish-owned shops in Germany were badly vandalized. Windows were smashed, doors kicked in and stock looted. It has been estimated that ninety-one Jews were killed during these incidents.

Hugh Greene, the *Daily Telegraph* reporter in Berlin, observed the violence first hand: 'Mob law ruled in Berlin throughout the afternoon and evening and hordes of hooligans indulged in an orgy of destruction. I have seen several anti-Jewish outbreaks in Germany during the last five years, but never anything as nauseating as this.'[194]

Robert Smallbones, the British Consul General in Frankfurt, sent a report to the Foreign Office on the pogrom in Wiesbaden: 'The violence began at six in the morning [10 November], with the burning of all synagogues. During the day, organized groups of both political formations – both the Brownshirts [SA] and the black-shirted SS – visited every Jewish shop and office, destroying windows and equipment.'[195] The involvement of the storm troopers was not spontaneous, but was ordered and controlled by the SS. These men were used as part of the terror system when required and were not acting autonomously, as is often supposed.[196]

Hedwig Müller, who came from Recklinghausen, and was not Jewish, observed the violence in her own neighbourhood:

Nobody knew what was going on when it started. On the opposite side of our street there was a Jewish shop, owned by an old couple, who sold second-hand clothes. We knew the family well. In the middle of the night we were suddenly woken by the sound of a shop window being smashed. My father, who was seventy, went to the window, opened it and shouted at those carrying out the attack: 'What are you doing?' My mother and I were scared as we could see they were storm troopers. We told our father to close the window, because we were afraid they would go crazy and attack us. We also saw the storm troopers break into the flat of a local Jewish woman who had small children. They threw a slashed mattress and bed clothes out of her window.[197]

Fritz Hennig, a Nazi Party member from Bitterfeld, recalled that as he drove through the streets on *Kristallnacht* he felt very uncomfortable with the level of vandalism he was witnessing. He told a friend who was travelling with him: 'Anyone who attacks Jews, smashes a window and steals a fur coat for his wife is not a patriotic German.'[198] Adina Koor, a Jewish schoolgirl from Hamburg, recalled: 'At the far end of the street where I lived stood the liberal synagogue, an impressive building. In the morning [of 10 November] on the way to school I saw thick clouds of smoke coming from the top of the building. Men dressed in Nazi uniforms patrolled the streets.'[199]

Goebbels met Hitler on the morning of 10 November and they agreed to issue a proclamation that 'all demonstrations and acts of revenge against Jewry should cease immediately'.[200] Later that day, at a secret press conference for German journalists, Hitler stressed that his 'peace propaganda' had been counterproductive, because it fed an impression that he desired peace at any price. He now wanted to make it absolutely clear to the German public that 'there are things that must be achieved by force'.[201]

Hitler decided there needed to be new, discriminatory anti-Jewish measures, especially in the economic sphere. Göring was instructed to convene a conference at the Air Ministry to 'summarize the decisive steps' on the solution of the 'Jewish question'. The meeting took place between 11 a.m. and 2.30 p.m. on 12 November, chaired by Göring. Hitler chose not to attend, because he did not want to be closely associated with the minutiae of the 'Jewish question'. Those present included Adolf Eichmann, Kurt Daluege and Reinhard Heydrich, representing the police apparatus; Wilhelm Frick, Bernhard Lösener and Wilhelm Stuckart of the Interior Ministry; Lutz von Krosigk, the Finance Minister; Walther Funk, the Economics Minister; Franz

Gürtner, the Justice Minister; Emil Schumburg and Ernst Woermann from the Foreign Ministry; and Goebbels representing the Ministry of Propaganda.

Detailed minutes of the conference have survived. Revealing a shameless contempt for Jewish life, Göring told the meeting that during *Kristallnacht* 'I would have preferred it if you had killed 200 Jews and not destroyed so many things of value.' This was a sideswipe at Goebbels, who was seen as the instigator of the mob violence.

Several solutions to the so-called Jewish question were put forward. Göring suggested creating Jewish ghettos, but Heydrich opposed this, because he thought they would breed crime and be impossible to police. Goebbels suggested banning Jews from all theatres, cinemas and circuses and other public places, including even walking in forests.

Outrageously, it was decided that the Jews should pay for all the damage caused by Nazi violence during *Kristallnacht* through an 'atonement tax' of 1 billion Reichsmarks. The tax was so successful that it brought in 6 per cent of all Reich revenue during 1938. It was also agreed that any insurance claims made by Jews would be honoured, but the money would go to the state instead of the claimants. Finally, it was decided that, as of 1 January 1939, all Jews would be prohibited from running a business or working in a trade.[202]

The British Cabinet Foreign Policy Committee met on 14 November to discuss *Kristallnacht*. Lord Halifax pointed out that while many Germans might desire peace, the same was not true of 'the crazy persons who had managed to secure control of the country'. In such circumstances, he saw 'no useful purpose' in resuming political discussions with the current German government. He urged Chamberlain to correct the false impression of the British that 'we are decadent, spineless and could with impunity be kicked about'. It was agreed that the British government would distance itself from its previous policy of openly appeasing Hitler.[203]

On 30 November the Czechoslovakian parliament elected Emil Hácha as its new president. Using an Enabling Act, democracy was suspended in favour of a pro-Nazi authoritarian state, which greatly increased the power of the president. The general public knew little about 66-year-old Hácha, a lawyer by occupation and the President of the Supreme Administration Court. Before his appointment he had taken very little interest in politics, but he made it clear that as president he was prepared to follow the Nazi line in domestic and foreign affairs.[204]

The ruins of the Tielshafer Synogue in Berlin, destroyed on Kristallnacht.

On 6 December Ribbentrop arrived in Paris for a two-day visit. During a meeting with Georges Bonnet, the French Foreign Minister, Ribbentrop stressed the importance of Franco-German friendship and he hoped that measures could be taken to improve trade between the two nations. The discussion then turned to progress on a guarantee to be given to Czechoslovakia by the four powers. Ribbentrop expressed doubts as to its workability. In his opinion a new guarantee might lead the Czech government to lapse back into its old anti-German stance. It would be better if London and Paris recognized Czechoslovakia as now being in the German sphere of influence.[205]

A Franco-German declaration was issued at the end of the meeting, featuring three rather optimistic clauses: (1) the governments of Germany and France fully share the conviction that peaceful and good neighbourly relations between the Germans and the French constitute the most essential elements in the consolidation of the situation in Europe and in the preservation of general peace; (2) both governments state that between their countries no questions of a territorial nature are outstanding and they solemnly recognize as final the frontier between their countries as it now exists; (3) both governments are resolved, without prejudice to their special relations with third powers, to remain in contact with each other on all questions concerning both their countries, and to confer together should the future evolution of these questions lead to international difficulties.[206] This declaration was Bonnet's idea. He had been rather jealous that Chamberlain had persuaded Hitler to sign a joint Anglo-German declaration on 30 September and gained huge propaganda value from it.

During these discussions, Bonnet allegedly told Ribbentrop that France was willing to recognize Eastern Europe as Germany's exclusive sphere of influence. In effect, the French were seemingly offering Hitler permission to take over the rest of Czechoslovakia. This was not mentioned in Ribbentrop's official record of his meeting with Bonnet, but Ribbentrop did refer to it six months later in order to embarrass the French government. Bonnet denied ever having made such a statement. He may well have been telling the truth, for Paul Schmidt, who took the minutes of the meeting, made no mention of Bonnet promising Germany a free hand in Eastern Europe.[207]

On 13 December Chamberlain gave a speech to the Foreign Press Association on the deteriorating situation in Europe. Only two alternatives were available to him, he said. The first was to decide that war was inevitable and throw all the energies of the country into preparation for it. The second was to make a prolonged and determined effort to eradicate the possible causes of war through personal contact and discussion. 'I had a message from Halifax that he didn't like the speech,' a weary Chamberlain commented a few days later, 'as he thought it laid too much emphasis on appeasement and was not stiff enough on the dictators.'[208]

On 15 December Andor Hencke, the German chargé d'affaires in Czechoslovakia, had a message for the German Foreign Ministry: the new Czech government wanted to reach a settlement on its relationship with Germany. Czech ministers were now prepared to 'fulfil all fundamental demands by Germany which affect its future'. It was hoped that the country would be able to retain an outward appearance of independence, even though it would now be in effect a vassal state of Germany.[209]

On 17 December Wilhelm Keitel, the chief of the OKW, issued a supplementary directive for the *Wehrmacht* to prepare for the 'liquidation of the Rump Czech State'. Hitler gave the following instructions to the *Wehrmacht*: (1) the military action was to be prepared on the assumption that the army would face no resistance; (2) it would be presented as a peaceful action; and (3) the action could be carried out using the peacetime *Wehrmacht*, without reinforcement through mobilization. However, no precise date for the operation was set.[210]

This was the last major order issued by Hitler during the anxiety-ridden year of 1938, when Europe came closer to war. The crisis had been caused solely by Hitler's aggressive determination to crush Czechoslovakia and it had been averted only by his last-minute decision to accept a negotiated settlement.

Chamberlain's desperation to try and satisfy Hitler's demands, a tactic endorsed by the French government, left Hitler more convinced than ever that Britain and France would not go to war to stop him from gaining territory at the expense of Europe's smaller nations. Ironically, their determination to maintain peace at any price had only encouraged Hitler to push ahead with his own unalterable plan to gain even more 'living space' for his newly created Greater German Reich.

1939
·
HITLER'S RACIAL WAR
·

In his New Year message for 1939 Hitler adopted a decidedly optimistic tone. He outlined three key aims for the coming year. First, to transform the German people into a National Socialist Community. Second, build up and strengthen the *Wehrmacht*. Third, carry on implementing the Four-Year Plan. He thanked Mussolini for playing such a crucial role in brokering the Munich Agreement. 'It was Germany's one desire,' he concluded, 'that it might be possible during the year to contribute towards general European appeasement.'[1]

Two articles by the British novelist H. G. Wells appeared in the *News Chronicle* entitled '1939 – What Does It Hold?' Hitler, Goebbels and Göring were 'certifiable lunatics', he wrote, and then went on to suggest that if the three of them could be put into a plane and it crashed, the world would be a much safer place.

These articles were heavily criticized in the German press. Ribbentrop asked the German ambassador to make a formal complaint about them to the Foreign Office. Dirksen met Lord Halifax, the British Foreign Secretary, who thought the comments made by Wells were 'the most shocking insult to the Führer' that he had seen in the British press. He promised to do everything in his power to prevent such insults from ever again appearing in print.[2]

On 4 January, in his annual address to the United States Congress, President Roosevelt discussed the current international situation. 'A war which threatened to envelop the world in flames has been averted,' he said, 'but it has become increasingly clear that world peace is not assured.' He promised US policy would not 'encourage, assist or build up an aggressor'.[3] The British press interpreted the speech as a direct attack on Hitler's aggressive foreign policy. Chamberlain issued a statement endorsing Roosevelt's comments.[4]

Ultimately, the real drama of 1939 would be Germany's invasion of Poland, but in January this was not even viewed as a possibility. In *Mein Kampf* Hitler devoted little space to the Polish question. When discussing the notion of the German people gaining more 'living space' (*Lebensraum*), he looked to the conquest of the Soviet Union. The ten-year German-Polish Non-Aggression Pact of 1934 remained operative, although there remained two main issues to be resolved: (1) the status of the Free City of Danzig, and (2) the small strip of land called the Polish Corridor, which gave Poles access to the Baltic Sea, but separated East Prussia from the rest of Germany. Even so, a negotiated settlement of both these issues between Germany and Poland seemed quite possible. Everyone knew that Danzig was a German city. In the long run Hitler hoped to incorporate it into the Reich, bringing it under German control. Similarly, the Polish Corridor question also seemed ripe for revision.

Once the Sudetenland had been ceded to Germany after the Munich Agreement, Polish armed forces occupied the Czech province of Teschen, with Hitler's blessing. Further cooperation with Poland seemed to suit Hitler's plans. However, on 5 January, when the Polish Foreign Minister Józef Beck visited the Berghof, Hitler told him bluntly: 'Danzig is German, will always be German. It will sooner or later become part of Germany.' Adopting a more conciliatory tone, he promised Beck that no fait accompli would be engineered in Danzig. If Germany and Poland worked together a negotiated settlement could be achieved, he added. Beck said that he doubted whether Polish public opinion would support a settlement of the Danzig question that went in Germany's favour.[5]

In Berlin, the President of the Reichsbank Hjalmar Schacht and seven other bank directors sent a detailed memorandum to Hitler on 7 January. They warned him that his rearmament programme was causing inflationary pressure to build up in the German economy. Their advice was for Hitler to change course by cutting public expenditure on armaments and encouraging exports. Hitler was unimpressed and made it clear to them that he was not prepared to tolerate any opposition to his war plans. He summarily dismissed Schacht along with Friedrich Dreyse, the Reichsbank Vice-President, and its director Ernst Huelse. In a letter to Schacht on 19 January Hitler wrote: 'I wish to take advantage of your leaving the office of the Reichsbank board of directors to express to you the sincere and cordial appreciation of your service in this position throughout the long and difficult years on behalf of Germany and my own. Your name will be tied to the initial period of the epoch of national restoration.' Schacht was offered the post of Minister without Portfolio, which he duly accepted. Loyal Nazi Walther Funk became the new President of the Reichsbank. Hitler also ordered the Reichsbank to extend credit to the state whenever he deemed it necessary. With these changes, the Reichsbank changed

overnight from an international bank into a body that issued unlimited loans to Hitler's government.[6]

Between 11 and 14 January the British Prime Minister Neville Chamberlain, accompanied by Lord Halifax, was on a four-day state visit to Rome. On 16 November 1938 the British government had finally ratified the Anglo-Italian Agreement. With the door to direct negotiations with Hitler in abeyance, Chamberlain was keen to explore whether Mussolini might restrain Hitler from further acts of unilateral aggression. As Mussolini was by now firmly in the German camp nothing concrete emerged from these talks. Mussolini and Ciano were not impressed by their British guests. 'How far apart we are from these people,' Ciano noted in his diary. 'It is another world. We were talking about it after dinner with Il Duce. "These men are not made of the same stuff," he was saying, "as the Francis Drakes and the other magnificent adventurers who created the Empire. These are the tired sons of a long line of rich men, and they will lose their empire."' They also made jokes about Chamberlain always carrying his umbrella around with him.[7]

Ciano briefed Hans von Mackensen, the German ambassador to Rome, about the Chamberlain-Halifax visit, telling him that the British government was worried about the growing military strength of the Axis powers. Chamberlain cannot have been reassured, when, during his talks with them, Mussolini said that the keystone of Italian foreign policy was his loyalty to Adolf Hitler.[8]

At a naval conference on 17 January Admiral Erich Raeder presented Hitler with Plan Z, an ambitious long-term expansion of the German navy (*Kriegsmarine*), with the eventual aim of challenging the supremacy of the Royal Navy. Plan Z was agreed by Hitler on 27 January and scheduled for completion by 1948. It aimed to build a German fleet strength of ten battleships (of which only four were ever built), four aircraft carriers (none was completed), five heavy cruisers (only three were completed), fifteen heavily armoured cruisers, which the British called 'pocket battleships' (only three came into service), and thirteen light cruisers (only six became operational). Plan Z was over-ambitious, but it gave a clear signal that a showdown with Britain was now being factored into future German rearmament projects. Plan Z was abandoned within a year as being economically unrealistic. Above all, it failed to prioritize the building of submarines (U-boats), which the Germans would require in the event of a war with Britain and France.[9]

Josef Beck, the Polish Foreign Minister.

When the Czech Foreign Minister František Chvalovský met Hitler in the new Reich Chancellery on 21 January he gave a solemn promise to adhere to a policy of cooperation with the German government. In reply Hitler said that he was deeply unhappy about current developments in Czechoslovakia. He pointed out there had been no purge of the followers of ex-President Beneš in the civil service, the press or the army. If the 'spirit of Beneš' was not ruthlessly purged then the 'annihilation of Czechoslovakia' would soon follow. Hitler was equally unimpressed by the Czech government's failure to deal with the Jewish question.[10] Shortly after this meeting, the Czech government intensified its purge of civil servants and Jews from government posts. Several officials of the Beneš era were also dismissed, including General Ludvík Krejčí, the Chief of the General Staff.[11]

On 30 January Hitler delivered his annual speech to members of the Reichstag. They once again met in the Kroll Opera House in central Berlin for what was described as the 'First Reichstag of the Greater German Reich'. Reichstag deputies voted to extend the Enabling Act to 30 January 1943, under the new 'Law on the Tenure of the Reichstag'. This gave Hitler the power to decide when the Reichstag would next convene. If he wanted to, he could delay calling it for years.

Hitler then delivered one of his most important and prophetic speeches. He began by highlighting the need for Germans to acquire more 'living space' to cope with overpopulation. The 'so-called democratic powers', he said, were still refusing to return the German colonies to the Reich, so Germany's future economic needs could be met only through an increase in imports or an expansion of territory.

Hitler then issued two ominous warnings. The first was directed at the Christian churches. He was not hostile to religion, he said. After all, when faith leaders objected to his creation of a Reich Church in 1933, he quickly abandoned the idea in response to their criticisms. He emphasized that the churches received huge sums through state funding and tax exemptions. However, if the opposition of church leaders continued, Hitler warned that he would consider removing state funding. He further promised to 'deal relentlessly with those priests, who instead of serving the Lord, see their mission in propagating divisive comments on our present Reich, its institution and its leading men'.

Hitler then turned to Germany's existential struggle with the Jews, promising that National Socialism 'would wrestle the Jewish enemy to the ground' on the international stage. He mocked the 'tales of pity' coming from democratic politicians concerning the plight of

Jews, while refusing to allow them entry into their own countries. In the years before 1933, Hitler said he had been a prophet on many political issues, but Jews in Germany had laughed at him when he had predicted that he would one day lead the German nation. 'Once again,' he added chillingly, 'I will be a prophet: should the international Jewry of finance [*Finanzjudentum*] succeed, both within and beyond Europe, in plunging mankind into yet another world war, then the result would not be the Bolshevization of the earth and the victory of Jewry, but the annihilation [*Vernichtung*] of the Jewish race in Europe.'[12]

At this time, a flood of alarming intelligence reports reached the British government indicating that Germany was planning a surprise military attack on the Netherlands or possibly Switzerland. These reports came from Admiral Wilhelm Canaris, the chief of the German military intelligence service, who was a member of the clandestine opposition to Hitler. Lord Halifax thought these warnings were genuine and so did the cabinet who voted for Chamberlain to publicly reaffirm Anglo-French solidarity in the event of a German threat to Western Europe. On 6 February Chamberlain told a packed House of Commons: 'I find it necessary to clearly state that the solidarity of interests that unites France and England is such that any threat directed against France's vital interests wherever it may come from must trigger Great Britain's immediate cooperation.'[13]

The intelligence warnings of an imminent German attack in Western Europe proved false. This did not mean that Hitler was not contemplating his next dramatic move in foreign policy. At a secret meeting in the Kroll Opera House with senior army commanders on 10 February, Hitler expressed disappointment with the 'wait and see' attitude of some of his officers during the Czechoslovakian crisis. He then admitted that his foreign policy was very carefully planned and moved step by step. The events of 1938, he added, were in fact staging posts along a pre-determined – and very long – road. His foreign policy successes had not come about through chance but were attributable to his single-minded ability to seize opportunities whenever they arose. Solving Germany's 'living space' problem was now his dominant foreign policy objective.[14]

The Western Powers were concerned that Hitler had not yet honoured his pledge made at the time of the signing of the Munich Agreement to join in the Anglo-French guarantee to respect the remainder of Czechoslovakia. The British and French governments now asked the German government to do so. In public, Hitler claimed

[*overleaf*] Hitler delivering his speech in the Kroll Opera House on 30 January 1939.

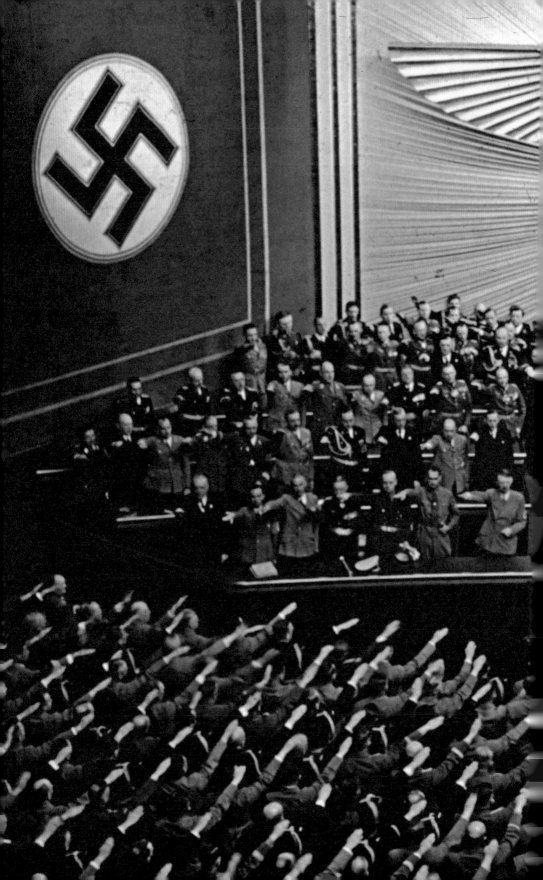

that all of the internal nationality disputes within Czechoslovakia would first have to be resolved before he would even consider joining such guarantee. In private, Hitler was waiting for an opportune moment to incorporate the Czech lands into his Greater German Reich.

With this in mind, Hitler met Professor Vojtech Tuka, the extreme right-wing leader of the Slovak People's Party, at the Reich Chancellery on 12 February. Tuka told Hitler, whom he addressed as 'my Führer', that it was becoming impossible for the Slovaks to coexist with the Czech state. In response, Hitler told him that he had only recently become aware of the Slovak people's desire for independence – in fact, he had mistakenly assumed the Slovaks wanted a reunion with Hungary. If Slovakia had declared independence during the Czech crisis of 1938, Hitler added, then he would have readily agreed to it. He promised Tuka he would support Slovakian independence from now on.[15]

On 17 February Hitler delivered a speech at the official opening of the International Automobile and Motorcycle Exhibition on Kaiserdamm in Berlin. He did not promise that soon every German would own a Volkswagen, but did pledge to press ahead with the construction of the first factory devoted exclusively to producing his much-hyped People's Car. He then brought up what he saw as a more negative aspect of car ownership: the huge increase in road deaths and injuries, pointing out that 7,000 people were killed and more than 30,000 seriously injured every year in car accidents. He promised that in future the drivers responsible would be punished ruthlessly by German courts.[16]

On 28 February the German Foreign Ministry sent a reply – largely written by Hitler – to the British and French governments in which Germany flatly refused to guarantee the remainder of the Czechoslovak state. Such a pledge would be destabilizing, it was argued, and would only aggravate differences between the Czech government and Germany. It might also incite fresh disagreements with bordering nations such as Poland and Hungary.[17] And so, under the guise of seeking stability, Hitler wriggled out of the promise he made at Munich.

In Czechoslovakia by now the Slovakians and the Ruthenians were agitating for independence. Emil Hácha, the elderly Czech president, dismissed the autonomous Ruthenian government on 6 March. On the night of 9 March Hácha declared martial law in Slovakia and on the next day removed its government and ordered the police to arrest Jozef

Tiso, the Prime Minister of the Autonomous Slovak Region, along with the Slovak nationalist leaders Ferdinand Ďurčanský and Vojtech Tuka. These were ill-judged moves by Hácha as he was offering Hitler an ideal pretext and opportunity for German troops to occupy what remained of Czechoslovakia.

On 11 March Hitler sent Arthur Seyss-Inquart, the Austrian Nazi Governor of Austria, and Josef Bürckel, the Reich Commissioner of Austria, accompanied by five German generals to Bratislava in Czechoslovakia. They pushed their way into a cabinet meeting of the new Slovak government and ordered its members to declare independence. The acting Prime Minister Karol Sidor refused to do so.

While a major crisis was about to erupt in Czechoslovakia, the Soviet leader Joseph Stalin delivered a remarkable speech in Moscow at the 18th Congress of the Soviet Communist Party on 10 March. A second imperialist world war had begun in July 1937, Stalin declared,

Hitler with the Czech President
Emile Hácha, photographed on 16 March
1938, after his ordeal in the new Reich
Chancellery in the early hours of the
previous day.

when Japan had invaded China. The capitalist democratic states, through their appeasement policy, were now intent on extending this war into Europe by allowing the aggressor states – Germany and Italy – to victimize Eastern European nations. In doing so, Britain and France had abandoned collective security. 'Let us take Germany, for example,' Stalin continued, 'Austria has been ceded to her, in spite of the pledge to protect the former's independence. The Sudetenland was abandoned, and Czechoslovakia was left to her fate, in violation of all [treaty] obligations.' The alleged military weakness of the Soviet Union was constantly highlighted by democratic countries, Stalin added, in order to encourage Germany to push eastwards, but he had a stark warning for the Western Powers: the Soviet Union would not allow itself to be 'drawn into a conflict by warmongers who are accustomed to have others pull their chestnuts out of the fire'.[18]

Meanwhile, Jozef Tiso, deposed Slovak Prime Minister, and his former Foreign Minister Ferdinand Ďurčanský were summoned to meet Hitler in Berlin. By 6.40 p.m. on 13 March they were sitting in Hitler's office in the Reich Chancellery. Hitler told them he had demonstrated enormous self-control during the crisis in Czechoslovakia, but now he was determined to resolve the Czech question once and for all, and in 'a matter of hours, not days'. First, he needed to know: did Slovakia want independence or not? Tiso said that he would have to return to Bratislava to discuss the matter with his colleagues, but he was certain they would want to declare Slovakian independence.[19]

On the following day, Tiso issued the following telegram, addressed to Hitler: 'In the name of the legal Slovak government I have the honour to inform Your Excellency that the sovereign Slovak nation has today thrown off the intolerable Czech yoke and, in accordance with the wishes of the overwhelming majority of the population, the independence of our state has been proclaimed.'[20]

Under pressure, Emil Hácha, the President of Czechoslovakia, asked for a meeting with Hitler on 13 March. He was invited to Berlin on the following day to discuss the crisis, but due to a serious heart condition the frail president declined Germany's offer of a plane. Instead, he travelled by special train, departing from Prague at 4 p.m. and transferring to a German special train at the border. As a result, he arrived at Berlin's Anhalter Station at 10.40 p.m., some ninety minutes late.

Hácha was accompanied by his Foreign Minister František Chvalovský. His teenage daughter Milada was chaperoned by Alois

Havelka, the wife of his Deputy Prime Minister. A military guard of honour greeted Hácha at the station and he was given the finest suite at Berlin's opulent Hotel Adlon, near to the Brandenburg Gate. A box of expensive chocolates and a huge bouquet of flowers were presented to Milada, personal gifts from the Führer.

At midnight Hácha and Chvalovský waited nervously in the huge reception hall of the new Reich Chancellery for a meeting with the Führer. At this time, Hitler was sitting in his private projection room watching a new film with the ironic title *A Hopeless Case* (*Ein hoffnungsloser Fall*). It was a romantic comedy, a genre Hitler liked, in which a determined medical student at Berlin University resists the amorous advances of her professor. Hitler knew Hácha had arrived, but he decided to keep him waiting until the end of the film.

At 1.15 a.m. Hácha and Chvalovský were finally summoned into Hitler's enormous study. This vast room, dimly lit by large standing lamps, offered a gloomy atmosphere for discussions. In the room sitting on comfortable chairs and sofas were Göring, Ribbentrop and Weizsäcker, plus General Wilhelm Keitel, Chief of the Armed Forces High Command, Otto Meissner, Chief of the Reich Chancellery, along with the Foreign Ministry official Walther Hewel, Otto Dietrich, Hitler's press chief, and his interpreter Paul Schmidt. Also, on the premises, though not in the room, were Dr Theodor Morell, Hitler's personal physician, and Hitler's private secretaries.

What followed was reminiscent of a harrowing Hollywood gangster movie. It began pleasantly enough. Hácha greeted Hitler enthusiastically, thanked him for agreeing to meet him. Hácha then delivered a deeply obsequious short statement of loyalty to Hitler, claiming never to have been interested in politics. He was merely a dedicated lawyer who had felt it his patriotic duty to lead his country during a time of crisis. He now firmly believed the destiny of Czechoslovakia lay in the Führer's hands. He explained that his dismissal of the Slovak government had been perfectly legal and he 'would not be shedding any tears' over the announcement of Slovakian independence.

In reply, Hitler adopted the calm but intimidating persona that had served him well in the past when he needed to intimidate someone. He told Hácha that he could be of great benefit to his country. The remainder or 'rump' of Czechoslovakia could only survive by being totally loyal to Germany, but it was now clear to Hitler that the new government under Hácha had failed to get rid of the old administration loyal to Beneš. He then listed several instances when the Czechoslovakian

[*overleaf*]   German troops in Prague,
15 March 1939.

377

government had gone against his wishes. In spite of Hácha's obvious sincerity, he said, he had no confidence that the current Czechoslovakian government as a whole could be trusted to do what he wanted.

Then he came to the main point: 'Tomorrow at 6 a.m., the German army will enter Czechoslovakia from all sides and the German air force will occupy all the airfields.' If Czech forces resisted, he continued, they would be completely annihilated. Hácha appeared frozen in a state of shock after Hitler delivered this devastating news. In response, Hácha said he accepted resistance was futile, but how did Hitler think that the whole of Czechoslovakia could be restrained in the space of just four hours? Hitler advised him to get in touch with members of his government by telephone immediately.[21]

At 2.15 a.m. Hácha and Chvalovský were escorted by Göring and Ribbentrop to an adjacent room. Hácha was summarily presented with

a pre-prepared document, agreeing to Bohemia and Moravia – the remaining parts of Czechoslovakia's 'rump' – being incorporated into the Greater German Reich as a 'Protectorate'. If Hácha didn't sign the document, Göring said, then the *Luftwaffe* would bomb Prague. At this point the elderly President fainted or had a mild heart attack. (Nobody was quite sure afterwards.) Göring left the room to find Dr Morell, who quickly administered one of his famous injections of vitamins, possibly laced with amphetamines. At any rate, Hácha revived sufficiently enough to make a telephone call to Prague. There were initially problems with the line connecting Berlin to Prague, but at 3.30 a.m. Hácha finally got through to Jan Syrový, the Czech War Minister. He urged Syrový to send orders to the Czechoslovak army not to offer any resistance to the imminent German occupation. Amazingly, this message was sent to every Czech army commander before the German troops had even crossed the border.[22]

Dr Morell gave Hácha another reviving injection and the Czech President was summoned back to Hitler's study. At 3.56 a.m. Hácha and Chvalovský signed the document, accepting German demands and agreed to release to the press the following statement: 'The Czechoslovak President declared that, in order to serve this object and to achieve ultimate pacification, he confidently placed the fate of the Czech people in the hands of the Führer of the German Reich.'[23] Afterwards, an ecstatic Hitler demanded that his two secretaries, Christa Schroeder and Gerda Daranowski, plant a kiss on each of his cheeks, saying: 'This is the greatest day of my life. I shall go down as the greatest German ever!'[24]

A solution to the rump state of Czechoslovakia could have been achieved peacefully, but Hitler chose bullying, intimidation and force instead. At the Nuremberg trials Ribbentrop said that he had talked at length

German tanks rumble through Prague after the German occupation, 22 March 1939.

with Hitler about why he had decided on the military occupation of Czechoslovakia. Ribbentrop claimed to have told Hitler that his actions to occupy Czechoslovakia using the armed forces would have 'considerable repercussions' in Britain and France.[25] Ribbentrop said Hitler seemed unconcerned and refused to accept any restriction on his chosen course of action.

At 6 a.m. on 15 March German troops crossed the Czech border into Bohemia and Moravia. By 9 a.m. they were in a snow-covered Prague. It was yet another bloodless German invasion. Hitler set off by motorcade in freezing blizzard conditions to visit his new conquest, entering Prague late in the afternoon. There were no cheering crowds this time. He spent the night at Hradčany Castle, before issuing a decree proclaiming the establishment of the Reich Protectorate of Bohemia and Moravia. It was allowed a limited measure of self-government, but it was ruled over by the newly appointed Reich Protector, who was the former German Foreign Minister Konstantin von Neurath. The two pro-Nazi Sudeten German Party leaders Konrad Henlein and Karl Frank were appointed as Head of Civil Administration and Secretary of State, respectively. Himmler soon arrived to establish a strong SS and Gestapo presence in the occupied area. Hácha, who had recovered from his ordeal in Berlin, was persuaded by Hitler to stay on as President of the Protectorate, a position he held until the end of the Second World War. Hácha remained critical of Nazism, however, and secretly maintained contact with the exiled government of Edvard Beneš.[26]

On 23 March, Slovakia signed a formal Treaty of Protection in Berlin. Ruthenia was awarded to Hungary, whose troops had occupied it the day before, and renamed the Republic of Carpatho-Ukraine. An appeal by its government to Hitler to be 'protected' was flatly rejected.

The German invasion of what remained of Czechoslovakia was deeply humiliating for the British and the French governments. The annexation of an area occupied by non-Germans proved all Hitler's talk of settling German grievances was entirely hollow. The notion that an ideologue like Hitler could be restrained by endless memoranda and carefully crafted negotiated agreements now seemed a deeply flawed illusion. When the details emerged about Hácha's personal ordeal at the Reich Chancellery, the public mood in Britain against the policy of appeasement hardened. Hitler had broken his promise. For even formerly loyal upper-class appeasers this was just not cricket. In France, Daladier told the French Chamber of Deputies that France must prepare for war.

Chamberlain did not immediately seem to grasp that the policy of appeasement had lost all credibility. Hitler's march into Prague was a national humiliation. At the cabinet meeting on the day of the German occupation Chamberlain seemed more concerned to stress that the guarantee to the rump of Czechoslovakia was null and void when German troops entered. He then delivered an ill-judged speech in the House of Commons during which he tried to dismiss the German occupation as a setback and even declared his intention to continue with the policy of appeasement.

After being denounced by his Tory, Liberal and Labour critics in parliament and then by the formerly pro-appeasement sections of the British press, Chamberlain delivered a much more critical assessment of Hitler's actions during a speech on 17 March in his home city of Birmingham. He began by defending his decision to sign the Munich Agreement, because at that time peace in Europe had been saved. He admitted, however, that for appeasement to work 'it was essential that no power should seek to obtain a general domination of Europe'. Next came his first words of warning about the probable direction of Hitler's foreign policy. He raised a key question: was Hitler's expansion of his Third Reich just the beginning of a plan to dominate the whole world by force? If so, then he promised Britain would resist Hitler 'to the utmost of its power'.[27]

France, Britain and the Soviet Union all formally condemned Germany's actions. Robert Coulondre, the French ambassador to Germany, met Weizsäcker at the German Foreign Ministry on 18 March. He placed a 'Note' from the French government on his desk. It challenged the legal basis of the German occupation, arguing that it had been forced upon the President of Czechoslovakia through bullying and intimidation, and also stressed that it breached the Munich Agreement and the spirit of the Franco-German Non-Aggression Agreement of 6 December 1938. Weizsäcker calmly read the 'Note', put it back in its envelope and then pushed it across the desk, telling Coulondre that he refused to officially accept it on behalf of the German government.[28] On that same day Nevile Henderson, Britain's ambassador to Germany, delivered a similar official 'Note' from the British government which argued that Germany's actions amounted to a complete repudiation of the Munich Agreement, but also that Hitler's military operations had been 'devoid of any legality'.[29]

On the following day Maxim Litvinov, the Soviet Foreign Minister, delivered yet another 'Note' of protest to the German ambassador to the Soviet Union in Moscow. It stated that the Soviet Union could not allow events in Czechoslovakia to pass without comment. Litvinov pointed out that Hácha had no right to terminate the independent existence of the Czechoslovakian state without the agreement of the Czech people. It was unlikely they would have agreed to the destruction of their country in a free democratic vote. The Germans had previously argued that self-determination was paramount, Litvinov continued, but in this instance they had ignored this principle and seemed prepared to do so whenever it suited them. It was the same when it came to events in Slovakia, Litvinov added. Germany's actions had encouraged Hungary to invade Ruthenia.[30]

Undeterred by this flurry of angry notes from other nations, Hitler returned from Prague to Berlin on 19 March, where he was given a triumphant welcome. Goebbels had meticulously planned the festivities, with searchlights creating a 'Tunnel of Light' on the Unter den Linden, followed by an extravagant firework display. On the balcony of the Reich Chancellery Hitler was loudly cheered by a huge crowd gathered below. However, beyond these celebrations the German people were much less euphoric about the occupation of Prague than they were about the *Anschluss* a year before. Many feared that it made a war in Europe much more likely.[31]

On 20 March Ribbentrop summoned the Lithuanian Foreign Minister Juozas Urbšys to Berlin. He informed him that the German government demanded the immediate return of the Memel territory (or Klaipėda Region) on the northern frontier of East Prussia, which had a population of 140,000. The area had been placed under French control at the 1919 Paris Peace Conference, but then after January 1923 it came under Lithuanian control even though it still had a German-speaking majority. After Hitler came to power pro-Nazi activists called for national self-determination.

At 1.00 p.m. on 23 March 1939 the Lithuanian government in Vilna signed a treaty in the German Foreign Ministry voluntarily transferring the Memel territory to the Greater German Reich. On the following day Hitler arrived at the seaport of Świnoujście (Schweinemünde in German) in the Memel territory at 2.30 p.m., aboard the German pocket battleship MS *Deutschland*. Standing on the balcony of the city's main theatre Hitler welcomed 'our old German comrades as the newest citizens of the Greater German Reich'. The transfer of the Memel territory to Germany proved to be the last of Hitler's 1930s bloodless occupations.[32]

The huge reviewing stand for the military parade on the Unter den Linden in Berlin on 20 April 1939 to mark Hitler's 50th Birthday.

With alarming swiftness, Hitler now turned his attention to Poland. Encouraged by Goebbels, the German press now depicted Poland as the 'old enemy of Germany'. Józef Lipski, the Polish ambassador to Germany, met Ribbentrop at the Foreign Ministry on 21 March. Ribbentrop warned him that Hitler was 'becoming increasingly amazed at Poland's attitude'. Germany was willing to renounce its claim to the Polish Corridor, he said, provided the Free City of Danzig was returned to Germany. An agreement should also be reached to establish railway and road links to connect Germany and East Prussia. Only then would Germany guarantee Poland's revised frontiers. Lipski promised to go back to the Polish government and tell them of Ribbentrop's demands, which he felt amounted to an ultimatum.[33]

Hitler issued a directive to the commander-in-chief of the army on 25 March, making it clear that he did not want to solve the Danzig question by force in case it drove the Poles 'into the arms of the British'. For now at least, he wanted negotiations to continue and to isolate Poland diplomatically.[34]

Lipski met Ribbentrop once again on 26 March. He presented him with a memorandum from the Polish Foreign Minister Józef Beck. It stated the Poles categorically rejected Germany's demand for Danzig to be incorporated into the Greater German Reich. However, the Polish government was willing to discuss road and railway links in the Polish Corridor, which separated Germany from East Prussia, and to enter into a joint Polish-German agreement on the treatment of the population of Danzig.[35]

Relations between Germany and Poland were beginning to rapidly deteriorate largely due to German provocation. In Warsaw on 29 March Beck summoned Hans-Adolf von Moltke, the German ambassador to Poland, and told him bluntly that if Germany made any attempt to alter the status quo in Danzig, then Poland would regard this as an act of war. The same would apply to any breach by Germany of the treaty that protected the Danzig Senate. Beck would continue to use his influence to do all he could to bring about a peaceful solution, he told Moltke, but he emphasized it was clear that a distinct tipping point had now been reached in German-Polish relations.[36]

In Britain Chamberlain feared that a German attack on Poland was imminent. On 30 March the British government asked Beck if he had any objection to a British guarantee of Polish independence. Beck readily agreed to British protection. Chamberlain issued the following statement to the House of Commons on the following day:

In the event of any action which clearly threatened Polish independence, and which the Polish government accordingly considered it vital to resist with their national forces, His Majesty's government would feel themselves bound at once to lend the Polish government all support in their power. They have given the Polish government an assurance to this effect. I may add that the French government have authorized me to make it plain that they stand in the same position in this matter as do His Majesty's government.[37]

When news of these British and French military guarantees to Poland reached Hitler he was furious. 'I'll cook them a stew they'll choke on,' he said.[38] On 13 April further Anglo-French guarantees were accepted by Greece, Romania and Turkey, although they were turned down by Denmark, the Netherlands and Switzerland.

For Chamberlain Poland was yet another foreign country about which he knew nothing. He gave no consideration to how the Western Powers were supposed to defend Poland in the event of a German attack. Poland was not a democracy like Czechoslovakia had been. It was under right-wing nationalist military rule, although it was not totalitarian. French ministers regarded Beck as a slippery character who was just as likely to reach an accommodation with Hitler as remain loyal to the Western Powers. The Polish government was also determined to oppose Soviet help. In effect the decision as to whether Britain and France went to war was now firmly in the hands of the unpredictable Polish government, thus narrowing the diplomatic options available to the Western Powers. It ought to have been obvious to anyone who looked at a map of Europe in 1939 that Poland could only resist a German military attack with the assistance of the Red Army, the Soviet fighting force created by the communist government after the Bolshevik Revolution of 1917.

The Conservative MP Winston Churchill was highly sceptical as to whether guaranteeing to protect Poland and other small nations threatened by Germany was the right diplomatic move. He felt that only a British alliance with the Soviet Union stood any chance of deterring Hitler. Such an agreement would force Hitler to fight a war on two fronts, east and west. However, Chamberlain, a lifelong anti-communist, had no stomach for any kind of collaboration with Stalin's Soviet Union. 'I have a considerable mistrust of the Soviet Union,' he told the cabinet on 5 April, 'and I have no confidence of receiving active support from that country.'[39] Chamberlain felt an alliance with the Soviet Union would push Europe into opposing blocs that would ensure war broke out. Similarly, he resisted strong calls in the press to include Winston Churchill, Hitler's most well-known British critic in his cabinet, as he felt this would antagonize Hitler even further.

Nevertheless, Chamberlain asked the British chiefs of staff to produce a report on the 'Military Value of the Soviet Union'. Their conclusion was that, while the numerical strength of the Red Army was impressive, it was cancelled out by military, administrative and economic weaknesses. The chiefs of staff saw only two advantages to a British alliance with the Soviet Union. First, it would prevent Germany from drawing on the Soviet Union's economic resources. Second, it would act as a restraint on Japan in the Far East. Relations between the Soviet Union and Japan had been deteriorating for some time, especially after Japan signed the Anti-Comintern Pact against international communism. His military chiefs' lukewarm assessment of the benefits of cooperation with the Soviet Union added weight to Chamberlain's own desire not to pursue an alliance with Stalin.[40]

There was little evidence of Hitler being worried about the Anglo-French guarantee of Poland. At Wilhelmshaven in Lower Saxony on 1 April Hitler gave an uncompromising speech at the launch of the enormous Bismarck-class battleship *Tirpitz*. He delivered a bitter attack on the Anglo-French guarantee of Poland's independence and said that the Great War had been caused, not by Germany, but by Britain's 'policy of encirclement'. Germany never really lost the war, he added, but it was stabbed in the back at home. After laying down its arms, Germany was then burdened with the unjust and imposed Treaty of Versailles. Now, at long last, Germany had broken free of this treaty and was strong enough to protect its own rights. Hitler also rejected any suggestion that Germany's vital interests needed to be discussed with the British government beforehand. In a stirring conclusion, he said:

> When I came to power, Germany was torn and impotent at
> home and abroad, a toy of foreign will. Today we have order at
> home and our economy is flourishing. Abroad we are perhaps
> not popular, but we are respected. That is the decisive factor.
> Above all, we have given millions of our fellow Germans
> [*Volksgenossen*]* the greatest happiness they could have wished for;
> their homecoming to the Greater German Reich. And secondly,
> we have given great happiness to Central Europe, namely, peace

---

* A Nazi term, meaning 'racial comrades'.

protected by German power. And this power shall not be broken by any force in the world. That is our oath.[41]

On 3 April the *Wehrmacht* High Command (OKW) received an order from Hitler entitled 'Directive for the *Wehrmacht*, 1939–40'. Only five copies were printed. The *Wehrmacht* was told to make detailed preparations and plan for Case White (*Fall Weiss*), the code name for an attack on Poland. The date of the attack was set as 1 September 1939.[42]

On 6 April an interim Anglo-Polish Treaty of Assistance was signed in London. The two countries were prepared to transform the British guarantee into a temporary pact of mutual assistance, with the fine details of a formal alliance worked out later. The treaty stressed that it was not directed against any specific country, but everyone knew that it aimed to halt a German attack on Poland.[43]

International tension escalated even further on 7 April when Italy began a five-day military and naval campaign, which ended in the occupation of the Kingdom of Albania. On 12 April Zog I, King of the Albanians, and his government were deposed. The king and his Hungarian-born Queen went into exile, taking a large amount of gold bars with them. Mussolini, aping Hitler, created the Italian Protectorate of Albania. This sudden attack once again revealed the vulnerability of small nations in the face of their more aggressive and powerful neighbours. It also showed Chamberlain's idea of Mussolini acting as a restraining influence on German aggression was another illusion. Not wanting to completely alienate the Italian government, Chamberlain did not renounce the Anglo-Italian Agreement.

The military plan for Case White was prepared by the Chief of the General Staff Franz Halder on 11 April. A negotiated settlement with Poland was still possible, he said, but if the Polish government continued to adopt a threatening attitude then the aim would be to destroy Polish military strength with a surprise attack. The Polish army could not be considered a 'serious opponent' for the *Wehrmacht* and a swift victory was confidently predicted. At the outbreak of hostilities Germany would announce the incorporation of Danzig into the Greater German Reich. The diplomatic aim would be to isolate Poland and attempt to confine the conflict to a German-Polish war. Poland would not only be defeated but 'liquidated'. Intervention by the Soviet Union was not expected. British restraint and political disputes inside the French government made it unlikely that those two nations would become directly involved either. The assumption was Germany could defeat Poland without the active intervention of the Western Allies and the Soviet Union.[44]

The US President Franklin D. Roosevelt, who was emerging as a vociferous critic of the military aggression of Hitler and Mussolini, sent a public note to the two dictators on 14 April in which he observed that three nations in Europe (Austria, Czechoslovakia and Albania) and one in Africa (Abyssinia) had been deprived of their independence though he did not name them directly. Roosevelt also cited the 'occupation of another independent nation in the Far East', an obvious reference to the Japanese invasion of Manchuria in 1931. There were reports of further acts of aggression against independent nations being planned, Roosevelt added, and he asked Hitler directly if he would 'give assurance that your armed forces will not attack or invade the territory' of thirty-one countries, which he listed. In conclusion, he offered American mediation in any further international disputes.[45]

Göring met Mussolini twice during a visit to Rome. In the first meeting on 15 April Göring relayed Hitler's congratulations on Italy's invasion of Albania, before giving Il Duce an update on Germany's current military strength. The German navy, he said, was not yet strong enough to take on the British navy. The *Luftwaffe* was expanding, but new bomber aircraft would be needed before it could contemplate offensive operations in the west. Göring was certain that in the event of a war Britain and France would support each other. He also predicted that Germany would not be ready to take on the Western democracies militarily until the spring of 1940 at the very earliest.[46]

In their second meeting, the following day, they discussed Roosevelt's telegram. Göring interpreted it as a sign that Roosevelt was suffering from 'an incipient mental disease'. Mussolini said the most sensible course of action was not to reply at all. Göring agreed. Mussolini then joked about Roosevelt's very poor grasp of geography, because he had mentioned countries that were already occupied by Britain and France in his list of potential German military victims.

Their conversation then turned to the Soviet Union. Stalin's speech in Moscow on 10 March was deeply significant, Göring said. Stalin had been highly critical of Britain and France in the speech. It seemed clear that the Soviets were not prepared to be used as cannon fodder by the Western democracies. Göring told Mussolini he would ask Hitler to consider some kind of rapprochement between the Soviet

Union and the Axis powers. Mussolini observed that the Japanese would have to be consulted first, but he thought an agreement with the Soviet Union would completely scupper the British guarantee to Poland and their policy of encirclement. A war in Europe was now unavoidable, Mussolini felt, but he was unsure when would be the best time for the Axis powers to seize the initiative. Göring suggested they should wait until 1942 or 1943.[47]

In Moscow Litvinov, the Soviet Foreign Minister, met Sir William Seeds, the British ambassador to the Soviet Union, on 16 April. Litvinov offered to sign a tripartite pact of mutual assistance between the Soviet Union, Britain and France, with an additional guarantee offered to Poland, and all the states in the Baltic if desired, and to any other nations feeling menaced by Hitler's Germany. When the British government eventually replied to this offer on 8 May it amounted to a rebuff, principally because Poland was opposed to the idea of being protected by the Soviet Union.[48]

In Berlin on 17 April Ernst von Weizsäcker at the German Foreign Ministry noted a quite remarkable occurrence: 'For the first time since he assumed charge of his post here, the Russian ambassador called on me today.' The man in question was Alexei Merekalov who had ostensibly wanted to discuss contracts for the delivery of war material from the Škoda Works in the former Czechoslovakia, but the conversation soon turned to 'the present situation in Central Europe'. Germany had always wanted cordial economic ties with the Soviet Union, Weizsäcker told him. Merekalov observed that ideological differences exerted little effect on Soviet-Italian relations, and he saw no reason why Germany could not return to cordial relations with the Soviet Union if both sides were willing.[49]

On 19 April, in a conversation with Grigore Gafencu, the Romanian Foreign Minister, Hitler offered a glimpse into his foreign policy thinking at this time. His life's ambition, he said, was to destroy the Treaty of Versailles. The world had no right to complain about his methods. The current differences between Germany and Poland were so minute as to be ridiculous. The Polish government had embarked on a course that was incomprehensible. He had already made a very generous offer to the Poles to settle any outstanding issues through negotiation. If Britain wanted a war over the German-Polish dispute, then it could have one, he added, although it would be a great personal disappointment, because Hitler had been 'a great Anglophile' since his youth.[50]

On 20 April Goebbels organized a lavish celebration for Hitler's fiftieth birthday. Many Germans lined the streets of Berlin. The high point of the festivities was an impressive display of German military power. It began at 11 a.m., moving past Hitler's reviewing stand and through the Brandenburg Gate, and went on for five hours. Ambassadors from Britain, France, Poland and the United States were invited, but refused to attend.

This was followed by a birthday reception in the grand Mosaic Hall of the Reich Chancellery. Hitler was lavished with gifts, including fifty letters written by his hero Frederick the Great, a new Volkswagen, several works of art, and a scale model of the new Victory Arch, designed by Albert Speer. Hitler was 'completely overcome' with this gift, Speer later recalled. 'He shook my hand without saying a word, before telling the other guests in a euphoric voice about the significance of this structure for the future history of the Reich.'[51]

Hitler used his speech to the Reichstag on 28 April to answer his critics regarding his foreign policy, in particular Chamberlain and Roosevelt. He began with a bitter attack on the British government and went on to deny that the German occupation of Prague had anything whatsoever to do with the Munich Agreement. He denounced Britain's 'new policy of encirclement' of Germany. Because the British government placed no trust in his promises, he announced he was unilaterally ending the Anglo-German Naval Agreement of 1935. He then pointed out that Britain had built its empire using 'brutal force in many instances', and had singularly failed to solve the Irish and Palestinian problems, too, so he would take no moral lectures from Chamberlain.

He described reports that Germany intended to attack Poland were 'inventions of the international press'. Poland had signed an agreement with Britain, which, under certain circumstances, would compel it to take military action against Germany. This invalidated the German-Polish Non-Aggression Pact of 1934, which Hitler said was now 'null and void'.[52] Hitler then turned to the vexed issue of German-Polish relations. Yes, he had demanded the return of Danzig to Germany, but he had promised to leave the Polish Corridor alone, provided road and rail links between Germany and East Prussia could be agreed. However, the Polish government had rejected these proposals and refused to negotiate.

Hitler finally gave a lengthy response to President Roosevelt. With a mixture of sarcasm, irony and wit, he went point by point through Roosevelt's telegram, offering an answer to each of his questions.

He denied that he was a warmonger, pointing out the United States had participated in six armed interventions since 1918 and the Soviet Union in ten. In comparison, Germany had managed to solve its grievances concerning the Treaty of Versailles without resorting to war. Furthermore, Roosevelt's telegram had mentioned a nation in Africa (presumably Abyssinia) that had lost its freedom. But, Hitler said, all the people of Africa had already lost their freedom before 1935 and most were now under the rule of the democratic nations.

Hitler then read out the names of each of the nations that Roosevelt had claimed Germany was planning to invade: Finland, Estonia, Latvia, Lithuania, Sweden, Norway, Denmark, the Netherlands, Belgium, Great Britain and Ireland, France, Portugal, Spain, Switzerland, Liechtenstein, Luxembourg, Poland, Hungary, Romania, Yugoslavia, the Soviet Union, Bulgaria, Greece, Turkey, Iraq, the Arabias, Syria, Palestine, Egypt and Iran. Hitler said he had asked each of their governments whether they felt menaced by Germany. Every country contacted had replied '*Nein*' ('No'). Admittedly, some countries had not replied at all, but 'those were occupied by the military forces of Britain and France'. This led to huge laughter and cheering. He next quoted the Irish Taoiseach Éamon de Valera, who said that it was the military aggression of the British government which the Irish people feared more than anything else. The British government continued to deny the Palestinians their freedom, Hitler added, but were furthering the cause of the Jews in the Middle East. And so, in conclusion, Hitler stated that he was willing to give an assurance of Germany's entirely peaceful intentions to each and every one of the nations listed in Roosevelt's telegram.

As he sat down, the cheering in the Reichstag was deafening. Many German listeners considered it to be the best speech he had ever given and most of the international press agreed.[53] The German chargé d'affaires in France felt that the speech had a 'reassuring effect on the French population'. Its tone was considered moderate, serious and dignified, while the jokes at Roosevelt's expense were viewed in France with 'a certain amount of malicious pleasure'.[54]

On 3 May Stalin suddenly dismissed his Foreign Minister Maxim Litvinov. He replaced him with his close political ally Vyacheslav Molotov. This new appointment was headline news in the Soviet press, although Litvinov's dismissal was relegated to the 'News in Brief' on the back page. The Nazi press had long derided Litvinov for being Jewish, referring to him as the 'Jew Finkelstein'. By replacing him with Molotov Stalin was clearly signalling to France and Britain the possibility of a rapprochement with Germany. Stalin was annoyed by the slow progress of negotiations towards an alliance with the Western Powers. He was particularly angry over the British proposal to link the alliance to the already failed procedures of the League of Nations.[55] Two days later Georgi Astakhov, the Soviet chargé d'affaires in Berlin, met Julius Schnurre of the German Economic Policy Department of the Foreign Ministry. Astakhov made the case that the replacement of Litvinov with Molotov represented a significant change in Soviet foreign policy. He asked whether the German government was now willing to resume the trade negotiations that had been broken off in February. Schnurre replied that he could not yet give an answer to that question.[56]

The Polish Foreign Minister Józef Beck delivered an eagerly awaited and brave speech to the Polish parliament on 5 May. He was more bullish than any leader of a small state had ever been towards Adolf Hitler. On the Danzig question, he said, Germany and Poland had cooperated on trade in the area for centuries. Yes, the population of Danzig was predominantly German, but it was heavily dependent on trade with Poland, just as Poland's seaborne trade depended upon the port city of Danzig. Poland was no threat whatsoever to the freedom of Danzig's German population. Furthermore, although the so-called Polish Corridor was an ancient Polish territory, the Polish government allowed Germans to freely travel and trade in the area without the need of customs or passport control. The Danzig question and the Polish Corridor (which the Poles called *Pomorze*) were complex issues. It was not just a simple matter of Poland giving in to German demands. Peace is 'a valuable thing', Beck concluded, but not 'peace at any price'.[57]

On the same day the Polish government sent a reply to the German government's note of 27 April, which had renounced the German-Polish Non-Aggression Pact of 1934 as having no legal force. The Germans' unilateral renunciation of the pact was unjustified, argued the Poles, because that pact had never ruled out either government concluding agreements with third parties. The Polish government emphasized once again that it was willing to sign a joint guarantee of Danzig's independence, and to discuss road and rail links through the Polish Corridor, but that the incorporation of Danzig into the Greater German Reich remained wholly unacceptable.[58]

At the Berghof on the same day Hitler met Monsignor Cesare Orsenigo, the Apostolic Nuncio to Germany. Orsenigo delivered a personal proposal from the Pope for a conference of the five great

European powers to try to solve the outstanding political questions of the era. Hitler replied that he did not think it was necessary as there was no danger of war in Europe. After all, Germany had no direct demands on Poland. The gravest danger to European peace at that time was Britain which was always interfering in those countries with which Germany had a dispute. It was doing the same thing again with Poland. The result was, he concluded, that 'Poland was now adopting a megalomaniacal attitude'.[59]

On 6 May Weizsäcker sent a circular to a number of German embassies abroad, offering instructions on how best to respond to Beck's recent speech to the Polish parliament. He outlined four points to make to refute it: (1) a great many lapses of memory crept into Beck's account of German-Polish conversations; (2) it made no contribution towards reaching an understanding between Germany and Poland; (3) the Führer's offer of a negotiated settlement was not mentioned by Beck; and (4) Beck's speech should be interpreted as the relatively insignificant pronouncement of a weak government.[60]

Meanwhile in Britain, at a Foreign Policy Committee meeting on 16 May, Lord Ernle Chatfield, the Minister for Coordination of Defence, argued strongly in favour of an Anglo-Soviet Agreement being concluded as soon as possible. If the Soviet Union stood aside during a European war it might 'secure an advantage from the exhaustion of the western powers', he added. Worse still, perhaps, was the distinct possibility of a Nazi-Soviet Agreement should the British and French negotiations with the Soviet Union fail.[61]

On 24 May Chamberlain met with his cabinet to discuss whether to begin serious negotiations towards some kind of Anglo-Soviet alliance. The cabinet was strongly in favour, but Chamberlain still found the idea distasteful. The cabinet won, however, and Chamberlain was forced to back down. 'In the present circumstances,' he said, 'it was impossible to stand out against the conclusion of an agreement.' Nevertheless, for the sake of appearances, he hoped that any such alliance between Britain and the Soviet Union could be concealed under the banner of the League of Nations. Bowing to pressure from his cabinet and from the British public, the Prime Minister had finally agreed to open negotiations for an alliance with Stalin.[62]

On 20 May Friedrich-Werner von der Schulenburg, the German ambassador to the Soviet Union, met the new Soviet Foreign Minister Vyacheslav Molotov. Before the meeting Ribbentrop had advised him to exercise 'extreme caution' during their conversation. A wary Molotov

[overleaf] The signing of the German-Italian 'Pact of Steel', on 22 May 1939.

made it clear that before the Soviet Union would resume trade talks with Germany, he would prefer some kind of wider political dialogue. Schulenburg felt that the Soviet Union might be using Germany as a political pawn to put pressure on the Western Powers to stop dawdling and sign a military alliance with the Soviet Union as soon as possible before Hitler beat them to it.[63]

On 22 May a Pact of Friendship and Alliance between Germany and Italy was signed in the new Reich Chancellery. The so-called 'Pact of Steel' was a bluntly phrased military alliance that seemingly tied Mussolini unconditionally to Germany. The protocol accompanying the agreement stated that 'the time has come to strengthen the close relationship and homogeneity, existing between National Socialist Germany and Fascist Italy'. Both sides pledged to 'act side by side and with their armed forces to secure their living space'. Each promised to consult the other about their plans and to come to one another's aid in time of war. Article V promised that 'in the event of war neither nation would conclude a separate armistice or peace'.[64]

On the following day Hitler addressed a group of leaders of the *Wehrmacht*, *Luftwaffe* and naval commanders of the *Kriegsmarine* in the Reich Chancellery. The only other member of the Nazi elite present was Göring. Minutes of the meeting have survived, taken by Lieutenant Colonel Rudolf Schmundt, although no copies were circulated at the time, because the meeting took place in the strictest secrecy. Hitler began by saying that 'Danzig was not the subject of dispute at all.' It was really a question of 'expanding our living space in the East'. He had decided to attack Poland at the earliest opportunity. 'We cannot expect a repetition of Czechoslovakia,' he added. 'There will be war. Our task is to isolate Poland. Success in isolating her will be vital.' He would issue the final order when to strike, but above all 'It must not come to a simultaneous showdown with the West.' However, if a war between Germany and Poland could not be contained, 'then the fight must be primarily against England [Britain] and France'. Hitler then turned to the Soviet Union and made a prediction: 'It is not ruled out that Russia might disinterest herself in the destruction of Poland.'[65]

Some of Hitler's top military brass felt uneasy about Germany risking a wider war in Europe. General Georg Thomas, the Head of the Defence Economy and Armament Office in the OKW, delivered a confidential lecture to his staff at the Foreign Ministry on 24 May. The strength of the *Wehrmacht* had increased from seven to fifty-one divisions between 1935 to 1939, he said, including five armoured divisions and four light ones. Added to this, the German navy now had two battleships, two heavy cruisers, seventeen destroyers and fifty-seven submarines. Plus the *Luftwaffe* had twenty-one squadrons. All of which amounted to a formidable fighting force, Thomas said, but he stressed it was still not strong enough to take on the combined might of Britain, France and the Soviet Union simultaneously.[66]

On 26 May Ribbentrop composed for Schulenburg some instructions as to how to proceed in further talks with the Soviet government. The time was ripe, Ribbentrop wrote, to consider a normalization of German-Soviet relations. It should be emphasized that Germany had no aggressive intentions towards the Soviet Union and that if the Soviets would stop being so hostile towards Germany, then both countries could come to some sort of diplomatic agreement. A copy of this note of advice was sent to Hitler, who decided to tread much more cautiously than Ribbentrop desired. Hitler felt a public rebuff from the Soviet Union would be humiliating. In the end, Ribbentrop's instructions were never sent to Schulenburg in Moscow.[67]

In his first major public speech as Soviet Foreign Minister in front of the Supreme Soviet in Moscow on 31 May, Molotov reprimanded the Western democracies for their hesitancy in concluding an alliance. The Soviet Union would not be drawn into conflicts started by warmongers, he warned. The Soviet government would only sign a defensive agreement with Britain and France if it guaranteed the security of states in Central and Eastern Europe and also made clear the exact form and scope of any military aid that was to be offered by each of the signatory nations. The latest Anglo-French proposals, which had been submitted on 27 May and which attempted to involve the moribund League of Nations, were totally unacceptable. Pointedly, Molotov made clear that the Soviet Union had not rejected the possibility of talks, with Germany and Italy, and the German-Soviet trade talks could be resumed.[68]

In the first week of June 1939 the German Foreign Ministry sent one of its research assistants – Adam von Trott zu Solz, a former Rhodes Scholar at Oxford University – on an eight-day fact-finding mission to assess current British attitudes towards Germany. He talked to Halifax and Chamberlain during his visit. Halifax told him that public opinion had now shifted in Britain concerning the aims of Hitler's foreign policy. There was now 'a definite emotional readiness for war', although the British government was still willing to accept any 'peaceful way out'. When Trott zu Solz met Chamberlain, he asked him why Britain decided to guarantee Poland's independence. The Prime Minister replied: 'Do you believe I enter into these obligations gladly? Herr Hitler forces me into it.' The British people had been 'passionately stirred' ever since the occupation of Prague, Chamberlain added. He now personally believed that Hitler's ultimate aim was conquest and promised that Britain would fight Germany should it attack another independent nation.[69]

Throughout June trade talks continued between Germany and the Soviet Union. During these conversations it soon became clear that Molotov was keen to begin political negotiations. He noted that the German-Soviet Neutrality and Non-Aggression Pact (the so-called Treaty of Berlin), which had been signed on 24 April 1926, had never been officially rescinded. It could now easily be converted into a German-Soviet Non-Aggression Pact.[70] Heartened by this news, Weizsäcker told Schulenburg that he was willing to send Julius Schnurre to Moscow to conclude a new German-Soviet trade agreement.[71]

On 17 June Hitler met with the Saudi Arabian ruler Ibn Saud's special envoy Khalid al-Hud al-Gargani at the Berghof. Hitler said he felt sympathy for the Arabs for two reasons: 'because Germany had no territorial aspirations in Arabia' and 'because we have the same enemies – the Jews', adding that he would not rest until 'the last Jew had left Germany'. In reply, al-Gargani said that the Prophet Mohammad had acted in the same way and driven all the Jews out of Arabia.[72]

On 28 June Schulenburg told Molotov that the German government would welcome a normalization of relations with the Soviet Union. Molotov replied that it was Soviet foreign policy to maintain good relations with all nations and he expressed optimism about the current trade talks. After the meeting, Schulenburg informed the Foreign Ministry of his suspicion that the Soviet government was using the trade talks as a bargaining chip to push Britain and France to hurry up and sign a military alliance. This, he felt, was the outcome that the Soviet government really desired.[73]

On the following day Hitler decided that it was unacceptable for the Soviet government to make the continuation of trade talks contingent on the start of political negotiations. He ordered the trade talks to cease. There is no clear indication as to why Hitler so abruptly changed his mind.[74] It was a bizarre decision, because a German-Soviet agreement had the advantage of completely isolating Poland. According to reports from the German Embassy in Moscow, talks between the Soviet Union, Britain and France concerning an alliance had been deadlocked for some time and were going nowhere. The key sticking point was the flat refusal of Poland, Rumania and the Baltic states to accept any kind of Soviet military assistance.

The Soviet government's growing frustration over the slow pace of these talks was increasingly evident. Andrei Zhdanov, Second Secretary of the Communist Party and the Head of the Propaganda and Agitation Department of the Central Committee, wrote an article in *Pravda* on 29 June entitled 'The British and French Governments Do Not Want an Equal Agreement with the USSR'. 'What they [Britain and France] want is a treaty in which the USSR would play a part of a hired labourer bearing the brunt of the obligations on his shoulders,' Zhdanov wrote. 'No self-respecting country will accept such a treaty unless it wants to be a plaything in the hands of people who are used to having others pull their chestnuts out of the fire.'[75] Schulenburg, the German ambassador to the Soviet Union, was convinced that this article had been written on 'orders from above'. It indicated that Stalin doubted the sincerity of the British and French negotiators, whom he believed were raising the issue of a guarantee over the Baltic states solely in order to create further delay.[76]

In London on 29 June Lord Halifax gave a speech at Chatham House, during which he said: 'In the past we have always stood out against the attempt by any single power to dominate Europe at the expense of other nations, and British policy is, therefore, only following the inevitable line of its own history, if such an attempt were to be made again.' It was the firm resolve of the British government, he added, 'to stop aggression'. As for Hitler's claim that the British wanted to isolate Germany, this was completely untrue. Germany was isolating itself through its own actions. As for the German demand for *Lebensraum*, Halifax argued that every nation had this problem to a greater or lesser degree, but that it could be solved through economic improvement within nations, not by external military territorial expansion.[77]

Meanwhile, in Germany, away from all this feverish diplomatic activity, something very sinister was occurring. Sterilization had been introduced in Germany on 1 January 1934 to prevent the so-called 'racially unfit' from procreating. Now, in the summer of 1939, to further 'purify' the German race, Dr Karl Brandt was selected to administer a new programme of mass murder through involuntary euthanasia.

Hitler's new Reich Chancellery would supervise the programme, which was to be led by Philipp Bouhler. It would take place in secret, administered by a department set up in a Berlin villa with the address Tiergartenstraße 4, hence it became known as the *Aktion T4* programme. *T4* began by concentrating on infants under the age of five, but was soon extended to disabled and mentally ill patients of all ages. Hitler personally signed an order sanctioning the *T4* programme on 1 October (backdated to 1 September). This is clear evidence of Hitler's willingness to sanction genocide.

The *T4* programme was a very important step on the way towards the Final Solution. It used many of the methods of murder that would later be employed in the later extermination camps. It operated under the strictest secrecy at a number of former hospitals (Bernburg, Grafeneck, Hadamar, Hartheim and Sonnenstein) and a former jail facility (Brandenburg). All of them were turned into killing centres, specially outfitted with gas chambers disguised as showers and with crematoria to burn the bodies. The programme was run by civilian administrators, some of whom had SS affiliations, but ordinary doctors and nurses were also involved. When murder by lethal injection proved too slow, doctors turned to the use of carbon monoxide gas. Around eighteen or twenty people were led into shower rooms by the nursing staff and told to undress. The doors were closed and the lethal gas was administered. After about ten minutes the room was cleared of gas and SS men would place the dead on stretchers and carry them to the ovens. Mobile gas vans were used, too. The first gassing experiment at Brandenburg was administered personally by Dr Albert Widmann, a chemist and an SS officer working for the Kripo, the Criminal Police Department of the Reich.

Elaborate administrative measures were used to cover up these murders. The concerned relatives of murdered patients were informed their loved ones had been transferred to another hospital for further treatment, but they were never told its name or location. After the murders, death certificates citing death by natural causes were sent by post, informing relatives that the body of their loved one had been cremated and they could collect the ashes. About 70,000 adults and 20,000 children were murdered in this forced euthanasia programme, which operated from 1939 to 1941. *Aktion T4* showed Hitler that it was possible to organize mass murder in a secretive, planned and organized manner.[78]

Meanwhile, there was no let-up in the diplomatic manoeuvring between Germany and the Soviet Union. On 22 July Weizsäcker informed Schulenburg in Moscow that Hitler had changed his mind again on the negotiations. He was now willing to not only support the signing of a trade agreement with the Soviet Union, but also to give his permission for the political negotiations to begin.[79] Hitler seems to have finally realized he could seriously discomfort Britain and France by coming to an agreement with Stalin.

A truly decisive moment came on 26 July when Julius Schnurre at the German Foreign Ministry invited Georgi Astakhov, the Soviet chargé d'affaires, and Yevgeniy Barbarin, the Head of the Soviet Trade Delegation, to dinner at a lavish restaurant in Berlin which served Baltic specialities. Astakhov reminded Schnurre of the good relations that had existed between Germany and the Soviet Union before 1933. At the core of good relations

then was the 1922 Treaty of Rapallo under which each side renounced all financial and territorial claims against each other. Afterwards relations became normalized and secret German rearmament was assisted by the Soviet Union in the Weimar era. Schnurre now outlined the three stages necessary for there to be some kind of new arrangement between the former friends, namely, a German-Soviet Non-Aggression Pact: (1) the re-establishment of collaboration in the economic field; (2) the normalization of political relations; and (3) the re-establishment of good relations, as existed in the 1920s, or else a new arrangement concentrating on the current vital political interests of both parties.

The Soviet Union favoured a rapprochement that addressed the vital interests of both countries, Astakhov said. He promised to relay the details of their conversation to the Soviet Foreign Ministry. Then

Philipp Bouhler, Chief of the Chancellery of the Führer, was a key figure in instigating the Aktion T4 Euthanasia Programme.

he asked: 'If a high-ranking Soviet personage discussed these questions with a high-ranking German personage, would the German put forward similar views?' And Schnurre replied: 'Oh yes. Certainly.'[80]

German-Soviet diplomatic talks now moved fast. In Berlin Ribbentrop had a lengthy conversation with Astakhov himself on 2 August, informing him that Germany desired detailed conversations on the 'remoulding of German-Russian relations'. Germany was 'favourably disposed towards Moscow', he added, and would not complicate matters, as the democratic powers were currently doing. The transformation of German-Soviet relations would be possible on three conditions: (1) non-interference in the internal affairs of both countries; (2) the Soviet Union must abandon its policy directed against vital German interests; and (3) all conversations between Berlin and Moscow would have to be conducted in the strictest secrecy or else they would be immediately discontinued.[81]

In Moscow, Molotov invited Schulenburg to meet him on 4 August. The Soviet Union had always desired a trade agreement with Germany, Molotov told him, and he was pleased this was nearing conclusion. He promised to appraise Stalin of Germany's desire for a normalization of political relations.[82]

On that same day the crisis over Danzig had escalated. Several incidents were widely reported at customs posts on the border, engineered by pro-Nazi elements. Polish customs inspectors were henceforth given permission to carry guns to enforce compliance with trade regulations. It was yet another sign that the Polish government would not yield to intimidation by Germany.[83]

On 8 August, Hitler met Count István Csáky, the Hungarian Foreign Minister, at the Berghof. The meeting had been arranged after the Hungarian Prime Minister had informed Hitler that Hungary would not participate in a war against Poland. Hitler told Csáky that the current approach of Poland was 'sheer madness'. He hoped that the Poles would see reason at the last minute, but he was now anticipating a war on two fronts, which would be 'concluded with lightning speed'.[84]

Mussolini was concerned about the possibility of war over Poland. Ciano, the Italian Foreign Minister, began a three-day diplomatic mission to Germany on 11 August. Mussolini had sent him to find out whether Hitler approved of his own idea of a Munich-style conference to seek a German-Polish negotiated settlement over Danzig and the Polish Corridor. The atmosphere between Ciano and Ribbentrop was deeply strained from the beginning.

On the first day, Ciano met Ribbentrop at his estate in Fuschl am See near Salzburg in the afternoon. Ribbentrop told him that Hitler's decision to attack Poland was now irreversible. Ciano noted in his diary: 'He [Ribbentrop] rejects any solution which might give satisfaction to Germany and avoid a struggle. I am certain that even if the Germans got more than they ask for they would attack [Poland] just the same, because they are possessed by the demon of destruction.'[85] In the evening, Ciano and Ribbentrop dined at the White Horse Inn in St Wolfgang. 'During the dinner hour not a word is exchanged,' Ciano commented. 'We are distrustful of each other. But I, at least, have a clear conscience. He has not.'[86]

The next day Ciano had talks with Hitler at the Berghof. He found the Führer cordial but rather cool and very determined to go to war. Poland would be defeated quickly, Hitler said, and the Western Powers would not get involved. Ciano was worried the conflict might escalate into a wider European war and Italy would be dragged into it. Ciano outlined Italy's military weaknesses and reiterated Mussolini's view that Italy would not be ready for war until 1942 at the very earliest. Ciano then suggested that a conference could settle the Danzig question in Germany's favour, without the need of war, but Hitler would not contemplate even attending such a meeting. Ciano then tried to pin down Hitler on the exact date of Germany's attack on Poland. Expect something to happen 'by the end of August at the latest', Hitler replied. 'I return to Rome completely disgusted with the Germans, with their leader, with their way of doing things,' Ciano wrote in his diary. 'They have betrayed us and lied to us. Now they are dragging us into an adventure which we have not wanted, and which might compromise the [Italian] regime and the country as a whole.'[87]

Britain and France, unaware of the clandestine German-Soviet negotiations, had not yet given up hope of signing an alliance with the Soviet Union even though the talks were not getting anywhere. On 23 July, Molotov demanded the immediate opening of military talks between the British and the French. An Anglo-French military mission was put together in some haste. Former Foreign Secretary Anthony Eden volunteered to lead the party but this offer was flatly rejected by Chamberlain. In the end, the British delegation was led by an upper-class admiral with a farcical sounding long name: Sir Reginald Plunkett-Ernle-Erle-Drax. In fact, he had a distinguished naval career in the Great War but he was not very well known by the general public nor even, it seems, by many of the senior Royal Navy Staff.

He was accompanied by Air Marshal Sir Charles Burnett and Major-General T. G. Heywood, plus a retinue of minor officials.

The quickest way to Moscow was by air. A plane could have taken them there in a day, with refuelling stops. A train journey was ruled out because the quickest route required a change in Berlin. That left travelling by sea as the final alternative. The fastest route by sea was by a speedy warship, but Halifax felt this would give too high a profile to the mission – yet another sign that the British government was going through the motions. The British delegation finally sailed on a slow-moving chartered merchant ship, *The City of Exeter*, with a top speed of thirteen knots per hour (fifteen miles per hour). The party set sail on 5 August and seemed to enjoy the journey, particularly the large curry dinners served by Indian waiters. The party arrived in Leningrad on 10 August, then caught the midnight train to Moscow, reaching the Soviet capital on 12 August a full week after departure.

Impatient for the talks to begin, the French delegate General Joseph Doumenc, a specialist in mechanized warfare, had already put together his negotiation team in early July. He was advised by Bonnet, the French Foreign Minister, to proceed quickly to Moscow. Doumenc suspected that the British government was spinning out the negotiations in order to play for time.[88] The prior instructions Drax had received from Lord Halifax prior to his departure was to 'go very slowly' during the talks add weight to Doumenc's concerns.[89]

The sluggish and slipshod approach of the British delegation led the Soviet government to question the sincerity of the Anglo-French mission from the start. Ivan Maisky, the Soviet Union's ambassador to Britain, had lunch with Drax shortly before his departure. When Maisky had asked why they were not going to Moscow by plane, Drax had replied: 'You see, there are nearly twenty of us and a lot of luggage, it would be uncomfortable in the plane.'[90] At a time of international crisis, it seems comfort rather than speed had been prioritized. Worse still, when Drax arrived in Moscow, he did not even possess the necessary accreditation documentation that Soviet military protocol required for a person to conduct negotiations. It took another two days for the accreditation of Drax to arrive from London. Doumenc at least had a letter of introduction signed by the French Prime Minister Daladier.

In contrast, the Soviet military negotiating team included several high-ranking officers in the Red Army, most notably Marshal Kliment Voroshilov, the People's Commissar (Minister) for Defence, and

Left to right, Ribbentrop, Count Ciano, the Italian Foreign Minister and Hitler.

General Boris Shaposhnikov, the Chief of the General Staff of the Red Army. The talks began in the Spiridonovka Palace, but it was not until the third meeting on 14 August that Voroshilov got to the heart of the matter by asking the British and French delegations: would Poland and Romania allow Soviet troops to enter their territory to engage with German troops? The British and French did their best to prevaricate on this question, to the point of telling blatant lies, but they were finally forced to admit, a few days later, that the answer was a firm no. The Polish government did not trust the Soviet Union and its ministers were worried that if they allowed Russian soldiers into Poland, they were unlikely ever to leave. Voroshilov said that if Poland and Rumania would not allow Soviet troops to assist them in the event of German aggression, then there was really no hope of a military alliance. These futile talks continued until 17 August when Voroshilov insisted they must be adjourned until the Polish and Romanian governments agreed to receive Soviet military assistance in the event of a German attack. The talks were never resumed.[91] As the Poles refused Soviet help, it made it easier for Stalin not to give it. The question for Stalin now became simple: why fight a war to save anti-Soviet Poland and thereby start a German-Soviet War?

In a confident mood Hitler spoke to his military commanders on 14 August at the Berghof. He told them he doubted whether the 'men of Munich' (meaning Chamberlain and others who signed the Munich Agreement of 1938) would go to war to save Poland: 'The men I got to know in Munich are not the kind that starts a world war.' Britain was not rich enough to sustain a conflict on the scale of the Great War, he added, while the Soviet Union was not prepared to, as he put it, pull the 'chestnuts out of the fire' for the Western democracies. Hitler predicted Switzerland, the Netherlands and Belgium would remain neutral. Hungary would support Germany in spirit if not materially, he said, while Italy and Spain would not want the Western democracies to win.[92]

In Berlin, on the same day, Ribbentrop sent a telegram to Schulenburg in Moscow requesting a meeting with Molotov. The Soviet Union now held the diplomatic initiative. Schulenburg was instructed to make absolutely clear to Molotov that no conflict of interests existed between Germany and the Soviet Union. To stress that Western Powers were the enemies of both National Socialism and the Soviet Bolshevism, that Britain, France and their allies were really trying to drive the Soviet Union into a war with Germany, while standing by

safely on the sidelines. In these circumstances, Ribbentrop was now prepared to visit Moscow to conduct high-level German-Soviet negotiations in person.[93]

Schulenburg read out Ribbentrop's telegram to Molotov at a meeting with him on the next day. Molotov warmly welcomed Germany's desire to improve relations. He then asked if the German government was prepared to sign a non-aggression pact with the Soviet Union and use its influence to improve Soviet relations with Japan. At the same time Molotov gave no indication of wanting to rush things, making clear that if Ribbentrop came to Moscow it must be to discuss concrete terms which would require detailed preparation on both sides beforehand.

Molotov regarded the personal intervention of Ribbentrop as decisive: it demonstrated how serious the Germans were about some kind of pact. He was pleased that the trade talks between Germany and the Soviet Union were going so well, too. Molotov promised Schulenburg that Stalin himself would be informed of these latest developments. Schulenburg's memorandum of this meeting with

Nazi stormtroopers march through Danzig, May 1939.

[overleaf] Stalin (*white jacket*) celebrates the signing of the German-Soviet Non-Aggression Treaty with Ribbentrop (*left*) and Molotov (*extreme right*).

Molotov is crucial, because it makes clear that the first suggestion of a Soviet-German non-aggression pact came from the Soviet Union.[94]

Ribbentrop was extremely pleased with Molotov's response. He asked Schulenburg on 16 August to inform him of the German desire to take up his offer of a Non-Aggression Pact. The Führer, he added, wanted the pact to be signed as 'soon as possible', because the Polish situation was coming to a crisis. Ribbentrop was prepared to visit Moscow any time after 18 August.[95] On 19 August Schulenburg informed Ribbentrop that the Soviet government had agreed to his visit. He was invited to go to Moscow one week after the signing of the trade agreement, which was to take place the following day. This meant that Ribbentrop would arrive on 26 or 27 August.[96]

Hitler quickly realized that the Soviet timeline of events interfered with his own firm plan to attack Poland. On the spur of the moment, in a shrewd diplomatic move, he wrote a personal telegram to Stalin. It was sent at 6.45 p.m. on 20 August:

> In my opinion it is desirable, in view of the intentions of the states to enter into a new relation to each other, not to lose any time. I therefore again propose that you receive my Foreign Minister on Tuesday 22 August, but at the latest Wednesday, 23 August. The Reich Foreign Minister has full powers to draw up and sign the Non-Aggression Pact, as well as the protocol. A longer stay by the Reich Foreign Minister in Moscow than one or two days at most is impossible in view of the international situation. I should be glad to hear your early answer.[97]

Hitler now impatiently awaited Stalin's reply, while those around him worried that he was on the verge of a physical and nervous collapse. Stalin's response arrived at the Berghof by teleprinter at 10.30 p.m. on 21 August. Stalin wrote:

> I hope the German-Soviet Non-Aggression Pact will mark a decided turn for the better in the political relations between our countries. The people of our countries need peaceful relations with each other. The assent of the German government to the conclusion of a Non-Aggression Pact provides the foundation for eliminating political tension and for the establishment of peace and collaboration between our countries. The Soviet government has authorized me to inform you that it agrees to Herr von Ribbentrop arriving in Moscow on 23 August.[98]

Hitler's close ally Albert Speer was with the Führer at the Berghof when Stalin's message came through. He recalled how Hitler had at first stared into space after reading the telegram, then banged on the dining table and shouted: 'I have them! I have them!'[99]

Hitler once again gathered his military commanders together at the Berghof on 22 August. 'I have called you together,' he said, 'to give you a picture of the political situation in order that you may have some insight into the individual factors on which I have based my irrevocable decision to act and in order to strengthen your confidence.' He then expressed concern that 'a criminal or a lunatic' might try to assassinate him, because he was the key to everything. 'Essentially, all depends on me,' he said, 'on my existence, because of my political talents. Furthermore, the fact that probably no one will ever again have the confidence of the whole German people as I have. There will probably never again in the future be a man with more authority than I have. My existence is therefore a factor of great value.'

He went on to say that in his view it was 'highly probable' that the Western democracies would not fight. 'Our enemies are little worms,' he said. 'I saw them at Munich.' The destruction of Poland was now his top priority: 'Close our hearts to pity! Act brutally! Eighty million people must obtain their right. The stronger man is right. Be strong and remorseless! Be steeled against any signs of compassion.'[100]

On that same day Chamberlain composed a letter to Hitler: 'Whatever may prove to be the nature of the German-Soviet Agreement, it cannot alter Great Britain's obligations to Poland, which His Majesty's Government have stated publicly and plainly and which they are determined to fulfil.'[101]

The British ambassador to Germany Nevile Henderson delivered Chamberlain's letter in person at the Berghof at 1 p.m. on 23 August. Hitler read it, then became 'excitable and uncompromising'. He handed Henderson an uncompromising reply, asserting that although Germany was prepared to settle the Danzig and Polish Corridor questions through negotiation, the decision of the British government to offer an unconditional guarantee to Poland had encouraged Polish intransigence, and was encouraging acts of violence against German-speaking citizens in Danzig. The German government was not prepared to stand by and passively accept this state of affairs for much longer.[102]

Soon after Henderson left, Hitler informed the Chief of the General Staff Franz Halder of the precise date and time of Germany's proposed attack on Poland: Saturday, 26 August at 4.30 a.m. Halder noted in his diary: 'Y-Day = 26 August. There will be no more orders regarding Y-Day and X-hour [the start of the attack]. Everything is to roll automatically.'[103] Later that same day the Danzig Senate, led by the Nazi Gauleiter Albert Forster, voted for Danzig to return to the Reich.

The landmark Treaty of Non-Aggression between the German government and the Union of Soviet Socialist Republics was finally signed in Moscow on 24 August at 2 a.m. by Ribbentrop and Molotov, with Stalin and Schulenburg also present. Germany and the Soviet Union were now obligated to desist from any act of violence or aggression towards each other for the next ten years. Both parties also agreed not to participate in any grouping of nations that was directly or indirectly aimed at the other party.

The Soviets requested an additional secret protocol to the pact, carefully mapping out German and Soviet spheres of influence in Eastern Europe. In the event of a territorial rearrangement in the Baltic states (Estonia, Latvia and Lithuania), it was agreed that the northern border of Lithuania would represent the boundary of the Soviet Union and Germany. The spheres of influence would be bounded by the line of the rivers Narew, Vistula and San. This turned the non-aggression pact into a cynical aggression pact: a joint agreement that ensured Poland would soon cease to exist. Germany and the Soviet Union had overcome their ideological differences to unite in practical self-interest, better defined by the German word: Realpolitik.[104]

A brief drinks party followed the signing of the pact. On the menu were black tea, sandwiches, caviar, vodka and vintage Crimean sparkling wine. Glasses were clinked, cigarettes were lit, smiles were exchanged. Then the traditional lengthy Russian toasts began. Stalin proposed a drink in honour of Hitler: 'I know how much the German nation loves its Führer. I should therefore like to toast his health.' Ribbentrop proposed a toast to Stalin. Molotov raised his glass to Ribbentrop. Stalin concluded by telling Ribbentrop: 'The Soviet government takes the new pact very seriously. I can guarantee on my word of honour that the Soviet Union will not betray its partner.'[105]

In August 1942 Stalin would recall this historic moment at a meeting with Winston Churchill in Moscow. He tried to explain to Churchill why he had signed the non-aggression pact with Hitler: 'We formed the impression that the British and French governments were not resolved to go to war if Poland were attacked, but that they hoped the diplomatic line-up of Britain, France and Russia would deter Hitler. We were sure it would not.'[106]

In a speech to a packed House of Commons on 24 August 1939

Chamberlain described the German-Soviet Treaty of Non-Aggression as a 'surprise of a very unpleasant character', because the negotiations by Britain and France with the Soviet Union 'had been seemingly progressing well, but the Soviet government had been conducting secret negotiations with the German government simultaneously'. In spite of the treaty, Chamberlain reiterated that 'our obligations to Poland and to other countries remained unaffected'. As for Hitler's recent letter to him, 'it amounted to a restatement of the German thesis that in Eastern Europe Germany should have a free hand'.[107]

At 1.30 p.m. on 25 August Hitler met British ambassador Henderson in the new Reich Chancellery fully realizing that the invasion of Poland was due to begin at dawn on the following day. Hitler outlined to Henderson a far-ranging offer to the British government, guaranteeing the British Empire and offering German assistance in the event of war. In return, the British were to allow him to settle the Polish question in his own manner. Henderson promised to pass on this offer to the British government.

A number of messages now served to weaken Hitler's resolve to go ahead with the attack on Poland. The French ambassador Robert Cou-londre informed Hitler in person of the French determination to fight if Poland was attacked. At the same time the news arrived that Britain and Poland had signed an Agreement of Mutual Assistance. Now if Britain or Poland became engaged in hostilities with an unspecified 'European Power', in consequence of aggression by the latter, the other contracting party would at once give it all of the support and assistance within its power. It was a clear and binding agreement, ensuring the British government would go to war if Poland was attacked.[108]

Earlier on that fateful day Hitler had sent a letter to Mussolini informing him that a war with Poland was likely to begin soon and that he hoped he could still count on Italy's support, according to the terms of the so-called Pact of Steel signed in May. A reply was delivered in person by the Italian ambassador Bernardo Attolico about 6 p.m. Mussolini wrote:

> If Germany attacks Poland and the conflict remains localized, Italy will afford Germany every form of political and economic assistance requested, but if Germany attacks Poland and the latter's allies [Britain and France] open a counter-attack against Germany, I inform you in advance that it will be opportune for me not to take any initiative in military operations, in view of the present state of Italian war preparations.

Mussolini then outlined an impossible wish list of military supplies that he would like Germany to deliver, including: 7 million tons of petrol, 6 million tons of coal, 2 million tons of steel, 1 million tons of timber, and numerous other items. After Attolico had left, Hitler commented: 'The Italians are behaving just as they did in 1914.'

Hitler now faced the prospect of a war with Britain and France without Italian support. This rattled him. He suddenly decided to postpone the invasion of Poland. This decision was given to the leading *Wehrmacht* commanders Halder and Keitel, then conveyed to the *Luftwaffe* and the navy chiefs. Halder noted in his diary: 'The Führer is rather shaken.'[109] Case White was officially postponed at 8.30 p.m. on 25 August. Only Hitler could have stopped such a massive invasion on the spur of the moment.[110]

On the next day, the French Prime Minister Édouard Daladier sent Hitler a letter warning him that France would go to war with Germany if Germany attacked Poland: 'If the blood of France and of Germany flows again,' he wrote, 'as it did twenty-five years ago in a longer and even more murderous war, each of the two peoples will fight with confidence in its own victory, but the most certain victors will be the forces of destruction and barbarism.' In reply, Hitler argued that Germany had no territorial claims against France, so there was absolutely no reason why France should go to war over Danzig.[111]

On the same day, regaining his composure, Hitler summoned Halder once again to give him a new and final date for the German

attack on Poland: Friday, 1 September at 4.45 a.m. In fact, this was the original date mentioned in the first draft of Case White. Hitler now planned to drive a wedge between Britain and Poland. He was determined to go to war and because the Polish Foreign Minister Józef Beck refused to give in to his demands, war was now inevitable whatever happened.

A 'mystery man' now emerged as an intermediary between Göring and the British Foreign Office, with the aim of preventing war. His name was Birger Dahlerus, a Swedish businessman and a contact of Göring's. Dahlerus met Halifax at the Foreign Office twice on 25 and 26 August. He asked him to write a letter to Göring emphasizing the British government was still willing to work towards a negotiated settlement of the German-Polish dispute. Halifax obliged with a bland message expressing a desire for peace without making any promises. Dahlerus delivered this letter to Göring in person.

Göring then took Dahlerus to meet Hitler in the early hours of 27 August. Hitler, who had been woken up by Göring, came downstairs to deliver a twenty-minute tirade to Dahlerus which amounted to several insults directed at the British and the Poles. Then Hitler outlined a six-point plan for Dahlerus to present to the British government. It offered a German pact with Britain; Danzig and the Polish Corridor to be transferred to Germany; a promise to offer Poland a guarantee of its new frontiers; a demand for German colonies to be returned to the Reich; the issuing of guarantees to the German minority in Poland; and a German pledge to defend the British Empire.[112]

The British government was now faced with two conflicting offers from Hitler. The first (communicated via Henderson) wanted Britain to give Hitler a free hand to crush Poland in return for a guarantee of the Empire. The second (delivered by Dahlerus) outlined a comprehensive negotiated settlement of the Danzig and Polish Corridor questions and offered a similar far-ranging guarantee to the British Empire. Chamberlain told Dahlerus that both offers were completely unacceptable. Halifax decided the amateur diplomat Dahlerus was now unnecessary and insisted that future negotiations should go through the proper diplomatic channels. The only part of Hitler's proposals that the British government felt inclined to accept was for negotiations to begin between the Germans and the Poles.

Due to the repeated insistence of Dahlerus that Hitler desired a negotiated settlement, Henderson asked the Germans to open negotiations with the Polish government during a meeting with Hitler on

Newspaper seller in London with papers announcing the German invasion of Poland, 1 September 1939.

28 August. The British government wanted a settlement of differences between Germany and Poland, Henderson explained, but Britain's undertaking to guarantee Poland's independence still remained intact and it would be honoured if the Germans attacked.[113]

On the following day Hitler met Henderson again and told the British ambassador that he was willing to open up a diplomatic dialogue with the Poles. Then came a familiar request: he wanted the British to persuade the Polish government to send an emissary 'with full powers' to Germany to conclude an agreement over Danzig and the Polish Corridor. The Polish representative had to arrive in Berlin by midnight on 30 August.[114]

Howard Kennard, the British ambassador to Poland, wrote to Lord Halifax on 30 August, commenting on this proposal:

> I feel sure that it would be impossible to induce the Polish
> government to send Colonel Beck or any other representative
> immediately to Berlin to discuss a settlement based on a
> proposal by Herr Hitler. They would certainly sooner fight
> and perish rather than submit to such humiliation, especially
> after the examples of Czechoslovakia, Lithuania and Austria. I
> would suggest that if negotiations are to be between equals, it is
> essential that they should take place in some neutral country or
> even possibly Italy.[115]

Halifax told Henderson to inform Hitler that the British government would not advise the Polish government to send a representative to Berlin, as this request was 'wholly unreasonable'. Halifax added that the German government should follow formal diplomatic protocol on the matter and submit its written proposals to the Polish ambassador in Berlin, who would then transmit them to Warsaw.[116]

Late on the evening of 30 August Henderson delivered Halifax's reply. Ribbentrop then proceeded to read out, at top speed, a new detailed sixteen-point German plan for a negotiated settlement with Poland. Henderson asked Ribbentrop for a text of these proposals, but Ribbentrop said that it was too late, because a Polish representative had not arrived. In response, Henderson asked Ribbentrop why he could not simply follow normal diplomatic procedure and invite the Polish ambassador in Berlin to meet him. A very angry Ribbentrop replied that he would not do that, but that he might respond if the Polish ambassador contacted him first. Henderson felt that Ribbentrop's behaviour at this meeting had been deeply unpleasant and very similar to Hitler at his worst.[117]

German armoured divisions causing devastation in Poland.

These German proposals were, of course, not serious at all. Hitler wanted the Poles to either capitulate or to be seen as rejecting Germany's generous offer of a peaceful negotiated settlement. As Hitler later put it: 'I needed an alibi, especially with the German people, to show them that I had done everything to maintain peace. This explains my generous offer about the settlement of the Danzig and [Polish] Corridor questions.'[118]

At 12.40 p.m. on 31 August Hitler issued 'Directive No. 1 for the Conduct of War' to his senior armed forces commanders. He made it clear to them that the political possibilities had now been completely exhausted and that as a last resort he had decided upon 'a solution by force'. Case White would begin at 4.45 a.m. on 1 September. The real responsibility for these hostilities should be 'placed unequivocally upon England [Britain] and France', he added.[119]

The Polish ambassador to Germany Józef Lipski finally went to see Ribbentrop at the Foreign Ministry at 6 p.m. on 31 August. He told him that Poland was willing to negotiate on the basis of Ribbentrop's proposals, as conveyed verbally to Henderson. Ribbentrop asked Lipski if he had full powers to negotiate there and then. 'No,' Lipski replied. On hearing this, Ribbentrop abruptly ended the conversation and showed him to the door.

In Moscow Vyacheslav Molotov delivered a speech to the Supreme Soviet on the same day. He began by explaining that the triple alli-

ance talks with Britain and France had failed, because Poland had repeatedly rejected the offer of Soviet military assistance. As a result of this breakdown of trust, the Soviet Union had decided to conclude a Treaty of Non-Aggression with Germany. 'The art of politics does not consist of increasing the country's enemies,' Molotov said. 'On the contrary, the art of politics in this sphere is to reduce the number of such enemies and make the enemies of yesterday good neighbours.'[120]

In the evening a German radio announcer read out Hitler's sixteen-point peace proposals and confirmed they had been rejected by the Polish government. In reality, of course, they had never been formally submitted. After the broadcast Wilhelm Hosenfeld, a teacher in the German city of Fulda, was not the only German thinking that 'The Führer's proposals were acceptable, modest and would serve to preserve the peace.'[121]

The German battleship SMS *Schleswig-Holstein* firing the opening salvo against Danzig during the attack on Poland.

At 8 p.m. a small German unit, dressed in civilian clothes, spear-headed by six armed SS men led by SS Major Alfred Helmut Naujocks of the SD (security service), captured a 380-feet-high German radio-transmitting tower on the outskirts of Gleiwitz (modern Gliwice), three miles inside the German border. A Polish speaker with Naujocks' group named Karl Hornack soon announced: 'Attention! Here is Gleiwitz! The radio station is in Polish hands!' He claimed to represent the mythical 'Polish Freedom Committee' and demanded the Polish population in Germany rise up against Hitler's regime. It remains unclear how much of this speech was broadcast, if any. In Berlin, Heydrich claimed he never heard anything. To further incriminate the Poles, the SS killed an ethnic Pole, provided by the Gestapo, who had previously lived in Berlin called Franciszek Honiok. His dead body was planted in the rear door of the adjacent building to the radio tower. Within hours, German national radio was running the story of the brutal 'Polish attack' on Gleiwitz. No one outside Germany believed the story but it was used by the German government to provide a justification for the German attack on Poland.[122]

The German army waiting to attack Poland on that night consisted of 102 divisions, but only 60 were fully equipped and ready. Numerically, it was still much weaker in manpower than the French army. Added to this, the German navy was still vastly inferior to the British Royal Navy. Only the *Luftwaffe* was stronger than its enemies. The ammunition supply for the German army during the Polish campaign would last just four to five weeks.[123]

The German attack on Poland began at 4.45 a.m. on 1 September. The German cruiser *Schleswig-Holstein*, which had docked earlier in Danzig harbour, fired shells at Polish armament dumps on the island of Westerplatte.[124] At the same time, divisions of the German army, numbering 1.5 million men, crossed the western frontier of Poland in a three-pronged attack from East Prussia in the north, across Slovakian territory in the south, and in the west stretching from Silesia to Pomerania, cutting through the Polish Corridor. Around 51,000 Slovakian troops participated in the invasion in the south.

The Germans had 2,750 modern tanks and 2,315 planes, including the screeching Junkers Ju-87 or Stuka (from *Sturzkampfflugzeug*, 'dive-bomber'). Mobile artillery guns were also deployed with devastating results. Among those who crossed the Polish border on that first day was Lieutenant Wilhelm Prüller, aged twenty-three, who noted: 'It's wonderful now to be a German, we've crossed the border [...] The

German *Wehrmacht* is marching. If we look back, or in front of us, or left or right, everywhere the motorized *Wehrmacht*.'[125]

Facing these formidable forces the Polish army lined up thirty-nine divisions consisting of 1 million men, trying to defend the entire 1,750-mile Polish frontier in the west. Marshal Edward Śmigły-Rydz, the Polish army commander-in-chief, had decided on this strategy. It turned out to be a suicide mission. The small number of 210 operational Polish tanks was supplemented by 670 light tankettes (about the size of a car and seen as more cost-effective than full-size, turreted tanks). In addition, there were 400 battle-ready aeroplanes which had been dispersed in anticipation of the German attack. Overall, the Germans enjoyed a numerical superiority of 5:1 in artillery, 3:1 in tanks and 5:1 in aircraft. Stories of the Polish cavalry charging armoured tanks with lances were the creation of German propaganda but the Polish armed forces were at an enormous military disadvantage.

The *Wehrmacht* split into two army groups for the Battle of Poland consisting of: Army Group North, containing the 3rd and 4th armies, was led by Field Marshal Fedor von Bock and Army Group South, commanded by Field Marshal Gerd von Rundstedt, was made up of the 8th, 10th and 14th armies. Their chief aim was to smash the Polish border defences, then trap the Polish army between the two German army groups in a dramatic pincer movement.

The main spearhead of the attack would be the forces of Army Group South. Its key aim was to defeat the bulk of the Polish army,

push east towards Lvov, and then assault Warsaw from the west and south. Army Group North had a more complicated logistical task, because it needed to operate in two battle zones, separated by the Polish Corridor. It had the more limited objective of capturing the Polish Corridor and Danzig. Once this was achieved, Army Group North would unite with the 3rd Army, drive into Poland and head for Warsaw, too.

In their attack on Poland the Germans unleashed a new kind of warfare intended to bring about a swift victory, the *Blitzkrieg*, meaning 'lightning war'. There's some dispute as to when the term *Blitzkrieg* was first used. The American *Time* magazine referred to a *Blitzkrieg* in its 25 September 1939 issue, but the term was used before that in a German periodical called *Military Weekly* in 1938. Official German military documents never use the term *Blitzkrieg* and Hitler claimed he never used the term either.[126]

At the heart of the *Blitzkrieg* strategy was the deployment of five Panzer divisions each with around 300 modern tanks. A Panzer division could assault, penetrate and smash through defence positions. It was extremely difficult to defend against them without similar modern equipment. These Panzer divisions were supplemented by four fully motorized divisions and four other lightly motorized divisions. Behind these mechanized forces were the traditional infantry divisions, on foot, with 300,000 horses deployed. In spite of the *Blitzkrieg* mythology, the German army was not a fully mechanized army. If it had been, Germany would probably have won the Second World War.

Above the advancing tanks flew ultra-modern *Luftwaffe* planes able to mount devastating bombing raids. This immense concentration of power, coordinated by electronic communications such as radio, telephone and telegram, produced a military juggernaut never before seen on a European battlefield. *Blitzkrieg* worked very effectively in Poland, because the weather was good and the ground was firm and flat. It was a strategy best suited to short wars in good weather on good roads.[127]

There was intense fighting during the initial German strike over the border, but even by the end of the first day Army Group North had sealed off the southern part of the Polish Corridor, trapping two Polish infantry divisions and a cavalry division. Army Group North, with its devastating Panzer divisions, made rapid progress against dogged Polish resistance. In charge of two of its armoured divisions was General Heinz Guderian, who had predicted in his book *Achtung – Panzer!* (1937) that concentrated tank warfare would prove unstoppable.[128]

German Panzer units travelling unimpeded through the Polish countryside.

[overleaf] The German Army marches into Warsaw after a comprehensive victory over Poland.

Germany's attack on Poland had been planned as a racial war. 'The Poles', Hitler had told Goebbels, 'were more animals than men, totally dull and formless.'[129] In fact, the invasion of Poland marks a decisive moment in the evolution of a much more radical version of Nazi anti-Semitic policy. Around 1.8 million Jews would soon fall into German hands. Up until September 1939 the solution to the so-called Jewish question had been emigration, but the outbreak of war would restrict the available routes out of Europe. A new solution was therefore required. The SS, led by Himmler, and its security intelligence wing the SD, led by Heydrich, planned to extend Nazi racial policies to the newly occupied territories.

In the vanguard of this Nazi racial war was the SS Special Task Force of the Security Police, the *Einsatzgruppen der Sicherheitspolizei*. These paramilitary death squads operated in a limited form after Austria and Czechoslovakia were annexed. However, their aim during the Polish campaign was much more wide-ranging: to purify the 'living space' occupied by the German armed forces, and to murder the leading political elites and intelligentsia of Poland. The SS was planning a murderous expedition that would turn Hitler's regime into a criminal one, carrying out extrajudicial killings at will.

Dr Werner Best, a senior Gestapo administrator, created a total of five *Einsatzgruppe* units for the Polish campaign. (This was later expanded to seven.) Around 2,000 men were recruited from SS and Gestapo personnel, supplemented by 2,250 volunteers from the ordinary civilian Order Police, bringing the total to 4,250 men. Each killing unit was assigned to the five *Wehrmacht* armies for the attack on Poland.

The leaders of each *Einsatzgruppe* tended to be university-educated, middle-class SS men already in prominent positions in the Gestapo and the security police or employed as guards in the concentration camps. In addition, there were three SS battalions from the *Totenkopf* or 'Death's Head' division. Back in June the leaders of the *Einsatzgruppen* had undergone a two-week training course at the SS/SD Security Service School in Bernau near Berlin. They were told that their mission in Poland was to make sweeping arrests of saboteurs, Jews and the Polish intelligentsia, including civil servants, teachers, academics, the judiciary and cultural figures.[130]

The *Einsatzgruppen* carried out numerous summary executions during the Polish campaign, but created some confusion among German army officers as to who was giving them their orders. The *Einsatzgruppen* reply was that they were acting on orders from Hitler to carry out 'certain ethnic tasks'.[131] On 3 September Himmler ordered the *Einsatzgruppen* to kill all 'insurgents', which he defined as people endangering life or property – in practice, for the *Einsatzgruppen*, this meant anyone.[132]

The *Einsatzgruppen* were not alone in carrying out massacres in Poland. German soldiers also participated in numerous arbitrary murders of civilians, with the agreement of their commanding officers. They torched residential homes with flamethrowers. On 10 September, for instance, Field Marshal Fedor von Bock told his troops that if they were fired upon from a house, they were to burn down that house with the inhabitants still inside. By the time the German invasion of Poland ended the *Wehrmacht* had burned to the ground 531 towns and villages.[133]

The crimes of the *Einsatzgruppen* during the Polish campaign have been extensively examined by historians. The most accurate estimate is that they murdered 16,336 people in summary executions. This figure is based on painstaking research by the Polish historian Szymon Datner, although his statistics do not distinguish between mass shootings by the *Einsatzgruppen* and those carried out by the army, police units and the SD. The victims were primarily members of the Polish intelligentsia, nationalists, Catholic priests, Jews and Gypsies.[134]

The mood was sombre in Berlin on 1 September. There was none of the enthusiasm for war that there had been in 1914. In the morning Hitler received a telegram from Mussolini asking him to release Italy from its obligations under the Pact of Steel. At 9.40 a.m. Hitler agreed to this in a friendly-worded telegram. Mussolini then suggested that Hitler should attend a peace conference on 5 September involving Britain, France, Germany and Poland. It was the best way, he said, to negotiate an armistice between Germany and Poland and also to discuss all of the outstanding clauses of the Treaty of Versailles that still needed to be revised.[135]

Hitler was driven to the Reichstag, which was still meeting at the Kroll Opera House. There he delivered a strangely subdued speech, offering his familiar attacks on the unjustness of the Treaty of Versailles and the unreasonableness of the Western Powers before explaining why he had decided to go to war:

> In my talks with Polish statesmen [...] I formulated at last the German proposals. For two whole days I sat with my government and waited to see whether it was convenient for the Polish government to send a plenipotentiary or not [...] I can no

longer find any willingness on the part of the Polish government
to conduct serious negotiations with us […] I have therefore
resolved to speak to Poland in the same language that Poland for
months past has used toward us.

Hitler promised that he would now be 'the first soldier of the
German Reich' and wear his grey uniform, and 'not take it off again until
victory was secured, or I will not survive the outcome'.[136] Looking on
from the public gallery was Eva Braun, who was in tears. 'If something
happens to him,' she told her sister, 'I will die, too.'[137]

Germany's *Blitzkrieg* was clearly sufficient to trigger the Anglo-
French guarantee of Poland's independence. The people of Britain and
France fully expected their nations to issue a joint declaration of war
straightaway. However, this did not happen for two reasons. First, the
British and the French wanted to give Mussolini's tentative idea of an
international conference a proper chance to succeed in the hope that
it might settle the matter peacefully. Second, the French government
made it clear to the British that it needed more time, perhaps until
5 September, to fully mobilize its army.[138] This lengthy delay proved
deeply embarrassing for the Western Powers.

On 1 September Chamberlain told the cabinet: 'Our conscience
is clear and there could be no question of where our duty lay.'[139]
The British government sent a telegram to the German government,
warning of the possibility of a war unless German troops withdrew
from Poland. There was absolutely no expectation of this happening.
Later that day Chamberlain told the House of Commons: 'Eighteen
months ago in this House I prayed that the responsibility might not
fall upon me to ask this country to accept the awful arbitrament of war.
I fear that I may not be able to avoid that responsibility.'[140]

The idea that Mussolini was seriously trying to persuade Hitler to
end his occupation of Poland is a myth. On 4 September Mussolini
told Hans von Mackensen, the German ambassador in Italy, that '[he]
never had the remotest thought of engaging in any action that was
conditioned on the withdrawal of German troops. No person in the
world could seriously think of proposing such a thing. He had rejected
such an idea with outright indignation.'[141]

By now the majority of the British public believed that Britain
needed to fight Hitler. The tense and sombre mood in the House
of Commons at 7.45 p.m. on 2 September, as the Prime Minister
rose to speak, reflected this. As one Labour MP noted: 'We waited
there exactly like a court awaiting the verdict of the jury.'[142] When

Chamberlain, whose voice betrayed some emotion, seemed to tentatively endorse the idea of a conference if Germany agreed to withdraw its troops from Poland, the anger of MPs boiled over. After Chamberlain had left the debating chamber, Lord Halifax told him that his government would fall on a vote of no confidence on the following day unless an ultimatum was sent to the German government by midnight.

At 11.30 p.m. on 2 September the British cabinet met in emergency session. Chamberlain told them that it was impossible for the government to delay any longer, nor could he wait for the French to coordinate a declaration of war. It was agreed that the British ambassador to Germany Nevile Henderson would deliver an ultimatum to the German government, in person, at 9 a.m. on the following morning, saying that unless Germany promised to withdraw its troops from Poland by 11 a.m. a state of war would exist between Britain and Germany.[143]

The wording for this ultimatum was adapted from a similar one sent by the British to the Germans in 1914. Back then Britain had been asking Germany to withdraw its troops from Belgium. This was now changed to Poland. The stakes could not have been higher. Of course, Britain was not going to war to save Poland, but to prevent Hitler from dominating Europe by force and to preserve the existing balance of power in the world. The French government had by now decided to present a similar ultimatum, on the same day, but with a later expiry time of 5 p.m.

At exactly 9 a.m. on 3 September Nevile Henderson delivered the British ultimatum to the German Foreign Ministry, but Ribbentrop was not there to receive it. Instead, Henderson handed it to Hitler's interpreter Paul Schmidt, the eye witness to so many of the key events on the road to war. 'I regret that on the instructions of my government,' Henderson told Schmidt, 'I have to hand you an ultimatum for the German government.' He regretted delivering it to Schmidt, because 'you have always been anxious to help'.[144]

Schmidt hurried along the Wilhelmstraße to the new Reich Chancellery, where he found Hitler seated at his desk, along with several other members of the Nazi elite, most notably Goebbels, Göring and Ribbentrop. Schmidt read out the British ultimatum slowly. 'When I finished there was dead silence,' he later recalled. 'Hitler sat staring into space, then he looked at Ribbentrop, who was standing by the window, and said: 'What now?' After a short pause, Ribbentrop replied: 'I assume that within the hour the French will hand us a similar ultimatum.'[145] Göring then spoke: 'If we lose this war, Lord have mercy on us.' Goebbels remained silent. [146]

At 11.15 a.m. Neville Chamberlain gave a live radio broadcast on the BBC from the cabinet room at 10 Downing Street:

> This morning the British ambassador in Berlin handed the German government a final note stating that, unless we heard from them by eleven o'clock that they were prepared at once to withdraw their troops from Poland, a state of war would exist between us. I have to tell you now that no such undertaking has been received, and that consequently this country is at war with Germany.

At 12.06 p.m. Chamberlain told the House of Commons: 'This is a sad day for all of us and to none is it sadder than to me. Everything that I have worked for, everything that I hoped for, everything that I have believed in during my public life has crashed into ruins.'[147]

Chamberlain then announced that two of his biggest critics would be returning to government: Anthony Eden as Secretary of State for Dominion Affairs and Winston Churchill as First Lord of the Admiralty. Churchill had held this position before (1911–15) and the Admiralty sent a three-word message to all the ships of the Royal Navy: 'Winston is back!' On that same day Australia and New Zealand also declared war on Germany. The British-controlled government of India soon followed, but without consulting the Indian nationalist leaders. Three days later South Africa declared war on Germany, too.[148]

In Munich Unity Mitford, the British friend of Hitler, felt completely shattered after hearing the news of Britain's declaration of war. She lunched at the Osteria Bavaria in a very distressed state and later confessed that she had wanted to kill herself there and then. After lunch she visited the pleasant surroundings of the *Englischer Garten* (English Garden). She walked through this beautiful public park before sitting down on a bench. Then she calmly took a pearl-handled pistol (a gift from Hitler) out of her handbag, placed it against her right temple and fired. The bullet lodged in her brain. Amazingly, she was still alive, but was left paralysed in her right arm and leg. Hitler visited her frequently in hospital, even paying her hefty hospital bills. He offered her the choice of German nationality or returning to Britain. She decided on the latter and Hitler arranged her safe passage in January 1940.[149]

At 9 p.m. on 3 September Hitler boarded his special armoured train in Berlin's *Stettiner Bahnhof* and set off for Poland. During the next three weeks the *Führersonderzug* (which was named *Amerika* in 1940 and *Brandenburg* in 1943) became the 'Führer Headquarters' during the Polish campaign. The first carriage contained a spacious living room complete with sleeping compartments and a bathroom. A command carriage contained communications equipment and a large conference table for meetings.[150]

On the evening of 5 September General Franz Halder noted in his diary: 'Enemy as good as beaten.' The Germans had by this stage sealed off the Polish Corridor. Army Group South had destroyed the Polish Łódź army. Franciszek Kornicki, a Polish pilot, described the scene at a local hospital in the midst of this battle: 'It was a terrible place, full of wounded and dying men lying everywhere on beds and on the floor, in rooms and corridors, some moaning in agony, others lying silent.'[151]

The ancient city of Kraków fell to the 14th Army attached to Army Group South on 6 September. The Pomeranian army was soon defeated, too. Victory over these two huge Polish armies ensured the Germans' success in the early Battle of the Borders. The diaries of German soldiers reveal how brutal they could be towards the civilian population. For instance, when a German soldier called Gerhard encountered sniper fire in a rural village on 10 September, his entire unit torched the local houses with flamethrowers:

> Soon burning houses were lining our route. And out of the flames there sounded the screams of people who had hidden in them and were unable any more to rescue themselves. The animals were bellowing in fear of death, a dog howled until it was burned up, but worst of all was the screaming of the people. It was dreadful. It's still ringing in my ears even today. But they shot at us, so they deserved death.[152]

German soldiers were shocked by the large number of Jews living in Poland. What most surprised them was that Polish Jews looked nothing like the assimilated Jews of Germany. A Private Grömmer described the Jews he saw as 'beasts in human form. In their beards and kaftans, with their devilish features, they make a dreadful impression on us. Anyone who was not a radical opponent of the Jews must become one here.'[153] The Polish Jews suffered all manner of humiliations from the brutal German invaders. 'If a bearded Jew was caught, his life was in danger,' Rabbi Shimon Huberband observed. 'They tore out his beard along with pieces of his [face] flesh or cut it off with a knife and a bayonet. The occupiers were particularly savage towards anything symbolic of Judaism.'[154]

There was some Polish barbarity, too, most notably on 4 September ('Bloody Sunday') in the city of Bydgoszcz, known to the Germans as Bromberg, when 254 ethnic Germans were brutally killed. Overall, it is estimated that during the Polish campaign some 4,000 ethnic Germans were murdered.[155] Goebbels inflated this figure to 5,400 for propaganda purposes. In February 1940, on Hitler's instructions, this figure was increased even further to a wildly inaccurate 58,000. News of the killing of ethnic Germans by Poles only helped to fuel and justify the much more numerous instances of German brutality.[156]

Mass executions of Polish civilians did provoke some criticism. Admiral Wilhelm Canaris, the head of military intelligence, protested to General Keitel, Chief of the Armed Forces High Command, about the high number of extrajudicial killings in Poland. He was informed that Hitler had ordered them to be carried out.[157] General Johannes Blaskowitz, the commander-in-chief of the 8th Army, protested about the activities of the *Einsatzgruppen* execution squads. When Hitler saw Blaskowitz's memorandum on the subject, he observed: 'You can't run a war on Salvation Army lines.'[158] On 4 October Hitler issued a general amnesty for all German army or SS personnel who had been convicted of offences against civilians in Poland, including murder and rape. On 17 October Hitler decreed that the SS and the police operating in Poland were no longer subject to military jurisdiction when engaged in 'special tasks'.[159]

One of the most surprising aspects of letters home from German soldiers in Poland is the frequent mention of a methamphetamine drug with the trade name Pervitin. It was freely available over the counter in German chemist shops but was used extensively by German troops in Poland. Some even asked relatives to send them more tablets. 'I am dog-tired,' wrote the German soldier Heinrich Böll* to his parents, 'because last night I only slept two hours, and tonight again I won't have more than three hours of sleep, but I've got to stay awake. The Pervitin will soon start working, by the way, and help me over my tiredness.'[160] The use of Pervitin was not officially sanctioned by the *Wehrmacht* during the initial stages of the Polish campaign, but officers turned a blind eye to its use. Doctors attached to army groups were soon openly supplying troops with the drug. As one medical officer put it: 'I'm convinced that in big pushes, where the last drop has to be squeezed from the team, a unit supplied with Pervitin is superior.'[161]

---

* In 1972 he would win the Nobel Prize for Literature.

On 8 September Hitler issued a command order to his government ministers, concerning the conduct of propaganda during the war. He viewed propaganda as vital in strengthening the will of the people towards victory, while destroying the morale of the enemy. Hitler assigned this activity to the Ministry of Propaganda. Psychological propaganda was crucial in domestic politics, he argued, but it could also be used to influence public opinion abroad. Ribbentrop, the Foreign Minister, and Goebbels, the Minister of Propaganda, disagreed so often about the best use of propaganda that Hitler lost patience with them both. 'I forbid once and for all that I be approached on such differences of opinion or disputes at any time in the future,' he said, 'unless the two ministers come to see me together to present the case.'[162]

In Poland, meanwhile, German Army Groups North and South were advancing at full throttle. On 8 September the first German Panzer divisions reached the outskirts of Warsaw with Field Marshal Walther von Richenau's fully armoured 10th Army at its epicentre. The retreat of the Poznań and Pomorze armies provided the climax of Germany's Polish campaign, known as the Battle of the Bzura, between 9 and 19 September. Amazingly, after being pushed back, the Polish army mounted a counter-attack against the German 8th Army on 9 September, capturing 1,500 German POWs. This victory was short-lived, however, as reinforcements from the fearsome 10th Army arrived, soon supplemented by the 4th Army. Around 20,000 Poles were killed during this battle and 100,000 Polish soldiers surrendered.[163]

In Berlin on 9 September Ribbentrop met Hiroshi Ōshima, the Japanese ambassador to Germany, and told him: 'The fate of Japan was now, as in the past, closely bound up with the fate of Germany. If Germany should be defeated in the present war, the Western democracies would quickly form an extensive coalition, which would oppose any expansion by Japan.' He further emphasized that close collaboration between Germany, Italy and Japan need not be affected by the Nazi-Soviet Pact. 'Oshima agreed with my statements on every point,' Ribbentrop noted.[164]

On the same day Hitler issued 'Directive No. 3 for the Conduct of War'. He ordered that the operations against the Polish army and air force would continue until it was safe to assume that the Poles had been defeated. Once this was clear, the main strength of the army and air force could then be transferred to the west. In operations there, Hitler insisted that his personal consent was required before any troops crossed the western borders of Germany and before every air attack.

The *Luftwaffe* could support naval operations, but no offensive action at sea was to be undertaken against the French navy yet.[165]

Ribbentrop informed Molotov on 15 September that the 'destruction of the Polish army is rapidly approaching'. He predicted that Warsaw would be occupied 'in the next few days'. The German government agreed to adhere to the 'spheres of influence' outlined in the secret protocol of the Non-Aggression Pact with the Soviet Union. Ribbentrop expected the Red Army to begin its military intervention soon. He advised that a joint German-Soviet communiqué should be released as follows: 'In view of the obvious splitting apart of nationalities living in the former Polish state, the Reich government and the government of the USSR consider it necessary to bring to an end the intolerable conditions existing in these territories. They regard it as their joint task to restore peace and order in these their natural spheres of influence and to bring about a new order by creation of natural frontiers and viable economic organization.'[166]

On the following day Molotov confirmed that military action by the Red Army was imminent. However, he felt that a joint communiqué along the lines suggested in Ribbentrop's draft was unnecessary. The Soviet Union, Molotov said, should justify its own military intervention in Poland as follows: 'The Polish state has disintegrated and no longer existed; therefore, all agreements concluded with Poland are null and void; third powers might try to profit from the chaos that has arisen; the Soviet Union considered itself obligated to intervene to protect its Ukrainian and White Russian brothers and make it possible for these unfortunate people to work in peace.' Molotov accepted that this statement might prove rather 'jarring to German susceptibilities', but the Soviet government needed to justify its action abroad. It did not want to be seen as openly collaborating with the Germans in the partition of Poland before world opinion.[167]

On 17 September at 6 a.m., in a move that shocked the world, and particularly the Western Powers, 466,000 Red Army troops swept across the 800-mile eastern Polish border. The Red Army was organized into two army groups: the Byelorussian Front and the Ukrainian Front. They faced Polish army forces of 300,000 supplemented by 12,000 members of the Border Defence Corps. Molotov summoned the Polish ambassador in Moscow and told him that since Poland no longer existed, the Red Army had decided to intervene to protect Russian citizens in western Belorussia and western Ukraine.[168] Hitler hoped that Stalin's intervention in Poland would lead the Allies to now declare war on the Soviet Union, but the British government neatly avoided doing this by stating that the British guarantee to Poland covered only German aggression.

The Red Army eventually overcame the dogged Polish defenders after nineteen days, with a loss of just 734 soldiers. Stalin gained 201,000 square miles of territory, 5 million Poles, 4.5 million ethnic Ukrainians, 1 million Belorussians and 1 million Jews. In addition, 200,000 Polish prisoners of war were captured. About 50,000 Poles were killed during the Soviet invasion.

Stalin was just as determined as Hitler to exterminate the Polish military leadership. While Hitler conducted racial war in one part of Poland, Stalin conducted a class war against the Polish bourgeoisie. In April 1940 the Soviet secret police (NKVD) murdered 4,443 Polish officers in mass shootings in the Katyn forest near Smolensk. A further 11,000 Polish 'counter-revolutionaries' were also murdered. Added to this, it is estimated that 1.5 million Polish citizens were deported to Soviet labour camps, where around a third of them died.[169]

The German government pressed for a joint communiqué on the Soviet intervention and Stalin finally agreed to the wording of this on 18 September. It read:

> In view of the internal incapacity of the Polish state and of the splitting apart of the nationalities living in the former territory, the Reich government and the USSR consider it necessary to bring to an end the intolerable political and economic conditions existing in these territories. They regard it as their joint task to restore peace and order in these, their natural spheres of interest, and to bring about a new order by the creation of natural frontiers and viable economic organizations.

This joint action was, it added, in the 'spirit of the Nazi-Soviet Non-Aggression Pact'.[170]

The Polish government fled from Warsaw to Romania on 18 September. Poland was now completely leaderless. A Polish government-in-exile was formed on 30 September, following an initiative by diplomats in Paris and London.

Molotov met Schulenburg, the German ambassador to the Soviet Union, in Moscow on 20 September. He told him that the Soviet government had changed its mind on the future political structure of the Polish area. Stalin had originally entertained the idea of a residual Polish state, but this had given way to agree to a partitioned Poland.[171]

Hitler issued 'Directive No. 4 for the Conduct of War' on 25 September. No final decision regarding the 'political future' of the areas occupied by German troops had yet been determined, it said. However, the Polish population was needed only as a source of cheap labour.[172]

Himmler amalgamated all of the security and police forces in the Greater German Reich to form the Reich Main Security Office (*Reichssicherheitshauptamt* or RSHA) on 27 September, with its headquarters in Berlin. The RSHA was designed to deal with 'enemies of the Reich' inside Germany and also in the newly occupied territories. It merged the secret police (Gestapo), the criminal police (Kripo), the uniformed police force (Orpo) and the security service (SD) into one centralized agency. Regional police authorities were subordinated under the umbrella of the RSHA.[173]

Germany and the Soviet Union signed the German-Soviet Frontier Treaty on 28 September. Poland was formally partitioned. The demarcation line followed the rivers Pisa, Narew, Bug, Vistula and San. In a further secret protocol it was agreed that anyone of German descent on the Soviet side could move to the German side of the border. A similar offer was made to Ukrainians and White Russians on the German side who wanted to move to the Soviet side of the partition line. Lithuania was now added to the Soviet sphere of influence, while the provinces of Lublin and East Warsaw became German-occupied territory.[174]

The Siege of Warsaw was declared at an end over German radio on 27 September. On the next day the Polish garrison in the city, commanded by General Walerian Czuma, formally surrendered. Among the Germans killed in action during the siege was the former commander-in-chief of the German army involved in the famous 1938 sex scandal Colonel-General Werner von Fritsch, who died on 22 September. News of his death was kept at a minimum. Hitler sent no wreath to his funeral.

The *Wehrmacht* entered Warsaw as a conquering army on 1 October and the plunder of Jewish property began. As Helena Szereszewska recalled in her memoirs: 'The Germans are now coming for our furniture almost every day. They had teams of Jews to carry the furniture downstairs and load it into a lorry. These teams were not volunteers.'[175]

The last operational unit of the Polish army surrendered on 6 October after the four-day Battle of Kock, near Lublin. It had taken the *Wehrmacht* just thirty-six days to achieve an overwhelming victory over Poland. It had been an unequal struggle. The Polish army fought bravely but the huge German military equipment advantage told in the end. The huge aerial bombing showed that in the coming struggle civilians would be on the front line. During the triumphant victory parade through Warsaw on 5 October Adolf Hitler told a group of foreign journalists: 'Gentlemen, you have seen the ruins of Warsaw. Let that be a warning to those statesmen in London and Paris who still think of continuing the war.'[176]

The number of casualties is heavily disputed. It is estimated that 70,000 Polish soldiers were killed in the invasion of Poland by Germany and the Soviet Union, along with up to 80,000 civilians who died in bombing raids. In addition, 16,376 Poles were arbitrarily executed by the *Einsatzgruppen* and the *Wehrmacht*. The *Einsatzgruppen* appear to have focused more of their attention on killing Jews than did the regular soldiers of the *Wehrmacht* who also participated in the atrocities.[177] A total of 700,000 Polish prisoners of war were captured. The German army officially listed 11,000 killed, with 3,400 missing, presumed dead. German equipment losses were also large, with 5,000 transport vehicles, 246 aircraft and 236 tanks lost.[178]

On 30 September Hitler issued his 'Directive No. 5 for the Conduct of War'. Poland would now be organized under a military government, it said, controlled by the commander-in-chief of the army. In Western Europe the war at sea against Britain and France would be stepped up. For air warfare, offensive actions in the North Sea against British and French naval forces would now be permitted.[179]

Hitler met Count Ciano, the Italian Foreign Minister, at the New Reich Chancellery on 1 October. Poland would have been conquered even more quickly if he had been willing to sacrifice more German lives, he boasted. Warsaw did not make the heroic last stand it had promised, he added. Hitler felt that the German army losses were very light due to the modern training of the infantry and the use of heavy artillery, but also by having heavily armoured divisions, supported by the *Luftwaffe*, spearheading the attack. He described the lack of any action on the Western Front as 'a farce'. The battle in the west had so far been 'of no consequence whatsoever'.[180] The betrayal of Poland by Britain and France was the real darkest hour of the Second World War for the Western Allies. It amounted to a continuation of the policy of appeasement by other means.

On 6 October Hitler delivered a lengthy speech to the Reichstag. Europe should be grateful to Germany and the Soviet Union for bringing order to the chaos resulting from the disintegration of the Polish state, he began. He now wanted to spare his people further suffering by offering a peace settlement to Britain and France. He saw no reason why the war should continue. The Poland of the Treaty of Versailles 'would never rise again'. If Britain and France were waging war to prevent the new German order then millions of people would die in vain, he added, because he was certain Germany would triumph in the west. Hitler then proposed a conference of the leading European nations to settle all the remaining differences. If the Western democracies did not accept his generous offer, 'then we shall fight. There will never be another November 1918 in German history.'[181] Even now Hitler and a great many other Germans still felt the shame of losing the First World War.

On the next day, the French government responded to Hitler's speech by declaring that France would not lay down its arms until guarantees for real peace were in place. It was not until 12 October when the British government responded to Hitler's 'peace offer'. Chamberlain told the House of Commons that Hitler's proposals were vague and uncertain. They contained no promise to right the wrongs done to Czechoslovakia and Poland and furthermore Chamberlain had no confidence in Hitler's promises any more. On the following day the German government issued a statement which stated that by turning down Hitler's offer of peace, Chamberlain had chosen war.[182]

Hitler issued the 'Annexation Decree on the Administration of the Occupied Polish Territories' on 8 October. It signalled the destruction of the Polish state. Hitler had only delayed this decree in the hope that he might be able to use it as a bargaining chip if France and Britain had decided to negotiate peace terms. Hitler had worked out no detailed governmental plans for Poland before the German invasion began. Once victory was assured, the German-occupied areas were divided into three zones. The first two were sub-divided into: (1) Reichsgau Danzig-West Prussia and East Prussia in the north, also containing the former Polish Corridor, to be controlled by the Nazi Gauleiter of Danzig Albert Forster; and (2) Warthegau (also known from 29 January 1940 as Reichsgau Wartheland) in the south, including East Prussia, Posen and East Upper Silesia, under the leadership of the former Senate President of Danzig Arthur Greiser. On 2 November these areas became part of the Greater German Reich.

Greiser, a fanatical Nazi, was determined to 'Germanize' the Warthegau ruthlessly by expelling Poles and Jews, sending Polish men to Germany to act as forced labourers and the women to work as domestic servants or on farms. In a speech on 6 October Greiser outlined his long-term objective for the new province he now governed: 'In ten years' time, there will be no patch of land which will not be German; every homestead will belong to German colonists.'[183] This was no easy task. Out of a population of 4.9 million, 4.2 million were Polish, 435,000 Jewish and 325,000 – fewer than 10 per cent – were ethnic Germans.

Forster took a far less fanatical approach to the policy of 'Germanization' in his Reichsgau Danzig-West Prussia area. He understood that by expelling Poles he would only create ghost towns. Instead, he reclassified nearly all the Poles who lived in his region as 'ethnic Germans', which spared them from deportation. When Himmler heard about this he complained bitterly to Hitler that Forster's decision was racially suspect, but Hitler refused to interfere with Forster's administration as he viewed him as a loyal Nazi.

The Catholic Church, viewed as a symbol of Polish identity, was ruthlessly suppressed and 1,700 Polish priests ended up in Dachau concentration camp. By 1941 the Catholic Church had effectively been outlawed in the Reichsgau Wartheland.[184]

The third German-occupied area, which contained most of the central Polish territory, was renamed the General Government (*Generalgouvernement*). It had a population of 11 million and came into existence through a decree issued on 12 October. It was originally called the General Government of the Polish Occupied Lands, but this name was dropped as it implied that the Polish state still existed.

The infamous German-occupied General Government region, which included the major cities of Lublin, Warsaw and Kraków, was placed under the control of the committed Nazi Hans Frank as governor, with Arthur Seyss-Inquart, the former Governor of Austria, as his deputy. The General Government was administered by zealous Nazi officials filled with anti-Jewish and anti-Polish prejudice. For this reason, the General Government soon became an extremely brutal experimental laboratory for racial engineering and genocide. As Goebbels noted: 'The Führer's judgement on Poland is annihilatory. More animals than human beings. The filth of the Poles is unimaginable. They would be pushed into their reduced state [in the General Government] and left entirely to themselves.'[185]

The General Government was never incorporated into the Greater German Reich. In this area, Polish culture was wiped out, Polish schools, universities, archives, publishing companies and museums closed down and its residents reduced to living way below a subsistence level. Every non-German who lived in the General Government area had no civil rights and no protection under the law whatsoever. It was effectively a lawless Nazi colony. It was here the ghettoization of Jews would be developed and the death camps of the Holocaust would be constructed.[186]

On 7 October Hitler appointed Himmler as Reich Commissioner for the Consolidation of German Nationhood (RKFVD). The main aim of Himmler's new role was to assist in the 'purification' and 'Germanization' of the newly annexed areas of what was formerly Poland, meaning mass deportations and ethnic cleansing. He set up a complex bureaucracy to manage this process, drawing on work undertaken by the SS Race and Settlement Office and the Office of Racial Policy of the Nazi Party. However, a major obstacle to Himmler's grandiose 'Germanization' plans soon became apparent: there were not enough Germans available to be resettled in the newly occupied areas. With Poles and Jews often being transported from the Warthegau and dumped in the General Government the logistical and food problems increased. Adolf Eichmann, the head of the 'Jewish desk' of the Gestapo at the Reich Security Main Office (RSHA), wanted to deport large numbers of Jews from Germany, Austria, and Bohemia and Moravia to the General Government. To this end he set up the Reich Central Office for Jewish Emigration.

On 30 October Himmler gave instructions for all Jews in the Warthegau to be forcibly transported to the General Government. Their houses would be given to incoming German settlers. Jews taken from Warthegau were temporarily confined to ghettos in the large cities of the General Government. Soon they were suffering from starvation and all the diseases associated with poverty and deprivation.[187]

Now that Poland had been defeated, Hitler's thoughts soon turned to an attack on Western Europe. On 9 October he signed 'Directive No. 6 for the Conduct of War', which made clear that he was 'determined to act vigorously and aggressively without delay' in the west. If Germany delayed its attack, he wrote, Britain and France would not allow Belgium and the Netherlands to remain neutral. Accordingly, Hitler issued an order to begin an 'attacking operation' through Luxembourg, Belgium and the Netherlands at 'as early a date as possible'. The key aim of this operation was to defeat the French army. The exact timing of the attack was dependent on the readiness of tanks and motorized units. The *Luftwaffe* would be used to prevent the French army from attacking German troops.[188]

On 15 October Admiral Erich Raeder produced a 'Memorandum on Intensified Naval Warfare against England [Britain]'. It was approved by Hitler and circulated to *Wehrmacht* and *Luftwaffe* commanders. In addition to sinking British merchant vessels, the German navy was now given authorization to sink any neutral ships that aroused suspicion, including those of Italy and Spain, and even vessels belonging to the Soviet Union and Japan. Furthermore, the *Luftwaffe* was now permitted to destroy the most vital British import harbours.[189]

Hitler met the famous Swedish geographer, explorer and travel writer Sven Hedin at the Reich Chancellery on 16 October. During his expeditions to Central Asia, he made the Transhimalaya mountain range known in the West. In his famous book *From Pole to Pole* Hedin charts his fascinating journey through Asia and Europe. Hitler told him that Britain was 'ruled by lunatics, who thought Britain was an island'. He complained that he had repeatedly offered Britain peace and friendship, but had received 'only slaps in return'. Britain needed to realize it should keep out of Germany's spheres of interest.[190]

At a meeting with his leading generals on 27 October Hitler set the date for the German attack on Western Europe as 12 November. It would begin with an assault on Belgium and the Netherlands. Several generals objected that the army was not ready for such an attack. On 7 November Hitler postponed the date of the attack. It was to be the first of fourteen further postponements of the attack on Western Europe that he ordered during the autumn and winter of 1939–40.[191]

On 8 November Hitler flew from Berlin to Munich for the annual commemoration of the 1923 Munich Beer Hall Putsch. He had to be back in Berlin sooner than expected, so his speech began earlier than usual at 8 p.m. in the Bürgerbräukeller during which he attacked the British government for rejecting his offer of peace and foolishly deciding to carry on the war. At 9.07 p.m. he abruptly ended his speech. He then left the beer hall, taking an overnight train from Munich's central station as it was too foggy to fly. At precisely 9.20 p.m. a time bomb suddenly exploded in the Bürgerbräukeller. It had been embedded in a pillar directly behind the speaker's podium. Eight people were killed and sixty-two injured in the incident. Hitler had escaped certain death by thirteen minutes.

On the next morning the Nazi Party newspaper *Völkischer Beobachter* blamed the 'British Secret Service' for this attempt on Hitler's life. The SS also suspected that British intelligence was involved. In a daring kidnapping raid in the Netherlands, led by Major Alfred Naujocks of the SD, two British MI6 agents – Major Richard Stevens and Captain Sigismund Payne Best – were seized and brought to Germany for interrogation.

On 12 November Himmler told the German press that Stevens and Best had planned the assassination attempt, which had been carried out by a German communist accomplice called Georg Elser, who had been captured while trying to cross the Swiss border. It made a good story, but no link was ever established between Elser and the two British intelligence officers.

Born in the village of Hermaringen in 1903, Elser was a skilled woodworker and qualified cabinet maker. He knew a great deal about electronics. He had voted for the Communist Party of Germany (KPD) before Hitler came to power, then briefly joined a left-wing group called the Red Front Fighters League (RFB), but he was not directly involved with any communist resistance groups at the time of the assassination attempt. Elser's bold plan to kill Hitler had taken shape over a year. He realized that security at the Bürgerbräukeller was extremely lax. In the months leading up to the attack he would frequently have an evening meal there, then sneak upstairs to hide in a storeroom until the beer hall closed. Elser worked diligently to create a space in the pillar behind the speaker's platform into which he could plant his deadly bomb. He created a very sophisticated timing device, too, which could run for 144 hours before detonating a bomb.

Elser was brutally interrogated by Gestapo and Kripo officers, but always maintained that he acted alone. When Hitler saw the interrogation transcript he said: 'What idiot conducted this investigation?' He refused to believe that Elser was a lone wolf. Elser underwent more questioning and several more beatings. His interrogators even tried hypnosis, but Elser stuck diligently to his story. He even recreated his timer and detonator in front of his interrogators. There seemed to be little doubt that he was telling the truth.

Eventually, Himmler, the head of the SS, under pressure for exposing the Führer to assassination at such a high-profile Nazi event, interrogated Elser himself. Himmler even violently beat Elser in an attempt to try and find out who his accomplices were. Even under this pressure, Elser stuck to his story. It was decided that there should be no trial as it would attract too much publicity. Elser was held under 'protective custody' in Sachsenhausen concentration camp, then transferred to Dachau concentration camp. He was given the status of 'special prisoner' and was kept in solitary confinement.[192]

Did Elser really act alone? This remains an intriguing question that has attracted historians over the years. The anti-Nazi pastor Martin Niemöller, a plausible witness and a prisoner with Elser at Sachsenhausen, claims to have heard that Elser was really in the SS and that the bomb attack had been ordered by Hitler himself as a propaganda exercise to blame Britain and increase German support for the war. However, the general consensus among respected historians is that Elser, the man who almost assassinated Hitler, acted alone.[193]

Adolf Hitler issued 'Directive No. 8 for the Conduct of War' on 20 November. It ordered the *Wehrmacht* to maintain a 'state of readiness' for an imminent attack on Western Europe. Furthermore, it argued that any planned attack must be able to be cancelled at 11 p.m. on the previous day. The code word for the Army High Command to begin the invasion would be 'Rhine' (meaning go through with the attack), or 'Elbe' (withhold the attack).[194]

Hitler spoke in front of 200 senior officers of the *Wehrmacht* in the Reich Chancellery on 23 November. The purpose of this secret conference, he said, was to give an idea of the thinking that 'governs my view of impending events and to tell you of my decisions'. It was to be one of his most revealing speeches. His chief war aim remained the conquest of *Lebensraum* – 'living space' – for the German people. This could only be achieved 'with the sword'. Before the conquest of Poland he admitted: 'I wasn't quite clear at the time whether I should start first

Munich's Bürgerbraükeller after the bomb blast on 8 November 1939, when an assassination attempt on Hitler's life was made by Georg Elser. Hitler left the hall just thirteen minutes before the explosion.

against the East and then in the West, or vice versa [...] Basically I did not organize the armed forces in order not to strike. The decision to strike was always in me. Earlier or later I wanted to solve the problem [of *Lebensraum*]. Under pressure it was decided that the East was to be attacked first. If the Polish war was won quickly it was because of the superiority of our armed forces.'

As for the Non-Aggression Pact with the Soviet Union, it would be cynically maintained only for as long as it served its purpose: 'We can oppose Russia only when we are free in the West.' The moment was now favourable for the attack in the west: 'I shall attack France and England [Britain] at the most favourable and earliest moment. Breach of the neutrality of Belgium and the Netherlands is of no importance. No one will question that when we have won.' Further to this, Hitler promised: 'I shall shrink from nothing and destroy everyone who is against me. I am determined to lead my life in such a way that I can meet death with equanimity when my time comes. Behind me stands the German people, whose morale can only deteriorate.' As the last factor,' he concluded, 'I must in all modesty describe my own person: irreplaceable. Neither a military man nor a civilian could replace me. Attempts at assassination may be repeated.'[195]

On the same day Hitler met two of his key military leaders, General Franz Halder and Field Marshal Walther von Brauchitsch, and sternly rebuked them for opposing his attack plan for Western Europe. Hitler had heard rumours of their opposition to the attack but did not know of their involvement in the so-called Zossen conspiracy, an abandoned plot to arrest Hitler in order to prevent him from starting a western offensive. Hitler told Brauchitsch and Halder that the Army High Command was 'full of defeatists'. Brauchitsch offered his resignation on the spot, but Hitler refused to accept it. However, he warned them that any further opposition to his plans by the General Staff would be brutally suppressed.[196]

Hitler issued 'Directive No. 9 on the Conduct of War against the Enemy's Economy' on 29 November. It argued that Britain was Germany's 'biggest enemy' and Britain's defeat was the prerequisite for a final victory in the war. To achieve this, Britain's economy had to be paralysed. Preparations would now be made as 'early as possible' to strike a 'paralysing blow' at Britain's economic strength. Once the Anglo-French army had been defeated, Hitler continued, the German navy and *Luftwaffe* should strike against Britain's economic strength. The navy would attack British shipping. London, Liverpool and

Manchester were highlighted as prime targets for bombing raids, along with Britain's coal-producing exporting ports, most notably Cardiff, Hull, Newcastle, Sunderland and Swansea, but other ports were included such as Belfast, Bristol, Glasgow and Southampton.[197]

In the weeks after the partition of Poland, Stalin was keen to increase Soviet domination over the spheres of influence assigned to the USSR under the secret protocols of the Nazi-Soviet Non-Aggression Pact. The Baltic states – Estonia, Latvia and Lithuania – were forced to sign treaties of mutual assistance, thereby allowing Soviet troops to be stationed on their territory.

On 5 October Stalin demanded that Finland let him lease Cape Hanko, on the Gulf of Finland, to have as a naval and air base, and also to acquire territory on the Karelian Isthmus to bolster security around Leningrad. In return, Finland was offered Soviet territory in Karelia. The Finnish government refused to accept these terms and broke off talks with the Soviet Union on 13 November. The Finnish government then terminated the Soviet-Finnish Non-Aggression Pact.

Without declaring war, the Soviet Union invaded Finland on 30 November, beginning fifteen weeks of fierce fighting known as the Finnish-Russian War or Winter War. It was the largest military conflict undertaken by the Red Army since the Russian Civil War (1918–21). As a result of these actions, the League of Nations expelled the Soviet Union on 14 December. The German government remained neutral, but secretly aided the Soviet Union.

The Finnish army deployed ten divisions with a total fighting strength of 130,000 men. The Red Army was split into four armies with a total of twenty-six divisions, composed of around 500,000 soldiers. The Finns had only 32 tanks and 114 aircraft against a Soviet tank force of 1,500, supplemented by 3,000 aircraft.

The Soviet High Command believed that a *Blitzkrieg*-style assault would bring about a swift victory, but from the beginning the Soviet campaign in Finland was a disaster. The first sign of trouble came when the mechanized Soviet 7th Army failed to break through Finnish defence fortifications on what became known as the 'Mannerheim Line', named in honour of Field Marshal Carl Gustaf Emil Mannerheim, the commander of the Finnish army who led its defence. The Red Army seriously underestimated the difficulties of fighting in extreme winter weather with temperatures often falling to -40°C. Finnish soldiers, imbued with a strong sense of patriotism, used guerrilla tactics to stem the Soviet advance, most notably by camouflaging snipers, dressed in white and throwing petrol bombs, stuffed with tar and rags, into the air vents of Soviet tanks. The Finns called these crude but effective devices Molotov cocktails, after the Soviet Foreign Minister who had signed a pact with Ribbentrop.

One of the most famous Finnish snipers, Simo Häyhä, reportedly killed 500 Soviet soldiers. The Red Army suffered horrendous casualties in the Soviet-Finnish War, with a total of 126,875 killed. In comparison, the Finns lost 25,904 dead or missing. Most Red Army soldiers simply froze to death in their inadequate winter clothing. Others starved, due to poor food supply. Fast-moving Finnish troops on skis and dressed suitably for the freezing weather proved formidable in the first five weeks of the war. But, of course, the small Finnish army could not sustain this early success, due to a lack of fresh troops and equipment. Even so, Stalin was furious about the Red Army's failure to achieve a swift victory. He replaced its commander Marshal Kliment Voroshilov with General Seymon Timoshenko on 8 January 1940. Timoshenko deployed twenty-seven new army divisions equipped with better winter clothing and supported by tanks, heavy artillery units and bomber aircraft.

The second Red Army offensive, which began on 1 February 1940, broke through the Mannerheim Line just ten days later. By the end of the month the Finnish government was seeking an armistice. On 12 March 1940 the Moscow Peace Treaty was signed by Finland and the Soviet Union. It was relatively generous to the Finns, offering them limited territorial losses, notably the Karelian Isthmus and the Mannerheim fortifications. Cape Hanko was leased to the Soviets as a naval base. Most importantly, however, Finland retained its independence.

The Winter War was a huge wake-up call for the Red Army. To the outside world it seemed to have exposed the Soviet Union's military weaknesses for all the world to see, but this proved to be a fatal misjudgement. In reality Stalin learned a great deal from the Finnish-Russian War. It led to dramatic changes in how the Red Army was organized. The political interference, a feature of the purged Red Army of the mid-1930s, was now greatly scaled down. The able Timoshenko undertook a full-scale review of the Soviet army, which he proposed turning into a much more professional force. With Stalin's approval, the unitary command structure, which had been expunged during Stalin's purges, was restored. The old officer corps was resurrected. More than a thousand army personnel were promoted to the ranks of general and admiral. The right of junior officers to challenge the orders of their superiors was abolished. A new training regime, based on strict military and tactical principles, replaced ideological indoctrination. Training was now focused upon attacking fixed defensive positions. Even the old army uniforms were reintroduced and these reforms would turn the Red Army into a highly effective fighting force.[198]

On 12 December Admiral Erich Raeder told Hitler of a recent meeting he held with the pro-Nazi Norwegian Vidkun Quisling who had warned Raeder that Britain might occupy Norway very soon. Raeder suggested to Hitler that a German takeover of Norway would scupper these plans. He recommended that they should cultivate Quisling. Hitler suggested he should speak with Quisling soon.[199]

While the Finnish-Russian War was raging on, nothing was happening on the Western Front. The German public had begun to refer to this uneasy period of inactivity as the 'sit-down war' (*Sitzkrieg*), while the British called it the 'Phoney War'. Hitler had long predicted that while Britain and France might declare war on Germany it would be a mere gesture and they would do nothing. This was now proving remarkably accurate. Neville Chamberlain was not cut out to be a vigorous war leader but the perfect leader of a 'Phoney War'. The British public, totally unaware that Hitler was planning a real war in Western Europe, entered into a strange, unsettling period. In fact, more British people thought that the war was over than felt it was shortly to begin.

There was no 'Phoney War' at sea. A naval battle between Britain and Germany had begun within hours of the declaration of war, when the British transatlantic liner SS *Athenia* was torpedoed by a German U-30 submarine, killing 117 civilian passengers and crew. On 17 September the aircraft carrier HMS *Courageous* was sunk by two torpedoes from a U-29 submarine off the coast of Ireland, with a loss of 519 of its crew. It was the first British warship sunk in the Second World War.

On 14 October the German navy scored another spectacular success. The battleship HMS *Royal Oak* was sunk near Scapa Flow in the Orkney Islands by a U-47 submarine. The U-boat commander, Günther Prien, became an instant national hero in Germany. A total of 833 British sailors lost their lives in this incident. By the end of November magnetic German mines around the British Isles sank a further twenty-nine British ships, including the new battlecruiser HMS *Belfast* and the destroyer HMS *Gipsy*.

A high-profile and unplanned British response to these escalating naval losses came in December 1939. A German pocket battleship, the *Admiral Graf Spee*, operating in the South Atlantic, had already sunk ten Allied ships. As a result, it was targeted on a search-and-destroy mission by the Royal Navy. On 13 December the *Admiral Graf Spee* came into conflict with the British cruiser HMS *Exeter*, the light cruiser HMS *Ajax* and the New Zealand light cruiser HMS *Achilles*. In this confrontation, the two British vessels were very badly damaged, but although the *Graf Spee*'s armour suffered only minor damage, its fuel system was totally crippled. The ship's commander Hans Langsdorff sailed into Montevideo in neutral Uruguay on 15 December for repairs. As a goodwill gesture, he released sixty-one British sailors he had captured during previous attacks.

The Uruguayan government informed Langsdorff that his vessel could dock only for seventy-two hours. In fact, under the Hague Convention, it should have stayed for only twenty-four hours. The BBC claimed in a radio bulletin that the aircraft carrier HMS *Ark*

The German cruiser the *Admiral Graf Spee*
is deliberately scuttled by its crew on
17 December 1939.

Royal and the battlecruiser HMS *Renown* were en route to join the hunt for the *Graf Spee*. It was fake news, designed to persuade Langsdorff to surrender. Only the cruiser HMS *Cumberland* managed to reach Montevideo, but too late. On 17 December Langsdorff blew up his pocket battleship spectacularly in Montevideo harbour. On 20 December he shot himself with a pistol while in custody in Buenos Aires. This first major naval battle of the Second World War was grandly called the Battle of the River Plate and highlighted by clever British propaganda. First Lord of the Admiralty Winston Churchill hailed it as a spectacular British victory. A total of seventy-two Royal Navy crew and thirty-six German sailors had been killed in the confrontation.

It hid the fact that Germany had come out on top in the early stages of the naval war. By the end of 1939 Britain had lost 422,000 tonnes of shipping against German losses of 224,000 tonnes. In percentage terms, this was 2 per cent of total British tonnage, but 5 per cent of the German total. In a war of attrition, the greater strength of the Royal Navy would count in the longer run. Had Hitler prioritized the expansion of his U-boat fleet, he might have possessed a force which could have mounted an even more effective economic blockade. At the start of the war the German navy only possessed twenty-nine fully functioning U-boats but this small force caused havoc.[200]

Hitler met Vidkun Quisling in Berlin three times between 14 and 18 December 1939. At these meetings, Quisling put himself forward as a potential pro-Nazi leader of Norway. He advised Hitler to invade Norway now or risk the British beating him to it. Hitler offered financial support, to the tune of 200,000 gold marks, for Quisling to mount an anti-British propaganda campaign in Norway. He then asked his *Wehrmacht* High Command to investigate how Germany might take possession of Norway.[201]

On 21 December Hitler and Stalin exchanged pleasant Christmas greetings. It was a turn of events that nobody could have predicted at the beginning of 1939. Hitler offered the Soviet leader 'best wishes for your personal well-being, as well as for the prosperous future of the peoples of the friendly Soviet Union'. Stalin replied: 'The friendship of the peoples of Germany and the Soviet Union, cemented in blood, has every reason to be lasting and firm.'[202]

On 31 December Joseph Goebbels delivered a New Year's Eve message live on German national radio. He described 1939 as 'a year burned into the book of history. It will surely give historians material to write about for decades to come.' He said it was the greatest year of triumph for the National Socialist government. He blamed the outbreak of the war on 'The London warmongering clique who gave Poland a blank cheque to oppose the German offer of a negotiated settlement of the Danzig and Polish Corridor questions.' When war came, he added, the British government 'did not lift a finger to support its Polish ally'. The British had seen Hitler's solution to the German-Polish problem as an excuse to begin a 'long-desired battle with the German people'. He concluded:

> It would be a mistake to predict what will happen in the New
> Year. That is all in the future. One thing is clear: It will be a hard
> year, and we must be ready for it. Victory will not fall into our
> laps. We must earn it, and not only at the front but at home as
> well. Everyone has to work and fight for it.[203]

The war that Hitler found himself involved in at the end of 1939 was not the one he had wanted or predicted. He expected the British government to abandon its long-standing policy of upholding a balance of power in Europe and hand to Germany a free hand to establish territorial dominance in Europe. He thought that Poland would accept German demands without a fight. He viewed the Soviet Union as his bitterest ideological enemy, but he was now entangled in a Nazi-Soviet Non-Aggression Pact.

A series of choices, some premeditated, others impulsive, had ended in the outbreak of war. Not all of them were made by Hitler alone. The most dominant view of historians on the events leading to the outbreak of the Second World War and the defeat of Poland was provided by Hugh Trevor-Roper who argued that Hitler's actions between 1933 and 1939 were the implementation of a carefully planned programme of expansion laid out in his book *Mein Kampf* published in 1925. This proposed a step-by-step plan for war, concentrating on the attainment of one objective at a time.

The interpretation offered in this book has told a different, less deterministic but more subtle and nuanced story. It has highlighted that Hitler was sometimes the prime mover and the key protagonist in the key events, but highlighted that he was more often a master of tactical political flexibility and improvisation. He was really at his most effective as a politician when he exploited events that he had not planned at all. He profited time and time again between 1933 and 1939 from the mistakes of others. This is evident in the story of how he came to power in 1933, the enactment of the Nuremburg Laws in 1935, the

Fritsch-Blomberg crisis, the *Anschluss*, the Czech crisis in 1938 and the events that led to the signing of the Nazi-Soviet Pact in 1939. Within a mind of dogmatic rigidity there existed in Hitler amazing political flexibility.

The numerous documents cited in this book should leave no one in any doubt that Hitler's foreign policy aimed to gain land through territorial expansion. At the same moment Hitler had decided on this course of action Neville Chamberlain became British Prime Minister and decided to try and find out what Hitler wanted and to accommodate his demands within a negotiated framework. Given Hitler's underlying war-like objectives Chamberlain needed to give the Nazi dictator a free hand to achieve German domination in Eastern and Western Europe in order to satisfy his true wishes.

The policy of appeasement was logical and reasonable to attempt to try and persuade Hitler to live in peace with Europe with his outstanding grievances satisfied. Chamberlain believed face-to-face negotiations with Hitler might work. Yet his desire for peace became an obstinate and dogmatic belief system which saw any other policy as unthinkable. Chamberlain was less likely to change his mind on foreign policy than Hitler. This mindset led Chamberlain to surround himself with an inner circle of advisers mostly composed of 'yes men' who endorsed his judgement rather than question it.

In essence Chamberlain's conduct of foreign policy was a crisis management strategy. The confrontation between Hitler and Chamberlain during their meeting in September 1939 was a total mismatch. Hitler ran rings around him and he never even realized it. Hitler's unscrupulous ability to move from contrived anger to the language of sweet reasonableness ended in him signing pieces of paper that Chamberlain thought were genuine but which Hitler knew were worthless.

After the occupation of Prague in March 1939, Hitler's duplicity was finally exposed for all the world to see. At that point Chamberlain should have abandoned appeasement and adopted a determined stance to stop Hitler but instead he opted for a dubious guarantee of Poland, a country Britain was incapable of defending. To make matters worse he delayed gaining an alliance with the Soviet Union with disastrous consequences.

At the end of 1939 the outcome of the Second World War remained uncertain. The chief culprit in bringing it about was Adolf Hitler, but the errors and misjudgements of his opponents had played a deeply significant role, too.

·

ACKNOWLEDGEMENTS
NOTES
BIBLIOGRAPHY
INDEX

·

Every book is a collaborative process. This book could not have been written without the advice and support of so many people. I'd like to mention some of them here. I would first like to thank my wonderful literary agent Georgina Capel for her advice and support throughout the whole process and the whole team at Georgina Capel and Associates, especially Irene Baldoni and Rachel Conway.

A sincere thanks is also due to Anthony Cheetham for persuading me to come to Head of Zeus in the first place and having faith that I could carry out such a huge project. The editorial team have been quite superb. The copy editing of Ian Pindar was meticulous, detailed and creative. The picture research and map creation, overseen by Juliet Brightmore, Clémence Jacquinet and Clare Gordon, was equally exemplary.

I have also benefitted from the support and advice of a number of friends and colleagues during the period of the completion of the book, including Peter Bierl, Paul and Annie McGann and all their wonderful family, Roger Moorhouse, Don Boyd, Dan Snow, Professor Peter Frankopan, Clare Mulley, Sir Richard J. Evans, Professor David Olusoga, Moira Kenny, John Campbell, Giles MacDonogh, Professor Jürgen Förster, Jakob Knab, Professor Kate Williams, Dr. Janina Ramirez, Dr Tom Beaumont, Professor Suzannah Lipscomb, Dr. David Clampin, Dr. Mike Benbough-Jackson, Dr. James Crossland, Dr.Gillian O'Brien, Cat Lewis, Tom Webber, Dr. Emma Vickers, Dr. Lucie Matthews-Jones, Dr. Chris Vaughan and Dr Alex Miles.

I would also like to thank the many people who follow my 'This Day in History' feature on Twitter – @FXMC1957 every day. They provide me with great support every day.

I must pay sincere gratitude to my family. Without the love and support of my wife Ann, my life would not have taken the course it did and led to achievements such as this. She's simply wonderful. I must also mention my lovely daughter Emily, son in law James, my beautiful grandchildren Martha and Veronica, my nephew Beninio, nieces Julie, Jane and Cathy, and cousins Paul, Cathy, Rob, Marie, Lily, Laura, Mark, John, Rose, Marie and everyone else in my vast extended family.

Finally, I must mention my brother Michael and my sister Carol. When I started to write up this book in February 2017 they were both alive and well. Sadly, Carol died suddenly after a heart attack on 12 May 2017 and then on 11 September 2018 my brother died of cancer. These were tremendously devastating blows to me. It has led me to endure a great deal of sadness, as they were my only two siblings. It is only fitting that I dedicate this book to their memory.

NOTES

SOURCE ABBREVIATIONS
USED IN NOTES

ADG-IFGB
Archiv Deutsches Gedächtnis,
Institute für Geschichte und
Biographie, Hagen [Hagen Oral
History Archive]

AP-IMT
Avalon Project. Yale University
[online archive of the Nuremburg
Trial Proceedings]

BA-MA
Bundesarchiv Marburg

BAB
Bundesarchiv Berlin-Lichterfelde

BAK
Bundesarchiv, Koblenz

BWBB
The British War Blue Book, 1939

DGFP
Documents on Germany Foreign
Policy 1918–1945 [files of the German
Foreign Ministry, Auswärtiges Amt,
Berlin]

DBFP
Documents on British Foreign Policy,
1919–1939

GWPA
German War Propaganda Archive

HCD
Hansard's Parliamentary Debates,
House of Commons, 5th series

IfZ
Institut für Zeitgeschichte, Munich

NA
National Archives, London

NSR
Nazi-Soviet Relations 1939–1941
[documents from the archives of the
German Foreign Ministry]

TA
Times Archives, London

INTRODUCTION

1 There are very few single-volume
or multi-volume English-language
histories of the Third Reich aimed at
the general reader. Perhaps the most
famous is William Shirer's *The Rise
and Fall of the Third Reich* (Simon and
Schuster, 1960). Originally a four-
volume history, it is better known in
its single-volume format. Shirer was
an American journalist who worked
in Berlin during the Nazi era and his
book is primarily a political history.
Adopting a deeply moralistic tone,
Shirer argues that Hitler's rule was the
inevitable result of Germany's unique
and distorted path of development.
Today most academic historians
consider it rather dated. A more
recent one-volume account is Michael
Burleigh's *The Third Reich: A New
History* (Macmillan, 2001). Adopting
a thematic framework, Burleigh
concentrates on Hitler's rise to power
– indeed, half the book is devoted to it.
The focus after 1933 is on mass murder,
resistance and collaboration. Burleigh
does not examine in detail Germany's
foreign or military policy. He
powerfully asserts that Nazi Germany
was a totalitarian dictatorship and
suggests that Hitler was trying to
create a new secular religion. Another
recent history is Richard J. Evans's
three-volume *The Third Reich Trilogy*
(Penguin, 2003–2008). These very
impressive books are thematically
structured and provide a much needed
social and cultural history of the Third
Reich. The first volume deals with
Hitler's rise to power; the second
explores domestic policy from 1933
to 1939; and the third covers 1939
to 1945 with extensive discussions
of the German home front and the
Holocaust.

2 The leading 'intentionalist' was
the British historian Hugh Trevor-
Roper, who portrayed Hitler as the
'master of the Third Reich', following
a consistent programme of ideas
outlined in *Mein Kampf*, especially
on foreign policy and the Holocaust.

See H. Trevor-Roper, *The Third
Reich: On the Rise and Fall of Nazi
Germany* (I. B. Taurus, 2016). This
view was challenged by 'structuralist'
historians, who mainly concentrated
on domestic policy. It was the German
historian Hans Mommsen who first
described Hitler as a 'weak dictator'
in 1966. See Mommsen's 'National
Socialism: Continuity and Change' in
W. Lacquer (ed.) *Fascism: A Readers
Guide* (University of California Press,
1979), pp. 151–92. The 'weak dictator'
thesis was expanded in detail by the
German historian Martin Broszat
in *The Hitler State: The Foundations
and the Internal Structure of the Third
Reich* (Routledge, 1981). He depicts
Hitler as presiding over bitter power
struggles within a chaotic system of
competing bureaucratic empires. For
a detailed discussion of the various
historical debates concerning aspects
of the Third Reich, see Ian Kershaw's
*The Nazi Dictatorship: Problems and
Perspectives* (Edward Arnold, 2000
edn).

3 A key advocate of the *Sonderweg*
theory was Hans-Ulrich Wehler. See
his *German Empire, 1871–1918* (Berg,
1985). See also Jürgen Kocka, *German
History before Hitler: The Debate about
the German Sonderweg* (Sage, 1998).

4 See Hannah Arendt, *The Origins of
Totalitarianism* (André Deutsch, 1951).
See also M. Burleigh, *Confronting the
Nazi Past: New Debates on Modern
German History* (Collins & Brown,
1996).

CHAPTER I

1 *Vorwärts*, 1 January 1933. See also
A. Tooze, *The Wages of Destruction:
The Making and Breaking of the Nazi
Economy* (Allen Lane, 2007), p. 32.

2 *Berliner Tageblatt*, 1 January 1933.

3 *Völkischer Beobachter*, 1 January
1933. See also V. Ullrich, *Hitler*, Vol. 1:
Ascent 1889–1939 (The Bodley Head,
2016), p. 349; I. Kershaw, *Hitler*, Vol.

1: *Hubris, 1889–1936* (Penguin, 1998), p.392; H. Turner, *Hitler's Thirty Days to Power: January 1933* (Bloomsbury, 1996), pp.1–2.

4 Turner, *Hitler's Thirty Days to Power*, p.31.

5 A. Bullock, *Hitler: A Study in Tyranny* (Penguin, 1952), p.81.

6 E. Hanfstaengl, *Hitler: The Missing Years* (Eyre & Spottiswoode, 1957), p.195.

7 For a more detailed examination of Schleicher's role, see P. Hayes, 'A Question Mark with Epaulettes?: Kurt von Schleicher and Weimar Politics', *Journal of Modern History*, Vol. 52 (1980), pp.35–65.

8 Kershaw, *Hitler*, Vol. 1, p.399.

9 Ibid., p.402.

10 J. Noakes and G. Pridham (eds.), *Nazism: A Documentary Reader*, Vol. 1: *The Rise to Power, 1919–1934* (Exeter: Exeter University Press, 1983), pp.115–16. (Hereafter *Nazism*, Vol. 1.)

11 Testimony of Franz von Papen, 18 June 1946, quoted in Avalon Project, Yale University: online archive of Nuremberg Trial Proceedings of the International Military Tribunal (Hereafter AP-IMT). See also AP-IMT, Affidavit of Baron Kurt von Schröder, 21 July 1946.

12 J. Toland, *Adolf Hitler* (Ware, Hertfordshire: Wordsworth, 1997), p.283.

13 F. von Papen, *Memoirs* (New York: E.P.Dutton, 1953), p.227.

14 AP-IMT. Testimony of Franz Von Papen, 18 June 1946.

15 Turner, *Hitler's Thirty Days to Power*, p.44.

16 Ullrich, *Hitler*, Vol. 1, p.351.

17 Institut für Zeitgeschichte, Munich (hereafter IfZ), Kurt Schröder interrogation, 18 June 1947, ZS/557.

18 Papen, *Memoirs*, pp.227–8.

19 Ullrich, *Hitler*, Vol. 1, p.352.

20 Kershaw, *Hitler*, Vol. 1, p.414

21 Turner, *Hitler's Thirty Days to Power*, pp.47–8.

22 Toland, *Adolf Hitler*, p.284.

23 *Frankfurter Zeitung*, 7 January 1933.

24 Ullrich, *Hitler*, Vol. 1, p.352.

25 Turner, *Hitler's Thirty Days to Power*, p.50.

26 Ullrich, *Hitler*, Vol. 1, p.356.

27 Ibid.

28 Turner, *Hitler's Thirty Days to Power*, pp.56–7.

29 For a detailed examination, see J. Leopold, *Alfred Hugenberg* (New Haven, CT: Yale University Press, 1977).

30 Toland, *Adolf Hitler*, p.284.

31 *Völkischer Beobachter*, 14 January 1933.

32 Turner, *Hitler's Thirty Days to Power*, p.67.

33 Ullrich, *Hitler*, Vol. 1, p.353.

34 Kershaw, *Hitler*, Vol. 1, p.417. At the meeting on 16 January 1933 Schleicher also expressed the view that he doubted whether Strasser would have brought many Nazi supporters with him, even if he had been won over.

35 Turner, *Hitler's Thirty Days to Power*, p.85.

36 Ullrich, *Hitler*, Vol. 1, p.355.

37 Ibid., p.359.

38 Turner, *Hitler's Thirty Days to Power*, p.70.

39 Ibid.

40 Papen, *Memoirs*, pp.225–6.

41 Toland, *Adolf Hitler*, p.285.

42 *Nazism*, Vol. 1, p.118, Ribbentrop diary notes, 18 January 1933.

43 Ullrich, *Hitler*, Vol. 1, p.359.

44 Turner, *Hitler's Thirty Days to Power*, p.78.

45 *Frankfurter Zeitung*, 21 January 1933.

46 Ullrich, *Hitler*, Vol. 1, pp.359–60.

47 *Der Angriff*, 21 January 1933.

48 Horst Wessel had been an activist in the Nazi storm troopers in Berlin. He was particularly disliked by communist paramilitaries after being involved in an attack on a local Communist Party headquarters, during which four communist workers were seriously injured. Wessel's landlady, the widow of a communist, became involved in a dispute with him over the non-payment of rent by his woman friend. A local communist and petty criminal called Albrecht 'Ali' Höhler agreed to help her deal with Wessel. Accompanied by the Communist Party member Erwin Ruckert, he went to Wessel's flat on 14 January 1930 and knocked on the door. When Wessel opened it, Höhler shot him in the head from point-blank range. Wessel was rushed to hospital, dying on 23 February 1930. The communists depicted Wessel as a violent man who had lived off the 'immoral' earnings of his woman friend, who was depicted as a prostitute. Goebbels chose to portray Wessel as 'a martyr' of the Nazi Party. A lavish funeral was held in his honour and a song was written about him called '*Die Fahne Hoch!*' ('Raise the Flag!'). It was known as the 'Horst Wessel Song' and became not merely an anthem of the Nazi Party, but a joint national anthem of Germany from 1933 to 1945.

49 *Vorwärts*, 23 January 1933.

50 Papen, *Memoirs*, p.235

51 Ibid.

52 Turner, *Hitler's Thirty Days to Power*, p.113.

53 Ibid., pp.114–16.

54 *Nazism*, Vol. 1, p.117. Testimony of Otto Meissner at the Nuremberg Trials.

55 Ibid., pp.116–17.

56 Toland, *Adolf Hitler*, pp.285–6.

57 Kershaw, *Hitler*, Vol. 1., p.418.

58 Toland, *Adolf Hitler*, p.286.

59 *Nazism*, Vol. 1, p.118.

60 Turner, *Hitler's Thirty Days to Power*, p.115.

61 Papen, *Memoirs*, pp.235–6.

62 *Nazism*, Vol. 1, p.118, Ribbentrop diary notes, 22 January 1933.

63 Papen, *Memoirs*, p.237.

64 *Nazism*, Vol. 1, p.117.

65 J. Fest, *Hitler* (Penguin, 1982), p.361.

66 Toland, *Adolf Hitler*, p.286.

67 *Frankfurter Zeitung*, 28 January 1933.

68 For Hugenberg's role in the drama of January 1933, see L. Jones, 'The Greatest Stupidity of My Life: Alfred Hugenberg and the formation of the Hitler cabinet, January 1933', *Journal of Contemporary History*, Vol. 27 (1992), pp.63–87.

69 Ullrich, *Hitler*, Vol. 1, p.364.

70 Fest, *Hitler*, pp.361–2.

71 *Nazism*, Vol. 1, p.119.

72 Ibid., p.120.

73 Cabinet meeting, 28 January 1933. For details, see A. Golecki (ed.), *Das Kabinett von Schleicher: 3 Dezember 1932 bis 30 Januar 1933* (Boppard am Rhein, Harald Boldt, 1986), pp.306–310.

74 Toland, *Adolf Hitler*, p.287.

75 Ibid., p.288.

76 *Nazism*, Vol. 1, p.117.

77 Papen, *Memoirs*, p.240.

78 *Nazism*, Vol. 1, p.121.

79 Toland, *Adolf Hitler*, p.289.

80 Papen, *Memoirs*, p.244.

81 Toland, *Adolf Hitler*, p.290.

82 Ullrich, *Hitler*, Vol. 1, p.370.

83 Fest, *Hitler*, p.366

84 Only six Nazis were added to the cabinet in 1933: Joseph Goebbels became Minister of Propaganda on 13 March; Kurt Schmitt became Minister for Economics; and Walter Darré became Minister for Food and Agriculture on 29 June. Ernst Röhm and Rudolf Hess became Ministers without Portfolio on 1 December. By the end of 1933 there was a total of eight Nazis in the cabinet, including Hitler, with eight conservatives remaining from the government formed on 30 January. Only Alfred Hugenberg of the old guard had resigned.

85 *Trials of The Major War Criminals before the International Military Tribunal*, 42 Vols (Washington, DC: US Government Printing Office, 1947–8), Vol. 14, p.399. (Hereafter IMT.)

86 Papen, *Memoirs*, pp.290–91.

87 IMT, Vol. 14, p.363.

88 Bundesarchiv, Koblenz (hereafter BAK), Lutz Schwerin von Krosigk to Hans Luther, 16 April 1952, N/1276/23.

89 Kershaw, *Hitler*, Vol. 1, p.438.

90 Ullrich, *Hitler*, Vol. 1, p.414.

91 Toland, *Adolf Hitler*, p.293.

92 R. J. Evans, *The Coming of the Third Reich* (Allen Lane, 2004), p.309.

93 Papen, *Memoirs*, p.260.

94 Toland, *Adolf Hitler*, p.296.

95 Papen, *Memoirs*, p.290.

96 IMT, Vol. 14, p.366.

97 Interview with Manfred von Schröder, quoted in L. Rees, *The Holocaust: A New History* (Viking, 2017), p.54.

98 M. Maschmann, *Account Rendered: A Dossier on My Former Self* (London/ New York: Abelard-Schumann, 1964), pp.10–13.

99 Interview with Gabriele Winckler, quoted in Rees, *Holocaust*, p.54.

100 Interview with Claus Moser by author (London, 3 August 2009).

101 Toland, *Adolf Hitler*, p.291.

102 Ibid.

103 Hermann Göring radio address, 30 January 1933, quoted in A. Rabinbach and S. L. Gilman, (eds.), *The Third Reich Sourcebook* (Berkeley: University of California Press, 2013). Document No. 17, p. 45. (Hereafter *Third Reich Sourcebook*.)

104 B. Blaine and R. Cottrell, *Uncertain Order: The World in The Twentieth Century* (Upper Saddle River, New Jersey: Prentice Hall, 2003), p.196.

105 Turner, *Hitler's Thirty Days to Power*, p.160.

106 Toland, *Adolf Hitler*, p.294.

107 *New York Times*, 31 January 1933.

108 Turner, *Hitler's Thirty Days to Power*, p.158.

109 Toland, *Adolf Hitler*, p.294.

110 D. Cesarani, *The Final Solution: The Fate of The Jews, 1933–1949* (Macmillan, 2016), p.31.

111 Turner, *Hitler's Thirty Days to Power*, p.159.

112 Kershaw, *Hitler*, Vol. 1, p.432.

113 Interview with Siegmund Weltlinger, quoted in R. Holmes, *The World at War: The Landmark Oral History from the Classic TV Series* (Ebury, 2011), p.35. (Hereafter *World at War*)

114 *Nazism*, Vol. 1, pp.127–8, cabinet meeting, 31 January 1933.

115 Fest, *Hitler*, p.394.

116 Ibid., p.388.

117 *Nazism*, Vol. 1, pp.131–4, Hitler's German radio speech, 1 February 1933.

118 Tooze, *The Wages of Destruction*, p.38.

119 Kershaw, *Hitler*, Vol. 1, p.442.

120 M. Fulbrook, *A History of Germany 1918–2014: The Divided Nation* (Chichester: John Wiley & Sons, 2015), p.69.

121 Kershaw, *Hitler*, Vol. 1, p.444.

122 Fest, *Hitler*, p.391.

123 Ullrich, *Hitler*, Vol. 1, p.418.

124 Evans, *The Coming of The Third Reich*, p.324.

125 Fest, *Hitler*, p.390.

126 Ibid., p.394.

127 Hitler speech, Stuttgart, 15 February 1933, quoted in: http://www.hitler.org/speeches.

128 Archiv Deutsches Gedächtnis, Institut für Geschichte und Biographie, Hagen (Hereafter ADG-IFGB). Interview with Alfred Haussen, 9 January 1994.

129 *Nazism*, Vol. 1, p.134.

130 Tooze, *The Wages of Destruction*, p.101.

131 *Nazism*, Vol. 1, p.138.

132 There is a huge literature on the controversy surrounding the Reichstag fire. The view that van der Lubbe acted alone is advanced in F. Tobias, *The Reichstag Fire* (New York: G. P. Putnam's Sons, 1964). For a more critical account, see B. Hett, *Burning the Reichstag: An Investigation into the Third Reich's Enduring Mystery* (Oxford: Oxford University Press, 2014).

133 Tobias, pp.36–44.

134 Ibid., p.47–50.

135 Toland, *Adolf Hitler*, pp.297–8.

136 Ibid., p.298.

137 Fest, *Hitler*, p.396

138 BAK. Lutz Schwerin von Krosigk to Fritz Tobias, 27 June 1970, N/127/40.

139 Papen, *Memoirs*, p.271.

140 Kershaw, *Hitler*, Vol. 1, p.458.

141 Toland, *Adolf Hitler*, p.299.

142 Ibid.

143 Papen, *Memoirs*, p.271.

144 P. Longerich, *Goebbels* (Vintage, 2015), p.289.

145 *Daily Express*, 3 March 1933.

146 W. L. Shirer, *The Rise and Fall of the Third Reich: A History of Nazi Germany* (Pan, 1961), pp.240–5.

147 *Nazism*, Vol. 1, p.141.

148 *Völkischer Beobachter*, 2 March 1933.

149 N. Wachsmann, *KL: The History of The Nazi Concentration Camps* (Little, Brown, 2016), p.30.

150 Quoted in Toland, *Adolf Hitler*, p.309.

151 D. Siemens, *Stormtroopers: A New History of Hitler's Brownshirts* (New Haven, CT: Yale University Press, 2017), pp.124–5.

152 ADG-IFGB. Interview with Lucie Baumann, 19 August and 30 September 1987.

153 Fest, *Hitler*, p.398.

154 V. Klemperer, *I Shall Bear Witness*, Vol. 1: *The Diaries of Victor Klemperer, 1933–1941* (Phoenix, 1998), p.6. (Hereafter *Klemperer Diaries*, Vol. 1.)

155 This view appears in Shirer, *Rise and Fall*, p.246, but it is repeated in nearly every other history of the Third Reich. See Kershaw, *Hitler*, Vol. 1, p.461; Ullrich, *Hitler*, Vol. 1, pp.424–5.

156 *Frankfurter Zeitung*, 6 March 1933.

157 *Daily Mail*, 7 March 1933.

158 Interview with Hans Kehrl, *World at War*, p.36.

159 *Nazism*, Vol. 1, pp.155–6, cabinet meeting, 7 March 1933.

160 Ullrich, *Hitler*, Vol. 1, pp.427–8.

161 J. Streicher, *Kampf dem Weltfeind, Reden aus der Kampfzeit*, Nuremberg, *Der Stürmer*, 1938, pp.143–8.

162 Kershaw, *Hitler*, Vol. 1, p.463.

163 Ibid., 469–70.

164 *Nazism*, Vol. 1, p.149.

165 Siemens, *Stormtroopers*, p.126.

166 *Nazism*, Vol. 1, p.149.

167 Ibid., p.152.

168 M. Burleigh, *The Third Reich: A New History* (Pan, 2001), p.159.

169 Ullrich, *Hitler*, Vol. 1, pp.430–31.

170 Ibid., p.413.

171 *Klemperer Diaries*, Vol. 1, p.15.

172 *Nazism*, Vol. 1, p.138.

173 Interview with Arnold Biegeleisen, quoted in J. Steinhoff, P. Pechel, D. Showalter (eds.), *Voices from the Third Reich: An Oral History* (Washington, DC: De Capo Press, 1994), p.43. (Hereafter *Voices from The Third Reich*.)

174 Evans, *Coming of the Third Reich*, pp.422–5.

175 Ibid., p.420.

176 Evans, *Coming of the Third Reich*, p.375.

177 Ibid., pp.375–6.

178 Longerich, *Goebbels*, p.212.

179 Papen, *Memoirs*, p.289.

180 Longerich, *Goebbels*, p.213.

181 Ibid., p.227.

182 Evans, *Coming of the Third Reich*, pp.394–5.

183 Ibid., p.401.

184 Ibid., p.406.

185 R. Grunberger, *A Social History of the Third Reich* (Penguin, 1971), p.478.

186 Evans, *Coming of the Third Reich*, p.407.

187 Burleigh, *The Third Reich*, p.206.

188 Grunberger, *A Social History of the Third Reich*, p.511

189 Ibid., p.496.

190 Evans, *Coming of the Third Reich*, p.409.

191 Longerich, *Goebbels*, p.217.

192 Kershaw, *Hitler*, Vol. 1, p.481.

193 Grunberger, *A Social History of the Third Reich*, p.455.

194 Evans, *Coming of the Third Reich*, pp.413–16.

195 Kershaw, *Hitler*, Vol. 1, p.465.

196 Hitler speech, Potsdam, 21 March 1933, *Third Reich Sourcebook*, p.45.

197 Toland, *Adolf Hitler*, pp.305–6.

198 Longerich, *Goebbels*, p.214.

199 Interview with Gottfried Fährmann, *Voices from the Third Reich*, p.xxxiv.

200 *Third Reich Sourcebook*, p.47.

201 *Nazism*, Vol. 1, p.155.

202 Evans, *Coming of the Third Reich*, p.352.

203 Ibid.

204 Toland, *Adolf Hitler*, p.307.

205 Otto Wels speech, 23 January 1933, *Third Reich Sourcebook*, pp.50–2.

206 *Nazism*, Vol. 1, pp.159–61.

207 Longerich, *Goebbels*, p.215.

208 Kershaw, *Hitler*, Vol. 1, p.477.

209 *Nazism*, Vol. 1, p.157.

210 Interview with Hugh Greene, *World at War*, p.40.

211 Kershaw, *Hitler*, Vol. 1, p.464.

212 T. Ryback, *Hitler's First Victims and One Man's Race for Justice* (The Bodley Head, 2015), p.19.

213 Wachsmann, *KL*, p.53.

214 Papen, *Memoirs*, p.295.

215 Wachsmann, *KL*, pp.52–6.

216 Rees, *Holocaust*, pp.69–70.

217 Ryback, *Hitler's First Victims*, p.41.

218 Ibid., p.146.

219 Ibid., pp.207–8.

220 Siemens, *Stormtroopers*, pp.136–7.

221 Ryback, *Hitler's First Victims*, pp.73–80.

222 Evans, *Coming of the Third Reich*, p.433.

223 Interview with Hans Peter Herz, *Voices from the Third Reich*, p.47.

224 Kershaw, *Hitler*, Vol. 1, p.411.

225 Evans, *Coming of the Third Reich*, p.433.

226 Cesarani, *The Final Solution*, pp.38–9.

227 Ibid., p.44.

228 Ibid., p.59.

229 Interview with Gaston Ruskin, *Voices from the Third Reich*, p.42.

230 Evans, *Coming of the Third Reich*, p.433.

231 *Daily Express*, 24 March 1933.

232 *New York Daily News*, 27 March 1933.

233 *Klemperer Diaries*, Vol. 1, pp.10–11.

234 Longerich, *Goebbels*, p.219.

235 Ullrich, *Hitler*, Vol. 1, p.442; Kershaw, *Hitler*, Vol. 1, p.473.

236 Cesarani, *The Final Solution*, p.44.

237 Evans, *Coming of the Third Reich*, p.436.

238 *Klemperer Diaries*, Vol. 1, p.12.

239 Ullrich, *Hitler*, Vol. 1, p.443.

240 Evans, *Coming of the Third Reich*, p.434.

241 ADG-IFGB. Interview with Friedrich Ernal 27 and 30 November 1984.

242 Evans, *Coming of the Third Reich*, p.438.

243 Ibid., p.437.

244 Toland, *Adolf Hitler*, p.310.

245 *Klemperer Diaries*, Vol. 1, p.14.

246 *Nazism*, Vol. 1, p.163.

247 C. Dams and M. Stolle, *The Gestapo: Power and Terror in the Third Reich* (Oxford University Press, 2014), p.7.

248 AP-IMT. Affidavit of Rudolf Diels.

249 Ullrich, *Hitler*, Vol. 1, pp.444–8.

250 *Nazism*, Vol. 2, p.136.

251 Hitler's speech, 1 May 1933, *Third Reich Sourcebook*, pp.54–5.

252 *Völkischer Beobachter*, 5 May 1933.

253 For details, see S. Baranowski, *Strength Through Joy: Consumerism and Mass Tourism in the Third Reich* (Cambridge: Cambridge University Press, 2007), pp.44–5.

254 ADG-IFGB. Interview with Walter Ehlery, 9 and 12 March 1982.

255 Kershaw, *Hitler*, Vol. 1, p.483.

256 Evans, *Coming of the Third Reich*, p.427.

257 W. Allen, *The Nazi Seizure of Power: The Experience of a Single German Town, 1922–1935* (New York: New Viewpoints, 1973), pp.203–4.

258 *Nazism*, Vol. 2, pp.45–9, Konstantin von Neurath, foreign policy paper, presented in cabinet, 7 April 1933.

259 Hitler speech, Berlin, 17 May 1933, quoted in N. Baynes (ed,), *The Speeches of Adolf Hitler: April 1922–August 1939* (Oxford: Oxford University Press, 1942), Vol. 2, pp.1041–58.

260 *The Times*, 18 May 1933.

261 Toland, *Adolf Hitler*, p.312.

262 Ullrich, *Hitler*, Vol. 1, p.479.

263 Ryback, *Hitler's First Victims*, pp.162–3.

264 Tooze, *The Wages of Destruction*, pp. 44–5.

265 Allen, *Nazi Seizure of Power*, p.229.

266 Kershaw, *Hitler*, Vol. 1, p.445.

267 Tooze, *The Wages of Destruction*, pp. 55–7.

268 Interview by author with Elizabeth Hartnagel, Stuttgart, 15 February 2008.

269 F. McDonough, *Sophie Scholl: The Real Story of the Woman Who Defied Hitler* (Stroud: The History Press, 2010), pp.27–8.

270 Ullrich, *Hitler*, Vol. 1, p.448.

271 Evans, *Coming of the Third Reich*, pp. 359–60.

272 Longerich, *Goebbels*, p.231.

273 Evans, *Coming of the Third Reich*, pp. 364–6.

274 *Nazism*, Vol. 1, pp.164–5.

275 Ibid., pp.170–1.

276 Ullrich, *Hitler*, Vol. 1, p.458.

277 Ibid., p.452.

278 Papen, *Memoirs*, p.303.

279 Ullrich, *Hitler*, Vol. 1, p.515.

280 *Klemperer Diaries*, Vol. 1, p.32.

281 Toland, *Adolf Hitler*, p.318.

282 *New York Times*, 10 July 1933.

283 See T. Childers, *The Third Reich: A History of Nazi Germany* (Simon & Schuster, 2017), pp.334–40.

284 Ullrich, *Hitler*, Vol. 1, pp.546–7.

285 Burleigh, *Third Reich*, pp.333–81.

286 Toland, *Adolf Hitler*, p.316

287 J. Conway, *The Nazi Persecution of the Churches, 1933–1945* (Vancouver: Regent College Publishing, 1968), p.20.

288 Burleigh, *Third Reich*, pp.219–27.

289 For full details of the trial see Tobias, *The Reichstag Fire*, pp.179–284.

290 Toland, *Adolf Hitler*, p.322.

291 Tobias, *The Reichstag Fire*, p.282.

292 Van Der Lubbe was guillotined on 10 January 1934, but after the Second World War his brother sought to overturn the guilty verdict. In 1967 a West German court changed the sentence from death to eight years in prison. In 1981 a further court ruling found him not guilty by reason of insanity. In 2008 a German court gave van Der Lubbe a posthumous pardon.

293 Toland, *Adolf Hitler*, p.323.

294 Tooze, *The Wages of Destruction*, pp.45–8.

295 Ibid., p.180–182.

296 Longerich, *Goebbels*, p.239.

297 Interview by Hitler with G. Ward Price, *Daily Mail*, 19 October 1933.

298 *Klemperer Diaries*, Vol. 1, p.46.

299 Hitler speech, Munich, 8 November 1933, Baynes (ed,), *Speeches of Adolf Hitler*, pp.1137–9.

300 Toland, *Adolf Hitler*, p.320.

301 Ibid., p.321.

CHAPTER 2

1 Kershaw, *Hitler*, Vol. 1, p.502.

2 L. Machtan, *The Hidden Hitler* (Oxford: The Perseus Press, 2001), p.206.

3 Fest, *Hitler*, p.451.

4 *Nazism*, Vol. 1, p.169.

5 Fest, *Hitler*, pp.440–42.

6 T. Snyder, *Black Earth: The Holocaust as History and Warning* (New York: Tim Duggan Books, 2015), pp.55–7.

7 Interview with Hitler, *Frankfurter Volksblatt*, 27 January 1934, quoted in M. Domarus, *The Essential Hitler: Speeches and Commentary* (Wauconda, IL: Bolchazy-Carducci, 2007), pp.170–76. (Hereafter: *Hitler: Speeches and Proclamations*)

8 See *Time*, 1 January 1934, 8 January 1934, 29 January 1934.

9 Hitler speech, Reichstag, 30 January 1934, *Hitler: Speeches and Proclamations*, pp.256–8.

10 Ullrich, *Hitler*, Vol. 1, p.461.

11 Machtan, *The Hidden Hitler*, pp.210–11.

12 Ullrich, *Hitler*, Vol. 1, p.461.

13 Interview with Hitler by G. Ward Price, *Daily Mail*, 17 February 1934. Extracts from the interview appeared in *Völkischer Beobachter* on 18 January 1934.

14 Fest, *Hitler*, p.455.

15 Toland, *Adolf Hitler*, pp.323–4.

16 Ibid., p.324.

17 Fest, *Hitler*, p.443.

18 *New York Times*, 12 May 1934.

19 Fest, *Hitler*, p.455.

20 Ullrich, *Hitler*, Vol. 1, p.462.

21 Papen, *Memoirs*, p.328.

22 Ibid., p.323.

23 Ibid., p.329.

24 *Time*, 29 January 1934.

25 Longerich, *Goebbels*, p.264.

26 *The New Republic*, 7 February 1934.

27 A. Speer, *Inside the Third Reich* (Weidenfeld and Nicolson , 1970), pp. 95–6.

28 Tooze, *Wages of Destruction*, pp. 59–62.

29 Interview with Hitler by Louis Lochner, Associated Press, 4 April, *Hitler: Speeches and Proclamations*, pp. 541–7.

30 Papen, *Memoirs*, pp. 330–1.

31 Longerich, *Goebbels*, p. 264.

32 Fest, *Hitler*, p. 456.

33 Ullrich, *Hitler*, Vol. 1, p. 462.

34 *Time*, 15 April 1934.

35 Machtan, *The Hidden Hitler*, pp. 185–6.

36 Hitler speech, Berlin, 1 May 1934, *Hitler: Speeches and Proclamations*, pp. 168–9.

37 R. Wittman and D. Kinney, *The Devil's Diary: Alfred Rosenberg and the Stolen Secrets of the Third Reich* (William Colling, 2016), p. 150. (Hereafter *The Rosenberg Diary*.)

38 Ibid.. p. 153.

39 See Tooze, *Wages of Destruction*, pp. 86–98.

40 Ibid., p. 97–8.

41 Ullrich, *Hitler*, Vol. 1, p. 463.

42 *Nazism*, Vol. 1, p. 174.

43 Toland, *Adolf Hitler*, pp. 326–8.

44 Ullrich, *Hitler*, Vol. 1, pp. 463–4.

45 Herbert Bose letter to Ministry of Propaganda, 17 June 1934. Bundesarchiv Berlin, NS 20/50 (Hereafter BAB). This file contains three copies of Papen's speech. It shows that Goebbels knew the contents of Papen's speech beforehand.

46 *Newsweek*, 30 June 1934.

47 Toland, *Adolf Hitler*, p. 335.

48 Papen, *Memoirs*, p. 310.

49 Ullrich, *Hitler*, Vol. 1, p. 463.

50 Ibid., p. 464.

51 Longerich, *Goebbels*, p. 265.

52 Kershaw, *Hitler*, Vol. 1, p. 511.

53 For Vicktor Lutze's role, see 'Notes on the Röhm Purge', *Frankfurter Rundschau* pp. 14–16, May 1957.

54 *Nazism*, Vol. 1, p. 177.

55 Kershaw, *Hitler*, Vol. 1, p. 512.

56 Papen, *Memoirs*, p. 313.

57 Ullrich, *Hitler*, Vol. 1, p. 466.

58 Longerich, *Goebbels*, pp. 264–5.

59 *Nazism*, Vol. 1, p. 513.

60 Fest, *Hitler*, pp. 462–3.

61 English-language histories of the Third Reich refer to the events of 30 June–2 July as the Night of the Long Knives. German historians tend to call it the Röhm Purge or the Röhm Affair.

62 IfZ, transcript of interview with Erich Kempka. ZS/253.

63 Speer, *Inside the Third Reich*, p. 91.

64 Toland, *Adolf Hitler*, p. 339.

65 Ullrich, *Hitler*, Vol. 1, p. 467.

66 Kershaw, *Hitler*, Vol. 1, p. 514.

67 Ibid., p. 515.

68 Papen, *Memoirs*, pp. 315–16.

69 Ibid., p. 321.

70 Speer, *Inside the Third Reich*, p. 94.

71 Interview with Erich Klausener, *Voices of the Third Reich*, pp. 29–30.

72 Papen, *Memoirs*, p. 320.

73 Ullrich, *Hitler*, Vol. 1, p. 468.

74 Machtan, *The Hidden Hitler*, p. 218.

75 *Rosenberg Diary*, p. 159.

76 Ibid., p. 160.

77 Fest, *Hitler*, p. 466.

78 Toland, *Adolf Hitler*, p. 347.

79 Rees, *The Holocaust*, p. 83.

80 Machtan, *The Hidden Hitler*, p. 215.

81 Ullrich, *Hitler*, Vol. 1, p. 469.

82 IfZ, official list of the dead of 30 June 1934 Munich, MA/131.

83 Siemens, *Stormtroopers*, p. 169.

84 *Nazism*, Vol. 1, p. 182.

85 *Daily Mail*, 2 July 1934.

86 Machtan, *The Hidden Hitler*, p. 221.

87 *The Nation*, 11 July 1934.

88 *Klemperer Diaries*, Vol 1., p. 90.

89 Machtan, *The Hidden Hitler*, p. 216.

90 Ullrich, *Hitler*, Vol. 1, p. 469.

91 Machtan, *The Hidden Hitler*, p. 221.

92 Fest, *Hitler*, p. 469.

93 Stanislaus Jaros to Adolf Hitler, 13 July 1934, quoted in Henrik Eberle (ed.), *Letters to Hitler* (Cambridge:

Polity Press, 2012), p. 143. (Hereafter *Letters to Hitler*.)

94 *Klemperer Diaries*, Vol. 1, p. 191.

95 *Nazism*, Vol. 1, p. 187.

96 Longerich, *Goebbels*, p. 268.

97 Snyder, *Black Earth*, pp. 77–9.

98 Burleigh, *The Third Reich*, p. 272.

99 P. Longerich, *Goebbels: A Life* (Oxford University Press, 2012), p. 176.

100 Toland, *Adolf Hitler*, pp. 354–5.

101 Longerich, *Goebbels*, p. 270.

102 Fest, *Hitler*, p. 475.

103 W. L. Shirer, *Berlin Diary: The Journal of a Foreign Correspondent, 1934–1941* (Sunburst Books, 1997), p. 12.

104 Ullrich, *Hitler*, Vol. 1, p. 474.

105 *Rosenberg Diary*, p. 161.

106 *Daily Mail*, 6 August 1934.

107 Toland, *Adolf Hitler*, p. 357.

108 Ullrich, *Hitler*, Vol. 1, p. 475

109 Hitler speech, Hamburg, 17 August 1934, *Speeches and Proclamations*, pp. 168–70.

110 Ullrich, *Hitler*, Vol. 1, p. 475.

111 *Klemperer Diaries*, Vol. 1, p. 101.

112 Cesarani, *The Final Solution*, p. 84.

113 Ibid., p. 90.

114 S. Friedländer, *Nazi Germany and the Jews*, Vol 1: *The Years of Persecution 1933–39* (Phoenix, 1998), p. 118.

115 Rees, *The Holocaust*, pp. 85–6; Tooze, *Wages of Destruction*, pp. 89–90.

116 Friedländer, *The Years of Persecution*, pp. 123–4.

117 Richard Fichte to Adolf Hitler, 2 February 1934, *Letters to Hitler*, pp. 118–19.

118 Friedländer, *The Years of Persecution*, p. 127.

119 Jakob Falkenstein to Adolf Hitler, 5 February 1934, *Letters to Hitler*, p. 120.

120 W. Wainwright, *Reporting on Hitler: Rothay Reynolds and the British Press in Nazi Germany* (Biteback, 2017), pp. 130–1.

121 Shirer, *Berlin Diary*, p. 13.

122 Toland, *Adolf Hitler*, p. 361.

123 S. Bach, *Leni: The Life and Work of Leni Riefenstahl* (New York: Vintage, 2007), p. 131.

124 Hitler proclamation, 5 September 1934, Nuremberg, *Hitler: Speeches and Proclamations*, pp.307–308.

125 Shirer, *Berlin Diary*, p.15.

126 Hitler speech, Nuremberg, 8 September 1934, *Hitler: Speeches and Proclamations*. pp.474–80.

127 Shirer, *Berlin Diary*, p.16.

128 *Klemperer Diaries*, Vol.1, p.120.

129 Toland, *Adolf Hitler*, p.366.

CHAPTER 3

1 *Observer*, 13 January 1935.

2 Ullrich, *Hitler*, Vol.1, p.496.

3 *Klemperer Diaries*, Vol.1, p.133.

4 Hitler interview with Pierre Huss, 16 January 1935, *Hitler: Speeches and Proclamations*, pp.547–9.

5 *Daily Mail*, 18 January 1935.

6 J. Butler, *Lord Lothian* (Macmillan, 1961), pp.330–8.

7 Shirer, *Rise and Fall*, p.350.

8 Ministerial Committee on Disarmament, 19 February 1935. National Archives, London (Hereafter NA), Cab 27/508, 35 DC (M).

9 D. Litchfield, *Hitler's Valkyrie: The Uncensored Biography of Unity Mitford* (Stroud: The History Press, 2015), p.202.

10 A. Joachimsthaler, *Hitlers Liste: Dokumente Privater Beziehungen* (Munich. F.A.: Herbig, 2003), p.522.

11 Litchfield, *Hitler's Valkyrie*, p.204.

12 Ibid., p.219.

13 Hitler speech, Berlin, 14 February 1935, *Hitler: Speeches and Proclamations*, p.338.

14 Hitler speech, Munich, 24 February 1935, ibid., pp.134–5.

15 Ullrich, *Hitler*, Vol.1, p.496.

16 *Daily Mail*, 2 March 1935.

17 *Newsweek*, 16 March 1935.

18 Kershaw, *Hitler*, Vol.1, p.549.

19 Ibid., pp.548–9.

20 Ibid., pp.550–1.

21 BAB, NS 26/12909. William Bruckner's notebook, 16 March 1935. This seems the only full account, because the official minutes of this meeting do not appear to have survived.

22 Ullrich, *Hitler*, Vol.1, p.498.

23 Ibid., p.499.

24 Kershaw, *Hitler*, Vol.1, p.552.

25 Hitler interview with G. Ward Price, *Daily Mail*, 18 March 1935. Ward believed Hitler sincerely did want peace. See also G. Ward Price, *I Knew These Dictators* (George G. Harrop & Co., 1937).

26 *Klemperer Diaries*, Vol.1, p.142.

27 A. Eden, *The Eden Memoirs: Facing the Dictators* (Cassell, 1962), p.168.

28 Ullrich, *Hitler*, Vol.1, p.501.

29 A. Bullock, *Hitler: A Study in Tyranny* (Penguin, revised ed., 1962), p.334.

30 Eden, *Facing the Dictators*, p.135.

31 For the full British account of the Anglo-German talks on 25–26 March 1935, see W. Medlicott, D. Deakin. M. Lambert, (eds), *Documents on British Foreign Policy, 1919–1939, 2nd Series, 1930–1937* (Her Majesty's Stationery Office, Series C. Vol.3, No.555, 1946), pp.1043–80. (Hereafter DBFP)

32 Kershaw, *Hitler*, Vol.1, p.555.

33 *Film-Kurier*, 29 March 1935.

34 Bach, *Leni Riefenstahl*, p.139.

35 R. Parkinson, *Tormented Warrior: Ludendorff and the Supreme Command* (New York: Stein and Day, 1979), p.224.

36 Ullrich, *Hitler*, Vol.1, p.500.

37 *Newsweek*, 27 April 1935.

38 Hitler speech, 1 May 1935, *Hitler: Speeches and Proclamations*, pp.135–9.

39 *Klemperer Diaries*, Vol.1, p.146.

40 A. Bullock, *Hitler and Stalin: Parallel Lives* (HarperCollins, 1991), p.584.

41 I. Kershaw, *Making Friends with Hitler: Lord Londonderry and Britain's Road to War* (Allen Lane, 2005), p.60.

42 Hitler interview with Edward Bell, *Daily Telegraph*, 10 May 1935.

43 Longerich, *Goebbels*, p.299.

44 Bullock, *Hitler*, p.335.

45 Hitler speech, Berlin, 21 May 1935, *Hitler: Speeches and Proclamations*, pp.512–14.

46 Shirer, *Rise and Fall*, p.355.

47 Shirer, *Berlin Diary*, p.24.

48 Ullrich, *Hitler*, Vol.1, p.516.

49 Ibid., p.286.

50 H. Görtemaker, *Eva Braun: Life with Hitler* (Penguin, 2012), p.52.

51 Ullrich, *Hitler*, Vol.1, p.614.

52 Toland, *Adolf Hitler*, p.375.

53 Görtemaker, *Eva Braun*, p.91.

54 Ibid., p.88.

55 Ibid., p.91.

56 Ibid., p.376.

57 Ibid., p.377.

58 Ibid., pp.94–8.

59 Toland, *Adolf Hitler*, pp.378–9.

60 Evans, *Third Reich in Power*, p.650.

61 M. Bloch, *Ribbentrop* (Abacus, 2003), pp.67–9.

62 Shirer, *Rise and Fall*, p.357.

63 Kershaw, *Hitler*, Vol.1, p.558.

64 Longerich, *Goebbels*, p.301.

65 *Klemperer Diaries*, Vol.1, p.155.

66 J. Noakes and G. Pridham (eds), *Nazism: A Documentary Reader*, Volume 2: *State, Economy, Society, 1933–1945* (Exeter: Exeter University Press, 1984), p.336. (Hereafter *Nazism*, Vol.2.)

67 Evans, *Third Reich in Power*, pp.538–9.

68 AP-IMT. Hjalmar Schacht Testimony, 30 April 1946.

69 Ullrich, *Hitler*, Vol.1, p.550.

70 IfZ, files of the Geheimes Staatsarchiv, Munich, MA 105990, File 427/2, Report of the Police Directorate, Munich, April–May 1935.

71 Evans, *Third Reich in Power*, p.542.

72 R. Heydrich, 'The Visible Enemy', *Das Schwarz Korps*, 15 May 1935, *Third Reich Sourcebook*, pp.197–9.

73 Ullrich, *Hitler*, Vol.1, p.549.

74 *Klemperer Diaries*, Vol.1, p.144.

75 AP-IMT, Julius Streicher testimony, 29 April 1946.

76 Evans, *Third Reich in Power*, p.540.

77 Kershaw, *Hitler*, Vol.1, p.562.

78 Ullrich, *Hitler*, Vol.1, p.550.

79 Rees, *Holocaust*, p.86.

80 Friedländer, *The Years of Persecution*, p.138.

81 *Nazism*, Vol. 2, p.337.

82 Rees, *Holocaust*, p.86.

83 *Klemperer Diaries*, Vol. 1, p.159.

84 Burleigh, *Third Reich*, p.294.

85 Cesarani, *The Final Solution*, p.103.

86 See H. T. Burden, *The Nuremberg Rallies, 1923–1939* (Pall Mall Press, 1967)

87 Hitler speech, Nuremberg, 13 September 1935, *Hitler: Speeches and Proclamations*, pp.480–2.

88 Hitler speech, Nuremberg, 14 September 1935, ibid., pp.465–6.

89 Friedländer, *The Years of Persecution*, p.146.

90 Ullrich, *Hitler*, Vol. 1, p.556.

91 Hitler Speech, Special Session of Reichstag, Nuremberg, 15 September 1935, *Hitler: Speeches and Proclamations*, pp. 266–71.

92 Rees, *Holocaust*, pp.88–9.

93 Friedländer, *The Years of Persecution*, p.147.

94 Kershaw, *Hitler*, Vol. 1, p.567.

95 *Nazism*, Vol. 2, p.340.

96 *C. V. Zeitung*, 16 September 1935, *Third Reich Sourcebook*, p.638.

97 Friedländer, *The Years of Persecution*, p.143.

98 Hitler speech to the *Wehrmacht*, Nuremberg, 16 September 1935, *Hitler: Speeches and Proclamations*, pp.309–11.

99 P. Burrin, *Hitler and The Jews* (Arnold, 1994), pp.48–50.

100 Friedländer, *The Years of Persecution*, p.151.

101 A. J. P. Taylor, *The Origins of the Second World War* (Penguin, 1954), pp.119–20.

102 N. Rose, *Vansittart: The Study of a Diplomat* (William Heinemann, 1978), p.178.

103 Longerich, *Goebbels*, p.307.

104 Shirer, *Rise and Fall*, p.358.

105 Taylor, *Origins of the Second World War*, p.126.

106 *The Times*, 16 December 1935.

107 P. Neville, *Hitler and Appeasement: The British Attempt to Prevent the Second World War* (Hambledon Continuum, 2006), p.55.

108 Interview with Hitler by Hugh Baillie, 28 November 1935, *Hitler: Speeches and Proclamations*, pp.554–7.

109 *Rosenberg Diary*, pp.188–9.

110 NA. Phipps to Hoare, 16 December 1935, FO371/18841. C8364/55/18. See also Minute by Orme Sargent on Sir Erich Phipps interview with Herr Hitler, 13 December (dated 18 December) 1935, FO371/18852/ c83329/55/18.

111 W. Churchill, 'The Truth About Hitler', *Strand Magazine*, November 1935.

CHAPTER 4

1 Hitler's New Year message, 1 January 1936 (read by Joseph Goebbels), quoted in Baynes (ed.), *The Speeches of Adolf Hitler*, Vol. 2, p.648.

2 O. Meissner, *Sraasssekretär, unter Ebert, Hindenburg, Hitler* (Hamburg: Hoffmann and Campe, 1950), p.408.

3 Toland, *Adolf Hitler*, p.380.

4 Interview between Hitler and Titaÿna, *Paris Soir*, 26 January 1936, *Hitler: Speeches and Proclamations*, pp.556–62.

5 Toland, *Adolf Hitler*, p.381.

6 Ullrich, *Hitler*, Vol. 1, p.507.

7 Kershaw, *Making Friends with Hitler*, pp. 145–50; Eden, *Facing the Dictators*, p. 332.

8 *The Times*, 31 January 1936.

9 *Daily Herald*, 30 January 1936.

10 *Manchester Guardian*, 31 January 1936.

11 *Daily Mail*, 30 January 1936.

12 Kershaw, *Making Friends with Hitler*, p.138.

13 Ibid., p.145.

14 Longerich, *Goebbels*, p.311.

15 Ullrich, *Hitler*, Vol. 1, p.561.

16 For a detailed examination, see G. Walters, *Berlin Games: How the Nazis Stole the Olympic Dream* (Harper Perennial, 2007), pp.64–84. See also J. Halasz, *Hitler's Winter Olympics: A Photo Book* (Foxley Books, 2009).

17 Longerich, *Goebbels*, p.311.

18 Shirer, *Berlin Diary*, p.31.

19 F. Hossbach, *Die Entwicklung des Oberbefehls über das Heer in Brandenburg, Preussen und im Deutschen Reich von 1655–1945* (Wurzbürg: Holzner Verlag, 1957), pp.97–8.

20 Hitler speech, Berlin, 14 February 1936, *Hitler: Speeches and Proclamations*, p.338.

21 J. Emerson, *The Rhineland Crisis, 7 March 1936: A Study in Multilateral Diplomacy* (Maurice Temple Smith, 1977), p.85.

22 Hitler interview with Bertrand de Jouvenel, *Paris Midi*, 28 February 1936. The publication of this interview in France was delayed until after the vote had taken place. Hitler was angry about this. A full English version of the interview appeared in the British *Daily Mirror* on 29 February 1936.

23 Ullrich, *Hitler*, Vol. 1, pp.508–9.

24 M. Gamelin, *Servir* (Paris: Plon, 1947), Vol. 2, p.199.

25 Ullrich, *Hitler*, Vol. 1, p.509.

26 Ibid. p.509.

27 Longerich, *Goebbels*, p.313.

28 B. Lossberg, *Im Wehrmachtführungsstab* (Hamburg: Nölke, 1950), p.11.

29 Shirer, *Berlin Diary*, p.32.

30 Toland, *Adolf Hitler*, p.383.

31 Eden, *Facing the Dictators*, p.340.

32 Shirer, *Berlin Diary*, pp.32–3.

33 Toland, *Adolf Hitler*, p.388

34 Emerson, *Rhineland*, p.97.

35 F. Hossbach, *Zwischen Wehrmacht und Hitler, 1934–1938* (Göttingen: Vandenhoeck & Ruprecht, 1965), p.97.

36 R. D. Challener, *The French Theory of the Nation at Arms, 1886–1939* (New York: Columbia University Press, 1955), pp. 216–17.

37 The Maginot Line was named after André Maginot (1877–1932), the French Minister of War who had sanctioned its construction.

38 J. P. Levy, *Appeasement and Rearmament: Britain, 1936–1939* (Oxford: Rowan & Littlefield, 2006), pp.21–56.

39 Emerson, *Rhineland*, pp.158–9.

40 NA. Cabinet Paper [CP73/36], 8 March 1936.

41 Bloch, *Ribbentrop*, p. 93.

42 House of Commons Debates, 9 March 1936, Vol. 308, cols 1812–1813. (Hereafter HCD.)

43 Toland, *Adolf Hitler*, p. 388.

44 *The Times*, 9 March 1936.

45 Interview between Hitler and G. Ward Price, *Daily Mail*, 11 March 1936, *Hitler: Speeches and Proclamations*, pp. 562–7.

46 *The Times*, 12 March 1936.

47 Quoted in Toland, *Adolf Hitler*, p. 389.

48 Ibid., p. 388.

49 Bloch, *Ribbentrop*, p. 94.

50 Emerson, *Rhineland*, pp. 195–200.

51 Ibid., p. 201.

52 Ibid., p. 208.

53 M. Hauner, *Hitler: A Chronology of His Life and Times* (Basingstoke: Palgrave Macmillan, 2008), p. 114.

54 Ibid.

55 Shirer, *Berlin Diary*, p. 36.

56 For the background to the proposals, see P. Schmidt, *Hitler's Interpreter* (Stroud: History Press, 2016), pp. 47–9.

57 I. Kershaw, *Hitler*, Vol. 2: *Nemesis, 1936–1945* (Penguin, 2000), p. 4. (Hereafter Kershaw, *Hitler*, Vol. 2.)

58 Emerson, *Rhineland*, p. 229.

59 Bloch, *Ribbentrop*, p. 100.

60 T. Jones, *A Diary with Letters, 1931–1950* (Oxford: Oxford University, 1954), pp. 197–201.

61 Bloch, *Ribbentrop*, p. 111.

62 A full and detailed account of the first fight of Max Schmeling and Joe Louis in June 1936 can be found in D. Margolick, *Beyond Glory: Max Schmeling vs. Joe Louis, and A World on The Brink* (Bloomsbury, 2006), pp. 123–201.

63 Longerich, *Goebbels*, p. 319.

64 See E. Maradiellos, 'The International Dimensions of the Spanish Civil War' in F. McDonough (ed.), *The Origins of the Second World War: An International Perspective* (Hambledon Continuum, 2011), pp. 311–26. See also, P. Preston, *A Concise History of the Spanish Civil*

War (Fontana Press, 1996). For German involvement see C. Leitz, 'Nazi Germany's Intervention in the Spanish Civil War', in P. Preston and A. Mackenzie (eds), *The Republic Besieged: Civil War in Spain* (Edinburgh: Edinburgh University Press, 1996), pp. 53–85. For Italian intervention, see J. Coverdale, *Italian Intervention in the Spanish Civil War* (Princeton: Princeton University Press, 1975). For Stalin's reasons for intervention, see Bullock, *Hitler and Stalin*, pp. 594–9. For French reasons for non-intervention see A. Adamthwaite, *France and the Coming of the Second World War* (Routledge, 1977). For the British position, see R. A. C. Parker, *Chamberlain and Appeasement: British Policy and the Coming of the Second World War* (Basingstoke: Macmillan, 1993).

65 See A. Krüger, 'The Nazi Olympics of 1936' in K. Young and K. B. Walmsley (eds.), *Global Olympics: Historical and Sociological Studies of the Modern Games* (Oxford: Elsevier, 2005), pp. 43–58.

66 Another 'half-Jew' Rudi Ball, an ice-hockey player, had competed for Germany at the Winter Olympics in February 1936.

67 Walters, *Berlin Games*, pp. 170–2.

68 Ullrich, *Hitler*, Vol. 1, p. 565.

69 Kershaw, *Making Friends with Hitler*, p. 174.

70 Walters, *Berlin Games*, p. 189.

71 Ibid., pp. 183–194.

72 B. Schirach, *Ich glaubte an Hitler* (Hamburg: Mosaik Verlag, 1967), pp. 217–19.

73 Walters, *Berlin Games*, p. 200.

74 Longerich, *Goebbels*, p. 321.

75 Archie Williams interview, *San Francisco Chronicle*, 12 June 1984.

76 Walters, *Berlin Games*, p. 298.

77 Ribbentrop received his letter of appointment on 24 July 1936.

78 *The Times*, 12 August 1936.

79 *Daily Telegraph*, 12 August 1936.

80 *Daily Mail*, 12 August 1936.

81 Kershaw, *Making Friends with Hitler*, p. 160.

82 Bloch, *Ribbentrop*, p. 106.

83 Kershaw, *Making Friends with Hitler*, p. 180.

84 For a detailed examination of the expansion of the Berghof, see D. Stratigakos, *Hitler at Home* (New Haven: Yale University Press, 2015).

85 Ullrich, *Hitler*, Vol. 1, p. 610.

86 Stratigakos, *Hitler at Home*, p. 81.

87 For a detailed account of Hitler's life at the Berghof, see Ullrich, *Hitler*, Vol. 1, pp. 608–635.

88 See Memorandum of Supreme Command of the German Army (Oberkommando des Heeres), presented at a military conference on the future planning of the German Army, 12 June 1936, Bundesarchiv Marburg, RH/2V 1021.

89 For details, see Tooze, *The Wages of Destruction*, pp. 203–14.

90 Adolf Hitler's Confidential Memorandum on Autarchy, August 1936. Source of English translation in *Documents on German Foreign Policy: From the Archives of the German Foreign Ministry* (Washington, DC: US Government Printing Office, 1957–1964), Series C (1933–1937), *Third Reich: The First Phase*, Vol. V: March 5–October 1936, Document No. 490, pp. 853–62. (Hereafter DGFP, followed by volume number, document number, page reference and document title)

91 Tooze, *Wages of Destruction*, pp. 222–3.

92 J. Boyd, *Travellers in the Third Reich: The Rise of Fascism Through the Eyes of Everyday People* (Elliot & Thompson, 2017), pp. 258–62.

93 Bloch, *Ribbentrop*, p. 109.

94 Ibid., p. 110.

95 Boyd, *Travellers in the Third Reich*, p. 260.

96 Ibid., pp. 261–2.

97 Bloch, *Ribbentrop*, pp. 109–112.

98 David Lloyd George, 'I Talked to Hitler', *Daily Express*, 17 September 1936.

99 Boyd, *Travellers in the Third Reich*, p. 262.

100 *Documents on German Foreign Policy*, Series C, Vol. 6: *Third Reich: The First Phase 1 November 1936–14 November 1937* (Washington, DC: US Government Printing Office, 1983), No. 47, pp. 83–8. British Government

View on Western Pact Negotiations, 19 November 1936.

101 Ibid., No,113, p.198, Ribbentrop to Hitler and Neurath, 19 December 1936.

102 Hitler speech, Bückeberg, 4 October 1936, *Hitler: Speeches and Proclamations*, pp.346–8.

103 J. Miller, *Belgian Foreign Policy between the Wars, 1919–1940* (New York: Bookman Associates, 1951), pp.226–41.

104 Emerson, *Rhineland*, pp.233–5.

105 Tooze, *Wages of Destruction*, p.224.

106 For a detailed study of the evolution of German–Italian relations, see E. Wiskemann, *The Rome–Berlin Axis* (Fontana, 1966).

107 Longerich, *Goebbels*, pp.325–7.

108 Toland, *Adolf Hitler*, pp.399–400.

109 Fest, *Hitler*, pp.501–502.

110 Bloch, *Ribbentrop*, p.120.

111 *Daily Telegraph*, 27 October 1936.

112 Bloch, *Ribbentrop*, pp.122.

113 Kershaw, *Making Friends with Hitler*, p.181.

114 Longerich, *Goebbels*, p.326

115 Shirer, *Berlin Diary*, p.41.

116 Bloch, *Ribbentrop*, pp.130–1.

117 For a detailed examination see M. Hitchens, *Abdication: The Rise and Fall of Edward VIII* (The Book Guild, 2016) and P. Ziegler, *King Edward VIII* (HarperPress, 2012).

118 Levy, *British Rearmament*, pp.36–7.

119 Bloch, *Ribbentrop*, pp.187–90.

120 DGFP, Series C, Vol. 6, No. 84, pp.158–9, Ribbentrop to Neurath, 10 December 1936.

121 L. Heston and R. Heston, *The Medical Casebook of Adolf Hitler: His Illnesses, Doctors and Drugs* (William Kimber, 1979), pp.32–3.

122 N. Ohler, *Blitzed: Drugs in Nazi Germany* (Allen Lane, 2016), pp.33–4.

123 Speer, *Inside the Third Reich*, p.106.

124 Heston and Heston, *Medical Casebook of Adolf Hitler*, p.32.

125 Ibid., p.19.

126 Ibid., p.101.

127 Ohler, *Blitzed*, pp.24–33.

CHAPTER 5

1 Toland, *Adolf Hitler*, p.402.

2 Ullrich, *Hitler*, Vol. 1, p.690.

3 DGFP, Series D, Vol. 6, No. 128, pp.251–2. Eden to Ribbentrop, 5 January 1937.

4 Ibid., No. 125, pp.244-5. Moltke to Foreign Ministry, 5 January 1937 .

5 Schmidt, *Hitler's Interpreter*, p.75.

6 Wiskemann, *Rome–Berlin Axis*, pp.95–9.

7 DGFP. Series D, Vol. 6, No. 164, pp.351–2. Ulrich von Hassell to Foreign Ministry, 30 January 1937.

8 HCD Vol. 319, cols, 92–161, Anthony Eden's statement, 19 January 1937.

9 DGFP, Series D, Vol.6, No. 148, pp. 300–303. Memorandum by Neurath, 20 January 1937.

10 Ibid., No. 153, pp.316–17. Minute by Ernst von Weizsäcker, Acting Director of the Political Department, German Foreign Office, 21 January 1937.

11 Hitler speech, Reichstag, 30 January 1937, *Hitler: Speeches and Proclamations*, pp.178–9.

12 *Daily Telegraph*, 1 February 1937.

13 *News Chronicle*, 1 February 1937.

14 DGFP, Series D, Vol. 6, No. 172, pp.364–5. Herbert von Richthofen to German Foreign Ministry, 3 February 1937.

15 Ibid., No. 174, p.366. Memorandum by Ernst von Weizsäcker, 3 February 1937.

16 Ibid., No. 193, p.402. Ulrich von Hassell to Neurath, 10 February 1937.

17 Bloch, *Ribbentrop*, pp.135–136.

18 DGFP, Series D, Vol. 6, No. 175, p.367. Ribbentrop to Neurath, 4 February 1937.

19 Ibid., No. 202, pp.422–4. Ribbentrop to Hitler and Neurath, 14 February 1937.

20 Bloch, *Ribbentrop*, p.137.

21 DGFP, Series D, Vol. 6, No. 185, pp.382–4. Memorandum by Hans-Heinrich Dieckhoff, 8 February 1937.

22 Ibid., No. 201, pp.414–22. Ribbentrop

to Hitler and Neurath, 14 February 1937.

23 Kershaw, *Making Friends with Hitler*, pp.194–5.

24 Wachsmann, *KL*, pp.144–7.

25 Kershaw, *Hitler*, Vol. 2, pp.39–49.

26 F. McDonough, *The Gestapo: The Myth and Reality of Hitler's Secret Police* (Coronet, 2015), pp.60–92.

27 DGFP, Series D, Vol. 6, No. 231, pp.481–2. The Ambassador to the Holy See to Neurath, 25 February 1937.

28 Ibid., No. 242, pp.494–5. Memorandum by Head of Political Division [Dumont], 3 March 1937.

29 Ibid., No. 260, pp.530–31. Neurath to the Apolistic Nuncio in Germany, 11 March 1937.

30 Ibid., No. 240, p.492. Memorandum by Otto von Erdmannsdorff, 2 March 1937.

31 *Der Angriff*, 5 March 1937.

32 DGFP, Series D, Vol. 6, No. 265, p.542. Memorandum by Neurath, 12 March 1937.

33 Ibid., No. 279, pp.564–5. Hans Luther to Foreign Ministry, 17 March 1937.

34 The actual date on the document was 14 March 1937.

35 J. Bentley, *Martin Niemöller* (Oxford: Oxford University Press, 1984), p.125.

36 Ullrich, *Hitler*, Vol. 1, p.651.

37 Longerich, *Goebbels*, pp.333–5.

38 DGFP, Series D, Vol. 6, No. 258, pp. 522–9. German Memorandum on the Western Pact, 10 March 1937.

39 Ibid., No. 263, pp.535–41. Italian Memorandum on the Western Pact, 11 March 1937.

40 Ibid., No. 288, pp.582–3. Memorandum by Neurath, 20 March 1937.

41 Ibid., No. 312. Report by Ulrich von Hassell on Germany and the Berlin–Rome Axis, 12 April 1937.

42 Ibid., No. 318, pp.653–7. Ernst Eisenlohr, German Minister to Czechoslovakia to Foreign Ministry, 15 April 1937.

43 Ibid., No. 322, pp.663–4. Memorandum by Neurath, 17 April 1937.

44 Ibid., No. 324, p. 665. Minute by Neurath, 17 April 1937.

45 Schmidt, *Hitler's Interpreter*, p. 72.

46 Gilbert, *Britain and Germany*, p. 102.

47 R. Griffiths, *Fellow Travellers of the Right: British Enthusiasts for Nazi Germany, 1933–1945* (Faber and Faber, 1983), p. 270.

48 Wiskemann, *The Rome–Berlin Axis*, pp. 100–101.

49 HCD, Vol. 323, cols, 307–310, Anthony Eden statement, 28 April 1937.

50 J. Corum, *The Luftwaffe: Creating the Operational Air War, 1918–1940* (Lawrence: University of Kansas Press, 1997), pp. 198–201.

51 *The Times*, 28 April 1937

52 *Times* Archives, London. Daniels to Dawson), 16 May 1937. (Hereafter TA.)

53 Hitler speech, Vogelsang Castle, 29 April 1937, Toland, *Adolf Hitler*, pp. 412–13.

54 Griffiths, *Fellow Travellers of the Right*, p. 280.

55 Bloch, *Ribbentrop*, p. 144.

56 Ibid.

57 Eden, *Facing the Dictators*, p. 504.

58 Hitler speech, Berlin, 1 May 1937, Ullrich, *Hitler*, Vol. 1, pp. 651–2.

59 DGFP, Series D, Vol. 6, No. 350, pp. 717–19. Memorandum by Neurath, 3 May 1937.

60 *The Times*, 31 January 1935.

61 Fest, *Hitler*, p. 507.

62 Griffiths, *Fellow Travellers of the Right*, p. 271.

63 See A. Hoehling, *Who Destroyed the Hindenburg?* (Little, Brown, 1962).

64 DGFP, Series D, Vol. 6, No. 360, pp. 738–9. Friedrich von Schulenburg to Foreign Ministry, 10 May 1937.

65 N. Henderson, *Failure of a Mission, Berlin 1937–1939* (Hodder & Stoughton, 1940), pp. 48–9.

66 DGFP, Series D, Vol. 6, No. 371, pp. 759–60. Memorandum of conversation between Field Marshal von Blomberg

and Stanley Baldwin, 13 May 1937 [Enclosure 1].

67 Ibid., pp. 760–763. Memorandum of Conversation between Field Marshal von Blomberg and Anthony Eden, 13 May 1937 [Enclosure 2].

68 Ibid., No. 371, pp. 763–4. Memorandum of a conversation between Field Marshal von Blomberg and Neville Chamberlain, 14 May 1937 [Enclosure 3].

69 *Chicago Tribune*, 20 May 1937.

70 *Hitler: Speeches and Proclamations*, pp. 431–3.

71 DGFP, Series D, Vol. 6, No. 380, pp. 777–82. Ribbentrop to Neurath, 21 May 1937.

72 Bloch, *Ribbentrop*, pp. 142–3.

73 Ibid, p. 143.

74 Hitler Interview with Abel Bonnard, *Le Journal De Paris*, 22 May 1937, *Hitler: Speeches and Proclamations*, pp. 567–70.

75 Kershaw, *Hitler*, Vol. 2, pp. 43–4.

76 Griffiths, *Fellow Travellers of the Right*, p. 281.

77 Wiskermann, *The Rome–Berlin Axis*, p. 103.

78 Hitler speech, Regensburg, 6 June 1937, *Hitler: Speeches and Proclamations*, p. 152.

79 DGFP, Series D, Vol. 6, No. 420, pp. 848–53. French Memorandum on the Western Pact, 10 June 1937.

80 Ibid., No. 430, pp. 868. German Ambassador in France to Foreign Ministry, 15 June 1937.

81 Henderson, *Failure of a Mission*, pp. 68–9.

82 *Nazi Aggression and Conspiracy: Nuremberg Prosecution Documents* (Washington, DC: US Government Printing Office, 1946), Vol. 6, C–175, pp. 1006–1011. (Henceforth *Nuremberg Documents*.) Directive for the Unified Preparation of the Armed Forces for War, Memorandum by Werner von Blomberg, 24 June 1937.

83 Hitler speech, Wurzburg, 27 June 1937, *Hitler: Speeches and Proclamations*, p. 153.

84 Bentley, *Martin Niemöller*, pp. 127–8.

85 Ibid., p. 132.

86 Ullrich, *Hitler*, Vol. 1, p. 655.

87 DGFP, Series D, Vol. 6, No. 474, pp. 926–9. British Memorandum on Western Pact, 16 July 1937.

88 Hitler speech, Munich, 19 July 1937, *Hitler: Speeches and Proclamations*, pp. 488–97.

89 Childers, *The Third Reich*, pp. 294–7.

90 DGFP, Series D, Vol. 6, No. 484, pp. 943–6. Sir Nevile Henderson to Anthony Eden, 20 July 1937. See also Henderson, *Failure of a Mission*, pp. 76–8.

91 Hitler speech, Breslau, 31 July 1937, *Hitler: Speeches and Proclamations*, pp. 497–500.

92 DGFP, Series D, Vol. 6, No. 505, pp. 991–93. Neurath to the German Missions in Great Britain, Italy, Belgium, Netherlands and to the Consulate in Geneva, 31 July 1937.

93 *Daily Mail*, 4 September 1937.

94 Hauner, *Hitler*, p. 123.

95 Hitler speech, Nuremberg, 7 September 1937, *Hitler: Speeches and Proclamations*, pp. 500–504.

96 Henderson, *Failure of a Mission*, pp. 70–71.

97 Hitler speech, Nuremberg, 10 September 1937, *Hitler: Speeches and Proclamations*, pp. 311–12.

98 Hitler speech, Nuremberg, 13 September 1937, *Hitler: Speeches and Proclamations*, pp. 384–90.

99 DGFP, Series D, Vol. 6, No. 551, pp. 1064–1066. Franz von Papen to Hitler, 14 September 1937.

100 Schmidt, *Hitler's Interpreter*, pp. 81–2.

101 Ullrich, *Hitler*, Vol. 1, p. 694.

102 Toland, *Adolf Hitler*, p. 418.

103 *Klemperer Diaries*, Vol. 1, p. 292.

104 Ullrich, *Hitler*, Vol. 1, p. 694.

105 DGFP, Series D, Vol. 6, No. 568, pp. 1086–1089. Hassell to Weizsäcker, 7 October 1937.

106 Hitler speech, Bückeberg, 3 October 1937, *Hitler: Speeches and Proclamations*, p. 155.

107 Griffiths, *Fellow Travellers of the Right*, p. 273.

108 Schmidt, *Hitler's Interpreter*, p. 85.

109 *The Times*, 14 October 1937.

110 DGFP, Series D, Vol. 6, No. 577, pp. 1097–1098. Memorandum by Kurt von Kamphoevener, 5 November 1937.

111 Toland, *Adolf Hitler*, p. 420.

112 Hossbach Memorandum, 10 November 1936, *Hitler: Speeches and Proclamations*, pp. 603–18.

113 Henderson, *Failure of a Mission*, p. 47.

114 *Nazism*, Vol. 2, p. 80.

115 Toland, *Adolf Hitler*, p. 412.

116 Kershaw, *Hitler*, Vol. 2, pp. 46–51.

117 *Nazism*, Vol. 2, p. 83.

118 Bloch, *Ribbentrop*, p. 153.

119 Ibid., p. 155.

120 Toland, *Adolf Hitler*, pp. 423–5.

121 Schmidt, *Hitler's Interpreter*, p. 87.

122 Toland, *Adolf Hitler*, p. 425.

123 Hitler speech, Augsburg, 21 November 1937, *Hitler: Speeches and Proclamations*, pp. 184–5.

124 Hitler speech, Allgäu, 23 November 1937, *Hitler: Speeches and Proclamations*, pp. 312–17.

125 Shirer, *Rise and Fall*, pp. 382–3.

126 *Klemperer Diaries*, Vol. 1, p. 295.

127 Toland, *Adolf Hitler*, pp. 425–6.

128 The report was sent to Hitler and Neurath on 2 January 1938.

129 Report by Ribbentrop on the German–English Relationship and the further treatment of the Chamberlain initiative, 28 December 1937 in Politiches Archiv des Auswärtgen Amtes, Berlin, R288852/A5522. See also Kershaw, *Making Friends with Hitler*, pp. 212–14.

CHAPTER 6

1 Hitler's New Year message, 1 January 1938, G. Shultze-Rhonhof, *1939: The War That Had Many Fathers: The Long Run-up to the Second World War* (Munich: Olzog Verlag, 2011), p. 389.

2 Shirer, *Rise and Fall*, p. 384.

3 Ullrich, *Hitler*, Vol. 1, pp. 699–703.

4 Ibid., p. 701.

5 Longerich, *Goebbels*, p. 373.

6 Shirer, *Rise and Fall*, p. 389.

7 Ullrich, *Hitler*, Vol. 1, p. 703.

8 Shirer, *Rise and Fall*, p. 388.

9 Kershaw, *Hitler*, Vol. 2, p. 55.

10 Ibid., p. 56.

11 Ullrich, *Hitler*, Vol. 1, p. 704.

12 The accuser, Otto Schmidt, was murdered in Sachsenhausen concentration camp on 30 October 1942. Fritsch never recovered his position. He was made commander of the artillery regiment that he had previously commanded. He was killed near Warsaw on 22 September 1939, during the German invasion of Poland.

13 Longerich, *Goebbels*, p. 399.

14 U. von Hassell, *The Ulrich von Hassell Diaries, 1938–1944: The Story of the Forces Against Hitler Inside Germany* (Barnsley: Frontline Books, 2011), p. 15.

15 *The Times*, 31 January 1938; *News Chronicle*, 31 January 1938.

16 Kershaw, *Hitler*, Vol. 2, p. 58.

17 Longerich, *Goebbels*, p. 374.

18 Bullock, *Hitler and Stalin*, p. 622.

19 Toland, *Adolf Hitler*, p. 430.

20 Fest, *Hitler*, p. 543.

21 Ibid., p. 544.

22 Bloch, *Ribbentrop*, pp. 166–7.

23 G. Gorodetsky (ed.), *The Maisky Diaries: Red Ambassador to the Court of St James, 1932–1943* (New Haven, CT: Yale University Press, 2015), pp. 99–100. (Hereafter *Maisky Diaries*.)

24 Papen, *Memoirs*, pp. 406–411.

25 Longerich, *Goebbels*, p. 374.

26 Bloch, *Ribbentrop*, p. 177.

27 AP-IMT. Affidavit of Kurt von Schuschnigg, concerning his visit to Berchtesgaden, 12 February 1938, dated 19 November 1945. See also K. von Schuschnigg, *Austrian Requiem* (Victor Gollancz, 1947), pp. 12–25.

28 Bloch, *Ribbentrop*, p. 178.

29 AP-IMT. Testimony of Arthur Seyss-Inquart, 10 June 1946.

30 Shirer, *Rise and Fall*, p. 404.

31 AP-IMT. Affidavit of Kurt von Schuschnigg concerning his visit to Berchtesgaden, 12 February 1938, dated 19 November 1945.

32 Kershaw, *Hitler*, Vol. 2, p. 71.

33 *The Times* 14 February 1938; *Manchester Guardian*, 14 February 1938.

34 *News Chronicle*, 16 February 1938.

35 *The Times*, 16 February 1938.

36 *Sunday Times*, 20 February 1938.

37 AP-IMT. Testimony of Arthur Seyss-Inquart, 10 June 1946.

38 F. McDonough, *Neville Chamberlain, Appeasement and the British Road to War* (Manchester: Manchester University Press, 1998), pp. 53–4.

39 *Maisky Diaries*, p. 101.

40 R. Parker, *Chamberlain and Appeasement: British Policy and The Coming of the Second World War* (Basingstoke: Palgrave Macmillan, 1993), p. 123.

41 *Maisky Diaries*, p. 103.

42 Hitler speech, Reichstag, Berlin, 20 February 1938, *Hitler: Speeches and Proclamations*, pp. 570–73.

43 Hitler speech, Munich, 24 February 1938, *Hitler: Speeches and Proclamations*, pp. 390–91.

44 Shirer, *Rise and Fall*, p. 409.

45 Bentley, *Niemöller*, pp. 138–41.

46 Kershaw, *Hitler*, Vol. 2, p. 73.

47 Schuschnigg, *Austrian Requiem*, pp. 35–6.

48 AP-IMT. Testimony of Arthur Seyss-Inquart, 10 June 1946.

49 Ullrich, *Hitler*, Vol. 1, p. 714.

50 Shirer, *Rise and Fall*, p. 423.

51 Ibid. p. 412.

52 Fest, *Hitler*, p. 547.

53 Bloch, *Ribbentrop*, pp. 187–8.

54 Shirer, *Rise and Fall*, p. 416.

55 Ibid. p. 419.

56 AP-IMT. Testimony of Arthur Seyss-Inquart, 10 June 1946. After the German occupation Schuschnigg was placed under house arrest. He was then sent to Sachsenhausen concentration camp and later moved to Dachau. American troops found him alive there on 4 April 1945.

57 Shirer, *Rise and Fall*, p. 421.

58 AP-IMT. Testimony of Arthur Seyss-Inquart, 10 June 1946.

59 Bullock, *Hitler*, p.455.

60 Childers, *Third Reich*, p.399.

61 ADG-IFGB. Interview with Emil Myles, 9, 11, 12 June 1987, pp.997–1086.

62 *The Times*, 15 March 1938.

63 *Manchester Guardian*, 12 March 1939.

64 Interview with Ferdinand Krones, *Voices of the Third Reich*, pp.95–6.

65 Tooze, *Wages of Destruction*, pp.245–7.

66 The reports of Gedye appeared in the *Daily Telegraph* every day from 12–18 March 1938. He was expelled from Austria on 28 March 1938.

67 Ullrich, *Hitler*, Vol. 1, p.661.

68 Cesarani, *Final Solution*, pp.143–150.

69 *Documents on German Foreign Policy*, Series. D. Vol. 2, *Germany and Czechoslovakia, 1937–1938* (Her Majesty's Stationery Office, 1950), pp.171–3. Ernst Woermann German chargé d'affaires in Great Britain, 17 March 1938 (Hereafter DGFP, Series D, Vol. 2.).

70 Fest, *Hitler*, p.551.

71 NA. Cab 27. 'Military Implications of German Aggression against Czechoslovakia', report by the Chiefs of Staff Sub-Committee, March 1938. Cab 23/95/37. Cabinet meeting, 22 March 1938.

72 *Maisky Diaries*, p.107.

73 DGFP, Series D, Vol. 2, No. 104, pp.192–3. Ernst Woermann German chargé d'affaires in Great Britain. 25 March 1938.

74 Ibid., No. 107, pp.197–9. Konrad Henlein's report of a meeting with Hitler, 28 March 1938.

75 Hitler speech, Graz, Austria, 3 April 1938, *Hitler: Speeches and Proclamations*, p.157.

76 Interview with Erich Kern, *Voices of the Third Reich*, p.97.

77 Hitler speech, Vienna, 9 April 1938, *Hitler: Speeches and Proclamations*, pp.162–3.

78 Kershaw, *Hitler*, Vol. 2, p.83.

79 DGFP, Series D, Vol. 2, No. 133, pp. 239–40. Memorandum of conversation between Adolf Hitler and Wilhelm Keitel on Case Green, 22 April 1938.

80 Ibid., No. 135, pp.242–3. Memorandum of the eight demands made by Konrad Henlein at Karlsbad, 24 April 1938.

81 Ibid., No. 143, pp.252–3. Theodore Kordt, German chargé d'affaires in Great Britain to German Foreign Ministry, 28 April 1938.

82 Hitler speech, Berlin, 1 May 1938, *Hitler: Speeches and Proclamations*, pp. 466–7.

83 DGFP, Series D, Vol. 2, No.144, pp. 253–4. Johannes von Welczeck to Foreign Ministry, 1 May 1938.

84 Ullrich, *Hitler*, Vol. 1, pp.723–4.

85 Toland, *Adolf Hitler*, p.461.

86 Ullrich, *Hitler*, Vol. 1, p.726.

87 Kershaw, *Hitler*, Vol. 2, p.97.

88 DGFP, Series D, Vol. 2, No. 155, pp.273–4. Memorandum by Ernst von Weizsäcker of conversation with Konrad Henlein, Berlin, 12 May 1938.

89 Ibid., No. 250, pp.403–409. Herbert von Dirksen to Foreign Ministry, 10 June 1938. Ever since 1935 (as Foreign Ministry records reveal) the Sudeten German Party was being subsidized to the tune of 15,000 Reichsmarks per month. See DGFP, Series D, Vol. 2, No. 375, pp.594–5. Foreign Ministry Personnel Department Memorandum, 19 August 1938.

90 Ibid., No. 170, pp.298–9. Memorandum by Ernst von Weizsäcker, 20 May 1938.

91 Ibid., No. 171, p.296. Minute by Ernst von Weizsäcker, 20 May 1938.

92 Ibid., No. 175, pp.299–303. Letter from Keitel to Hitler, containing revised draft for 'Case Green', 20 May 1938.

93 The conversation between Henderson and Ribbentrop is contained in two separate documents, dated 21 May 1938. See DGFP, Series D, Vol. 2, No. 184, pp.311–13, Memorandum by Ribbentrop, 21 May 1938 and DGFP, Series D, Vol. 2, No. 186, pp.315–17. Memorandum by Ribbentrop, 21 May 1938.

94 DGFP, Series D, Vol. 2, No. 193. Memorandum by Ribbentrop, 23 May 1938.

95 Ibid., No. 194, pp.326–8. Johannes von Welczeck to Foreign Ministry, 23 May 1938.

96 Ibid., No. 209, pp.340–43. Ernst Eisenlohr to Foreign Ministry, 25 May 1938.

97 Hitler speech, Fallersleben, 26 May 1938, *Hitler: Speeches and Proclamations*, pp.348–51.

98 Tooze, *Wages of Destruction*, pp.135–161. See also C. Clark, *The Conditions of Economic Progress* (Macmillan, 1940).

99 DGFP, Series D, Vol. 2, No. 212, pp.346–8. Herbert von Dirksen to Foreign Ministry, 26 May 1938.

100 Kershaw, *Hitler*, Vol. 2, p.727.

101 DGFP, Series D, Vol. 2, No. 221, pp. 357–62. Directive for Case Green, 30 May 1938.

102 Ibid., No. 234, pp.379–85. Excerpt from Strategic Study for 1938 by the Supreme Headquarters of the *Wehrmacht* (OKW), 2 June 1938.

103 Ibid., No. 282, pp.473–7. General Strategic Directive, signed by Adolf Hitler, 18 June 1938.

104 Ibid., No. 259, pp.420–422. Memorandum by Ernst von Weizsäcker, 20 June 1938.

105 Margolick, *Beyond Glory*, pp.240–351.

106 DGFP, Series D, Vol. 2, No. 280, pp.467–9. Memorandum by Kurt Tippelskirch, 5 July 1938.

107 Cesarani, *Final Solution*, p.167.

108 Friedlander, *The Years of Persecution*, p.249.

109 Kershaw, *Hitler*, Vol. 2, p.102.

110 Toland, *Adolf Hitler*, p.466.

111 DGFP, Series D, Vol. 2, No. 313, pp.512–14. Minute by Weizsäcker to Ribbentrop, 25 July 1938.

112 Ullrich, *Hitler*, Vol. 1, p.730.

113 *Maisky Diaries*, p.117.

114 Fest, *Hitler*, p.561; Kershaw, *Hitler*, Vol. 2, pp.102–103.

115 Ullrich, *Hitler*, Vol. 1, p.730.

116 Ibid.

117 DGFP, Series D, Vol. 2, No. 374, p.593. Minute by Weizsäcker, 19 August 1938.

118 Ibid., No. 379, pp. 599–601. Ribbentrop to Halifax, 21 August 1938.

119 Ibid., No. 380, pp. 601–602. Friedrich Schulenburg to Foreign Ministry. 22 August 1938. See also DGFP, Series D, Vol. 2, No. 381, pp. 604–605. Schulenburg memorandum, 23 August 1938.

120 Kershaw, *Hitler*, Vol. 2, p. 106.

121 Hitler interview with Alphonse de Châteaubriant, 31 August 1938, *Hitler: Speeches and Proclamations*, pp. 573–4.

122 DGFP, Series D, Vol. 2, No. 424, pp. 686–7. Military Conference, Berghof, 3 September 1938.

123 Shirer, *Rise and Fall*, p. 468.

124 Hitler opening proclamation to the Nuremberg Rally, 6 September 1938, *Hitler: Speeches and Proclamations*, pp. 351–3.

125 DGFP, Series D, Vol. 2, No. 436, pp. 704–710. Foreign policy memorandum, 6 September 1938.

126 *The Times*, 7 September 1938.

127 DGFP, Series D, Vol. 2, No. 439, pp. 712–14. Curt Bräuer, the German chargé d'affaires in France, 7 September 1938.

128 Ibid., No. 448, pp. 727–30. Military conference, Nuremberg, 9 September 1938.

129 *The Times*, 13 September 1938.

130 DGFP, Series D, Vol. 2, No. 469, p. 754. Foreign policy minute [unsigned], 13 September 1938.

131 Ibid., No. 487, pp. 786–98. Memorandum on the conversation between the Führer and Mr Chamberlain, the British Prime Minister, at Berchtesgaden, 15 September 1938, prepared by Paul Schmidt.

132 Schmidt, *Hitler's Interpreter*, p. 103.

133 DGFP, Series D, Vol. 2, No. 532, pp. 839–40. Minute by Foreign Ministry Secretariat, 19 September 1938.

134 Ibid., No. 489, p. 801. Henlein to Hitler, 15 September 1938.

135 Hitler interview with G. Ward Price, 16 September 1938, *Hitler: Speeches and Proclamations*, p. 575. For

the full interview see *Daily Mail*, 17 September 1938.

136 NA. Cab 23/95/37. Cabinet meeting, 17 September 1938.

137 Toland, *Adolf Hitler*, p. 478.

138 DGFP, Series D, Vol. 2, No. 554, pp. 863–4. Minute by Erich Kordt, Foreign Ministry, 21 September 1938.

139 Ibid., No. 562, pp. 870–9. Minutes of the conversation between the Führer and Mr Chamberlain, the British Prime Minister, on the afternoon of 22 September 1938.

140 DGFP, Series D, Vol. 2, No. 572, pp. 887–8. Chamberlain to Hitler, 23 September 1938.

141 Ibid., No. 573, pp. 889–91. Hitler to Chamberlain, 23 September 1938.

142 Ibid., No. 574, p. 892. Chamberlain to Hitler, 23 September 1938.

143 Ibid., No. 584. pp. 908–910. German memorandum of transfer of territory, 23 November 1938.

144 Ibid.

145 DGFP, Series D, Vol. 2, No. 583, pp. 890–908. Minutes of the conversation between the Führer and Mr Chamberlain, the British Prime Minister, on the evening of 23 September 1938.

146 NA. Cab 23/95/37. Cabinet meetings, (3), 24 September 1938.

147 Ullrich, *Hitler*, Vol. 1, p. 739.

148 NA. Cab 23/95/37. Cabinet meetings, (1) 25 September 1938.

149 Toland, *Adolf Hitler*, p. 483.

150 NA. Cab 23/95/37. Cabinet meetings, (1) 25 September 1938.

151 DGFP, Series D, Vol. 2, No. 619, pp. 944–5. Chamberlain to Hitler, 26 September 1938.

152 Schmidt, *Hitler's Interpreter*, p. 110.

153 Hitler speech, Berlin, 26 September 1938, *Hitler: Speeches and Proclamations*, pp. 618–36.

154 Fest, *Hitler*, p. 557.

155 Ibid.

156 DGFP, Series D, Vol. 2, No. 618, p. 943. Statement by the Prime Minister, 26 September 1938.

157 Ibid., No. 632, pp. 958–959. President Roosevelt to Adolf Hitler, 26 September 1938.

158 Ibid., No. 633, pp. 960–62. Hitler to Roosevelt, 27 September 1938.

159 Ibid., No. 620, pp. 946–8. Friedrich Schulenburg to Foreign Ministry, 26 September 1938.

160 Ibid., No. 634, pp. 963–5. Memorandum of the conversation between Hitler and Sir Horace Wilson in the presence of Ribbentrop and Mr Kirkpatrick of British Embassy, 27 September 1938.

161 Ibid., No. 635, pp. 966–8. Hitler to Chamberlain, 27 September 1938.

162 *The Times*, 28 September 1938.

163 Schmidt, *Hitler's Interpreter*, p. 113.

164 DGFP, Series D, Vol. 2, No. 661, pp. 993–4. Hans Mackenen, the German ambassador to Italy, 28 September 1938.

165 Ibid., No. 663, p. 995. Statement issued to press by Foreign Ministry, 28 September 1938.

166 Ibid., No. 667, pp. 998–9. Friedrich Schulenburg to Foreign Ministry, 29 September 1938.

167 Ibid., No. 670, pp. 1003–1008. Memorandum on the first meeting at Munich conference between Chamberlain, Hitler, Daladier, Mussolini, 29 September 1938.

168 Schmidt, *Hitler's Interpreter*, p. 116.

169 DGFP, Series D, Vol. 2, No. 674, pp. 1011–1014. Memorandum on the second meeting at the Munich Conference between Chamberlain, Hitler, Daladier and Mussolini, 29 September 1938.

170 DGFP, Series D, Vol. 2, No. 675, pp. 1014–1015. Munich Agreement, dated 29 September 1938 (although signed on 30 September 1938).

171 Toland, *Adolf Hitler*, p. 492.

172 Longerich, *Goebbels*, p. 389.

173 Henderson, *Failure of a Mission*. p. 171.

174 Schmidt, *Hitler's Interpreter*, p. 118.

175 Fest, *Hitler*, p. 566.

176 Schmidt, *Hitler's Interpreter*, p. 120.

177 *The Times*, 2 October 1938.

178 Neville Chamberlain Papers, University of Birmingham Library, 18/1/1074, Neville Chamberlain to Ida Chamberlain, 22 October 1938.

179 Interview with Peter Schober, *Voices of the Third Reich*, p.106.

180 Interview with Siegfried Fischer, *Voices of the Third Reich*, p.107.

181 Longerich, *Goebbels*, p.390.

182 For a detailed account, see Milan Hauner 'The Sudeten Crisis of 1938: Beneš and Munich' in F. McDonough (ed.), *The Origins of the Second World War: An International Perspective* (Continuum, 2011), pp.360–373.

183 Hitler speech, Saarbrücken, 9 October 1938, in Adolf Hitler, *My New Order*, ed. R. de Roussy de Sales (Reynal and Hitchcock, 1941), pp.539–45.

184 *Documents on German Foreign Policy*, Series D, Vol. 4: *The Aftermath of Munich: October 1938–March 1939* (Washington, DC: US Government Printing Office, 1951), No. 55, pp.60–63. Conversation between Ribbentrop and Chavalovský, the Czech Foreign Minister, 13 October 1938. (Hereafter DGFP, Series D, Vol. 4.)

185 DGFP, Series D, Vol. 4, No,61, pp. 69–72. Conversation between Hitler and Chavalovský, Munich, 14 October 1938.

186 Ibid., No. 67, pp.81–2. Conversation between Göring and Czech Minister Vojtěch Mastný (most likely 16 October 1938).

187 Ibid., No. 68, pp.82–3. Conversation between Göring and Dr Ferdinand Ďurčanský, Slovak Minister in Berlin (most likely 17 October 1938).

188 Ibid., No. 81, pp.99–100. Directive by Hitler to the *Wehrmacht*, 21 October 1938.

189 Childers, *Third Reich*, p.362.

190 Cesarani, *Final Solution*, p.183.

191 Ullrich, *Hitler*, Vol. 1, p.670.

192 Shirer, *Rise and Fall*, p.525.

193 ADG-IFBG. Interview with Hans Frankenberger, 10 February 1994.

194 *Daily Telegraph*, 11 November 1938.

195 NA. FO 771/21637, Robert Smallbones, telegram, 11 November 1938.

196 Siemens, *Stormtroopers*, pp.183–216.

197 ADG-IFBG. Interview with Hedwig Müller, 23 June 1996, pp.468–519.

198 ADG-IFBG. Interview with Fritz Hennig, 13 June 1983, pp.408.

199 M. Gilbert, *Kristallnacht: Prelude to Destruction* (HarperCollins, 2006), p.75.

200 Longerich, *Goebbels*, p.399.

201 Ibid.

202 R. Conot, *Justice at Nuremberg* (New York, NY: Harper and Row, 1983), pp.164–72.

203 NA. FP (36), Cab, 27/624, Cabinet committee on foreign policy, 14 November 1938.

204 DGFP, Series D, Vol. 4, No. 143, pp.173–7. Andor Hencke, the German chargé d'affaires in Czechoslovakia to Foreign Ministry, 2 December 1938.

205 Ibid., No. 370, pp.471–7. Conversation between Ribbentrop and French Foreign Minister Bonnet on 6 December 1938 in Paris.

206 Ibid., No. 369, p.470. Franco-German declaration of 6 December 1938.

207 Bloch, *Ribbentrop*, pp.228–30.

208 A. Roberts, *The Holy Fox: A Biography of Lord Halifax* (Weidenfeld & Nicolson, 1991), p.132.

209 DGFP, Series D, Vol. 4, No. 150, pp.182–3. Andor Hencke, the German chargé d'affaires in Czechoslovakia to Foreign Ministry, 15 December 1938.

210 Ibid., No. 152, pp.185–6. Directive by the Chief of Staff of the Supreme Command of the *Wehrmacht* (Wilhelm Keitel), 17 December 1938.

CHAPTER 7

1 *Goulburn Penny Post*, New South Wales, Australia, 2 January 1939.

2 The two articles by H. G. Wells appeared in the *News Chronicle* on 2 and 3 January 1939. For the diplomatic fall out see DGFP, Series D, Vol. 4, No. 290, pp.377–9. Herbert von Dirksen to Foreign Ministry, 5 January 1939.

3 Roosevelt speech, Washington, DC, 4 January 1939, http://www.presidency. ucsb.edu/ws/index.php?pid=15684.

4 DGFP. Series D, Vol. 4, No. 291, pp.379–80. Dirksen to Foreign Ministry, 9 January 1939.

5 Shirer, *Rise and Fall*, p.557.

6 Tooze, *Wages of Destruction*, pp.297–9; *Hitler: Speeches and Proclamations*, pp.353–357.

7 G. Ciano, *The War Diaries of Count Galeazzo Ciano, 1939–43* (Fonthill, 2015), p.39. [Hereafter *Ciano Diaries*]

8 DGFP. Series D, Vol. 4, No. 435, pp.560–61. Mackensen to Foreign Ministry, 18 January 1939.

9 See D. Wragg, *Plan Z: The Nazi Bid for Naval Supremacy* (Pen & Sword, 2008).

10 DGFP. Series D, Vol. 4, No. 156, pp.190–95. The meeting by the Führer and the Czechoslovak Foreign Minister Chvalovský, 21 January 1939.

11 DGFP. Series D, Vol. 4, No. 161, pp.203–206. The chargé d'affaires in Czechoslovakia [Hencke], 27 January 1939.

12 Hitler speech, Berlin, 30 January 1939, *Hitler: Speeches and Proclamations*, pp.185–7, pp.271–3, pp.395–400, pp.434–7.

13 *The Times*, 7 February 1939.

14 Kershaw, *Hitler*, Vol. 2, p.168.

15 DGFP. Series D, Vol. 4, No. 168, pp. 209–213. Conversation between Hitler and Vojtech Tuka, 12 February 1939.

16 Hitler speech, Berlin, 18 February 1939, *Hitler: Speeches and Proclamations*, pp.357–63.

17 DGFP. Series D, Vol. 4, No. 175, pp. 218–20. Note verbale from German Foreign Ministry to French Embassy, 28 February 1939. An identical reply was sent to the British Embassy. In a handwritten marginal note Ernst Weizsäcker points out that Hitler had personally drafted the reply.

18 *Documents on German Foreign Policy*, Series D, Vol. 6: *The Last Months of Peace: March–August 1939* (Her Majesty's Stationery Office, 1956) [hereafter DGFP, Series D, Vol. 6], No. 1, pp.1–3, Schulenburg to Foreign Ministry, 13 March 1939.

See also G. Roberts, 'Stalin and the Outbreak of the Second World War', in McDonough (ed.), *Origins of the Second World War*, pp. 409–428.

19 DGFP. Series D, Vol. 4, No. 202, pp. 243–5. Conversation between Hitler and Tiso, 13 March 1939.

20 Ibid., No. 209, p. 250. President Tiso to Hitler (undated, but most likely drafted by Wilhelm Keppler on 13 March 1939 at the Foreign Ministry).

21 Ibid., No. 228, pp. 263–9. Conversation between Hitler and Czechoslovak President Hácha in the presence of Ribbentrop, 15 March 1939, 1.15 a.m. to 2.15 a.m.

22 Hitler described the meeting with Hácha in DGFP. Series D, Vol. 4, No. 296, p. 379. Conversation between Hitler and Pái Teleki, the Hungarian Prime Minister, 29 April 1939.

23 DGFP. Series D, Vol. 4, No. 229, p. 270. Declaration by the German and Czechoslovakian governments, 15 March 1939.

24 Shirer, *Rise and Fall*, pp. 542–6.

25 AP-IMT. Testimony of Joachim von Ribbentrop, 29 March 1946.

26 Shirer, *Rise and Fall*, pp. 546–8.

27 *The British War Blue Book: Documents concerning German-Polish Relations and the Outbreak of Hostilities between Britain and Germany on September 3, 1939* (New York: Farrar and Rinehart, 1939), pp. 6–13. [Hereafter BWBB.]

28 DGFP. Series D, Vol. 6, No. 20, pp. 20–21. Memorandum by Weizsäcker, 18 March 1939.

29 Ibid., No. 26, p. 27. Henderson to Ribbentrop, 18 March 1939.

30 Ibid., No. 50, pp. 52–5. Litvinov's note on the Czechoslovak affair, 18 March 1939.

31 Kershaw, *Hitler*, Vol. 2, pp. 172–3.

32 Ullrich, *Hitler*, Vol. 1, pp. 753–4.

33 DGFP. Series D, Vol. 6, No. 61, pp. 70–72. Memorandum by Ribbentrop, 21 March 1939.

34 Ibid., No. 99, pp. 117–119. Directive from Hitler to the commander-in-chief of the army, 25 March 1939.

35 Ibid., No. 101, pp. 121–6. Memorandum by Ribbentrop, 26 March 1939.

36 Ibid., No. 118, pp. 147–8. Moltke to Foreign Ministry, 29 March 1939.

37 *The Times*, 1 April 1939.

38 Fest, *Hitler*, p. 578.

39 NA. CAB 23/98, cabinet meeting, 5 April 1939.

40 NA. CAB 27, 'The Military Value of the Soviet Union', report by the Chiefs of Staff sub-committee, April 1939.

41 BWBB, No. 20. Hitler speech, Wilhelmshaven, 1 April 1939, pp. 52–63.

42 DGFP, Series D, Vol. 6, No. 149, pp. 186–7. Directive for the *Wehrmacht*, 1939–1940 [for Case White], 3 April 1939.

43 BWBB, No. 18. Anglo-Polish communiqué, 6 April 1939, p. 49.

44 DGFP, Series D, Vol. 6, No. 185, pp. 223–7. Directive for the uniform preparation for war by the *Wehrmacht*, 1939–1940 [Case White], 11 April 1939

45 Ibid., No. 200, pp. 243–5. President Roosevelt to Hitler, Telegram, 15 April 1939. (An identical telegram was sent to Mussolini.)

46 Ibid., No. 205, pp. 248–253. Record of conversation between Göring and Mussolini, 15 April 1939.

47 Ibid., No. 206, pp. 258–62. Record of conversation between Göring and Mussolini, 16 April 1939.

48 Shirer, *Rise and Fall*, p. 583.

49 DGFP, Series D, Vol. 6, No. 2015, pp. 266–7. Memorandum by Weizsäcker, 17 April 1939.

50 Ibid., No. 234, pp. 290–293. Conversation between Hitler and the Romanian Foreign Minister Grigore Gafencu, 19 April 1939.

51 Ullrich, *Hitler*, Vol. 1, pp. 756–7.

52 Two official notes were sent from the Foreign Ministry on 27 April, ending both agreements. For the text to the Poles denouncing the 1934 Polish-German Pact, see DGFP, Series D, Vol. 6, No. 276, pp. 347–51. For the text to the British government renouncing the 1935 Anglo-German Naval Agreement, see DGFP, Series D, Vol. 6, No. 277, pp. 351–2.

53 Hitler speech, Berlin, 28 April 1939, *Hitler: Speeches and Proclamations*, pp. 636–46, pp. 684–701.

54 DGFP, Series D, Vol. 6, No. 290, pp. 366–8. Chargé d'affaires in France [Kurt Bráuer] to Foreign Ministry, 29 March 1939.

55 Ibid., No. 324. pp. 419–420. Chargé d'affaires in Moscow [Tippelskirch] to Foreign Ministry, 4 May 1939.

56 Ibid., No. 332, p. 429. Memorandum by Julius Schnurre, Economic Policy Department, 5 May 1939.

57 BWBB, No. 15. Speech, Jósef Beck, Poland, 5 May 1939, pp. 36–42.

58 DGFP, Series D, Vol. 6, No. 334, pp. 430–35. Memorandum from the Polish government on German renunciation of the 1935 German-Polish Agreement, 5 May 1939.

59 Ibid., No. 331, pp. 426–8. Visit of Papal Nuncio to Hitler at the Berghof, 5 May 1939.

60 Ibid., No. 335, p. 346. Circular by Weizsäcker, 6 May 1939.

61 NA. FP (36), FO 371/230066/C7401, Foreign Policy Committee meeting, 16 May 1939.

62 NA, CAB 23/98, cabinet meeting, 24 May 1939.

63 DGFP, Series D, Vol. 6, No. 424, pp. 558–60. Schulenburg to Weizsäcker, 22 May 1939.

64 Ibid., No. 426, pp. 561–4. Text of Pact of Friendship and Alliance between Germany and Italy, 22 May 1939.

65 Ibid., No. 433, pp. 574–80. Minutes of Military Conference, Berlin, 23 May 1939.

66 Shirer, *Rise and Fall*, pp. 594–5.

67 DGFP, Series D, Vol. 6, No. 441, pp. 589–92. Ribbentrop to embassy in Soviet Union (undated, but thought to be 26 May 1939 due to a marginal handwritten note).

68 Ibid., No. 463, pp. 624–6. Schulenburg to Foreign Ministry, 1 June 1939.

69 Ibid., No. 497, pp. 674–84. Memorandum of 'Fact-finding Mission to Britain' 1–8 June 1939 [Adam von Trott zu Solz].

70 Ibid., No. 490, pp. 659–62. Memorandum by embassy in Soviet Union [unsigned, but most likely written by Schulenburg], 7 June 1939.

71 Ibid., No. 514, p. 711. Weizsäcker to embassy in the Soviet Union, 12 June 1939.

72 Ibid., No. 541, p. 743. Record of conversation of Khalid al-Hud al-Gargani with Hitler, 17 June 1939.

73 Ibid., No. 579, pp. 805–807. Schulenburg to Foreign Ministry, 29 June 1939.

74 Ibid., No. 583, p. 810. Memorandum by Foreign Minister's personal staff, 29 June 1939.

75 Bullock, *Hitler and Stalin*, p. 676.

76 DGFP, Series D, Vol. 6, No. 582, pp. 808–809. Schulenburg to Foreign Ministry, 29 June 1939.

77 BWBB. No. 25. Lord Halifax speech, Chatham House, London, 29 June 1939, pp. 78–87.

78 For a detailed analysis, see Burleigh, *Third Reich*, pp. 345–404.

79 DGFP, Series D, Vol. 6, No. 700, pp. 955–6. Weizsäcker to embassy in the Soviet Union, 22 July 1939.

80 Ibid., No. 729, pp. 1006–1009. Memorandum by Karl Schnurre, 27 July 1939.

81 The conversation is detailed in two documents. See DGFP, Series D, Vol. 6, No. 759, p. 1048, Ribbentrop to the embassy in the Soviet Union, 3 August 1939; and DGFP, Series D, Vol. 6, No. 760, pp. 1049–50, Ribbentrop to the embassy in the Soviet Union, 3 August 1939.

82 DGFP, Series D, Vol. 6, No. 766, pp. 1059–62. Schulenburg to Ribbentrop, 4 August 1939.

83 Shirer, *Rise and Fall*, p. 606.

84 DGFP, Series D, Vol. 6, No. 784, pp. 1093–1101. Record of reception of the Hungarian Foreign Minister István Csáky, Berghof, 8 August 1939.

85 *Ciano Diaries*, p. 106.

86 Ibid.

87 Ibid.

88 J. Holland, *The War in the West: A New History*, Vol. 1: *Germany Ascendant, 1939–1941* (Corgi, 2015), p. 15.

89 Shirer, *Rise and Fall*, p. 648.

90 Maisky, *Diaries*, p. 211.

91 Shirer, *Rise and Fall*, pp. 645–51.

92 Halder's notes on Hitler's speech at the Berghof, 14 August 1939, *Hitler: Speeches and Proclamations*, pp. 648–50.

93 R. Sontag and J. Beddie (eds.), *Nazi-Soviet Relations, 1939–1941: Documents from the Archives of the German Foreign Office* (Washington, DC: US Government Printing Office, 1948), Ribbentrop to Schulenburg, 14 August 1939. [Hereafter NSR.]

94 NSR, Memorandum by Schulenburg, 16 August 1939, pp. 53–6.

95 NSR, Ribbentrop to Schulenburg, 16 August 1939, p. 58.

96 NSR, Schulenburg to Ribbentrop, 19 August 1939, p. 63.

97 NSR, Hitler to Stalin, 20 August 1939, pp. 66–7.

98 NSR, Stalin to Hitler, 21 August 1939, p. 69.

99 R. Moorhouse, *Devils' Alliance: Hitler's Pact with Stalin, 1939–1941* (The Bodley Head, 2014), p. 35.

100 Bloch, *Ribbentrop*, p. 266.

101 BWBB, No. 56, Chamberlain to Hitler, 22 August 1939, pp. 125–7.

102 BWBB, No. 60, Hitler to Chamberlain, 23 August 1939, pp. 132–5.

103 Fest, *Hitler*, p. 595.

104 NSR, Text of Treaty of Non-Aggression between Germany and Soviet Union, including Secret Protocol, dated 23 August 1939 (signed 24 August), pp. 76–8.

105 NSR, memorandum of conversation held on the night of August 23 to August 24 between Ribbentrop, Stalin and Molotov, 24 August 1939, pp. 72–6.

106 Shirer, *Rise and Fall*, p. 638.

107 BWBB, No. 64. Neville Chamberlain speech, House of Commons, 24 August 1939, pp. 138–45.

108 BWBB, No. 19. Agreement of Mutual Assistance between the United Kingdom and Poland, 25 August 1939, pp. 49–52.

109 Fest, *Hitler*, p. 597.

110 Shirer, *Rise and Fall*, pp. 660–82.

111 Ibid., p. 687.

112 Fest, *Hitler*, p. 599.

113 Shirer, *Rise and Fall*, pp. 688–96.

114 Ibid., pp. 695–700.

115 BWBB, No. 84. Sir H. Kennard to Halifax, 30 August 1939, pp. 181–2.

116 BWBB, No. 88. Halifax to Henderson, 30 August 1939, pp. 183–4.

117 Henderson, *Failure of a Mission*, pp. 269–72.

118 Shirer, *Rise and Fall*, p. 703.

119 Fest, *Hitler*, p. 599.

120 J. Degras (ed.), *Soviet Documents on Foreign Policy* (Oxford: Oxford University Press, 1939), pp. 361–71.

121 N. Stargardt, *The German War: A Nation Under Arms, 1939–1945* (The Bodley Head, 2015), p. 28.

122 For details see R. Moorhouse, *First to Fight: The Polish War 1939* (The Bodley Head, 2019), prologue. See also M. Hastings, *All Hell Let Loose: The World at War, 1939–1945* (HarperPress, 2011), pp. 3–4.

123 Fest, *Hitler*, pp. 614–15.

124 Ibid., p. 600.

125 Hastings, *All Hell Let Loose*, p. 4.

126 K-H Frieser, *The Blitzkrieg Legend: The 1940 Campaign in the West* (Annapolis, MD: Naval Institute Press, 2012), pp. 4–5.

127 For a detailed examination of the operation of the *Wehrmacht* in Poland, see R. Citino 'The Prussian Tradition, the Myth of the Blitzkrieg and the Illusion of German Military Domination, 1939–1941' in McDonough (ed.), *Origins of the Second World War*, pp. 126–32.

128 A. Roberts, *The Storm of War: A New History of the Second World War* (Allen Lane, 2009), p. 21.

129 R. Evans, *The Third Reich*, Vol. 3: *The Third Reich at War* (Allen Lane, 2008), p. 11.

130 Cesarani, *Final Solution*, pp. 237–58.

131 C. Browning, *The Origins of the Final Solution, 1939–1942* (Arrow, 2005), p. 19.

132 Ibid., p. 28.

133 Evans, *The Third Reich at War*, p. 20.

134 A. Beevor, *The Second World War* (Phoenix, 2012), p. 30.

135 Shirer, *Rise and Fall*, pp. 728–9.

136 Ibid., pp. 722–3.

137 Toland, *Adolf Hitler*, p.570.

138 K. Feiling, *The Life of Neville Chamberlain* (Macmillan, 1946), p.416.

139 TA, CAB 23/98, cabinet meeting, 1 September 1939.

140 *The Times*, 2 September 1939.

141 *Documents on German Foreign Policy*, Series D, Vol. 8: *The War Years: 4 September 1939–18 March 1940* (Washington, DC: US Government Printing Office, 1954), No. 1, pp.1–2, Mackensen to Foreign Ministry, 4 September 1939. [Hereafter DGFP, Series D, Vol. 8.]

142 Toland, *Adolf Hitler*, p.573.

143 TA, CAB 23/98, cabinet meeting [2], 2 September 1939.

144 Toland, *Adolf Hitler*, p.575.

145 Fest, *Hitler*, p.601.

146 Toland, *Adolf Hitler*, p.576.

147 *The Times*, 4 September 1939.

148 Beevor, *Second World War*, p.28.

149 Litchfield, *Valkyrie*, pp.297–309. Unity Mitford died on 28 May 1948 due to meningitis caused by the bullet still lodged in her brain.

150 Kershaw, *Hitler*, Vol. 2, pp.235–6.

151 Hastings, *All Hell Let Loose*, p.70.

152 Evans, *The Third Reich at War*, p.21.

153 Cesarani, *Final Solution*, p.248.

154 Ibid., p.249.

155 Kershaw, *Hitler*, Vol. 2, p.242,

156 Evans, *The Third Reich at War*, pp.8–9.

157 Cesarani, *Final Solution*, p.245.

158 Beevor, *Second World War*, p. 36.

159 Burleigh, *Moral Combat: A History of World War II* (HarperPress, 2010), p.133.

160 Ohler, *Blitzed*, pp.49–51.

161 Ibid., pp.64–5.

162 DGFP, Series D, Vol. 8, No. 30, pp.30–31. Command of the Führer, 8 September 1939.

163 Citino, 'Myth of the *Blitzkrieg*', pp.131–3.

164 DGFP, Series D, Vol. 8, No. 40. pp.36–8. Ribbentrop to the ambassador in Japan, 9 September 1939.

165 Ibid., No. 43, p.41. Führer's Directive No. 3 for the Conduct of War, 9 September 1939.

166 Ibid., No. 70, pp.68–70. Ribbentrop to embassy in Soviet Union, 15 September 1939.

167 Ibid., No. 78, pp.76–7. Schulenburg to Foreign Ministry, 16 September 1939.

168 Hastings, *All Hell Let Loose*, p.15.

169 Evans, *The Third Reich at War*, pp. 44–5.

170 DGFP, Series D, Vol. 8, No. 94, pp.95–6. Memorandum by official in the embassy in the Soviet Union, 18 September 1939.

171 Ibid., No. 104, p.105. Schulenburg to Foreign Ministry, 20 September 1939.

172 Ibid., No. 135, pp.135–6. Führer's Directive No. 4 for the Conduct of War, 25 September 1939.

173 McDonough, *Holocaust*, pp.30–31.

174 DGFP, Series D, Vol. 8, No. 157, pp.164–6. German-Soviet Boundary and Friendship Treaty, 28 September 1939.

175 Cesarani, *Final Solution*, p.250.

176 Beevor, *Second World War*, p.35.

177 Cesarani, *Final Solution*, p.244.

178 Evans, *The Third Reich at War*, p.7.

179 DGFP, Series D, Vol. 8, No. 170, pp.176–7. Führer's Directive No. 5 for the Conduct of War, 30 September 1939.

180 Ibid., No. 176, pp.184–94. Conversation between Hitler and Count Ciano in the Reich Chancellery, 1 October 1939.

181 *New York Times*, 7 October 1939.

182 Shirer, *Rise and Fall*, pp.772–3.

183 M. Mazower, *Hitler's Empire: Nazi Rule in Occupied Europe* (Allen Lane, 2008), p.81.

184 Evans, *The Third Reich at War*, p.34.

185 Kershaw, *Hitler*, Vol. 2, p.245.

186 *Hitler: Speeches and Proclamations*, pp.278–9.

187 McDonough, *Holocaust*, pp.30–33.

188 DGFP, Series D, Vol. 8, No. 224, pp.248–50. Führer's Directive No. 6 for the Conduct of War, 9 October 1939.

189 Ibid., No. 270, pp.307–308. Memorandum by Weizsäcker, 17 October 1939.

190 Ibid., No. 263, pp.293–297. Visit of Swedish Explorer Sven Hedin to Hitler, Berlin, 18 October 1939.

191 Shirer, *Rise and Fall*, pp.777–84.

192 To prevent Elser falling into Allied hands, he was executed by the SS in Dachau in April 1945.

193 R. Moorhouse, *Killing Hitler: The Third Reich and the Plots against the Führer* (Vintage, 2007), pp.36–58.

194 DGFP, Series D, Vol. 8, No. 377, pp.430–32. Führer's Directive No. 6 for the Conduct of War, 20 November 1939.

195 Ibid., No. 377, pp.439–47. Memorandum of Conference of Hitler with Principal Army Commanders, 23 November 1939.

196 Shirer, *Rise and Fall*, pp.791–2.

197 DGFP, Series D, Vol. 8, No. 299, pp.463–5. Führer's Directive No. 6 for the Conduct of War against the Enemy's Economy, 29 November 1939.

198 R. Overy, *Russia's War* (Penguin, 1999), pp.55–8. See also Roberts, *Storm of War*, pp.29–35 and Moorhouse, *Devils' Alliance*, pp.80–90.

199 DGFP, Series D, Vol. 8, No. 443, pp.519–21. Report of commander-in-chief of the navy [Raeder] to Hitler, 12 November 1939.

200 Roberts, *Storm of War*, pp.35–8.

201 Shirer, *Rise and Fall*, pp.811–15.

202 Ibid., p.805.

203 GWPA, Goebbels speech, German National Radio, 31 December 1939. See 'Jahreswechsel 1939/40, Sylvesteransprache an das deutsche Volk', *Die Zeit ohne Beispiel* (Munich: Zentralverlag der NSDAP, 1941), pp.229–39.

BIBLIOGRAPHY

BOOKS AND ARTICLES
Place of publication is London, UK, unless otherwise stated.

Adam, U. 'An Overall Plan for Anti-Jewish Legislation in the Third Reich', *Yad Vashem Studies*, Vol. 11 (1976), pp.33–55

Adamthwaite, A. *France and the Coming of the Second World War* (Routledge, 1977).

Allen, W. *The Nazi Seizure of Power: The Experience of a Single German Town, 1922–1945* (New York: Franklin Watts, 1984)

Aly, G. *Aktion T4 1939–1945. Die 'Euthanasie'-Zentrale in der Tiergartenstrasse 4* (Berlin: Rotbuch, 1989)
———— Chroust, P. and Pross, C. *Cleansing the Fatherland: Nazi Medicine and Racial Hygiene* (Baltimore: Johns Hopkins University Press, 1994)

Angress, T. and Smith, B. 'Diaries of Heinrich Himmler's Early Years', *Journal of Modern History*, Vol. 31 (1959), pp.206–24.

Aronson, S. *The Beginnings of the German Gestapo: The Bavarian Model in 1933* (Jerusalem: Israel Universities Press, 1970)

Arendt, H. *The Origins of Totalitarianism* (Andre Deutsch, 1951)
———— *Eichmann in Jerusalem: A Report on the Banality of Evil* (Penguin, 1994)

Ayçoberry, P. *The Social History of the Third Reich, 1933–1945* (The New Press, 1999)

Bach, S. *Leni: The Life and Work of Leni Riefenstahl* (New York: Vintage, 2007)

Bajohr, F. *'Aryanisation' in Hamburg: The Economic Exclusion of the Jews and the Confiscation of their Property in Nazi Germany* (New York: Berghahn, 2002)

Bankier, D. *The Germans and the Final Solution: Public Opinion under Nazism* (Oxford: Blackwell, 1996)
————(ed.) *Probing the Depths of German Anti-Semitism: German Society and the Persecution of the Jews, 1933–1941* (New York: Berghahn, 2000)

Baranowski, S. *The Confessing Church: Conservative Elites and the Nazi Elite* (Lewiston, NY: Edward Mellen Press, 1986)

Barkai, A. *From Boycott to Annihilation: The Economic Struggle of German Jews, 1933–1943* (Harrisburg, PA: Brandeis University Press, 1990)

Barnett, V. *For the Soul of the People: Protestant Protest against Hitler* (Oxford: Oxford University Press, 1992)

Bauer, Y. *The Holocaust in Historical Perspective* (Seattle: University of Washington Press, 1978)

Baynes, N. (ed.) T*he Speeches of Adolf Hitler*, 2 vols (Oxford: Oxford University Press, 1942)

Beevor, A. *The Second World War* (Phoenix, 2011)

Behnken, K. (ed.) *Deutschland Berichte der Sozial democratischen Partei Deutschlands (SOPADE), 1934–1940*, 7 vols (Frankfurt am Main: P. Nettlebeck, 1980)

Bentley, J. *Martin Niemöller* (Oxford: Oxford University Press, 1984)

Bergen, D. *Twisted Cross: The German Christian Movement in the Third Reich* (Chapel Hill, NC: University of North Carolina Press, 1996)

Berschel, H. *Bürokratie und Terror: Das Judenreferat der Gestapo Düsseldorf, 1935–1945* (Essen: Klartext, 2001)

Bethell, N. *The War Hitler Won: The Fall of Poland, September 1939* (New York: Holt, Rinehart & Winston, 1972)

Bessel, R. *Political Violence and the Rise of Nazism: The Stormtroopers in Eastern Germany, 1925–1934* (New Haven, CT: Yale University Press, 1984)
———— (ed.) *Life in the Third Reich* (Oxford: Oxford University Press, 1987)

Best, W. *Die deutsche Polizei* (Darmstadt: L. C. Wittlich Verlag, 1941)

Bielenberg, C. *Ride Out of the Dark: The Experience of An Englishwoman in Wartime Germany* (Boston: G. K. Hall, 1968)

Bloch, M. *Ribbentrop* (Abacus, 2003)

Bluel, H. *Strength Through Joy: Sex and Society in Nazi Germany* (Secker & Warburg, 1973)

Bonnet, G. *De Munich a la Guerre: Défense de la Paix* (Paris: Plon, 1967)

Browder, G. *The Foundation of the Nazi Police State: The Formation of Sipo and S.D.* (Lexington, KY: University Press of Kentucky, 1990)
———— *Hitler's Enforcers: The Gestapo and S.S. Security Service in the Nazi Revolution* (New York/Oxford: Oxford University Press, 1996)

Boyd, J. *Travellers in the Third Reich: The Rise of Fascism Through the Eyes of Everyday People* (Elliott & Thompson, 2017)

Bracher K. *The German Dictatorship: The Origins, Structures, and Effects of National Socialism* (Pelican, 1973)

Bramstedt, E. K. *Dictatorship and Political Police: The Technique of Control by Fear* (K. Paul, Trench, Trubner & Co., Ltd, 1945)

Bridenthal, R., Grossmann, A. and Kaplan, M. (eds) *When Biology Became Destiny: Women in Weimar and Nazi and Germany* (New York: Monthly Review Press, 1984)

Browning, C. *The Origins of the Final Solution. The Evolution of Jewish Policy 1939–1942* (Arrow, 2005)

Broszat, M. *The Hitler State: The Foundation and Development of the Internal Structure of the Third Reich* (Longman, 1981)

———, *et al* (eds) *Bayern in der NS-Zeit*, 6 vols. (Munich-Vienna: Oldenbourg, 1977–1983)

——— *Hitler and the Collapse of Weimar Germany* (Oxford: Berg, 1987)

Brustein, W. I. *Roots of Hate. Anti-Semitism in Europe before the Holocaust* (Cambridge: Cambridge University Press, 2003)

Bullock, A. *Hitler: A Study in Tyranny* (Penguin, revised edn, 1962)

——— *Hitler and Stalin: Parallel Lives* (HarperCollins, 1991)

Burleigh, M. *Death and Deliverance. 'Euthanasia' in Germany 1900–1945* (Cambridge: Cambridge University Press, 1994)

——— *Ethics and Extermination: Reflections on Nazi Genocide* (Cambridge: Cambridge University Press, 1997)

——— *The Third Reich: A New History* (Macmillan, 2000)

Burleigh, M. and Wippermann, W *The Racial State. Germany 1933–1945* (Cambridge: Cambridge University Press, 1991)

Burleigh, M. *Moral Combat: A History of World War II* (HarperPress, 2010)

Burden, H. T. *The Nuremberg Rallies, 1923–1939* (Pall Mall Press, 1967)

Burrin, P. *Hitler and the Jews: The Genesis of the Holocaust* (Arnold, 1994)

Butler, J. *Lord Lothian* (Macmillan, 1961)

Caplan, J. *Government without Administration: State and Civil Service in Weimar and Nazi Germany* (Oxford: Oxford University Press)

Cesarani, D. (ed.) *The Final Solution: Origins and Implementation* (Routledge, 1994)

——— *Eichmann: His Life and Crimes* (Heinemann, 2004)

——— *The Final Solution: The Fate of the Jews, 1933–1949* (Macmillan, 2016)

Challener, R. D. *The French Theory of a Nation at Arms, 1886–1939* (New York: Columbia University Press, 1955)

Childers, T. *The Nazi Voter: The Social Foundations of Fascism in Germany, 1919–1933* (Chapel Hill, NC: University of North Carolina Press, 1983)

——— *The Third Reich: A History of Nazi Germany* (Simon & Schuster, 2017)

Childers, T. and Caplan, J. (eds) *Re-Evaluating the Third Reich* (New York: Holmes and Meier, 1993)

Churchill, W. *The Second World War: Vol 1: The Gathering Storm* (Penguin, 2005)

Ciano, G. *The War Diaries of Count Galeazzo Ciano, 1939–43* (Fonthill, 2015)

Citino, R. *The German Way of War: From the Thirty Years' War to the Third Reich* (Lawrence, KS, University Press of Kansas, 2008)

Clark, C. *The Conditions of Economic Progress* (Macmillan, 1940)

Cohen E. *Human Behaviour in the Concentration Camp* (Free Association Books, 1988)

Conot, R. *Justice at Nuremberg* (New York, NY: Harper and Row, 1983)

Conway, J. *The Nazi Persecution of the Churches, 1933–1945* (Vancouver: Regent College Publishing, 1968)

——— *Hitler's Scientists* (Viking, 2003)

Corum, J. *The Luftwaffe: Creating the Operational Air War, 1918–1940* (Lawrence, University of Kansas Press, 1997)

Coverdale, J. *Italian Intervention in the Spanish Civil War* (Princeton: Princeton University Press, 1975)

Crew, D. (ed.) *Nazism and German Society 1933–1945* (Routledge, 1994)

Dahlerus, B. *The Last Attempt* (Hutchinson, 1948)

Dawidowicz, L. *The War against the Jews 1933–45* (Pelican, 1979)

de Roussy de Sales, R. (ed) *My New Order* (Reynal and Hitchcock, 1941)

Dedencks, M. *Heydrich: The Face of Evil* (Greenhill, 2006)

Degras, J. (ed.) *Soviet Documents on Soviet Foreign Policy* (Oxford: Oxford University Press, 1939)

Deschner, G. *Heydrich: The Pursuit of Total Power* (Orbis, 1981)

Diels, R. *Lucifer ante Portas … es spricht der erste Chef der Gestapo* (Stuttgart: Dt. Verl.-Anst., 1950)

Diest, W. *The Wehrmacht and German Rearmament* (Toronto: University of Toronto Press, 1981)

DGFP Documents on German Foreign Policy (Series C), 1933–1937, Vol. 1: *The Third Reich First Phase, January 30–October 14, 1933*; Vol. 2: *The Third Reich First Phase, October 15, 1933–June 13, 1934*; Vol. 3: *The Third Reich First Phase, June 14, 1934–March 31, 1935*; Vol. 4: *The Third Reich First Phase, April 1, 1935–March 4, 1936*; Vol. 5: *The Third Reich First Phase, March 5, 1936–October 31, 1936*; Vol. 6: *The Third Reich First Phase, November 5, 1936–November 14 1937* (Her Majesty's Stationery Office, 1957–83)

——— Documents on German Foreign Policy (Series D), 1937–1941, Vol. 1: *From Neurath to Ribbentrop, September 1937–September 1938*; Vol. 2: *Germany and Czechoslovakia, 1937–1938*; Vol. 3: *The Spanish Civil War*; Vol. 4: *The Aftermath of Munich, October 1938–March 1939*; Vol 5.: *Poland, the Balkans, Latin America and the Smaller Powers, June 1937–March 1938*; Vol. 6: *The Last Months of Peace, March–August 1939*; Vol. 7: *The Last Days of Peace, August 9–September 1939*; Vol. 8: *The War Years, September 4, 1939–March 18, 1940* (Her Majesty's Stationery Office, 1949–54)

Dodd, W and Dodd, M. *Ambassador Dodd's Diary* (Gollancz, 1939)

Domarus, M. *The Essential Hitler: Speeches and Commentary* (Wauconda, IL: Bolchazy-Carducci, 2007)

Duhnke, H *Die KPD von 1933 bis 1945* (Cologne: Kiepenheuer & Witsch, 1972)

Eberle, H. (ed.) *Letters to Hitler* (Cambridge: Polity Press, 2012)

Eden, A. *The Eden Memoirs: Facing the Dictators* (Cassel, 1962)

Eley, G. *From Unification to Nazism: Reinterpreting the Nazi Past* (Allen & Unwin, 1986)

Emerson, J. *The Rhineland Crisis, 7 March 1936: A Study in Multilateral Diplomacy* (Maurice Temple Smith, 1977)

Engelmann, B. *In Hitler's Germany: Daily Life in the Third Reich* (New York: Pantheon, 1986)

Evans, R. J. (ed.) *The German Underworld: Deviants and Outcasts in German History* (Oxford: Oxford University Press, 1988)
——— *Rituals of Retribution: Capital Punishment in Germany 1600–1987* (Oxford: Oxford University Press)
——— *The Third Reich*, 3 vols, Vol. 1: *The Coming of the Third Reich*; Vol. 2: *The Third Reich in Power*; Vol. 3: *The Third Reich at War* (Allen Lane, 2003–2008)
——— *The Third Reich in History and Memory* (Little, Brown, 2015)

Fahlbusch, M. and Haar, I. (eds) *German Scholars and Ethnic Cleansing, 1920–1945* (New York: Berghahn, 2004)

Farquharson, J. *The Plough and the Swastika: N.S.D.A.P. and Agriculture in Germany, 1928–1945* (Bloomington, IN: Indiana University Press)

Feiling, K. *The Life of Neville Chamberlain* (Macmillan, 1946)

Feldman, M (ed.) *A Fascist Century: Essays by Roger Griffin* (Basingstoke: Palgrave, Macmillan, 2008)

Fest, J. *Hitler* (Penguin, 1982)

Fischer, C. *Stormtroopers: A Social, Economic and Ideological Analysis, 1929–1935* (Routledge, rev. edn, 2014)
——— (ed.) *The Rise of National Socialism and the Working Classes in Weimar Germany* (New York: Berghahn, 1996)

Fraenkel. E. *The Dual State: A Contribution to the Theory of Dictatorship* (Clark, NJ: The Lawbook Exchange, 2006 edn)

Frei, N. *National Socialist Rule in Germany: The Führer State, 1933–1945* (Oxford: Blackwell, 1993)

Friedländer, S. *Nazi Germany and the Jews*, Vol 1: *The Years of Persecution 1933–39* (Phoenix, 1998)

Frieser, K-H *The Blitzkrieg Legend: The 1940 Campaign in the West* (Annapolis, MD: Naval Institute Press, 2012)

Fröhlich, E. (ed.) *Die Tagebücher von Joseph Goebbels*, Vol. 1: *Aufzeichnungen 1923–1941*, 9 vols; Vol. 2: *Diktate 1941–1945*, 15 vols (Munich: K. G. Saur, 1993–2000)

Fulbrook, M. *A History of Germany, 1918–2014: The Divided Nation* (Chichester, John Wiley & Sons, 2015)

Gamelin, M. *Servir* (Paris: Plon, 1947), 3 vols

Garbe, D. *Zwischen Widerstand und Martyrium: Die Zeugen Jehovas im 'Dritten Reich'* (Munich: Oldenbourg, 1994)

Gebauer, T. *Das KPD-Dezernat der Gestapo Düsseldorf* (Hamburg: Disserta Verlag, 2011)

Gellately, R. *The Gestapo and German Society: Enforcing Racial Policy 1933–1945* (Oxford: Clarendon Press, 1990)
——— *Backing Hitler: Consent and Coercion in Nazi Germany* (Oxford: Oxford University Press, 2001)

Gellately, R. and Fitzpatrick, S. (eds) *Accusatory Practices: Denunciations in Modern European History, 1789–1989* (Chicago: University of Chicago Press, 1997)

Gellately, R. and Stolfus, N. (eds) *Social Outsiders in Nazi Germany* (Princeton, NJ: Princeton University Press, 2001)

Gerlach, W. *And the Witnesses were Silent: The Confessing Church and the Persecution of the Jews* (Lincoln, NB: University of Nebraska Press, 2000)

Gerhart, U and Karlauf, T. (eds) *The Night of the Broken Glass: Eyewitness Accounts of Kristallnacht* (Polity, 2012)

Gerwarth, R. *Reinhard Heydrich* (Munich: Siedler, 2011)

Gilbert, M. *Kristallnacht: Prelude to Destruction* (HarperCollins, 2006)

Glass, J. *Life Unworthy of Life: Racial Phobia and Murder in Hitler's Germany* (Basic Books, 1997)

Goldhagen, D. *Hitler's Willing Executioners: Ordinary Germans and the Holocaust* (Abacus, 1996)

Gordon, S. *Hitler, Germans and the Jewish Question* (Princeton, NJ: Princeton University Press, 1984)

Gorlitz, W. (ed.) *The Memoirs of Field Marshal Keitel* (New York: Stein and Day, 1966)

Gorodetsky, G. (ed.) *The Maisky Diaries: Red Ambassador to the Court of St James, 1932–1943* (New Haven, CT: Yale University Press, 2015)

Görtemaker, H. *Eva Braun: Life with Hitler* (Penguin, 2012)

Graber, G. *History of the SS* (Robert Hale, 1978)

Graml, H. *Antisemitism in the Third Reich* (Oxford: Oxford University Press, 1992)

Grau, G. (ed.) *Hidden Holocaust? Gay and Lesbian Persecution in Germany 1933–45* (New York: Continuum, 1995)
——— (ed.) *Homosexualität in der NS-Zeit: Dokumente einer Diskriminierung und Verfolgung* (Frankfurt am Main: Fischer, 1993)

Gregor, N. (ed.) *Nazism, War and Genocide. Essays in Honour of Jeremy Noakes* (Exeter: University of Exeter Press, 2005)

Griffiths, R. *Fellow Travellers of The Right: British Enthusiasts for Nazi Germany, 1933–1939* (Faber & Faber, 1983)

Gruchmann, L. *Justiz im Dritten Reich 1933–1940: Anpassung und Unterwerfung in der Ära Gürtner* (Munich: Oldenbourg, 1988)

Grunberger, R. *A Social History of the Third Reich* (Penguin, 1971)

Hake, S. *Popular Cinema in the Third Reich* (Austin, TX: University of Texas Press, 2001)

Halasz, J. *Hitler's Winter Olympics: A Photo Book* (Foxley Books, 2009)

Hale, O. *The Captive Press in the Third Reich* (Princeton, NJ: University Princeton Press, 1964)

Hall, C. 'An Army of Spies? The Gestapo Spy Network, 1933–1945', *Journal of Contemporary History*, Vol. 44 (2009)

Hamilton, R. *Who Voted for Hitler?* (Princeton, NJ: University Princeton Press, 1964)

Hanfstaengl, E. *Hitler: The Missing Years* (Eyre & Spottiswoode, 1957)

Hart-Davis, D. *Hitler's Games: The 1936 Olympics* (Century, 1996)

Hartmanns-Gruber, F. (ed.) *Akten der Reichskanzlei: Regierung Hitler, 1934–1945*, 5 vols (Munich: Oldenbourg, 1999–2012)

Hastings, M. *All Hell Let Loose: The World at War, 1939–1945* (HarperPress, 2015)

Hassell, U. *The Ullrich von Hassell Diaries, 1938–1944: The Story of the Forces Against Hitler Inside Germany* (Barnsley: Frontline Books, 2011)

Hauner, M. 'Did Hitler want World Domination?', *Journal of Contemporary History*, Vol. 13 (1978)
———— *Hitler: A Chronology of His Life and Times* (Basingstoke: Palgrave Macmillan, 2008)

Hayes, P. 'A Question Mark with Epaulettes?': Kurt von Schleicher and Weimar Politics, *Journal of Modern History*, Vol. 52 (1980)

———— *Industry and Ideology: IG Farben in the Nazi Era* (Cambridge, MA: Harvard University Press, 1987)

Helmreich, E. *The German Churches under Hitler: Background, Struggle and Epilogue* (Detroit: Wayne State University Press, 1979)

Henderson, N. *Failure of a Mission, Berlin 1937–1939* (Hodder & Stoughton, 1940)

Henry, F. *Victims and Neighbours: A Small Town in Nazi Germany Remembered* (South Hadley, MA: Bergin & Garvey, 1984)

Herbert, U. 'The Real Mystery in Germany: The Working Class During the Nazi Dictatorship', in Burleigh, M. (ed.), *Confronting the Nazi Past* (Collins and Brown, 1996)

Heston, L. and Heston, R. *The Medical Casebook of Adolf Hitler: His Illnesses, Doctors and Drugs* (William Kimber, 1979)

Hett, B. *Burning the Reichstag: An Investigation into the Third Reich's Enduring Mystery* (Oxford: Oxford University Press, 2014)

Heydrich, L. *Leben mit einem Kriegsverbrecher* (Pfaffenhofen: Verlag W. Ludwig, 1976)

Hiden, J. and Farquharson, J. *Explaining Hitler's Germany: Historians and the Third Reich* (Totowa, NJ: Barnes and Noble, 1983)

Hildebrand, K. *The Third Reich* (Allen & Unwin, 1984)

Hinz, B. *Art in the Third Reich* (New York: Pantheon, 1979)

Hitchens, M. *Abdication: The Rise and Fall of Edward VIII* (The Book Guild, 2016)

Hoehling, A. *Who Destroyed the Hindenburg?* (Little, Brown, 1962)

Hoffmann, H. *Hitler Was My Friend* (Frontline, 2014)

Holland, J. *The War in the West: A New History*, Vol. 1: *Germany Ascendant, 1939–1941* (Corgi, 2015)

Holmes, R. *The World at War: The Landmark Oral History from the Classic TV Series* (Ebury, 2011)

Horn, D. 'The Hitler Youth and Educational Decline in the Third Reich', *History of Education Quarterly*, Vol. 16 (1976)

Hossbach, F. *Die Entwicklung des Oberbefehls über Heer in Brandenburg, Preussen und im Deutschen Reich von 1955–1945* (Wurzbürg: Holzner Verlag, 1957)
———— *Zwischen Wehrmacht und Hitler, 1934–1938* (Göttingen: Vandenhoeck & Ruprecht, 1965)

Housden, M. *Resistance and Conformity in the Third Reich* (Abingdon: Routledge, 1997)

IMT *Trials of the Major War Criminals before the International Military Tribunal*, 42 vols (Nuremberg: International Military Tribunal, 1947–1949)
———— *Nazi Conspiracy and Aggression (Documents from the Nuremberg Trials of the Major War Criminals)*, 8 vols (Washington, DC: US Government Printing Office, 1946–1948)

Jäckel, E. *Hitler's World View: Blueprint for Power* (Cambridge, MA: Harvard University Press, 1981)

Jacobsen, H (ed.) *General Franz Halder: Kriegstagebuch, 1939–1943*, 3 vols (Stuttgart: W. Kohlhammer, 1962–1964)

Joachimsthaler, A. *Hitlers Liste: Dokumente Privater Beziehungen* (Munich. F.A.: Herbig, 2003)

Johnson, E. *The Nazi Terror: The Gestapo, Jews and Ordinary Germans* (John Murray, 1999)
———— and Reuband, K. *What We Knew: Terror, Mass Murder and Everyday Life in Nazi Germany* (John Murray, 2005)

Johnson, G. (ed) *Our Man in Berlin: The Diary of Sir Edward Phipps, 1933–1937* (Basingstoke: Palgrave Macmillan)

Jones, L. 'The Greatest Stupidity of My Life: Alfred Hugenberg and the formation of the Hitler Cabinet,

January 1933', *Journal of Contemporary History*, Vol. 27 (1992)

Jones, T. *A Diary with Letters, 1931–1950* (Oxford: Oxford University Press, 1954)

Kaplan, M. *Between Dignity and Despair: Jewish Life in Nazi Germany* (Oxford: Oxford University Press, 1998)

Kater, M. *Doctors under Hitler* (Chapel Hill, NC: University of North Carolina Press, 1989)
——— *The Twisted Muse: Musicians and Their Music in the Third Reich* (Oxford: Oxford University Press, 1997)

Keegan, J. *The Second World War* (Pimlico, 1989)

Kershaw, I. *The Hitler Myth: Image and Reality in the Third Reich* (Oxford: Oxford University Press, 1987)
——— *Popular Opinion and Political Dissent in the Third Reich: Bavaria 1933–1945* (Oxford: Oxford University Press, 1983)
——— *The Nazi Dictatorship: Problems and Perspectives of Interpretation* (4th edn, Arnold, 2000)
——— *Hitler*, Vol. 1: *Hubris, 1889–1936* (Penguin, 1998)
——— *Hitler*, Vol. 2: *Nemesis, 1936–1945* (Penguin, 2000)
——— *Making Friends with Hitler: Lord Londonderry and Britain's Road to War* (Allen Lane, 2005)

Klee, E. *'Euthanasie' im NS-Staat: die 'Vernichtung lebensunwerten Lebens'* (Frankfurt am Main: Fischer, 1983)

Klemperer, V. *I Shall Bear Witness: The Diaries of Victor Klemperer, Vol. 1: 1933–41* (Phoenix, 1998)

Kochan, L. *Pogrom: November 10, 1938* (André Deutsch)

Kogon, E. *The Theory and Practice of Hell: The German Concentration Camps and the System Behind Them* (New York: Berkeley, 1964)

Koonz, C. *Mothers in the Fatherland: Women, the Family and Nazi Politics* (Methuen, 1988)

Krausnick H. and Broszat M. *Anatomy of the SS State* (Paladin, 1973)

Krosigk, L. *Es geschah in Deutschland* (Tübingen: Wunderlich, 1951)

Kruger, A. 'The Nazi Olympics of 1936' in Young, K. and Walmsley, K. B. (eds) *Global Olympics: Historical and Sociological Studies of the Modern Games* (Oxford: Elsevier, 2005)

Lang, J. von *Die Gestapo: Instrument des Terrors* (Hamburg: Rasch und Röhring, 1990)
——— and Sibyll, C. (eds) *Eichmann Interrogated: Transcripts from the Archives of the Israeli Police* (Washington, DC: Da Capo Press, 1999)

Leitz, C. *Nazi Foreign Policy, 1933–1941* (Routledge, 2004)

Leopold, J. *Alfred Hugenburg* (New Haven, CT: Yale University Press, 1977)

Levy, J. P. *Appeasement and Rearmament: Britain, 1936 to 1939* (Oxford: Rowman & Littlefield, 2006)

Lewy, G. *The Catholic Church and Nazi Germany* (Washington, DC: Da Capo Press, 2000)
——— *The Nazi Persecution of the Gypsies* (Oxford: Oxford University Press, 2000)

Lifton, R. *The Nazi Doctors: A Study of the Psychology of Evil* (Macmillan, 1986)

Litchfield, D. *Hitler's Valkyrie: The Uncensored Biography of Unity Mitford* (Stroud: The History Press, 2015)

Longerich, P. *Heinrich Himmler: A Life* (Oxford: Oxford University Press, 2012)
——— *Goebbels* (Vintage, 2015)

Lossberg, B. *Im Wehrmachtführungsstab* (Hamburg: Nölke, 1950)

Lubrich, O. (ed.), *Travels in the Third Reich: Foreign Authors Report from Germany* (Chicago: University of Chicago Press, 2010)

Lukacs, J. *The Hitler of History: Hitler's Biographers on Trial* (Weidenfeld & Nicolson, 2000)

Machtan, L. *The Hidden Hitler* (Oxford: The Perseus Press, 2001)

Maschmann, M *Account Rendered: A Dossier on My Former Self* (London/New York: Abelard-Schumann, 1964)

Mann, R. *Protest und Kontrolle im Dritten Reich: Nationalsozialistische Herrschaft im Alltag einer rheinischen Grosstadt* (Frankfurt am Main: Campus, 1987)

Manstein, E. *Lost Victories: The War Memoirs of Hitler's Most Brilliant General* (TBS The Book Service, 2004)

Mason, T. *Social Policy in the Third Reich: The Working Class and the 'National Community'* (Oxford: Oxford University Press, 1993)

Mazower, M. *Hitler's Empire: Nazi Rule in Occupied Europe* (Allen Lane, 2008)

McDonough, F. *Hitler and the Rise of the Nazi Party* (Pearson, 2012)
——— *Neville Chamberlain, Appeasement and the British Road to War* (Manchester: Manchester University Press, 1998)
——— *Opposition and Resistance in Nazi Germany* (Cambridge: Cambridge University Press, 2001)
——— with Cochrane, J. *The Holocaust* (Basingstoke: Palgrave Macmillan, 2008)
——— *Sophie Scholl: The Real Story of the Woman Who Defied Hitler* (Stroud: The History Press, 2010)
——— (ed.), *The Origins of the Second World War: An International Perspective* (Continuum, 2011)
——— *The Gestapo: The Myth and Reality of Hitler's Secret Police* (Coronet, 2015)

McElligott, A and Kirk, T. (eds) *Working Towards the Fuhrer: Essays in Honour of Sir Ian Kershaw* (Manchester: Manchester University Press, 2003)

Medlicott, W. Deakin, D. and Lambert, M. (eds) *Documents on British Foreign Policy, 1919–1939, 2nd Series, 1930–1937* (Her Majesty's Stationery Office, Series C. Vol. 3, No. 555, 1946)

Meissner, O. *Sraasssekretär, unter Ebert, Hindenburg, Hitler* (Hamburg: Hoffmann and Campe, 1950)

Merson, A. *Communist Resistance in Nazi Germany* (Lawrence & Wishart, 1985)

Miller, J. *Belgian Foreign Policy between the Wars, 1919–1940* (New York: Bookman Associates, 1951)

Minuth, K. (ed.) *Akten der Reichskanzlei: Die Regierung Hitler, 1933–1934*, 2 vols (Boppard am Rhein: Harald Boldt, 1983)

Mommsen, H. 'Hitler's Reichstag Speech, 30 January 1939', *History and Memory*, Vol. 9 (1977)

Moorhouse, R. *First to Fight: The Polish War 1939* (The Bodley Head, 2019)
—————— *Killing Hitler: The Third Reich and the Plots against the Führer* (Vintage, 2007)
—————— *The Devil's Alliance: Hitler's Pact with Stalin, 1939–1941* (The Bodley Head, 2014)

Margolick, D. *Beyond Glory: Max Schmeling vs. Joe Louis and a World on the Brink* (Bloomsbury, 2006)

Mühlberger, D. *Hitler's Voice: The Völkischer Beobachter, 1920–1933*, 2 vols (Oxford: Peter Lang, 2004)

Müller-Hill, B. *Murderous Science: Elimination by Scientific Selection of Jews, Gypsies and Others in Germany 1933–45* (Oxford: Oxford University Press, 1997)

Müller, I. *Hitler's Justice: The Courts of the Third Reich* (Cambridge, MA: Harvard University Press, 1991)

Neville, P. *Hitler and Appeasement: The British Attempt to Prevent the Second World War* (Hambledon Continuum, 2006)

Noakes J. and Pridham, G (eds) *Nazism 1919–1945: A Documentary Reader*, 4 vols, Vol. 1: *The Rise to Power, 1919–1934*; Vol. 2: *State, Economy, Society, 1933–1938*; Vol. 3: *Foreign Policy, War and Racial Extermination*; Vol. 4: *The German Home Front in World War II* (Exeter: Exeter University Press, 1983–98)

Ohler, N. *Blitzed: Drugs in Nazi Germany* (Allen Lane, 2016)

Overy, R. *Göring: Hitler's Iron Knight* (I.B. Taurus, 2011)
—————— *Interrogations: Inside the Minds of The Nazi Elite* (Penguin, 2002)

Owings, A. *Frauen: German Women Recall the Third Reich* (Penguin, 1995)

Padfield, P. *Himmler: Reichsführer-SS* (New York: H. Holt, 1990)
—————— *War Beneath the Sea: Submarine Conflict 1939–1945* (John Murray, 1995)

Papen, F. von *Memoirs* (New York: E. P. Dutton, 1953)

Parker, R. *Chamberlain and Appeasement: British Policy and the Coming of the Second World War* (Basingstoke: Macmillan, 1993)

Parkinson, R. *Tormented Warrior: Ludendorff and the Supreme Command* (New York: Stein and Day, 1979)

Pehle, W. (ed.) *November 1938: From 'Kristallnacht' to Genocide* (Oxford: Berg, 1991)

Penton, M. *Jehovah's Witnesses and the Third Reich: Sectarian Politics under Persecution* (Toronto: University of Toronto Press, 2004)

Peukert, D. *Die KPD im Widerstand: Verfolgung und Untergrundarbeit an Rhein und Ruhr 1933–1945* (Wuppertal: Peter Hammer, 1980)
—————— *Inside Nazi Germany: Conformity, Opposition and Racism in Everyday Life* (Batsford, 1987)

Pine, L. *Nazi Family Policy 1933–1945* (Oxford: Berg, 1997)
—————— *Hitler's 'National Community': Society and Culture in Nazi Germany* (Bloomsbury, 2011).
—————— *Education in Nazi Germany* (Oxford: Berg, 1997)

Plant, R. *The Pink Triangle: Nazi War against Homosexuals* (New York: Henry Holt & Co., 1986)

Preston, P. *A Concise History of the Spanish Civil War* (Fontana Press, 1996)

Preston, P. and Mackenzie A. (eds), *The Republic Besieged: Civil War in Spain* (Edinburgh: Edinburgh University Press, 1996)

Proctor, R. *Racial Hygiene. Medicine under the Nazis* (Cambridge, MA: Harvard University Press, 1988)

Rabinbach, A. and Gilman, S. L. (eds) *The Third Reich Sourcebook* (Berkeley: University of California Press, 2013)

Rauschning, H. *Hitler Speaks: A Series of Political Conversations with Adolf Hitler on His Real Aims* (Whitefish, MT: Kessinger Publishing, 2010)

Reed, D. *The Burning of the Reichstag* (New York: Convici Friede, 1934)

Rees, L. *The Holocaust: A New History* (Viking, 2017)

Ribbentrop, J. *The Ribbentrop Memoirs* (Weidenfeld & Nicolson, 1954)

Rich, N. *Hitler's War Aims: Ideology, the State and Course of Expansion*, Vol. 1 (New York: W. Norton & Company, 1973)

Roberts, A. *The Holy Fox: A Biography of Lord Halifax* (Weidenfeld & Nicolson, 1991)
—————— *The Storm of War: A New History of the Second World War* (Allen Lane, 2009)

Rose, N. *Vansittart: The Study of a Diplomat* (William Heinemann, 1978)

Rürup, R. (ed.) *Topographie des Terrors: Gestapo, SS und Reichssicherheitshauptamt auf dem 'Prinz-Albrecht-Gelände': Eine Dokumentation* (Berlin: Willmuth Arenhövel, 1987)

Ryback, T. *Hitler's First Victims and One Man's Race for Justice* (The Bodley Head, 2015)

Schacht, H. *Account Settled* (Weidenfeld & Nicolson, 1949)

Schleunes, K. A. *The Twisted Road to Auschwitz* (Champaign, IL: University of Illinois, 1970)

Schmidt, P. *Hitler's Interpreter* (Stroud: History Press, 2016)

Schirach, B. *Ich glaubte an Hitler* (Hamburg: Mosaik Verlag, 1967)

Schoppmann, C. *Days of Masquerade: Life Stories of Lesbians during the Third Reich* (New York: Columbia University Press, 1996)

Schuschnigg, K. von *Austrian Requiem* (Victor Gollancz, 1947)

Shirer, W. L. *Berlin Diary: The Journal of a Foreign Correspondent, 1934–1941* (Sunburst Books, 1997)
———— *The Rise and Fall of the Third Reich: A History of Nazi Germany* (Folio, 2004 edn)

Shultze-Rhonhof, G. *1939: The War That Had Many Fathers: The Long Run-up to the Second World War* (Munich: Olzog Verlag, 2011)

Siemens, D. *Stormtroopers: A New History of Hitler's Brownshirts* (New Haven, CT: Yale University Press, 2017)

Smith, H. *Last Train from Berlin* (New York: Alfred Knopf, 1942)

Snyder, T. *Black Earth: The Holocaust as History and Warning* (New York: Tim Duggan Books, 2015)

Speer, A. *Inside the Third Reich* (Weidenfeld & Nicolson, 1970)

Sofsky W. *The Order of Terror: The Concentration Camp* (Princeton, NJ: Princeton University Press, 1993)

Sontag, R. and Beddie, J. (eds) *Nazi-Soviet Relations, 1939–1941: Documents from the Archives of the German Foreign Office* (Washington, DC: US Government Printing Office, 1948)

Stargardt, N. *The German War: A Nation Under Arms, 1939–1945* (Bodley Head, 2015)

Steinhoff, J., Pechel, P. and Showalter,
D. (eds) *Voices from the Third Reich: An Oral History* (Washington, DC: Da Capo Press, 1994)

Stephenson, J. *Women in Nazi Germany* (Longman, 2001)

Stone, D. (ed.) *The Historiography of the Holocaust* (Basingstoke: Palgrave Macmillan, 2004)

Taylor, A. J. P. *The Origins of the Second World War* (Penguin, 1954)

Thalmann, R. and Feinerman, E. *Crystal Night: 9–10 November 1938* (Thames & Hudson, 1974)

The British War Blue Book: Documents concerning German-Polish and the Outbreak of Hostilities between Britain and Germany on September 3, 1939 (New York: Farrar and Rinehart, 1939)

The Polish White Book: Official Documents concerning Polish-German and Soviet Relations, 1933–1939 (Hutchinson, 1939)

The Trial of Adolf Eichmann: Record of Proceedings in the District Court of Jerusalem, 9 vols (Jerusalem: Israel Minister of Justice, 1992–95)

Tobias, F. *The Reichstag Fire* (New York: G. P. Putnam's Sons, 1964)

Toland, J. *Adolf Hitler* (Ware, Hertfordshire: Wordsworth, 1997)

Tooze, A. *The Wages of Destruction: The Making and Breaking of the Nazi Economy* (Allen Lane, 2007)

Trevor-Roper, H. (ed.) *Hitler's War Directives, 1939–1934* (Pan, 1983)

Turner, H. *German Big Business and the Rise of Hitler* (Oxford: Oxford University Press, 1985)
———— *Hitler's Thirty Days to Power: January 1933* (Bloomsbury, 1996)

Ullrich, V. *Hitler*, Vol. 1: *Ascent: 1889–1939* (The Bodley Head, 2016)

Vandana J. *Gender and Power in the Third Reich: Female Denouncers and the Gestapo, 1933–1945* (Basingstoke: Palgrave, 2003)

Wachsmann N. *Hitler's Prisons: Legal Terror in Nazi Germany* (New Haven, CT: Yale University Press, 2004)
———— *KL: The History of the Nazi Concentration Camps* (Little, Brown, 2015)

Wainwright, W. *Reporting on Hitler: Rothay Reynolds and the British Press in Nazi Germany* (Biteback, 2017)

Walters, G. *Berlin Games: How the Nazis Stole the Olympic Dream* (Harper Perennial, 2007)

Ward Price, G. *I Knew These Dictators* (George G. Harrop & Co., 1937)

Warlimont, W. *Inside Hitler's Headquarters, 1939–1945* (Novato, CA: Presidio, 1964)

Weinberg, G. *The Foreign Policy of Hitler's Germany: The Road to World War II* (New York: Enigma Books, 2005)

Weinreich, M. *Hitler's Professors. The Part of Scholarship in Germany's Crimes against the Jewish People* (New Haven, CT: Yale University Press, 1999)

Weizsäcker, E. *Memoirs* (Gollancz, 1951)

Welch, D. *Third Reich: Politics and Propaganda* (Routledge, 2002)

Wheeler-Bennet, J. *Munich: A Prologue to Tragedy* (Macmillan, 1948)

Wildt, M. *An Uncompromising Generation: The Leadership of the Reich Security Main Office* (Madison: University of Wisconsin Press, 2009
———— (ed.) *Die Judenpolitik des SD 1933–1939: Eine Dokumentation* (Munich: Oldenbourg, 1995)

Wiskemann, E. *The Rome–Berlin Axis* (Fontana, 1966)

Wittman R. and Kinney D. *The Devil's Diary: Alfred Rosenberg and the Stolen Secrets of the Third Reich* (William Collins, 2016)

Wragg, D. *Plan Z: The Nazi Bid for Naval Supremacy* (Pen & Sword, 2008)

Ziegler, P. *King Edward VIII* (HarperPress, 2012)

INDEX